THE CROSS OF GOLD

MONEY AND THE CANADIAN BUSINESS CYCLE

1867 - 1913

The CROSS of GOLD

Money and the Canadian Business Cycle, 1867-1913

by Georg Rich

Carleton University Press
Ottawa, Canada
1988

ISBN 0-88629-082-1 (casebound)
0-88629-080-5 (paperback)

Printed and bound in Canada

Carleton Library Series # 153

Canadian Cataloguing in Publication Data

Rich, Georg, 1939-
The cross of gold: money and the Canadian business cycle, 1867-1913

(The Carleton library; 153)
Bibliography: p.
ISBN 0-88629-082-1 (bound)
ISBN 0-88629-080-5 (pbk.)

1. Money—Canada—History. 2. Canada—Economic conditions—1867-1918. 3. Gold standard. I. Title. II. Series.

HC114.R53 1988 332.4'971 C88-090398-8

Distributed by: Oxford University Press Canada,
70 Wynford Drive,
Don Mills, Ontario,
Canada. M3C 1J9
(416) 441-2941

Cover Design: Robert Chitty

Acknowledgements

Carleton University Press gratefully acknowledges the support extended to its publishing programme by the Canada Council and the Ontario Arts Council.

This book is published with the help of a grant from the Social Science Federation of Canada, using funds provided by the Social Sciences and Humanities Research Council of Canada.

To Ruth, Daphne and Clemens

THE CARLETON LIBRARY SERIES

A series of original works, new collections, and reprints of source material relating to Canada, issued under the supervision of the Editorial Board, Carleton Library Series, Carleton University Press Inc., Ottawa, Canada.

CONTENTS

LIST OF CHARTS

LIST OF TABLES

PREFACE

Early in the 1970s, Ted English and Tom Rymes, two of my former colleagues at Carleton University, suggested that I compile for the Carleton Library Series a compendium of important journal articles and other relevant documents on the Canadian balance of payments since Confederation. After sifting through the available literature, I gradually came to realize that there was a dearth of analytically oriented research on Canadian monetary history. I was particularly struck by an almost complete absence of research on the operation of the pre-1914 Canadian gold standard, even though Jacob Viner (1924) had provided an admirable impetus with his seminal study of the price-specie-flow mechanism. Aside from Viner's work, existing research on the pre-1914 Canadian gold standard tends to be descriptive, with an abundance of studies on the structure and development of banking, as well as on the evolution of monetary and banking legislation. Considering this lacuna in Canadian monetary history, I felt that a monograph on the operation of the pre-1914 Canadian gold standard would make a more useful contribution to the existing literature than a book of readings. The present study draws together the results of these efforts. A summary of my research was already provided in an earlier paper (Rich, 1984).

Although I toyed briefly with the idea of writing a comprehensive monetary history of the pre-1914 period, I decided to restrain my ambitions by confining my investigation to the cyclical aspects of the operation of the gold standard. My study addresses the question of whether and to what extent the fetters imposed by the gold standard on domestic money creation compelled the Canadian government and the chartered banks to act in a manner designed to stabilize cyclical fluctuations in economic activity. In order to answer this question, I show that it is necessary to reopen the debate initiated by Viner and to take a fresh look at the operation of the price-specie-flow mechanism.

The need to limit the scope of my study was all the more important as I left academe in 1977 for the world of central banking. Repeated difficulties of reconciling the demands of my current employer, the Swiss National Bank, with my desire to fill a major gap in Canadian monetary history accounts for the length of time required to complete this project. Whatever imperfections this study may possess, I hope that it will stimulate further research on the pre-1914 period.

Interest in the history of the pre-1914 Canadian gold standard already appears to be growing. In two stimulating papers that I received after completing my study, Dick and Floyd (1987a; b) have also re-examined the operation of the Canadian price-specie-flow mechanism prior to 1914. The Canadian evidence, they maintain, accords with the monetary approach to balance-of-payments analysis, as applied to the gold standard by McCloskey and Zecher (1976; 1984), but is at variance with the classical price-specie-flow doctrine. In the present study, I have intentionally made parsimonious use of the term "monetary approach to balance-of-payments analysis." In my opinion, the Canadian evidence does not lend full support to either the classical doctrine or the McCloskey-Zecher model. The classical doctrine, I argue, fails to recognize the importance of bank reserve management as a determinant of cyclical movements in the Canadian money supply and Canadian economic activity. McCloskey and Zecher's model is also inadequate because of their insistence on the effectiveness of international arbitrage as a means of equalizing prices across countries. McCloskey and Zecher's perfect-arbitrage view of the world does not do justice to pre-1914 Canadian realities. Nonetheless, I assign an important role to money in balance of payments adjustment, but I leave it to the reader to decide whether the approach followed in this study should bear a classical or monetary label.

This book could not have been written without the kind assistance of various individuals and institutions. I am greatly indebted to my former colleague, Tom Rymes, who encouraged me to embark on this venture and patiently read the drafts of the manuscript. I would also like to express my deep gratitude to Messrs. Michael Huband and Freeman Clowery, Bank of Montreal, Ms. Jane Nokes, Bank of Nova Scotia, and Mr. Bertwing C. Mah, California State Banking Department, whose generous support enabled me to plug various gaps in the published statistics on Canadian banking. Furthermore, Professor Irving Stone from City University of New York was kind enough to prepare a special tabulation of data on Canadian bond issues in London, compiled by the late Matthew Simon. In addition, the manuscript has greatly benefited from the scrutiny of Keith Acheson, Michael Bordo, Derek Chisholm, Trevor Dick, Jack Galbraith, Irwin Gillespie, Susan Howson, Ed Neufeld, Gilles Paquet, Soo Bin Park, Angela Redish, Anna Schwartz, Ron Shearer, Alexandre Swoboda, John Taylor, Peter Temin, Geoffrey Wood, and several anonymous referees, whose comments and suggestions resulted in a much improved product. Needless to say, this project could never have materialized without the painstaking efforts of my research assistants, Peter Balon, Jamie Corbet, Paul Geddes, Sushama Gera, Patricia Hamilton, Sue Hill, and Yasmin Sheik. I also owe many thanks to my secretaries, Miss

Sylvia Eberle and Mrs. Barbara Grässli, for their excellent typing assistance, as well as to my colleagues, Jean-Pierre Béguelin and Pia Schaad, for helping me with the charts.

Chapter 6 is a slightly shortened and modified version of an article, "Canadian Banks, Gold, and the Crisis of 1907," that appeared in the January 1989 issue of *Explorations in Economic History*. I would like to thank Academic Press for their permission to reprint my article. Last but not least, I am greatly indebted to the Social Sciences Research Council for awarding me two research grants in support of this study, as well as to Carleton University for financial support in the form of a GR-6.

CHAPTER 1

INTRODUCTION

1.1. AIM AND SCOPE OF STUDY

The aim of this book is to investigate the relationship between money and the Canadian business cycle under the pre-1914 gold standard. Although various studies exist on pre-1914 Canadian business cycles, little is known about the monetary causes of cyclical instability. This lacuna in research on Canadian monetary history is unfortunate since the pre-1914 period offers a perfect opportunity to study the stabilizing or destabilizing role of a laissez-faire monetary system that severely restricted the government's scope for managing the domestic money stock.

Prior to 1914, the Canadian money stock was managed largely by the commercial banks, rather than an official monetary authority. The Bank of Canada, Canada's central bank, was not established until 1935. The government was authorized to issue notes, known as Dominion notes, but government money only played a minor role as a means of payment. The bulk of the media of exchange employed by the Canadian public was issued by the chartered banks, Canada's commercial banks. The government's ability to manage the money stock was closely circumscribed by law. In particular, the government was not permitted to act as a lender of last resort to the banking system. It assumed this role only after the outbreak of World War I. With the passage of the Finance Act of 1914, the government acquired the power to provide advances to the chartered banks against specified collateral (see Shearer and Clark, 1984).

Advocates of the gold standard tend to argue that the pre-1914 fetters on government or central-bank management of the money stock were highly effective in forcing stabilizing behaviour upon monetary authorities. In their opinion, the gold standard compelled or induced the suppliers of money to expand the money stock at a pace consistent with a stable price level and steady real economic growth.

As far as inflation trends are concerned, the performance of the pre-1914 gold standard was indeed remarkable. Throughout the period under study, Canadian inflation trends were modest, ranging from roughly −1 percent per year in the period 1868-96 to slightly less than 3 percent in the period 1897-1913. The inflation record of other major gold-standard countries was similar to that of Canada. Over the periods 1872-96 and 1896-1913, the United States, the United Kingdom, Germany and France, taken together, saw wholesale prices change by annual averages of −2.3 and 2.0 percent respectively.[1] Thus, under the pre-World War I gold standard, trend movements in the price level were negligible as compared with the high inflation rates recorded in the second half of the twentieth century.

While the gold standard kept trend movements in prices clearly within bounds, its performance as a cyclical stabilizer was less satisfactory, as indicated by substantial short-run swings in the price level and output. Assessing the performance of the pre-1914 gold standard, Bordo (1981, 13-16) concludes that in the United States and United Kingdom, short-run variability of the price level and output was stronger before World War I than in the post-World War II period. However, both variables were less stable in the interwar period than either before 1914 or after 1945. Furthermore, Bordo investigates the short-run volatility of the money stock and finds close conformity to the patterns observed for prices and output. In both countries, money growth was more variable before 1914 than after 1945.

Canadian output and prices follow a similar pattern. Table 1-1 describes the variability of Canadian real GNP, the GNP deflator and wholesale prices since 1870. Two measures of variability are employed: standard deviations; and coefficients of variation (standard deviation divided by the mean) of annual rates of change in output and prices. Bordo (1981, Table 1) relies exclusively on the coefficient of variation as a measure of variability. Bordo's procedure may be criticized on the ground that it tends to bias the results against the pre-1914 period. As indicated earlier, the mean annual inflation rates recorded before World War I were very low. A mean inflation rate near zero implies that the coefficient of variation will assume a value close to infinity even if price fluctuations from year to year were very small. For this reason, it is advisable to examine standard deviations in addition to coefficients of variation.

The variability of Canadian output growth and inflation recorded under the pre-1914 gold standard is compared with that observed in the periods 1919/20-1938/39 and 1950/51-1984/85. The pre-1914 period is divided into two subperiods to take account of the shift in price trends around 1896. Table 1-1 illustrates that real GNP growth also changed dramatically at that time.

From 1870/71 to 1895/96, real GNP — on average — grew at a relatively modest pace of 2.5 percent. In the mid-1890s, a surge in exports of natural resources ushered in a boom — commonly known as the wheat boom. As a result, real GNP in the period 1896/97-1912/13 expanded at more than double the rate recorded in the earlier subperiod. This experience contrasts sharply with that of the United States, where average real growth amounted to roughly 4 percent in both subperiods.[2]

As regards the variability of real GNP growth, the evidence of Table 1-1 largely confirms Bordo's results. On the whole, the variability of real growth was highest in the interwar period and lowest after 1950. Thus, the pre-1914 gold standard performed better than the monetary system of the interwar period, but not as well as that of the post-1950 period. However, even within the pre-1914 period the patterns revealed by Table 1-1 were not uniform. The

TABLE 1-1
VARIABILITY OF CANADIAN REAL GNP AND PRICES
(Annual Rates of Change)

	Mean (Percent)	Standard Deviation (Percent)	Coefficient of Variation (Ratio)
Real GNP			
1870/71-1895/96	2.5	4.9	2.0
1896/97-1912/13	6.6	4.0	0.6
1919/20-1938/39 a)	2.9	7.4	2.6
1950/51-1984/85 a)	4.5	2.5	0.6
GNP Deflator			
1870/71-1895/96	-0.3	4.3	-14.8
1896/97-1912/13	2.1	2.0	0.9
1919/20-1938/39 b)	-0.9	5.6	-5.9
1950/51-1984/85 b)	5.0	3.6	0.7
Wholesale Prices			
1870/71-1895/96	-1.3	4.6	-3.7
1896/97-1912/13	2.4	2.3	0.9
1919/20-1938/39	-2.3	9.6	-4.2
1950/51-1984/85	4.4	5.4	1.2

a) For the period 1926-85, real GDP, valued at 1981 prices.
b) For the period 1926-85, GDP deflator.

Sources for Table 1-1

Real GNP and GNP Deflator: Urquhart (1987, Table 9) for 1870-1926; Bank of Canada for 1926-85.

Wholesale Prices: Dominion Bureau of Statistics (1954, 14-16) and Urquhart and Buckley [1965, series J 34 (general index excluding gold)], for 1870-1957. For 1957-85, the index of industrial selling prices is employed (International Monetary Fund, *International Financial Statistics*).

variability of real growth was more pronounced before 1896 than in the years immediately preceding World War I. While the standard deviation of real growth was higher in the period 1896/97-1912/13 than after 1950, the coefficients of variation were identical for the two subperiods. Contrary to Bordo's evidence, Table 1-1 suggests that the variability of pre-1914 Canadian inflation was relatively low, especially in the subperiod 1896/97-1912/13. Furthermore, the two measures of variability yield conflicting results. In particular, one cannot conclude unambiguously that the variability of prices was lower after 1950 than before 1914. The difference between Bordo's evidence and Table 1-1 is explained, for the most part, by his reliance on coefficients of variation as a measure of variability.[3]

Consequently, at least in the short run, the stabilizing powers of the gold standard were not as effective as its advocates tend to claim. Similar conclusions may be drawn from an analysis of cyclical movements in the Canadian money stock. Analyzing Canadian monetary experience in the post-Confederation period, Hay (1967) concludes that the pattern of the money stock was consistently procyclical, both before and after World War I. Hay's evidence implies that destabilizing movements in the Canadian money stock did not arise as a result of the shift to a managed financial system during World War I, but were already a prominent feature of the laissez-faire regime in force prior to 1914.

While there is little doubt that the stabilizing powers of the gold standard were far from perfect, existing research does not provide an answer to the question why the laissez-faire Canadian system tended to generate destabilizing movements in the money stock. This gap in existing research is attributable to the fact that students of pre-1914 Canadian business cycles have shown little interest in the monetary sources of cyclical instability. The bulk of existing research rests on a simplistic Keynesian approach that abstracts almost entirely from possible monetary forces behind the Canadian business cycle.[4] The monetary aspects of cyclical instability were largely ignored until the late 1960s, when Hay (1967), Macesich (1970), and others began to investigate the cyclical pattern of the Canadian money stock. Keynesian economists tend to argue that cyclical fluctuations in Canadian economic activity, for the most part, are imported from abroad, with exports and investment serving as the main links between Canadian and foreign business cycles. In contrast to the Keynesian school of thought, monetarists emphasize the destabilizing role of procyclical movements in the money stock. However, both Keynesian and monetarists tend to agree that the Canadian business cycle was triggered largely by foreign disturbances. For example, Hay concurs with the Keynesian view about the foreign origin of the Canadian business cycle, but departs from the Keynesian analysis in that he stresses the importance of money in the cycle-transmission process.

Although Hay and other monetarists open up a promising line of research, they have not pushed their monetary analysis of the Canadian business cycle very far. In particular, their studies offer few insights into the causes and effects of the procyclical movements in the pre-1914 Canadian money stock. On the following pages, an attempt is made to extend research on the pre-1914 Canadian gold standard in four directions:

(a) The study traces the sources of cyclical and long-run variation in the Canadian money stock. It demonstrates how the laissez-faire Canadian financial system generated destabilizing swings in the money stock despite the fetters imposed by the gold standard on money creation by the government and chartered banks. Reserve management of the chartered banks is identified as the principal source of monetary instability, while the behaviour of the Canadian government was largely stabilizing. The reasons for the stabilizing or destabilizing behaviour of the government and the chartered banks are also examined.

(b) The study twines two distinctly different strands of research by emphasizing the linkages between monetary business-cycle analysis and Viner's (1924) seminal study of the price-specie-flow mechanism. I show that money could not have played a destabilizing role if the price-specie-flow mechanism had operated as Viner suggested. The evidence presented in this study indicates that the relationship between the Canadian money stock and the balance of payments — in the short run — was not as close as Viner believed, although the two magnitudes were closely linked in the long run.

While Viner's conclusions are partly refuted by this study, I do not follow McCloskey and Zecher (1976; 1984) in dismissing altogether the classical price-specie-flow doctrine. Through analyzing the operation of the gold standard within the framework of the monetary approach to balance-of-payments theory, McCloskey and Zecher have recently cast doubt on the empirical relevance of that doctrine. In their opinion, the gold standard was ruled by the law of one price, that is, international arbitrage equalized prices of similar commodities (and assets) across the gold-standard world. Inasmuch as price differentials between national markets did exist, they mirrored transportation costs and trade impediments. Arbitrage, McCloskey and Zecher maintain, not only linked national prices of traded commodities, but a high degree of substitutability of traded for non-traded commodities ensured that the law of one price applied to non-traded commodities too. An important implication of McCloskey and Zecher's analysis is that an exogenous increase in an individual country's money supply did not affect domestic interest rates and the price level either in the short or long run.[5] Instead, any attempt to expand the domestic money supply was frustrated by an instantaneous outflow of capital and gold. However, the McCloskey-Zecher postulate of perfect international arbitrage does not accord well with the pre-1914 Canadian evidence. The cyclical behaviour of Canadian interest rates, in particular, cannot be adequately explained within the framework of the McCloskey-Zecher approach.

(c) As far as the available data permit, I examine the effects of the procyclical movements in the Canadian money stock on economic activity. The focus of the analysis is on the cyclical pattern of pre-1914 Canadian interest rates. As I demonstrate in Chapters 2, 5 and 6, interest rates in Canada were much more stable than in the United States, a phenomenon widely discussed by contemporary observers of financial markets. The monetary analysis of the cycle-transmission process developed in this study is shown to account for the remarkable stability of pre-1914 Canadian interest rates. The study seeks to demonstrate that the cyclical stability of Canadian interest rates constituted an important element in the cycle-transmission process. In essence, the behaviour of the chartered banks was similar to that of a central bank striving to keep interest rates stable. The chartered banks accommodated a foreign-induced cyclical expansion in economic activity by augmenting the domestic money stock. Owing to the constraints of the gold standard, however, the banks' ability to create money had limits. Accommodative behaviour of the banks, in due course, generated balance-of-payments deficits, as suggested by the classical price-specie-flow doctrine. The resulting outflows of gold and other reserve assets did not prevent destabilizing movements in the money stock, but precluded unlimited money creation by the chartered banks.

Although this study assigns an important destabilizing role to money, I do not purport to offer a complete monetary analysis of the pre-1914 Canadian business cycle. The study identifies the channels through which the procyclical movements in the Canadian money stock were likely to impinge on economic activity, but it does not supply conclusive evidence that money was a significant destabilizing force. In particular, I am unable to offer more than cryptic evidence on the relative importance of monetary and real channels in the cycle-transmission process because annual estimates of Canadian GNP for the pre-1914 period (Urquhart, 1987) did not become available until I had virtually completed my research project. Nonetheless, these estimates are used to some extent in the subsequent analysis.

(d) Finally, the study makes a contribution to improving existing Canadian monetary statistics for the pre-1914 period. The most important innovations are revised statistics on monetary balance-of-payments flows and trade in non-monetary gold, as well as new data on domestic and foreign borrowing by the Dominion government. The study shows that a major obstacle to measuring correctly pre-1914 monetary balance-of-payments flows lies in the existence of foreign branches and agencies of the Canadian banks.[6] Before World War I, the Canadian banks already operated a far-flung network of foreign branches. The bank's foreign branches posed a variety of reporting problems that tend to mar pre-1914 Canadian monetary statistics.

1.2 THE STRUCTURE OF THE PRE-1914 CANADIAN FINANCIAL SYSTEM

The Dominion of Canada was established in 1867 when the provinces of Ontario, Quebec, New Brunswick and Nova Scotia were joined in Confederation. Upon Confederation, the new Dominion acquired from the provinces jurisdiction over banking and monetary matters. The gold standard, which had already been adopted by the former provincial regimes, was retained after

Confederation. The value of the Canadian dollar was defined in terms of gold, with United States and British gold coins declared legal tender in Canada. The public was required to accept U.S. ten-dollar pieces (eagles) at ten Canadian dollars and British one-pound coins (sovereigns) at $4.86 2/3. Despite their legal-tender status, eagles and sovereigns were not used much by the non-bank public (households and firms, including non-bank financial intermediaries) as media of exchange.[7] The bulk of the gold coins imported from the United States and Britain wound up in the vaults of the government and the chartered banks. Canadian gold coins were not minted until the very end of the period under study. In 1908, the British Royal Mint opened a branch in Ottawa and undertook to process gold received from all parts of Canada. At first, the Ottawa Mint only issued sovereigns, but in 1912 it also started to produce small quantities of Canadian gold coins. While Canadian gold coins only played a minor role, the government, throughout the pre-1914 period, issued subsidiary silver and bronze coins possessing limited legal-tender status (Beckhart, 1929, 291-92).

Besides gold and subsidiary coin, Dominion notes issued by the government carried legal-tender status. Dominion notes were redeemable in specie upon demand[8] and were held by both the chartered banks and the non-bank public. Although specie comprised United States, British and Canadian gold coins, as well as Canadian subsidiary coin,[9] it appears that the government typically redeemed the Dominion notes in eagles or sovereigns. The government was also obliged to maintain a minimum reserve against outstanding Dominion notes. Prior to 1880, the minimum required reserve was to be held in specie, thereafter entirely in gold.[10] However, it does not appear that before 1880, the monetary reserve of the government included substantial amounts of subsidiary coin.[11]

Before the Bank of Canada was established, the chartered banks shared with the government the privilege of issuing notes. Though not legal tender, bank notes were redeemable in specie or Dominion notes upon demand. While bank notes were a very popular medium of exchange in Canada, Dominion notes did not circulate widely outside the banking system. The non-bank public used Dominion notes only because the government possessed a monopoly for issuing small-denomination notes of $4 and less. On the whole, the circulation of Dominion notes outside the banking system was restricted to the small denominations. Since the non-bank public showed little interest in the government currency, the share of Dominion notes in the aggregate Canadian money stock was very small indeed. Between 1873 and 1913, Dominion notes never accounted for more than 5 percent of the Canadian money stock, defined to include bank notes, as well as demand and notice deposits held by the non-bank public, in addition to the government notes.[12] However, Dominion notes were used extensively by the banks as a reserve asset and as a means of settling domestic clearing-house balances.

While the government was expected to comply with a minimum gold reserve requirement, asset and liability management of the chartered banks was not subject to tight legal restrictions. In particular, the chartered banks were completely unfettered by minimum reserve requirements against their notes and deposits, save for a marginal cash reserve requirement imposed on bank notes in July, 1913 (see below).[13] Nevertheless, the banks kept on hand ample reserves of gold and Dominion notes to safeguard the redemption of their liabilities.

Another important feature of pre-1914 Canadian banking legislation was the relaxed approach to regulating the issue of bank notes. In this regard, Canadian legislation differed fundamentally from that of the United States. The U.S. bank note issue, for all practical purposes, was a government money in disguise. After the passage of the U.S. National Banking Act in 1863, the issue of bank notes became virtually the exclusive privilege of the national banks.[14] The Act compelled the national banks to deposit with the Treasury specific U.S. government bonds as a collateral against their note issue. The required deposits of bonds amounted to at least 111 percent of the bank-note circulation. Since U.S. national bank notes were backed by government bonds, they did not differ much from the notes issued directly by the Treasury.[15]

In Canada, by contrast, bank notes, like bank deposits, were not secured by special collateral such as government bonds, but by the the issuing bank's total assets. The Canadian Bank Act did not oblige the chartered banks to hold government bonds. It merely stipulated that the note circulation was not to exceed a bank's paid-up capital. Moreover, in case of insolvency, the notes constituted a first lien on the assets of the issuing bank. In 1891, in an effort to improve the protection of the note holders, the government also established a bank circulation redemption fund guaranteeing the redemption of the notes in the event of bank failures. Each bank was required to remit to the fund a sum equalling 5 percent of the average circulation in the previous year. The banks earned interest of 3 percent of their contributions to the fund.

In practice, the statutory ceiling set by the banks' paid-up capital did not significantly restrain the supply of bank notes. Until the mid-1890s, the note circulation never exceeded two-thirds of aggregate bank capital and, therefore, remained well below its statutory ceiling. The onset of the wheat boom caused the growth in demand for bank notes to accelerate, both absolutely and relative to bank capital. By 1902, the note issue had expanded to such an extent that it approached its statutory ceiling, especially during the crop-moving season (see also Chapter 6). In 1908, in response to public concern about the seasonal elasticity of the note issue, the banks were authorized to issue notes in excess of the statutory ceiling, but only during the crop-moving season from September 1 to February 28. However, the excess issue was not to rise above 15 percent of the banks' paid-up capital and surplus.[16] Moreover, in July, 1913, the banks were permitted to issue notes beyond the statutory ceiling provided the excess issue was fully backed by gold or Dominion notes deposited in a fund called the central gold reserves. The 1913 revision of the Bank Act, in effect, imposed on the banks a 100-percent cash reserve requirement on notes issued in excess of the statutory ceiling.[17]

On the whole, the Canadian banks were free to adjust the supply of bank notes to changes in demand. Many contemporary observers praised the Canadian bank-note system for its ability to accommodate seasonal and other peaks in demand. U.S. national bank notes, by contrast, did not display much seasonal variation (Beckhart, 1929, 375-77).

Despite[18] the relaxed regulatory environment, the pre-1914 Canadian banking system was remarkably resistant to financial crises. During the period under study, bank failures were rare events indeed and suspensions of specie payments by the Canadian government and the chartered banks were practically unknown. In this regard, Canadian experience contrasts sharply with that of the United States. The U.S. government and the majority of banks were forced to lift convertibility of their liabilities into gold upon the outbreak of the Civil War and did not resume specie payments until January 1, 1879. Moreover, in the United States, the financial panics of 1893 and 1907 triggered wide-spread bank failures and compelled a host of commercial banks to suspend temporarily specie payments. In Canada, the crisis of 1907 was associated with a liquidity squeeze that prompted the government to act informally as a lender of last resort to the banking system (see Chapter 6), but there were no bank failures or suspensions of specie payments.

A reason for the stability of the Canadian financial system lay in the prevalence of well-capitalized banks with nation-wide branch networks. Although the number of chartered banks — about 50 in the mid-1870s — was still 24 at the end of 1913 (Neufeld, 1972, Table 4:2), banking in Canada was dominated by a few large institutions. Notably, the Bank of Montreal, Canada's largest financial institution before World War I, played a unique role in the Canadian financial system. The Bank accounted for one-fourth to one-fifth of aggregate chartered-bank assets (Neufeld, 1972, Table 4:6), acted as Canada's principal foreign exchange dealer, served as fiscal agent to governments (see Chapter 7), and provided banking services to other banks.

Provided governments and banks were prepared to furnish specie upon demand, the market exchange rates between the currencies issued by the various gold-standard countries could not deviate much from their par values. The amplitude of fluctuations about the par values was limited by the so-called gold export and import points. The price of New York exchange (i.e., cheques drawn on New York banks or bills and other drafts on New York residents) traded on the Montreal foreign exchange market normally remained within a range of ± 0.08 percent from the par value of Cdn. $1.00 per U.S. dollar. The difference between the gold export point of Cdn. $1.0008 (or between the gold import point of Cdn. $0.9992) and the par value was equivalent to the cost of shipping U.S. $1.00 worth of eagles from Montreal to New York. Montreal residents would have been foolish to purchase New York exchange at prices exceeding the gold export point since the desired exchange could normally be acquired at a price of Cdn. $1.0008 by trading Canadian dollars for eagles in Montreal and shipping the coins to New York for conversion into U.S. dollars. Thus, gold flows between the two cities ensured that the

Montreal price of New York exchange stayed within the gold points. In view of the tiny spread between the gold export and import points, the Montreal market price of New York exchange, for all practical purposes, was equivalent to the par value of Cdn. $1.00. For London, England, the price fluctuations were larger but still less than ± 1 percent about the par value of Cdn. $4.86 2/3.[19]

Endnotes — Chapter 1

1. Compounded annual rates of change in wholesale prices. See legend to Chart 4-3 for data on Canadian wholesale prices. For the United States, the United Kingdom, Germany and France, the rates of change are calculated from the unweighted means of the individual countries' price indices, as shown in Triffin (1964, 13).

2. For the United States, average annual growth in real GNP — corresponding to the rates presented for Canada in Table 1-1 — equalled 3.8 and 4.6 percent in 1870/71-95/96 and 1896/97-1912/13 respectively. Calculated from Friedman and Schwartz (1982, Table 4.8).

3. Note that the coefficient of variation in Canadian inflation, for the most part, was lower in the period 1950/51-1984/85 than in the two pre-1914 subperiods, while exactly the opposite conclusion may be drawn from a comparison of standard deviations. In addition, Bordo examined the period 1870-1913 as a whole (for the United States, the period 1879-1913), rather than the two subperiods shown in Table 1-1. Over 1870/71-1912/13, the mean annual rate of change in Canadian wholesale prices amounted to 0.2 percent, while the standard deviation equalled 4.3 percent, a lower value than that recorded for the post-1950 period. This yields a coefficient of variation of 22.7, which exceeds by far the ratio calculated for the post-1950 period but is of the same order of magnitude as the pre-1914 ratios reported by Bordo [1981, Table 1, row (2)] for the U.K. and the U.S. Thus, Bordo overstates the variability of pre-1914 prices.

4. Keynes (1936) himself did not deny that cyclical and other short-run changes in output could result from monetary disturbances.

5. Domestic interest rates fell and the domestic price level rose only if that country was large enough to make a significant imprint on world interest rates and prices.

6. In several U.S. states (e.g., New York), Canadian banks were only permitted to open agencies. Unlike a branch, an agency is not empowered to accept deposits on its own account. However, it may receive deposits on behalf of head office (Shearer, 1965, 329). For the sake of convenience, only the term «branch» is used in this study.

7. In 1913, less than $2 million worth of gold coin was estimated to be circulating outside the government and the chartered banks (Viner, 1924, 34). Government and bank holdings of gold amounted to over $100 million at that time (Table A-2).

8. Government notes were issued even before Confederation (Chapter 7). For the legal provisions governing the redemption of the Dominion notes, see *Statutes of the Province of Canada,* 29-30 Vict. Cap. 10, Section 1; *Statutes of Canada,* 31 Vict. Cap. 46, Section 8; 33 Vict. Cap. 10, Section 2. These provisions also assigned legal-tender status to the Dominion notes.

9. See Curtis (1931a, 9) for the definition of specie.

10. See *Statutes of the Province of Canada,* 29-30 Vict. Cap. 46, Section 10; *Statutes of Canada,* 33 Vict. Cap. 10, Section 4; 43 Vict. Cap. 13, Section 1.

11. The unpublished records of the Finance Department (see Chapter 7) contain no references that the government reserve included substantial amounts of subsidiary coin.

12. See Tables A-1 and A-2 for data on the Canadian money stock.

13. The chartered banks, however, were required to hold a minimum proportion of their cash reserves in Dominion notes (see Chapter 7).

14. In 1865, the U.S. government began to levy a tax of 10 percent on the note issue of state banks. This tax virtually eliminated state bank notes (Friedman and Schwartz, 1963b, 18-19).

15. National banks were required to value the eligible bonds at par or at the market price, whichever was lower. See Friedman and Schwartz (1963b, 20-25) for a detailed discussion of the regulations governing the issue of national bank notes. National bank notes were not tied mechanically to the supply of eligible bonds. Until 1908, the circulation of national bank notes remained well below the potential maximum (Goodhart, 1965, 518-19).

16. The so-called crop-moving provisions also required banks to pay to the government interest of 5 percent on the excess issue. From 1911 onwards, the note issue regularly rose above bank capital during the crop-moving season.

17. The central gold reserves were administered jointly by the Canadian Bankers' Association and the Minister of Finance. Excess issues under the crop-moving provisions were not subject to the 100-percent reserve requirement. See Shortt (1922) and Beckhart (1929, 375-87) for a more detailed discussion of the regulations governing the bank-note issue. Shortt (1922) provides an excellent survey of pre-1914 Canadian monetary and banking legislation.

18. Hayek (1978) and other proponents of privately issued money would substitute the word "because of" for "despite." Note that there are similarities between Canadian experience and that of Scotland under free banking before 1844. The Scottish free-banking system was also remarkably stable (see White, 1984). Interestingly, early Canadian banking legislation was shaped to a considerable extent by Scottish experience.

19. The gold points are calculated from Patterson and Escher (1914, 419 and 428). The data drawn from this source refer to the post-1900 period.

CHAPTER 2

MONEY AS A DESTABILIZING FORCE

2.1. REAL AND MONETARY VIEWS OF THE CANADIAN BUSINESS CYCLE

As indicated in the preceding chapter, both Keynesian and monetarist students of the Canadian business cycle tend to stress the vulnerability of the Canadian economy to cyclical fluctuations in the United States. The close correspondence between cyclical swings in Canadian and U.S. economic activity is clearly brought out by Table 2-1, which shows the dates of business-cycle turning points in the two countries. The cyclical turning points in economic activity are dated on the basis of the reference-cycle technique developed by the U.S. National Bureau of Economic Research (see Burns and Mitchell, 1946) and applied to Canadian data by Chambers (1958; 1964) and Hay (1966). The almost perfect coincidence of Canadian and U.S. reference-cycle turning points revealed by Table 2-1 is striking.[1] Note that the Canadian turning points did not systematically lead or lag their U.S. counterparts. On the contrary, leads and lags occurred with about equal frequency.

The strong correlation between national business cycles was not a unique North American phenomenon. In all the gold-standard countries, there was a close coincidence of cyclical turning points in economic activity. In an extensive study of pre-1914 business cycles, Morgenstern (1959, ch. 2) found a high degree of correlation between cyclical activity in Britain, France, Germany and the United States. In general, the parallelism of cyclical movements was very close within North America and Europe, but less so between the two continents. However, North American and European cycles were not out of phase in any fundamental sense. The turning points of major reference cycles coincided closely, but the United States and Canada witnessed a number of minor cycles that were not transmitted to Europe.

TABLE 2-1
CANADIAN AND UNITED STATES REFERENCE-CYCLE TURNING POINTS, 1873-1915

Turning Point	Date of Turning Point (Month/Year)		Lead (-) or Lag (+) in Months of Canadian Turning Point to U.S. Turning Point
	Canada	United States	
Peak	11/73[a)]	10/73	+ 1
Trough	5/79	3/79	+ 2
Peak	7/82	3/82	+ 4
Trough	3/85	5/85	- 2
Peak	2/87	3/87	- 1
Trough	2/88	4/88	- 2
Peak	7/90[a)]	7/90	0
Trough	3/91[a)]	5/91	- 2
Peak	2/93	1/93	+ 1
Trough	3/94	6/94	- 3
Peak	8/95[a)]	12/95	- 4
Trough	8/96[a)]	6/97	- 10
Peak	4/00	6/99	+ 10
Trough	2/01	12/00	+ 2
Peak	12/02	9/02	+ 3
Trough	6/04	8/04	- 2
Peak	12/06	5/07	- 5
Trough	7/08	6/08	- 1
Peak	3/10	1/10	+ 2
Trough	7/11	1/12	- 6
Peak	11/12	1/13	- 2
Trough	1/15	12/14	+ 1

a) Some uncertainty exists about the exact timing of these turning points (Chambers, 1964, 406).
Sources for Table 2-1
Chambers (1964) and Hay (1966).

2.1.1. Real Channels of Transmission

Until the 1960s, Canadian exports were widely considered to serve as the principal medium for the transmission of foreign cyclical disturbances. A prominent proponent of this view was the Royal Commission on Dominion-Provincial Relations (1940, 125-26). In its report, the Commission argued that a cyclical upswing in the United States typically led to a rise in Canadian exports and output. The impact on output of the increase in exports, in turn, was reinforced by a multiplier effect on consumption. Moreover, the Commission stressed the role played by induced investment in the cycle-transmission process. As a result of the cyclical rise in exports, Canadian firms were prompted to step up their investment and, thus, contributed further to the surge in domestic output.

Although the Commission echoed views that — for a long time — were popular among Canadian economists, its export-multiplier model does not accord well with the empirical evidence. In two important papers published three decades ago. Rosenbluth (1957; 1958) attempted to verify empirically the export-multiplier model, as well as alternative Keynesian theories of the transmission process. His empirical tests, based on data for the period 1903-54, suggest that the export-multiplier model suffers from two major shortcomings.

First, if exports had served as the major transmission channel, one would expect that cyclical movements in Canadian output were closely linked to cyclical movements in both Canadian exports and United States output. On the whole, this expectation is not borne out by the empirical evidence. Although the output fluctuations in the two countries were highly correlated, only a loose relationship existed between Canadian exports and U.S. output (Rosenbluth, 1958). Moreover, exports did not fully account for a marked decline in the cyclical sensitivity of Canadian to U.S. output recorded during the period studied by Rosenbluth. This decline reflected a reduction in the Canadian export multiplier, rather than a decrease in the sensitivity of Canadian exports to U.S. output.[2] The instability in the link between Canadian output and exports suggests that the export-multiplier model fails to capture all the channels that were instrumental in transmitting foreign cyclical disturbances to Canada.

Second, it is unclear to what extent induced investment amplified the impact on domestic output of cyclical movements in exports. As Taylor (1931, 3) suggested as early as the 1930s, the Canadian merchandise trade balance typically deteriorated (improved) during business-cycle expansions (contractions) since the procyclical swings in exports were more than offset by procyclical swings in imports. Rosenbluth (1957, 482) attributes the strong cyclical fluctuations in imports to the high import content of domestic investment in machinery and equipement, a component of Canadian aggregate demand that was very sensitive to cyclical fluctuations in domestic output. In so far as the additional investment elicited by a cyclical upswing led to a rise in demand for foreign products, it did not accentuate the fluctuations in Canadian output.

Considering the shortcomings of the export-multiplier model, Rosenbluth (1958) also explored alternative Keynesian explanations of the transmission process. In particular, he examined the possibility that Canadian investment decisions were influenced directly by business conditions in the United States. Due to the close links between the Canadian and U.S. business communities, it is conceivable that Canadian investment was sensitive to expectations about the state and future development of the U.S. economy.[3] Rosenbluth's evidence is inconclusive with regard to the importance of direct influences on Canadian investment. For example, during the early part of the period 1903-54, the sensitivity of Canadian investment to cyclical fluctuations in U.S. output increased, whereas the responsiveness of Canadian to U.S. output — as indicated earlier — declined.[4]

The decline in the export multiplier, Rosenbluth (1958, 37-40) maintains, is explained chiefly by the growing importance of the government sector after World War I. He claims that this led to a substitution of cyclically stable government expenditures for cyclically unstable consumption. Moreover, the introduction of unemployment insurance tended to curtail the cyclical variance of disposable income and consumption. While the growth of the government sector might well account for the observed decrease in the export multiplier, Rosenbluth's interpretation of the evidence is not entirely convincing. He does not attempt to verify econometrically the postulated relationship between the multiplier and the growth of the government sector, nor does he consider other factors that might have influenced the multiplier. A major defect of his analysis is his failure to take account of the monetary sector as a possible channel for the transmission of foreign cyclical disturbances. He does not appear to believe that such monetary variables as the money stock, interest rates and the exchange rate could have affected the size of the export multiplier.[5] The role played by the monetary sector in the transmission process is the central theme of the monetary approach to Canadian business-cycle analysis.

2.1.2. Monetary Channels of Transmission

The last two or three decades have witnessed a revival of interest in monetary interpretations of business cycles. The growing popularity of the monetary approach to business-cycle analysis owes much to Friedman and Schwartz's (1963a; b; 1970; 1982) seminal studies of United States monetary history.[6] Examining United States evidence for the period 1867-1960, Friedman and Schwartz (1963a) conclude that U.S. business cycles were predominantly a monetary phenomenon. The evidence suggests that movements in the U.S. money stock were distinctly procyclical. Moreover, the cyclical turning points in U.S. economic activity tended to follow those in the money stock with a long and variable time lag. Friedman and Schwartz take the lag to imply that the procyclical movements in the money stock were an important cause of the fluctuations in economic activity.[7]

Similar conclusions have been drawn from Canadian evidence for the post-Confederation period. Studying the monetary forces behind the Canadian business cycle, Hay (1967) finds that the Canadian money stock — like its U.S. counterpart — varied procyclically and consistently led economic activity. Prior to 1914, the lag between the cyclical turning points in Canadian economic activity and the money stock typically ranged from 4 to 26 months.[8] In his opinion, the evidence of a systematic lag suggests that money was an important source of cyclical instability. Considering the close linkages between the Canadian and United States economies, however. Hay (1967, 271-72) does not regard the procyclical swings in the Canadian money stock as the ultimate cause of the fluctuations in Canadian economic activity. In his view, the Canadian business cycle was generated by the cyclical gyrations in the U.S. money stock. The Canadian money stock mattered only in so far as it served to link Canadian economic activity to the U.S. money stock.

While Hay puts his finger on a potentially important avenue for the propagation of foreign cyclical disturbances, he does not offer a full-fledged model of the cycle-transmission mechanism. Cyclical fluctuations in Canadian economic activity, he maintains, were proximately determined by corresponding fluctuations in the Canadian money stock. Furthermore, the Canadian money stock was linked to its U.S. counterpart by means of a price-specie-flow mechanism (Hay, 1967, 271). To illustrate Hay's analysis of the transmission process, consider the effects of a cyclical expansion in the U.S. money stock. Such a disturbance, in the short run, caused U.S. interest rates to decline and aggregate demand to rise, eliciting an increase in U.S. prices and output. As a result of the surge in U.S. prices and output, Canadian exports rose and imports shrank. Furthermore, the drop in U.S. interest rates led to an inflow of capital to Canada. The attendant surplus in the Canadian balance of payments was settled by a transfer of monetary gold or U.S. dollars from the United States to Canada, boosting the Canadian monetary base and the money stock. The cyclical expansion in the Canadian money stock, in turn, affected domestic economic activity with a time lag of varying length.

As far as may be judged from the available data, it is doubtful whether Hay's analysis of the cycle-transmission process fully conforms to the empirical evidence. Hay (1967, 271) himself concedes that, while money seems to account for cyclical contractions in Canadian economic activity, his model performs poorly for reference-cycle expansions.[9] Besides this asymmetry, three further difficulties arise from Hay's analysis.

First, if the price-specie-flow mechanism had operated along the lines suggested by Hay, cyclical swings in the Canadian money stock should have been caused mainly by balance-of-payments surpluses or deficits. Hay does not investigate the relationship between the money stock and the balance of payments. Instead, he refers to Viner's (1924) study of the Canadian price-specie-flow mechanism to support his view of the cycle-transmission process. Although Viner, admittedly, concluded that the classical adjustment mechanism had operated efficiently and rapidly, it is unclear whether his results may be taken to imply that the Canadian money stock — over the business cycle — was closely related to the balance of payments.

Second, the evidence of a lag between Canadian economic activity and the money stock is not as firm as Hay claims since he employs a dubious procedure for identifying possible leads or lags. Following Friedman and Schwartz (1963a), Hay compares *rates of change* in the money stock with the *level* of economic activity.[10] Although it is not obvious why leads or lags between money and economic activity should be determined in this way, Hay (1967, 264) fails to justify his reliance on the Friedman-Schwartz procedure.

He probably employs it for the same reasons as Friedman and Schwartz, who advance statistical arguments in support of their procedure. They show that the cyclical turning points in the U.S. money stock, which frequently rose during both reference-cycle expansions and contractions, cannot be dated precisely unless the data are adjusted for trend. Various statistical techniques are available for eliminating the growth trend from a time series. A widely-used method is to fit a linear or non-linear trend line to the data and to treat the trend-adjusted values, that is, the deviations from the trend line, as the cyclical component of the time series. Alternatively, one may compute rates of change between successive observations of the time series and analyze the cyclical attributes of the rates of change.[11] Friedman and Schwartz (1963a, 36; 1982, 85-86) advocate dating the cyclical turning points in the money stock on the basis of growth rates, rather than trend-adjusted values, because the latter are sensitive to the choice of a specific functional form for the trend line and to variations in the length of the sample period.

While growth rates, admittedly, are less arbitrary than trend-adjusted values, the selection of an appropriate technique for dating the cyclical turning points in the money stock should be guided by theoretical considerations rather than statistical convenience. As Culbertson (1960) correctly points out, the Friedman-Schwartz procedure of comparing money growth with the activity level raises theoretical difficulties since it is biased in favour of the monetarist view as to the direction of causation.[12] To illustrate Culbertson's critique of that procedure, suppose that causation ran exclusively from economic activity to money, that is, the Canadian money stock adjusted passively to cyclical fluctuations in demand. Moreover, assume that the *level* of money demand was related to the *level* of economic activity (prices and output), as suggested by neoclassical and Keynesian macroeconomic models, and that the cyclical turning points in the level of money demand — if adjusted for trend — coincided perfectly with the reference-cycle turning points. An analysis of cyclical turning points in the trend-adjusted money stock, therefore, would not reveal any leads or lags to economic activity. An application of the Friedman-Schwartz procedure, however, would yield a radically different result. Had the money stock oscillated regularly about a trend, the turning points in its trend-adjusted values would necessarily have lagged the turning points in its growth rates. Moreover, the lag would have amounted to one-quarter of the length of a full reference cycle.[13] Thus, the Friedman-Schwartz procedure would produce a lag between economic activity and money even though the two magnitudes were perfectly correlated.[14] In view of this bias inherent in the Friedman-Schwartz procedure, the question arises whether Hay's evidence of a lag would still obtain if trend-adjusted values of the money stock were substituted for growth rates.

Third, Hay does not address the question whether the explanatory power of his monetary analysis is superior to that of the Keynesian approach. Procyclical movements in the money stock, by themselves, need not imply that money was an active destabilizing force. In such a small open economy as the Canadian one, the money stock could have adjusted passively to cyclical fluctuations in economic activity triggered by a Keynesian export-multiplier mechanism. Had money played a purely passive role, a monetary analysis of the Canadian business cycle would contribute nothing to understanding the causes of the fluctuations in economic activity.

Consequently, Hay's monetary analysis of the cycle-transmission process leaves a number of issues unsettled. In particular, he fails to show why the pre-1914 laissez-faire Canadian financial system generated destabilizing swings in the money stock, nor does he answer the question to what extent money played an active destabilizing role. In the following two sections, these issues are examined further. Particular attention is paid to Viner's analysis of the price-specie-flow mechanism and to the role of the balance of payments as a source of variation in the Canadian money stock.

2.2. THE BALANCE OF PAYMENTS AS A SOURCE OF VARIATION IN THE CANADIAN MONEY STOCK

2.2.1. Conceptual Problems

Under the pre-1914 gold standard, three factors were responsible for cyclical and long-run changes in the Canadian money stock: balance-of-payments surpluses or deficits, shifts in the monetary policy of the Dominion government, and movements in the reserve ratios of the chartered banks. The first two factors influenced the money stock through variations in the monetary base, while movements in the reserve ratios impinged on the money multiplier, that is, on the ratio of the money stock to the monetary base. In principle, the money multiplier also depended upon the preferences of Canadian non-banks as to the share of Dominion notes in the aggregate money stock. However, as I show in Chapter 3, changes in that share did not significantly influence the money multiplier since Dominion notes outside the banking system were an unimportant component of the money stock.

In order to analyze the relationship between the balance of payments and the money stock, it is useful to divide the monetary base (H) into two components, capturing the variation attributable to the balance of payments and to monetary policy. The monetary base, as commonly defined, encompasses reserves of the chartered banks and legal-tender money held by the non-bank public. I assume that pre-1914 Canadian bank reserves consisted of monetary gold (MGB), Dominion notes (DB) and secondary reserves (SR). Thus,

$$H = MGB + DB + SR + HC, \tag{2.1}$$

where HC stands for Dominion notes outside the banking system. The inclusion of secondary reserves in the monetary base is justified because SR was regarded as a close substitute for monetary gold. Students of the pre-1914 Canadian financial system (Johnson, 1910, 49-50; Viner, 1924; Beckhart, 1929, 416-17, 430; Shearer, 1965, 331) generally agree that the chartered banks held their reserves not only in the form of cash (monetary gold and

Dominion notes), but also in the form of secondary reserves, comprising call loans extended in New York and other foreign financial centres,[15] as well as deposits with foreign correspondent banks. These secondary reserves could be readily converted into gold if the chartered banks faced an unexpected drain of the precious metal.

Dominion notes were issued by the government either against monetary gold or on an uncovered basis. Therefore, aggregate Dominion notes (DB + HC) may also be expressed as:

$$DB + HC = MGG + UD, \tag{2.2}$$

where MGG denotes the monetary gold stock of the Dominion government and UD stands for uncovered Dominion notes, that is, the share of the aggregate note issue not backed by gold in government vaults. Substitution of identity (2.2) into (2.1) yields:

$$H = I + UD, \tag{2.3}$$

where

$$I = MGG + MGB + SR. \tag{2.4}$$

The sum of monetary gold and secondary reserves, as shown by identity (2.4), will be termed Canada's stock of international monetary assets (I).[16]

Identity (2.3) suggests that changes in the monetary base mirrored changes in either international monetary assets or uncovered Dominion notes. International monetary assets varied only if Canada ran a balance-of-payments surplus or deficit. Thus, the ''I'' term captures the influence of the balance of payments on the monetary base, while movements in the uncovered stock of Dominion notes were the result of discretionary monetary policy measures taken by the government.

In his study of the Canadian price-specie-flow mechanism, Viner only considered the balance of payments and movements in bank reserve ratios as possible sources of variation in the money stock. In other words, he assumed the monetary base to equal international monetary assets and disregarded entirely the role of monetary policy. His neglect of monetary policy was perfectly legitimate since his study was confined to the period 1900-13. As I show in Chapter 3, monetary policy was not an important source of variation in the money stock over this period. However, if the period under study is extended back to Confederation, the question arises whether the role of monetary policy may still be ignored. Therefore, I first review Viner's study and then turn to the role of monetary policy under the pre-1914 gold standard.

2.2.2. Viner's Analysis of the Price-Specie-Flow Mechanism

Viner's study constitutes one of the first attempts to verify empirically the classical adjustment mechanism under the gold standard, as described by the venerable price-specie-flow model. In Viner's opinion, Canadian experience between 1900 and 1913 provides an almost perfect opportunity for studying the operation of the classical adjustment mechanism. As indicated in the preceding chapter, towards the end of the nineteenth century, Canada experienced a remarkable surge in economic growth, which was followed by an enormous acceleration of capital imports from Great Britain and the United States. Viner felt that the massive capital inflow created conditions highly favourable to an empirical test of the price-specie-flow model. On the basis of Canadian experience, it was possible to investigate how the capital inflow had been translated into a real transfer of goods and services and how efficiently the classical adjustment mechanism had operated.

Before delving fully into Viner's analysis, I should note that he did not use the terms "monetary base" and "money stock." He investigated the relationship between bank reserves (cash and secondary) and an aggregate to be called the chartered banks' monetary liabilities. He assumed these monetary liabilities to include bank notes, as well as demand and notice deposits in the hands of Canadian non-banks. Monetary liabilities, as compiled by Viner, are virtually equivalent to Hay's money-stock series, which covers Dominion notes outside the banking system in addition to monetary liabilities. Moreover, as I indicate in Chapter 3, aggregate bank reserves were closely correlated with the monetary base, since HC only accounted for a minor share and H [equation (2.1)]. Therefore, Viner's investigation of the relationship between monetary liabilities and bank reserves was tantamount to analyzing the link between the money stock and the monetary base.

After a careful study of the interaction between the Canadian current account balance, prices, monetary liabilities and capital inflows, Viner concluded that the

> Canadian borrowings obtained transfer into Canada smoothly and without noticeable friction in the form of a net commodity and service import surplus, as the result of relative price changes (and shifts in demands) which were of the character indicated as to be expected by the older writers (Viner, 1960, 413).

In order to summarize Viner's account of the adjustment mechanism, suppose that there occurred a once-and-for-all increase in the Canadian foreign debt. Moreover, assume that the current account balance was zero initially. According to Viner, the capital inflow led to an increase in Canadian monetary liabilities and bank reserves as the Canadian borrowers converted their foreign exchange receipts into domestic money and deposited these funds with the chartered banks. However, despite the increase in their reserves, the chartered banks did not augment their lending to Canadian residents; instead, they allowed their reserves to rise relative to their monetary liabilities. The increase in bank reserve ratios implied that the capital inflow was associated only with a primary round of domestic money creation, resulting directly from foreign borrowing, but not with a secondary round, due to an expansion in the banks' Canadian loans (Viner, 1924, ch. 8).

As Canadian monetary liabilities increased, Canadian demand for goods and services also rose. Since the prices of Canadian imports were largely set abroad, the increase in demand elicited primarily a rise in the relative prices of non-traded goods. The relative prices of exportable goods also rose, but less than those of their non-traded counterparts. These relative price changes shifted demand from non-traded to imported and exportable goods. Thus, the current account tended to deteriorate in response to the capital inflow. Balance-of-payments equilibrium was restored when the cumulative value of the ensuing current account deficits exactly matched the increase in the Canadian foreign debt. As a result of these deficits, the initial change in Canadian monetary liabilities and relative prices was reversed. Since monetary liabilities and prices only changed temporarily, the current account balance in the new equilibrium was once again zero (Viner, 1924, chs. 9-11).[17]

In one respect, however, Viner found that the Canadian evidence did not conform to the classical doctrine. In the initial phase of the adjustment process, the capital inflow was not accompanied by an inflow of monetary gold, as the proponents of that doctrine would have argued. Instead, the chartered banks augmented their secondary reserves. Monetary gold, Viner argued, was imported only as a result of the subsequent increase in Canadian monetary liabilities since the chartered banks strove to maintain a stable ratio between their cash reserves and monetary liabilities. Thus, flows of monetary gold across the Canadian border were not directly related to the capital inflow, but were a consequence of the change in Canadian monetary liabilities. Viner's conclusions imply that the pre-1914 Canadian monetary system resembled a gold exchange rather than a pure gold standard. However, in his view, this did not render the price-specie-flow mechanism inoperative since "fluctuations in the [secondary] reserves played the same role in the Canadian mechanism as that assigned to gold movements in the classical doctrine" (1960, 414).

Why did the chartered banks fail to expand their domestic loans in response to the capital inflow and the attendant rise in their secondary reserve ratios? Viner contended that the banks, prior to 1914, kept interest rates on bank loans and deposits "practically constant" (1924, 175-76). Moreover, they were prepared to furnish any amount of loans demanded by their customers at the fixed interest rates. Thus, bank loans, Viner argued, were determined entirely by the non-bank sector. The banks, in turn, absorbed shifts in their monetary liabilities relative to their loans by varying their secondary reserves.

2.2.3. A Critique of Viner's Analysis

Even sixty years after its publication, the reader of *Canada's Balance* cannot fail to be impressed by Viner's imaginative and painstaking theoretical and empirical investigation. Although Viner's study no doubt ranks with the classics in balance-of-payments analysis, his account of the Canadian adjustment mechanism has not gone unchallenged. Two shortcomings of his analysis are particularly noteworthy.

First, his method of verifying the price-specie-flow model would be valid only if capital flows could be regarded as a truly exogenous variable. Viner's verdict as to the speed and smoothness of the adjustment mechanism depends crucially on the close positive correlation he uncovered between the current account deficit and capital inflows. In the presence of endogenous capital flows, it is conceivable that the correlation was merely the consequence of common factors impinging on the two variables. Therefore, the positive correlation does not necessarily indicate that the current account would have adjusted quickly if an exogenous capital inflow had occurred. A number of authors treating capital flows as an endogenous variable (Carr, 1931; Meier, 1953; Ingram, 1957; Stovel, 1959; Borts, 1964; Cairncross, 1968) have cast doubt on Viner's conclusions and have demonstrated convincingly that the evidence is consistent with alternative interpretations of the adjustment mechanism. For example, both the acceleration of capital inflows and the deterioration of the current account balance could have been explained by the shift to rapid economic growth observed around the turn of the century.[18] However, these studies do not refute the Viner analysis; they merely suggest that Viner failed to furnish sufficient empirical support for the price-specie-flow model. Viner himself later admitted that the evidence was consistent with alternative interpretations.[19]

Second, Viner's analysis of the link between the Canadian money stock and the balance of payments leaves much to be desired. A number of his critics have called into question his conclusion as to the unimportance of secondary money creation in the adjustment mechanism.[20] In reply to his critics, Viner conceded that "primary and secondary expansion of means of payment both contributed to the creation of a situation in which necessary import surpluses could develop" (1960, 429). However, he did not completely change his mind in this regard, for he continued to insist that primary money creation had played the dominant role in the adjustment mechanism (1960, 431).

If we consider the procedure Viner adopted for analyzing money creation by the chartered banks, his conclusions are hardly surprising. In his 1924 study, he did not examine the relationship between monetary liabilities and reserves of the chartered banks, but between a series, which he called foreign loan deposits, and reserves. He defined foreign loan deposits as the difference between the banks' monetary liabilities and loans to Canadian non-bank residents (1924, 187).[21] As Goodhart (1969, 148-51) has convincingly demonstrated, the Viner procedure is largely tautological since it effectively eliminates from the data on monetary liabilities much of the variation due to secondary money creation.

Later on, Viner sensed the inadequacies of his procedure, for he decided to compare bank reserves with both monetary liabilities and foreign loan deposits. Although even a cursory glance at the data suggests that monetary liabilities and reserves were not closely correlated, Viner stuck firmly to his conclusions as to the speed and efficiency of the Canadian adjustment mechanism. In his opinion, the adjustment mechanism had operated efficiently despite the existence in Canada of a fractional-reserve banking system. However, it is doubtful whether Viner correctly interpreted the available evidence. If he had carefully scrutinized the data, he would have noticed that over the period 1900-13, out of thirteen pairs of annual changes in monetary liabilities and reserves, five exhibited opposite signs.[22] Thus, it does not appear that the link between capital flows, bank reserves and monetary liabilities was as close as Viner suggested.

Furthermore, the evidence only lends partial support to Viner's assertion that the Canadian banks kept their loan and deposit rates practically constant. While Viner did not attempt to explain the alleged constancy of Canadian interest rates, most contemporary observers (e.g., Johnson, 1910, 87) believed that interest rates on domestic loans and deposits were fixed rigidly by collusive arrangements among the banks. Despite repeated assertions to the contrary, I doubt that price-fixing agreements were as important as was widely believed. According to Goodhart (1969, 143-44), Canadian bankers were quite candid about their restrictive practices. While they were prepared to admit that — for all practical purposes — deposit rates were set by the Canadian Bankers' Association, they regarded the market for bank loans as reasonably competitive. The views expressed by Canadian bankers are largely borne out by the available empirical evidence.

As far as interest rates on savings deposits are concerned, their variability was indeed very small, notably after the turn of the century. During the period examined by Viner, most banks continually offered 3 percent on their savings deposits, with that rate, in all likelihood, fixed by tacit collusion.[23] Interestingly enough, the government and the post office, which operated a network of savings banks at that time, also appear to have participated in the price-fixing cartel (Table 2-2). However, it is unclear to what extent collusive arrangements existed before 1900. Pre-1900 data on savings deposit rates are unavailable, except for the Bank of Montreal and the government and post office savings banks (Table 2-2). As far as may be judged from the available evidence, deposit rates were more volatile before the turn of the century than after. The Bank of Montreal, for example, adjusted its deposit rate six times between 1874 and 1888, but managed to keep it at a constant level of 3 percent from 1888 onwards. Moreover, prior to 1897, the rates posted by the Bank of Montreal and the government savings banks frequently deviated by as much as one percentage point. The message conveyed by Table 2-2 is confirmed by impressionistic evidence gathered from a perusal of the contemporary financial press (see Naylor, 1975, vol. 1, 85-95). Until the 1890s, the market for savings deposits appears to have been fairly competitive, with banks and non-bank financial intermediaries showing little hesitation to offer higher deposit rates than their competitors in order to attract profitable new business. Considering the disparities of deposit rates among financial institutions, I doubt that the price-fixing arrangements — if they existed at all — were very cohesive before the turn of the century.

TABLE 2-2
INTEREST PAID ON SAVINGS DEPOSITS AT GOVERNMENT SAVINGS BANKS AND BANK OF MONTREAL, 1867-1913
(Percent)

Month/Year	Government a)	Bank of Montreal b)
7/67 - 8/80	4.0	5.0
8/80 - 11/80	4.0	4.0
11/80 - 12/82	4.0	3.0
12/82 - 11/84	4.0	4.0
11/84 - 10/87	4.0	3.0
10/87 - 7/88	4.0	4.0
7/88 - 10/89	4.0	3.0
10/89 - 7/97	3.5	3.0
7/97 - 12/13	3.0	3.0

a) Government and post office savings banks.
b) No data are available prior to 1874

Sources for Table 2-2

Canada, Public Accounts for 1915, 39; Bank of Montreal Archives. Interest on Bank of Montreal savings deposits was payable annually from 1874 to 12/06, quarterly from 12/06 to 12/08, and semi-annually thereafter.

Owing to the fragmentary nature of the available data, it is difficult to determine and appraise the variability of pre-1914 Canadian bank loan rates. Monthly data exist for the average interest rate on domestic call loans granted by the chartered banks in Montreal. Unfortunately, this series only covers the period 1900-13. Chart 2-1 clearly indicates that — contrary to Viner's assertion — the Montreal call-loan rate was not constant but fluctuated between a low of 4 percent and a high of 6.5 percent. Furthermore, the averages shown in Chart 2-1 mask sizeable disparities among the call-loan rates posted by individual banks (see Canada, Board of Inquiry, 1915, 739). The marked variability of the Montreal call-loan rate both over time and across banks suggests that the market for bank loans was not fettered by rigid cartel arrangements.[24]

Nevertheless, Viner's analysis contains a grain of truth in so far as the Montreal call-loan rate was much less volatile than its New York counterpart. Likewise, the rate fluctuations recorded in Montreal were smaller than those in Boston, the nearest U.S. financial centre (Chart 2-1). As compared with the New York and Boston rates, the Montreal call-loan rate displayed only moderate seasonal and cyclical movements. Frequently, the Montreal banks did not change their rates for prolonged periods of time. Thus, the Montreal call-loan rate, though not constant, was remarkably stable in the face of the violent gyrations recorded in New York and Boston. As I show in Chapters

CHART 2-1
CALL-LOAN RATES IN MONTREAL, NEW YORK AND BOSTON, 1900-13

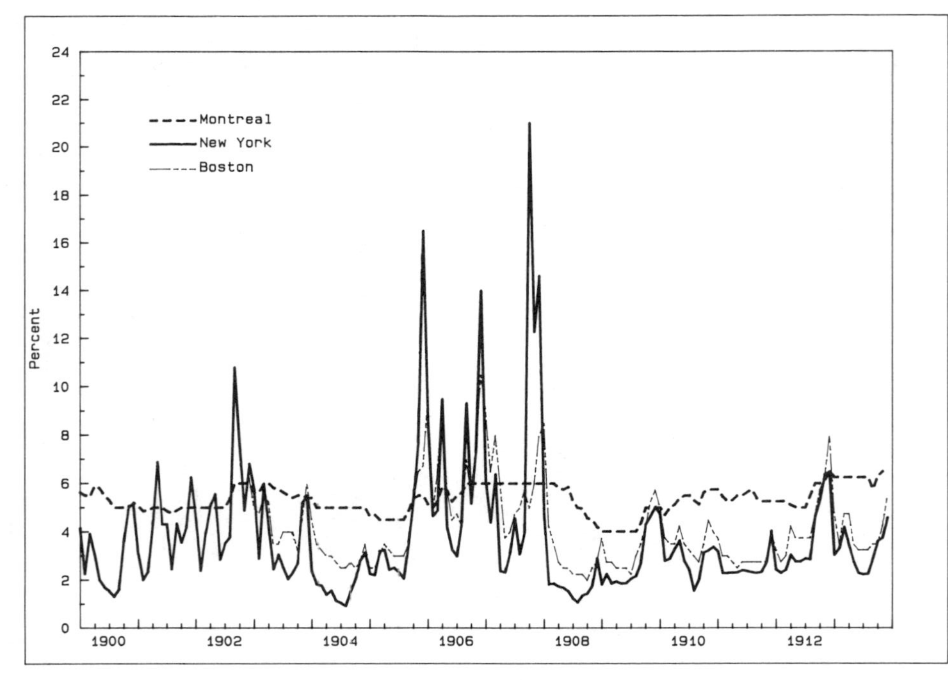

Sources for Chart 2-1

Monthly data on the Montreal call-loan rate are obtained from Canada, Board of Inquiry (1915, 739). For data on short-term interest rates in New York and Boston, see, respectively, Macaulay (1938, Appendix, table 10), and Goodhart (1969, table 14). The U.S. loan rates are monthly averages, while the Montreal call-loan rate refers to the first day following the end of the month.

4, 5 and 6 the relative stability of the Montreal call-loan rate, which puzzled many contemporary observers, may be explained without pleading collusive behaviour and other rigidities in the Canadian financial system. The reasons for the stability of that rate will become clear once the role of the Canadian money stock in the cycle-transmission process is properly understood.

2.2.4. The Influence of Monetary Policy

The term "monetary policy," as used in this study, circumscribes any policy measures bearing upon the note issue and the monetary gold stock of the Dominion government. In particular, I distinguish between automatic and discretionary systems of monetary policy, that is, between automatic and discretionary modes of managing the Dominion note issue and the official gold stock. Under an automatic system of monetary policy, the initiative for altering the note issue and the official gold stock was taken by the public rather than the government. Since the public could increase (lower) its aggregate holdings of Dominion notes only by converting gold into notes (notes into gold), an automatic change in the note issue was matched dollar for dollar by a change in the official gold stock. Discretionary movements in the note issue and in the official gold stock, in contrast, were instigated by the government and were associated with changes in the uncovered stock of Dominion notes.

As a result of the redemption and minimum reserve requirements for the Dominion notes, the scope for discretionary monetary policy was very limited in the pre-1914 period. Curtis (1931b, 106), Easterbrook and Aitken (1956, 462-67), and others have argued that pre-1914 Canadian monetary policy was largely automatic since the constraints of the gold standard ruled out effective discretionary management of the Dominion note issue. A re-examination of the evidence, however, suggests that pre-1914 Canadian monetary policy was not as automatic as has commonly been believed. Over the first two decades after Confederation, in particular, the government frequently experimented with discretionary monetary policy. On the whole, the purpose of these policy experiments was not to manage the liquidity of the Canadian banking system, let alone to stabilize prices or employment. Rather, the government attempted to reduce substantial budget deficits through partial monetization of the public debt. Thus, discretionary monetary policy was largely a debt management tool. Macroeconomic stabilization, by contrast, was not considered to be a government task prior to World War I.

In managing the note issue and the official gold stock, the government was severely hampered by a dearth of policy instruments. Prior to 1914, it was not empowered to discount bills or to make advances to the chartered banks, nor did it conduct open-market operations in securities. Its choice was limited to two instruments of discretionary monetary policy. To expand the uncovered issue, the government, from time to time, deposited Dominion notes with the chartered banks (note deposit policy). Issuing Dominion notes in this way did not raise any particular technical difficulties since the government held demand and time deposits with most chartered banks. These deposits served mainly as transactions balances but could also be employed for monetary policy purposes. For reasons to be discussed in Chapter 7, the government also conducted various kinds of discretionary gold transactions. It varied the uncovered issue by depositing or withdrawing gold with or from the chartered banks. Moreover, it frequently acquired — on a discretionary basis — sovereigns in the London gold market. In principle, discretionary changes in the note issue and the official gold stock were accompanied by movements in the Canadian monetary base. For example, if the government deposited Dominion notes or monetary gold with the chartered banks, bank cash reserves and, hence, the monetary base increased.[25]

The government also influenced the monetary base in indirect ways. During the period under study, the government typically ran budget deficits, which it financed, in large measure, by issuing bonds in the London capital market or by borrowing funds from London banks. Foreign borrowing by the government affected the monetary base through changes in international monetary assets. Thus, the question arises to what extent the monetary and budgetary policies of the Dominion government were responsible for cyclical movements in the monetary base and the money stock.

2.3. ACTIVE OR PASSIVE MONEY?

In order to analyze the stabilizing or destabilizing role of the Canadian monetary sector, it is useful to distinguish between direct and indirect effects of changes in the domestic money stock on domestic economic activity. I speak of direct monetary effects if changes in the Canadian money stock influenced domestic economic activity through changes in domestic relative to foreign interest rates. Indirect monetary effects, in contrast, were transmitted through movements in both foreign *and* domestic interest rates.

2.3.1. Direct Monetary Effects

As Mundell (1963) has shown, changes in the Canadian money stock do not directly affect domestic economic activity if exchange rates are fixed and if international capital flows are perfectly mobile between domestic and foreign markets. The implications of capital mobility for the cycle-transmission process may be analyzed within the framework of a standard open-economy macroeconomic model. For simplicity's sake, cyclical fluctuations in Canadian economic activity are assumed to reflect movements in output or real income, while prices are invariant to the business cycle.[26] The model incorporates three markets, that is, markets for Canadian output (y), nominal money (M), and financial assets bearing an interest rate (r). By virtue of Walras' Law, the market for financial assets is disregarded in the analysis. Output, the money stock and the interest rate are assumed to be endogenously determined.

Under conditions of perfect capital mobility, arbitrage between domestic and foreign financial markets operates such as to equalize Canadian and foreign interest rates. For the moment, assume that the foreign interest rate (r_f) is insensitive to changes in domestic economic conditions and, therefore, may be treated as an exogenous variable. Under these circumstances, the domestic interest rate is tied rigidly to the exogenous variable, r_f, as depicted by the horizontal RR-line drawn at $r=r_f$ in Chart 2-2. The loci of r and y, consistent with equilibrium in the output and money markets, are traced by the familiar Hicksian IS- and LM-lines respectively.

Now suppose that the Canadian economy is disturbed by a cyclical upswing in foreign economic activity and a corresponding rise in foreign demand for Canadian goods. The cyclical expansion in Canadian exports causes the IS-line to shift to the right. Provided the foreign interest rate remains unchanged, Canadian output will go up from y* to y**. Obviously, the sensitivity of Canadian output to the foreign cyclical disturbance is invariant to supply and demand conditions in the domestic money market since the equilibrium value of y is determined solely by the point of intersection between the RR- and IS-lines. All the Canadian money supply does is to adjust passively to the increase in money demand triggered by the output expansion, as manifested by a rightward shift in the LM-line. The rise in Canadian money demand is shown by the DD-line drawn on the lower panel of Chart 2-2. That line depicts the variation in money demand resulting from changes in output, given prices and the domestic interest rate.

The foregoing analysis implies that under conditions of perfect capital mobility, the Canadian government and the chartered banks are powerless to alter the money supply in a way that significantly accentuates or moderates the export-induced expansion in Canadian output. Perfect international capital mobility ensures that the money supply rises from M* to M**, regardless of any measures taken by the government and the banks. If, for example, an increase in bank lending were to push up the money supply beyond M**, capital would quickly flow out of Canada. The resulting balance-of-payments deficit, in turn, would cause the Canadian money stock to shrink to M**. Thus, procyclical movements in bank lending would not amplify the fluctuations in output.[27]

The conclusions drawn from the Mundellian analysis, however, are altered drastically if the assumption of perfect capital mobility is dropped. Since under conditions of imperfect capital mobility domestic interest rates are not tied rigidly to their foreign counterparts, changes in the Canadian money stock, triggered by a cyclical expansion in exports, may directly influence Canadian output. An export-induced increase in Canadian output may be associated with a rise or fall in domestic relative to foreign interest rates, depending on the way monetary authorities and the chartered banks react to the business-cycle expansion. Thus, domestic interest rates may moderate or amplify the impact on Canadian output of the foreign cyclical disturbance.

Even though there was some correlation between call-loan rates in Montreal and major cities of the Northeastern United States, the evidence of Chart 2-1 is incompatible with the assumption of perfect capital mobility. Therefore,

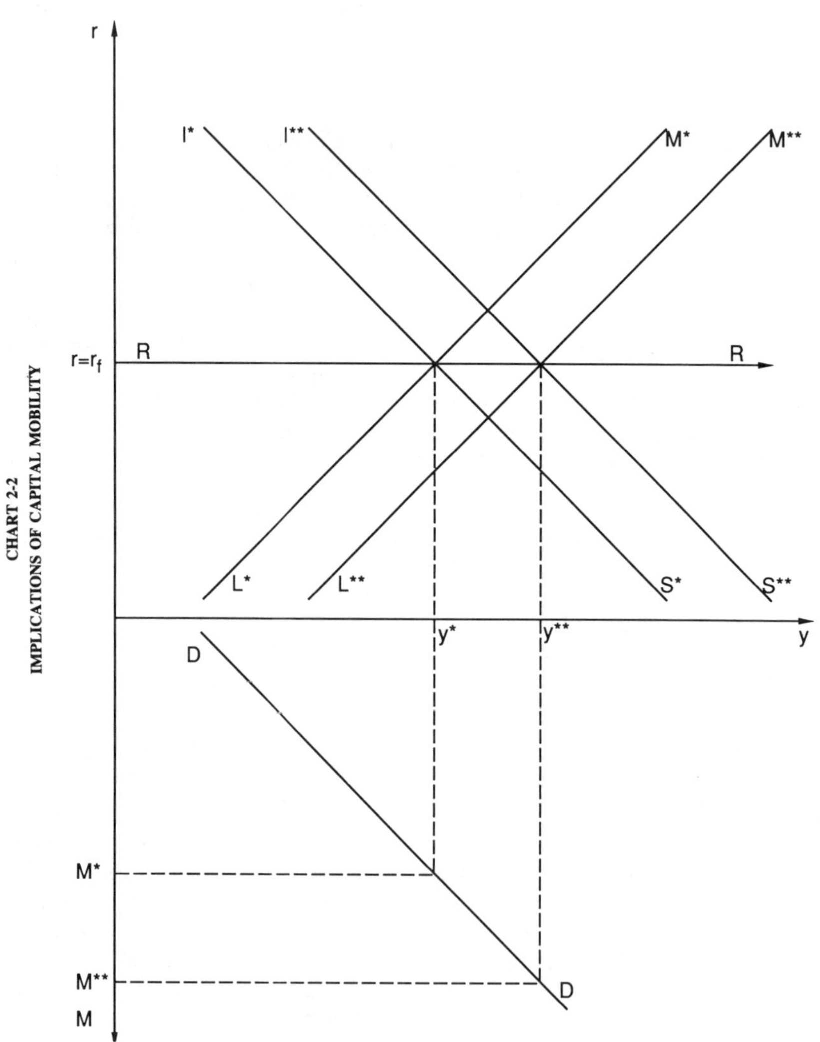

CHART 2-2
IMPLICATIONS OF CAPITAL MOBILITY

McCloskey and Zecher's assertion that the gold standard was ruled by the law of one price does not appear to be borne out by the Canadian evidence. Accordingly, the analysis of the cycle-transmission process presented in this study does not rest on a perfect-arbitrage view of the gold-standard world. On the contrary, the model to be presented in Chapter 4 explicitly allows for the possibility of changes in the Canadian money stock directly impinging on domestic economic activity. The explicit recognition of direct monetary effects is all the more important as one of the objectives of this study is to discover the reasons for the relative stability of Canadian interest rates.

2.3.2. Indirect Monetary Effects

Aside from direct monetary effects, indirect channels may have linked domestic economic activity and the money stock. A bank-induced expansion in the Canadian money supply, for example, might have influenced domestic economic activity through a simultaneous decrease in foreign and domestic interest rates — provided the balance-of-payments deficit, elicited by the increase in the money supply, led to a gold outflow from Canada that significantly lowered foreign interest rates through a rise in foreign money stocks. Needless to say, indirect monetary effects could have been present under conditions of both perfect and imperfect capital mobility.

Considering the relatively small size of the Canadian economy, I doubt that the indirect effects emanating from changes in the Canadian money stock were strong. Nonetheless, this book deals with both types of monetary effects. Although the indirect effects of the procyclical movements in the Canadian money stock, by themselves, were likely to be negligible, a study of such effects might still constitute a worthwhile endeavour. In a world in which national business cycles were closely synchronized, the combined indirect monetary effects emanating from a multitude of gold-standard countries could have acted as a powerful destabilizing force. As I show in Chapter 8, Canadian indirect monetary effects — though small if taken in isolation — were not negligible by comparison with those originating in other major gold-standard countries.

In principle, the indirect monetary effects could have moderated or amplified the impact of foreign cyclical disturbances on Canadian output, depending on the way the price-specie-flow mechanism operated in Canada. If, as suggested by Viner, the Canadian stocks of money and monetary gold were closely correlated, I would expect that the indirect monetary effects dampened the cyclical fluctuations in Canadian economic activity. In this case, a cyclical expansion in the Canadian money stock, resulting from an export-induced rise in Canadian economic activity, would have been associated with an inflow of monetary gold from abroad, diminishing the monetary base of other gold-standard countries and, thus, pushing up foreign interest rates. Consequently, to answer the question whether the indirect monetary effects were likely to be stabilizing or destabilizing, it is necessary to study the operation of the Canadian adjustment mechanism, notably the link between the Canadian money stock and international gold flows.

2.4. PLAN OF STUDY

This study starts with an investigation of the relationship between the pre-1914 Canadian money stock and the balance of payments. In Chapter 3, the cyclical attributes of the Canadian balance of payments, the monetary base and the money stock are analyzed. Furthermore, I identify the sources of cyclical variation in the Canadian money stock. To this end, new estimates of Canadian international monetary assets and the balance of payments on current account are presented. The estimation procedure is discussed in detail in Appendices A and B. I conclude that the procyclical pattern of the Canadian money stock was attributable largely to countercyclical movements in the reserve ratios of the chartered banks, while the overall balance-of-payments surplus and the monetary base varied countercyclically. The significance of discretionary monetary policy as a source of variation in the monetary base is also investigated. Finally, I explore the relationship between the Canadian money stock and international gold flows to identify possible indirect monetary effects on domestic economic activity.

Chapter 4 presents a theoretical model of the cycle-transmission process. The focus of the analysis is on the role played by bank reserve management in the propagation of foreign cyclical disturbances. Two hypotheses concerning the causes of the countercyclical swings in bank reserve ratios are specified. I then show that either of the two hypotheses — if incorporated in an open-economy macroeconomic model — accounts for the observed cyclical patterns of the Canadian money stock, economic activity and balance of payments, save for leads or lags between domestic economic activity and foreign cyclical disturbances produced by the model that conflict with the empirical evidence. The theoretical analysis also yields various propositions about the cyclical pattern of Canadian interest rates. In particular, I demonstrate that it is possible to infer from the observed cyclical patterns of Canadian interest rates the causes of the countercyclical swings in bank reserve ratios.

Chapter 5 examines further the consistency of the model with the empirical evidence. The cyclical patterns of Canadian interest rates are determined and the causes of the countercyclical movements in bank reserve ratios are inferred from these patterns. These results are in turn compared with those derived from an alternative approach, under which the causes of the countercyclical swings in bank reserve ratios are traced directly. I conclude that bank reserve management, in all likelihood, played an important role in the cycle-transmission process. The chartered banks tended to accentuate cyclical fluctuations in Canadian economic activity by keeping domestic interest rates relatively stable and by delaying the adjustment in these rates to foreign cyclical shocks.

In Chapter 6, the monetary analysis of the Canadian business cycle developed in the preceding chapters is applied to the crisis of 1907, an event that has received considerable attention in the existing literature. I demonstrate that the causes of the crisis may be readily identified if the analysis is extended to take account of seasonal movements in the Canadian balance of payments. The conclusions of this chapter differ fundamentally from existing interpretations of the crisis.

Chapter 7 traces pre-1914 Canadian monetary and budgetary policies. The emphasis is on the monetary policy experiments conducted by the Dominion government in the first twenty years after Confederation, a fascinating — and largely forgotten — episode in Canadian monetary history. Moreover, I examine the cyclical pattern of the Dominion-government budget deficit and foreign borrowing to ascertain the extent to which government policy impinged on the cyclical pattern of the monetary base.

The concluding Chapter 8 provides a summary of the principal results. In addition, it offers a brief comparison of Canadian with foreign experience in order to examine the stabilizing or destabilizing features of the pre-1914 Canadian gold standard from a global perspective and to highlight the significance of indirect effects of procyclical movements in the Canadian money stock.

Endnotes — Chapter 2

1. Using spectral analysis, Bonomo and Tanner (1972) also uncover a close correspondence between Canadian and U.S. business cycles. Their study, however, only covers the post-World-War-I period.

2. The cyclical sensitivity of Canadian exports only shrank temporarily during the 1900s and 1910s. Since quarterly data on Canadian and U.S. output were not available for the entire period under study, Rosenbluth also employed such indicators as bank debits and clearings, as well as railway freight-ton miles, to date the cyclical turning points in output.

3. Bryce (1939, 383-84) argued that U.S. business conditions directly affected Canadian investment. He calls this effect "contagion of spirits."

4. Rosenbluth (1958, 36-37) also examined the role of capital imports in the transmission process. This analysis, not surprisingly, is inconclusive since it makes little sense to investigate the role of capital imports within the framework of a model that does not include a monetary sector.

5. Moreover, Rosenbluth did not explicitly analyze the role of export and import prices in the transmission process. However, since his study is based largely on nominal values of exports and output, he indirectly took account of export prices.

6. More recently, proponents of real business-cycle theories have challenged the monetary approach to business-cycle analysis. They deny that monetary disturbances have real effects. Unlike the earlier Keynesian approach, real business-cycle models are rooted in the classical tradition. See McCallum (1986) for an excellent review of real business-cycle theories.

7. Friedman and Schwartz (1963a, 50-53) do not claim that causation ran exclusively from the money stock to economic activity. In their view, the procyclical movements in the money stock were both an effect and cause of the cyclical fluctuations in economic activity. However, a detailed investigation of individual U.S. business cycles (see their 1963b study) leads them to conclude that the money stock reacted not to contemporary but to past business conditions.

8. As a matter of fact, the longest lag — recorded early in the 1870s — amounted to 44 months. However, for the other pre-1914 reference cycles, the lags were at most 26 months (Hay, 1967, Table 3). In another study of cyclical movements in the Canadian money stock, Macesich (1970, Table 1) obtains results similar to Hay's, but his investigation does not cover the subperiod 1900-20.

9. Hay (1967, Table 6) finds that, for reference-cycle contractions, the rank correlation between the cyclical amplitude of the Canadian money stock and the cyclical amplitude of Canadian economic activity was statistically significant. However, no statistically significant rank correlation was obtained for reference-cycle expansions. Hay does not attempt to explain this asymmetry.

10. The same procedure is used by Macesich (1970).

11. On the problem of identifying the cyclical component of a time series, see also Mintz (1969). More sophisticated procedures are discussed by Beveridge and Nelson (1981).

12. Culbertson's critique is not addressed to Friedman and Schwartz (1963a), but to earlier statements by Friedman (see U.S. Congress, 1959; Friedman, 1960, 87-88).

13. Suppose that the level of the money stock (M) is related to time (t) and may be split up into a trend and a cyclical component, as indicated by the following equation:

$$\ln M = \nu_1 + \nu_2 t + \nu_3 \sin t, \qquad \text{(A)}$$

where $\nu_1 + \nu_2 t$ stands for the trend, and $\nu_3 \sin t$ for the cyclical component. The rate of change in the money stock is given by:

$$d \ln M/d\, t = \nu_2 + \nu_3 \cos t. \qquad \text{(B)}$$

If a full money cycle were assumed to last 2π units of time, equation (B) could also be written as:

$$d \ln M/dt = \nu_2 + \nu_3 \sin(t + \pi/2).$$

Adjusted for trend, the money stock would equal the cyclical component, $\nu_3 \sin t$. Thus, the turning points in $d \ln M/d\, t$ would lead the corresponding turning points in the trend-adjusted money stock by $\pi/2$ units of time.

14. Of course, no lag would be obtained if the rate of change in economic activity were compared with the rate of change in the money stock.

15. The available data on foreign call loans (see Curtis, 1931a, 52) include fixed-term loans maturing in 30 days or less.

16. I employ the term "international monetary assets," rather than "international monetary reserves," in order to distinguish the former clearly from bank reserves. Deposits of the Dominion government with foreign banks are not included in international monetary assets. Lindert (1967; 1969) has argued that in most countries the shift from a pure gold standard to a gold-exchange standard occurred well before World War I. As far as Canada is concerned, he claims that around the turn of the century, the government began to hold an increasing share of its international monetary assets in the form of deposits with the London branch of the Bank of Montreal (1967, 106-07). However, I have not been able to find any evidence in support of Lindert's view that the government considered these deposits to be part of its holdings of international monetary assets. As I show in Chapter 7, the Bank of Montreal, along with two British banks, acted as the government's fiscal agent in London, whose principal task was to manage the government's foreign debt. The deposits with the London branch of the Bank of Montreal and with the other foreign fiscal agents were transactions balances used mainly for debt management purposes.

17. Viner also analyzed the more realistic case of a permanent increase in the capital *inflow*. He clearly realized that there was a difference between a once-and-for-all change in Canada's foreign debt and a permanent increase in its growth (1924, 177-80). He ignored the implications of changes in interest payments on the foreign debt.

18. Some critics (e.g., Stovel, 1959, ch. 16) have taken Viner to task for focussing attention on the role of relative prices in the adjustment process. They argue that capital inflows affected the current-account balance primarily through changes in Canadian real income rather than relative prices.

19. According to Viner (1960, 429-30), it is "possible to argue that at times at least" the observed increase in the money stock was due to purely internal factors, rather than a capital inflow. The rise in the money stock caused the current account to deteriorate. Moreover, "the borrowings were engaged in to obtain the foreign funds necessary to liquidate trade balances already incurred." However, he felt this interpretation was "quite consistent with the orthodox

explanation.'' He also admitted that the current-account balance was likely to respond to an exogenous capital inflow with a lag (1960, 423).

20. To be precise, in his 1924 study, Viner argued that the importance of secondary money creation had increased somewhat towards the end of the period under study (1924, 189-90).

21. Viner (1924, 184-85) apparently believed that loans to Canadian residents were unrelated to the capital inflow.

22. See his Table VI (1960, 428). In 1902/03, 1906/07, 1910/11 and 1912/13, reserves (column 6) decreased, while monetary liabilities (column 1) increased. In 1907/08, reserves went up, while monetary liabilities fell.

23. See Johnson (1910, 87) and Beckhart (1929, 402). Beckhart states that ''there was an 'understanding' among the banks regarding the 3% rate but that there was nothing to prevent a bank from paying more and that no penalties could be imposed for any deviations.'' That rate applied to the minimum monthly balance of savings accounts.

24. Goodhart (1969, 141-45) discusses in detail the structure of the Canadian market for bank loans. He believes that contemporary observers overstated the importance of price-fixing arrangements in that market. It should also be noted that Canadian loan rates, prior to 1913, were seldom constrained by usury laws. Canadian usury laws stipulated that the banks could charge any rate on their loans ''but could not use legal process to recover interest in excess of 7%'' (Neufeld, 1972, 88).

25. Official purchases of sovereigns in Britain need not have diminished the monetary base. Had the government acquired the coins against funds on deposit with foreign banks, cash reserves of the domestic banks and the monetary base would have remained unchanged. In other words, the increase in the official gold stock, resulting from the purchase of precious metal, would have been associated with a simultaneous reduction in UD and an increase in I [identity (2.3)]. However, it is reasonable to assume that discretionary monetary policy normally altered the monetary base. As I show in Chapter 7, much of the observed variation in the uncovered issue was due to deposits of Dominion notes and monetary gold with the chartered banks. Moreover, sovereigns were usually acquired and imported by the Bank of Montreal on behalf of the government (see Chapter 7, note 29). The government paid for the sovereigns by lowering its deposits booked at the domestic branches of the Bank. The latter, in turn, saw its secondary reserves decrease as it drew on funds held with one of its correspondent banks in order to finance the purchase. Thus, the monetary base was likely to fall as a result of the import of sovereigns.

26. The assumption of fixed prices — which is blatantly unrealistic — is relaxed in Chapter 4. However, the subsequent discussion remains valid even if the model allows for cyclical movements in prices.

27. Perfect capital mobility, however, need not imply that the Keynesian export-multiplier model represents an adequate framework for analyzing the Canadian business cycle. The Mundellian analysis does not suggest that foreign cyclical disturbances were transmitted to Canada entirely through fluctuations in exports. Cyclical movements in foreign interest rates and prices could also have influenced Canadian output.

28. As I show in Chapter 5, there are doubts about the reliability of the available data on the Montreal call-loan rate. However, it is safe to conclude that the variability of short-term interest rates in Canada was much smaller than in the United States.

CHAPTER 3

THE SOURCES OF VARIATION IN THE MONEY STOCK

The evidence presented in the preceding chapter is at variance with Viner's thesis about a close link between the pre-1914 Canadian money stock and the balance of payments. Therefore, it is necessary to re-examine the sources of variation in the Canadian money stock. To this end, I determine the relative importance of four possible sources of variation: the balance of payments, discretionary monetary policy, bank reserve behaviour and the preferences of the Canadian non-bank public as to the composition of the money stock. The analysis proceeds in four steps: In Section 3.1, the cyclical patterns of the Canadian balance of payments are examined. Section 3.2 is devoted to an analysis of the link between the monetary base and the balance of payments. In particular, the relative importance of discretionary monetary policy and the balance of payments as sources of variation in the monetary base is determined. Section 3.3 focusses on the relationship between the money stock and the monetary base, while Section 3.4 is devoted to a re-examination of Viner's evidence on the relationship between the Canadian money stock and international gold flows.

3.1. CYCLICAL PATTERNS OF THE BALANCE OF PAYMENTS

3.1.1. The Canadian Balance of Payments: General Remarks

The cyclical patterns of the pre-1914 Canadian balance of payments may be determined with the help of Table 3-1, exhibiting data on the current account surplus (deficit), residual inflows (outflows) and the overall surplus (or deficit). Note that the current-account data shown in Table 3-1 exclude interest and dividend flows, for which reliable statistics are unavailable. The overall balance-of-payments surplus corresponds to annual first-differences in international monetary assets, as recorded in Tables A-1 and A-2. Residual inflows equal the difference between the overall and current-account surplus. They are used as a proxy for net inflows of non-monetary capital, corresponding to the difference between aggregate net capital inflows and net imports of monetary capital by the chartered banks in the form of net decreases in their secondary reserves.

Table 3-1 is based on the standard sources of data on the pre-1914 Canadian balance of payments (Viner, 1914; Hartland, 1955; 1960), except that it incorporates new estimates of the overall surplus, as well as non-monetary flows of gold and other precious metals. The data on the overall surplus shown in Table 3-1 are derived from revised estimates of the Canadian stock of monetary gold and secondary reserves, which are presented in Tables A-1 and A-2. The estimation procedures are discussed in Appendices A and B. The data on gold and secondary reserves are estimated from Curtis (1931a), the principal source of statistical information on pre-1914 Canadian banking (henceforth called Curtis data), as well as from published and unpublished data sources not previously employed in empirical studies of the pre-1914 Canadian balance of payments.

The data displayed in Table 3-1 suffer from a variety of breaks. The breaks in the overall-surplus series in 1888 and 1901 are attributable to the fact that, due to gaps in the existing primary data sources, I was compelled to estimate international monetary assets using three different procedures. For the period beginning with the third quarter of 1900, the revised estimates of international monetary assets are available quarterly and appear to be reasonably accurate. For the period 1887-1900, I was able to estimate an annual series that seems to be fairly complete too, but does not match the quality of the post-1900 quarterly data. The pre-1887 estimates rest almost entirely on Curtis and are marred by various omissions. Although the pre-1900 estimates of international monetary assets leave something to be desired, they seem to be adequate for analyzing cyclical movements in the Canadian overall balance of payments (see Appendix B). The current-account statistics suffer from a major break in 1900, attributable to a corresponding break in the existing estimates of the Canadian non-merchandise trade balance.

The exclusion of interest and dividend flows from the current-account estimates implies that Table 3-1 systematically understates the size of Canada's current-account deficits. Analogously, net capital inflows were larger than indicated by residual inflows. Due to Canada's role as an important borrower of foreign capital, net interest and dividend payments (payments minus receipts) to foreigners were a significant and rapidly growing item in the Canadian balance of payments. Adjusted for this item, the Canadian current account would likely have been in deficit during the entire pre-1914 period, save for a possible surplus in 1897. Nonetheless, I doubt that the cyclical attributes of the current-account balance and residual inflows would be altered very

TABLE 3-1

CANADIAN BALANCE OF PAYMENTS
(Millions of Dollars)

	Current Account Surplus (Excl. Interest and Dividends)	Residual Inflows	Overall Balance of Payments Surplus	Ref. Cycle
1868	-8.2			
1869	-1.7			
1870	-9.9			
1871	-21.9			
1872	-28.6	20.6	-8.0	
1873	-28.5	29.1	0.6	P/11
1874	-33.3	32.8	-0.5	
1875	-19.7	18.9	-0.8	
1876	-10.0	7.0	-3.0	
1877	-8.8	10.2	1.4	
1878	-6.9	4.9	-2.0	
1879	4.3	16.4	20.7	T/05
1880	5.6	0.4	6.0	
1881	-3.3	-2.9	-6.2	
1882	-15.4	1.4	-14.0	P/07
1883	-21.0	31.3	10.3	
1884	-15.6	12.3	-3.3	
1885	-12.5	15.2	2.7	T/03
1886	-14.5	10.5	-4.0	
1887	-13.7	11.5	-2.2	P/02
1888	-17.5	26.9	9.4a)	T/02
1888	-17.5	28.8	11.3	
1889	-22.9	8.3	-14.6	
1890	-20.8	15.0	-5.8	P/07

	Current Account Surplus (Excl. Interest and Dividends)	Residual Inflows	Overall Balance of Payments Surplus	Ref. Cycle
1890	-21.4	15.6	-5.8	
1891	-12.3	28.6	16.3	T/03
1892	-6.5	8.4	1.9	
1893	-0.5	-2.8	-3.3	P/02
1894	3.1	10.4	13.5	T/03
1894	4.2	9.3	13.5	
1895	3.9	-9.4	-5.5	P/08
1896	12.5	-11.7	0.8	T/08
1897	42.4	-30.8	11.6	
1898	19.2	-21.4	-2.2	
1899	15.0	-15.2	-0.2	
1899	14.9	-15.1	-0.2	
1900	18.5	-7.5	11.0	P/04
1900	23.3	-12.3	11.0	
1901	21.3	8.7	30.0b)	T/02
1901	21.3	-1.4	19.9	
1902	22.9	-16.2	6.7	P/12
1903	-14.4	18.2	3.8	
1904	-39.0	70.4	31.4	T/06
1905	-33.2	36.9	3.7	
1906	-52.1	53.1	1.0	P/12
1907	-119.5	102.4	-17.1	
1908	-29.7	147.9	118.2	T/07
1909	-66.8	94.8	28.0	
1910	-141.9	112.5	-29.4	P/03
1911	-213.6	248.8	35.2	T/07
1912	-316.9	310.3	-6.6	P/11
1913	-254.5	281.7	27.2	

a) Calculated from an estimate of international monetary assets for the end of 1888 (amounting to $33.3 million), derived on the basis of the estimation procedure employed for the period 1871-87 [sum of data for 1888IV in Table A-1, column (1), Table B-4, and Table B-5, columns (1) and (3)].

b) Calculated from an estimate of international monetary assets for the end of 1901 (amounting to $96.4 million), derived using the estimation procedure employed for the period 1887-1900 [sum of data for 1901IV in Table A-2, columns (1), (3) and (5), and Table B-6, column (3)].

Sources and estimation method for Table 3-1

Current-account surplus: Table A-3, column (7).
Residual inflows: Difference between overall balance-of-payments and current-account surplus.
Overall balance-of-payments surplus: Annual first differences in international monetary assets as shown in Tables A-1 and A-2, column (7).
Reference-cycle turning points: Table 2-1.

much if the data in Table 3-1 were adjusted for interest and dividend flows (see Appendix A).

As far as trend movements in the balance of payments are concerned, Table 3-1 suggests that Canada, before 1914, ran persistent — and frequently massive — current-account deficits. From 1868 to the end of the 1880s, the deficits varied considerably in the short run, but did not follow a noticeable upward or downward trend. Around 1890, the current-account balance began to improve significantly, with the deficit declining intermittently until the end of the decade. The striking improvement in the current-account balance was attributable to the wheat boom and the attendant surge in exports of natural resources. As Naylor (1975, vol. 1, 11-12) correctly points out, the term "wheat boom" is somewhat of a misnomer, for exports of mineral products, rather than wheat, served as the initial driving force behind the boom. However, he overlooks the fact that the marked temporary improvement in the current-account balance from 1896 to 1897 was due largely to a huge increase in wheat exports.[1] From 1897 to 1900, the impetus was provided by the Yukon gold rush that led to an almost fivefold increase in net exports of non-monetary gold (Table A-3). After the turn of the century, the surge in economic activity also caused import growth to accelerate. The transition to higher import growth was mirrored by a renewed shift in the trend of the current-account balance, as manifested by the mounting deficits recorded towards the end of the period under study.

The current-account deficits were more than offset by inflows of foreign capital. Therefore, the overall balance of payments was in surplus during much of the pre-1914 period. However, international monetary assets did not expand at a steady pace. Until the end of the 1880s, they fluctuated strongly in the short run, but did not follow a noticeable upward trend. The onset of the wheat boom and the attendant surge in real GNP growth also caused the growth in international monetary assets to accelerate. From the end of 1900 to the end of 1913, international monetary assets rose at an average annual rate of almost 12 percent (Tables A-1 and A-2).

3.1.2. Overall Balance-of-Payments Surplus

In order to identify the cyclical pattern of the Canadian balance of payments, I insert in Table 3-1 the dates of the Canadian reference-cycle turning points. The evidence clearly indicates that the overall surplus was inversely related to the reference cycle. The countercyclical pattern of the overall surplus was remarkably regular. Throughout the period under study, cyclical peaks (troughs) in the overall surplus tended to coincide with reference-cycle troughs (peaks). The only major departure of the overall surplus from its normal countercyclical pattern occurred during the reference-cycle expansion of 1896-1900. While the overall surplus, as usual, had risen during the preceding contraction, it shrank temporarily in 1898, only to increase again as the Canadian economy approached the cyclical peak of 1900. Another departure was the sharp transitory rise in the overall surplus in 1883. Moreover, during the contraction of 1873-79, the overall surplus did not increase until economic activity approached its cyclical trough.[2]

The striking inverse relationship between the overall surplus and the reference cycle was not a spurious phenomenon. On the contrary, the evidence suggests that the observed countercyclical pattern was statistically significant. In order to test the statistical significance of the countercyclical movements in the overall surplus, the reference cycle is split up into two pairs of cycle stages, that is, an expansion and contraction stage, on the one hand, as well as a boom and depression stage on the other. The expansion (contraction) stage is assumed to cover the period between a cyclical trough (peak) and the subsequent peak (trough). The boom stage is assumed to last from the midpoint of a cyclical expansion to the midpoint of the subsequent contraction. The depression stage is delineated analogously (see Appendix C for the details).

Considering the cyclical patterns revealed by Table 2-4, I would expect that the overall surplus tended to be higher during depressions than during booms. Therefore, I test the null hypothesis that the overall surplus or the growth in international monetary assets, on average, would be the same for booms and depressions. A rejection of the null hypothesis would point to a statistically significant countercyclical pattern for the overall surplus. The test of the null hypothesis is confined to the post-1900 period, for which quarterly data on international monetary assets are available (see Table A-2). To eliminate the scale effect arising from the rapid growth in international monetary assets after 1900, I employ rates of change rather than first differences in that aggregate. If the scale effect were not removed, the significance test would be biased against the cyclical fluctuations in the overall surplus observed in the early part of the sample period. Moreover, international monetary assets are smoothed by a seven-quarter moving average to reduce intra-cycle variation.[3] As indicated by Table 3-2, the null hypothesis is clearly rejected at the 99 percent level of significance. During depressions, the average quarterly growth in international monetary assets was almost four percentage points higher than during booms. The averages for expansions and contractions, by contrast, were not significantly different.

Chart 3-1 identifies possible leads or lags between the quarterly growth rates of international monetary assets and the reference cycle. Reference-cycle contractions are indicated by the shaded areas in the chart. The evidence strongly suggests that high (low) growth rates were clustered around reference-cycle troughs (peaks). Chart 3-1 does not reveal a consistent lead or lag pattern for the growth in international monetary assets. Moreover, when noticeable leads or lags occurred, they seldom exceeded two quarters.[4]

3.1.3. Current-Account Surplus

In order to avoid confusion concerning the direction of change in the current-account balance, I henceforth use the term "surplus," no matter whether the current account was actually in surplus or deficit. As I pointed out in Chapter

TABLE 3-2
CYCLICAL CHARACTERISTICS OF INTERNATIONAL MONETARY ASSETS, THE MONETARY BASE AND THE MONEY STOCK
(Arithmetic Means of Quarterly Rates of Change)

Estimation Period	Boom Stage	Depression Stage	t-values	Expansion Stage	Contraction Stage	t-values
	International Monetary Assets			International Monetary Assets		
1901III - 1913I	0.80	4.62	5.14 (52)	2.76	2.62	0.14 (52)
	Monetary Gold			Monetary Gold		
1872III - 1899III	0.30	1.32	2.48 (119)	1.00	0.59	0.93 (119)
1901III - 1913I	2.92	4.06	2.51 (52)	2.83	4.25	3.11 (52)
	Monetary Base			Monetary Base		
1901III - 1913I	0.80	4.14	5.00 (52)	2.55	2.35	0.24 (52)
	Money Stock			Money Stock		
1874III - 1886IV	1.00	0.62	0.82 (52)	2.24	-0.19	7.86 (51)
1887I - 1895III	1.18	1.56	1.79 (39)	1.37	1.21	0.66 (40)
1895IV - 1913I	2.28	2.40	0.55 (78)	2.65	1.86	4.20 (78)
	Deposits Abroad			Deposits Abroad		
1901III - 1913I	3.03	2.58	0.69 (52)	3.69	1.36	4.17 (52)
	Other Current Loans Abroad			Other Current Loans Abroad		
1901III - 1913I	0.95	1.70	0.48 (52)	3.69	-1.95	4.65 (52)

Sources and estimation methods for Table 3-2

See Table A-2 for post-1900 data on international monetary assets, monetary gold, the monetary base and the money stock. Quarterly data on the money stock for the period prior to 1900III are calculated in the same way as those for 1900III and subsequent quarters. Quarterly data on monetary gold for the period up to 1900II are drawn from the following sources: government gold: Table 7-1 and Curtis, 1931a, 92-93; bank gold: see Curtis, 1931a, 36. Data on deposits and other current loans abroad are obtained from Curtis, 1931a, 21 and 52. All the data are smoothed by a seven-quarter moving average centred on the fourth quarter covered by the average. The quarterly rates of change in turn are calculated from the smoothed data. In the case of government gold, the observation for 1880I is missing. I assume government gold at the end of 1880I to have equalled the average of the observations for 1879IV and 1880II. The quarterly rates of change are assigned to the various reference-cycle stages according to Appendix C, procedure 1. For the significance test, see Yamane (1973, 661-69). The numbers in parentheses denote degrees of freedom.

CHART 3-1

QUARTERLY GROWTH IN INTERNATIONAL MONETARY ASSETS, MONETARY GOLD STOCK AND MONEY STOCK, 1901III-1913I

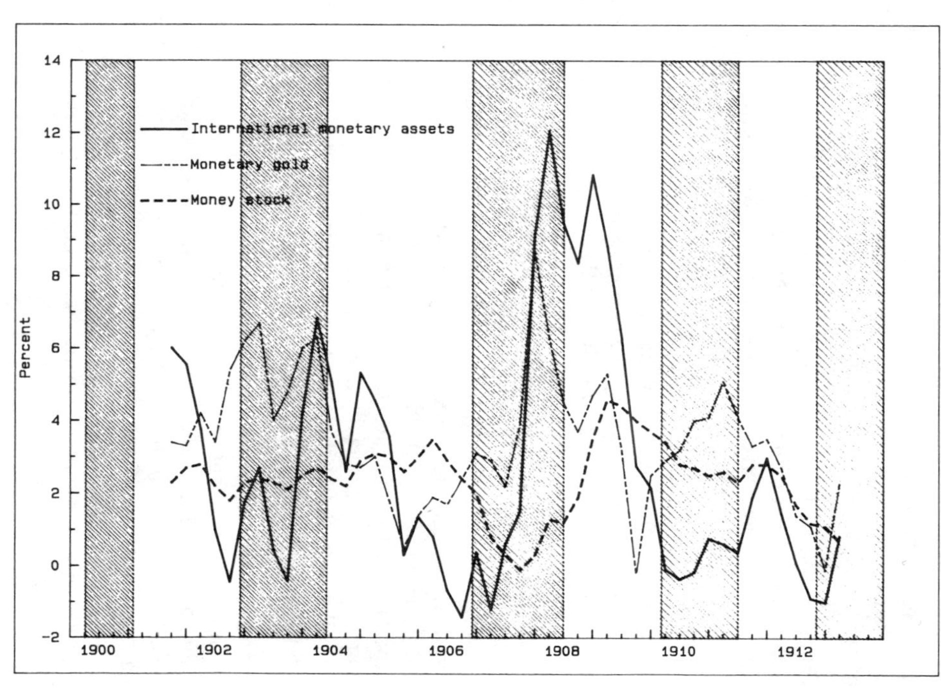

Sources for Chart 3-1

Table A-2. Monetary gold equals the sum of columns (1) and (3). The data are smoothed by a seven-quarter moving average and the quarterly growth rates are calculated from the smoothed series.

2, the current-account surplus, like the overall surplus, tended to rise during reference-cycle contractions and to decline during expansions. However, its countercyclical pattern was not as regular as that of the overall surplus. From 1868 to 1891 and from 1904 to 1913, the current-account surplus typically peaked near reference-cycle troughs. Similarly, the smallest surpluses tended to coincide with reference-cycle peaks. As far as may be judged from annual data, the current-account surplus did not systematically lead or lag the reference-cycle. From 1886 to 1889, it tended to lead cyclical movements in economic activity,[5] while a distinctive lag was recorded in 1883.[6] Moreover, from 1910 to 1911, the current-account surplus declined (or the deficit increased) significantly even though the economy plunged into a short recession.

From 1891 to 1900, the current-account surplus did not exhibit a discernible cyclical pattern. It increased steadily during both reference-cycle expansions and contractions, save for a large bulge in 1897 and 1898. From 1900 to 1904, it moved procyclically, with the sharp decline during the reference-cycle contraction of 1902-04 particularly noteworthy.

The countercyclical pattern of the current-account surplus mirrored strong procyclical fluctuations in Canadian merchandise imports. Merchandise exports also tended to move procyclically, but on the whole their cyclical variance was not as large as that of imports. The cyclical attributes of merchandise exports and imports (excluding trade in non-monetary precious metals) are described by Charts 3-2 and 3-3, showing the deviations in the two magnitudes from their respective growth trends. Trend-adjusted rather than actual values of imports and exports are used to time the cyclical turning points. Trend-adjusted values are more reliable indicators of cyclical movements in imports and exports than the unadjusted ones, since the two magnitudes followed strong upward trends, especially after 1895. Note that both magnitudes varied procyclically, with the cyclical turning points in imports frequently lagging those in exports.

As indicated by Charts 3-2 and 3-3, the deviations in the current-account surplus from its normal countercyclical pattern were due to two factors. First, from 1890 to 1901, merchandise exports and imports frequently did not vary procyclically. Exports, in particular, were insensitive to the business cycle. Instead, the wheat boom made a strong imprint on their growth pattern, notably after 1896. If trade in non-monetary gold is taken into account, export growth in the 1890s was even more dramatic than suggested by Charts 3-2 and 3-3. Moreover, imports declined relative to their growth trend over the reference-cycle expansions of 1891-93 and 1894-95, while the contractions of 1890-91 and 1895-96 saw import growth accelerate. Strong export growth throughout the 1890s, coupled with a failure of imports to rise over the reference-cycle expansions of 1891-93 and 1894-95, explains the steady improvement in the current-account balance from 1890 to 1901.

Second, from 1901 to 1904, both merchandise exports and imports moved procyclically, but the former fluctuated more strongly than the latter. For this

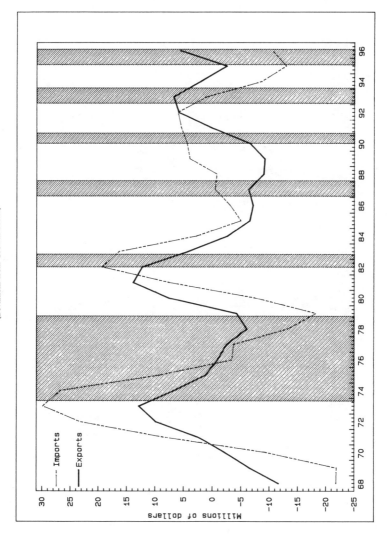

CHART 3-2
CANADIAN MERCHANDISE EXPORTS AND IMPORTS, 1868-96
(Deviations from Growth Trend)

CHART 3-3

CANADIAN MERCHANDISE EXPORTS AND IMPORTS, 1896-1913
(Deviations from Growth Trend)

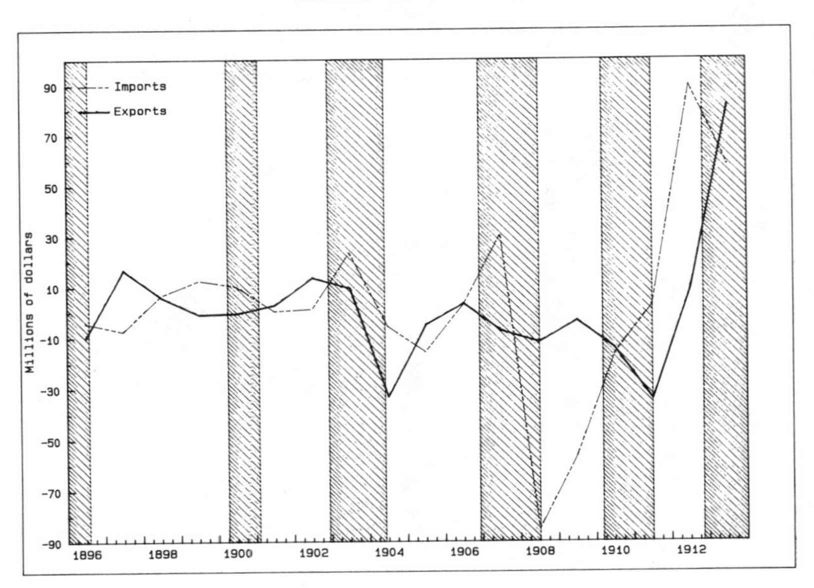

Sources and estimation methods for Charts 3-2 and 3-3

The charts depict the deviations in merchandise exports (XM) and imports (KM), as recorded in Table A-3, from their respective growth trends. The following log-linear trend lines are fitted to the data:

$$\ln XM = \underset{(123)}{4.17} + \underset{(9.76)}{0.0192}t,\ R^2 = 0.78, \text{ for 1868-1896,}$$

$$\ln XM = \underset{(20.7)}{3.09} + \underset{(15.5)}{0.0611}t,\ R^2 = 0.94, \text{ for 1896-1913,}$$

$$\ln KM = \underset{(82.7)}{4.47} + \underset{(3.63)}{0.0114}t,\ R^2 = 0.33, \text{ for 1868-1896,}$$

$$\ln KM = \underset{(11.1)}{1.92} + \underset{(21.4)}{0.0975}t,\ R^2 = 0.97, \text{ for 1896-1913.}$$

reason, the current-account surplus varied procyclically over this period. Similarly, a sharp temporary drop in export growth, combined with an only modest decline in import growth, accounts for the failure of the current-account surplus to rise over the reference-cycle contraction of 1910-11.

Unlike merchandise exports and imports, the non-merchandise trade surplus was insensitive to the business cycle. Therefore, cyclical movements in the current-account surplus were dominated by merchandise trade.

3.1.4. Residual Inflows

The relationship between residual inflows and the reference cycle was complex. From about 1885 to 1895 and from 1900 to 1913, residual inflows, like the overall surplus, varied countercyclically. However, the cyclical turning points in residual inflows and economic activity frequently did not coincide. In 1889, 1905 and 1910, residual inflows led the reference cycle, while in 1912 they peaked well after the trough in economic activity had been reached.

From 1872 to 1884, the fluctuations in residual inflows were irregular. Large inflows were recorded near the reference-cycle peak of 1873, but this does not imply that the pattern was consistently procyclical. From 1896 to 1899, the movements in residual inflows were the mirror image of those in the current-account surplus. Thus, it would appear that the sharp rise in exports, recorded in the initial phase of the wheat boom, was largely offset by a decline in capital inflows.[7]

3.2. SOURCES OF VARIATION IN THE MONETARY BASE

The cyclical patterns revealed by Table 3-1 are inconsistent with Hay's conjecture as to a close link between the Canadian money stock and the balance of payments. Since the overall surplus moved countercyclically, the balance of payments does not explain the procyclical swings in the money stock. One possible reason for the procyclical pattern of the money stock might have lain in discretionary monetary policy. Had monetary policy accounted for the procyclical swings in the money stock, I would expect that both the money stock and the monetary base were positively correlated with the reference cycle. In the following, I explore the importance of discretionary monetary policy as a source of variation in the monetary base.

3.2.1. The Significance of Discretionary Monetary Policy

Chart 3-4 traces the development of the aggregate and the uncovered stocks of Dominion notes over the period 1867-1913. The growth trend of the uncovered issue clearly suggests that pre-1914 Canadian monetary policy was not as automatic as has commonly been believed. Notably the infant years of the Dominion saw the government rely extensively on discretionary monetary policy, as manifested by a marked expansion in the uncovered issue from 1867 to 1885. Much of the increase in the uncovered issue was recorded immediately after Confederation and early in the 1880s. Up to the mid-1880s,

CHART 3-4
AGGREGATE AND UNCOVERED DOMINION NOTES, 1867-1913

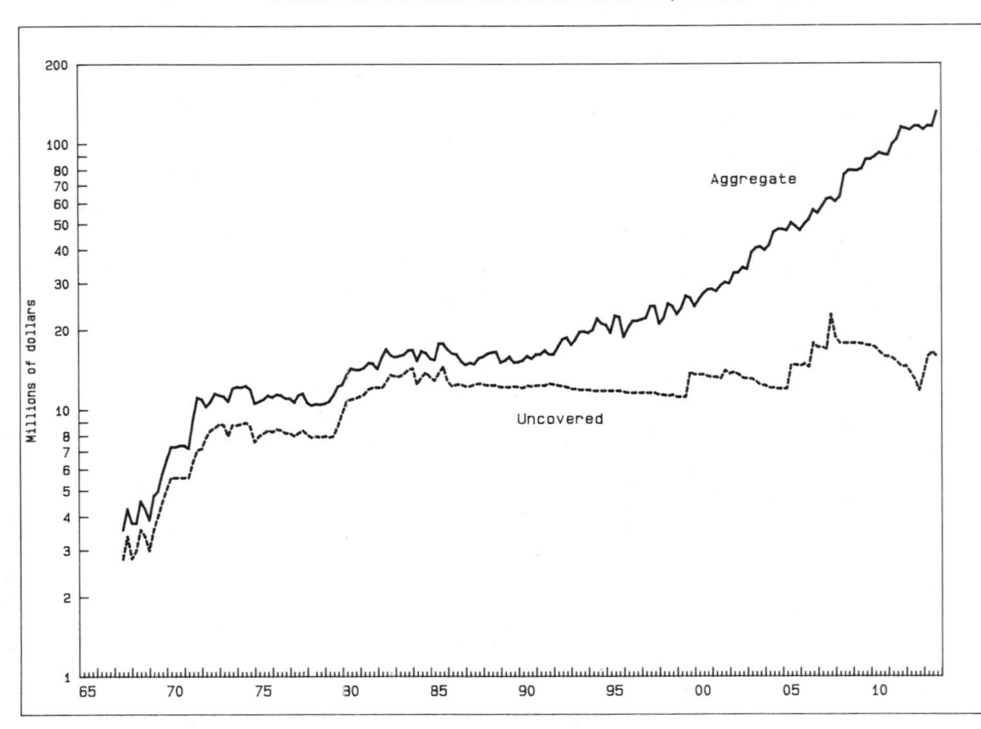

Sources for Chart 3-4
See Tables A-1 and A-2, columns (1) and (2), and Table 7-1. The data for the period 1887I-1900II are also available on a quarterly basis. Uncovered Dominion notes equal aggregate notes minus government gold.

the growth in the aggregate stock of Dominion notes was attributable largely to the strong expansion in the uncovered issue, while the official gold stock (equalling the difference between the aggregate and the uncovered stocks of Dominion notes) only rose slightly.[8]

Around 1885, the growth trend of the uncovered issue shifted dramatically. Although aggregate Dominion notes continued to surge, the growth in the uncovered issue came to a virtual standstill. From the mid-1880s to the eve of World War I, the uncovered issue fluctuated within a stationary band ranging from roughly $11 to $18 million. There was only one instance where the uncovered issue surpassed the upper limit of this band. In the autumn of 1907, the government decided to circulate temporarily over $5 million worth of additional Dominion notes, causing the uncovered issue to reach a record of $22.9 million at the end of the year. It was an emergency measure designed to alleviate a liquidity squeeze in the Canadian banking system (see Chapter 6). Thus, the evidence points to a significant shift in the stance of Canadian monetary policy in the mid-1880s. At that time, the Dominion government apparently abandoned monetary discretion in favour of a predominantly automatic system of monetary policy.

Similar conclusions may be drawn from an analysis of the sources of long-run variation in the Canadian monetary base. Data on that aggregate back to 1871 are presented in Tables A-1 and A-2. As may be recalled from Chapter 2, the monetary base is defined as the sum of international monetary assets and uncovered Dominion notes [equation (2.3)].[9] The two components of the monetary base in turn reflect the influence on that aggregate of the overall balance of payments and discretionary monetary policy. As a result of the policy experiments in the early part of the period under study, the share of uncovered Dominion notes in the monetary base increased intermittently until the mid-1880s. The shift to an automatic system of monetary policy was followed by a renewed decline in that share. The trend in the share of the uncovered issue may be brought out clearly by calculating averages for individual reference cycles. Over the reference cycle of 1887-90 (measured from peak to peak), that is, upon the shift to an automatic policy regime, uncovered Dominion notes averaged 28 percent of the monetary base. The average for the reference-cycle of 1910II-1912IV, by contrast, amounted to as little as 5 percent.[10]

3.2.2. The Sources of Cyclical Variation in the Monetary Base

Despite the rapid increase in the uncovered issue during the 1870s and early 1880s, discretionary monetary policy was not an important source of cyclical variation in the monetary base, either before or after 1885. Table 3-3 shows to what extent the balance of payments and discretionary monetary policy were responsible for cyclical movements in the monetary base. Due to the breaks in the series on the overall surplus, the period under study is divided up into subperiods delineated by the data breaks. For each subperiod, I have compiled the average annual contributions to base-money growth of the overall surplus and changes in the uncovered issue. Note that the first subperiod approximately covers the years of active discretionary management of the Dominion note issue. Thus, the average contributions calculated for the various subperiods should reveal the extent to which the shift to an automatic system of monetary policy impinged on the cyclical pattern of base-money growth. The subperiod 1896-1901, which saw the overall surplus move procyclically, is shown separately.

TABLE 3-3
CONTRIBUTION OF THE BALANCE OF PAYMENTS AND MONETARY POLICY TO CHANGES IN THE MONETARY BASE
(Millions of Dollars)

Annual Average	Boom Stage	Depression Stage	Entire Period
1872-1888			
Overall Surplus	- 2.8	5.0	0.4
Δ Uncovered Dominion Notes	0.2	0.4	0.3
Δ Monetary Base	- 2.6	5.4	0.7
1888-1896			
Overall Surplus	- 5.5	10.5	1.6
Δ Uncovered Dominion Notes	- 0.1	- 0.1	- 0.1
Δ Monetary Base	- 5.6	10.4	1.5
1896-1901			
Overall Surplus	-	-	8.5
Δ Uncovered Dominion Notes	-	-	0.4
Δ Monetary Base	-	-	8.9
1901-1913			
Overall Surplus	1.7	41.7	17.1
Δ Uncovered Dominion Notes	0.7	- 0.7	0.2
Δ Monetary Base	2.4	41.0	17.3
1901-1913 (excl. 1907 and 1908)			
Overall Surplus	4.4	22.5	11.0
Δ Uncovered Dominion Notes	0.1	0.4	0.2
Δ Monetary Base	4.5	22.9	11.2

Sources and estimation methods for Table 3-3

See Tables A-1 and A-2 for data on the monetary base and uncovered Dominion notes. Uncovered Dominion notes equal the difference between aggregate Dominion notes [column (2)] and the Dominion government gold reserve [column (1)]. The averages are based on annual first differences in the two magnitudes. Data on the overall surplus are obtained from Table 3-1. The annual observations are assigned to the boom and depression stage of the reference cycle according to Appendix C, procedure 3.

Table 3-3 corroborates my earlier conclusion that from the mid-1880s onwards, the contribution of discretionary monetary policy to base-money growth was insignificant. During the first subperiod, changes in the uncovered issue accounted for roughly one-half of the observed growth in the monetary base.[11] However, even before 1885, discretionary monetary policy did not strongly influence the cyclical pattern of the monetary base. As indicated by Table 3-3, the cyclical swings in base-money growth paralleled those in the overall surplus during the entire period under study. Except during the subperiod 1896-1901, therefore, base-money growth varied countercyclically, with cyclical peaks (troughs) typically attained during depressions (booms).

Although the balance of payments largely accounted for the cyclical movements in the monetary base, discretionary monetary policy — during the first subperiod — was a somewhat more significant source of cyclical variation in base-money growth than indicated by Table 3-3. The averages for booms and depressions presented in that table mask a modest procyclical pattern of the uncovered issue prior to 1885. According to Chart 3-4, much of the growth in the uncovered issue coincided with the reference-cycle expansion ending in 1873 and with the expansion of 1879-82. Therefore, the averages for booms and depressions do not bring out clearly the cyclical pattern of the uncovered issue.

To throw that pattern into sharp relief, I split up the reference cycle into a larger number of cycle stages than the two shown in Table 3-3. The expansion and contraction stages of the reference cycle are both subdivided at their midpoints, with the two halves of the expansion (contraction) phase called expansion (contraction) I and II. This procedure yields four, rather than two, cycle stages. Obviously, expansion II and contraction I, if joined together, match the boom stage of the reference cycle, while contraction II and expansion I overlap with the depression stage. According to Table 3-4, the growth in the uncovered issue varied procyclically during the first subperiod and typically attained a peak during the first half of a reference cycle expansion. Thus, during expansion I, discretionary monetary policy reinforced somewhat the impact on base-money growth of the large overall surpluses normally arising at that stage of the business cycle. In contrast to expansion I, expansion II saw discretionary policy neutralize slightly the effect of the balance of payments on base-money growth. As the economy passed from the first to the second half of a business-cycle expansion, the overall surpluses typically gave way to deficits, while the uncovered issue rose further, albeit at a slower rate. During contraction II, discretionary monetary policy once again amplified the impact of the balance of payments on base-money growth.[12] However, in all the four stages of the reference cycle, the contribution of discretionary monetary policy to base-money growth was minor compared with that of the balance of payments. The reasons for the procyclical movements in the uncovered stock of Dominion notes prior to 1885 and for the shift to an automatic monetary policy stance are explored in Chapter 7.

TABLE 3-4
CONTRIBUTION OF THE BALANCE OF PAYMENTS AND MONETARY POLICY TO CHANGES IN THE MONETARY BASE, 1872-88
(Millions of Dollars)

Annual Average	Expansion Stage		Contraction Stage	
	I	II	I	II
Overall Surplus	9.7	-6.3	0.8	-1.3
Δ Uncovered Dominion Notes	0.9	0.4	-	-0.3
Δ Monetary Base	10.6	-5.9	0.8	-1.5

Sources and estimation methods for Table 3-4

See legend to Table 3-3 for the data sources. The annual observations are assigned to the various reference-cycle stages as follows:

expansion I: 79, 80, 85, 88;
expansion II: 72, 73, 81, 82, 86;
contraction I: 74-76, 83, 87;
contraction II: 77, 78, 84.

After 1900, the growth in the uncovered issue once again moved procyclically and tended to neutralize somewhat the impact of the balance of payments on base-money growth. It should be noted, however, that the procyclical pattern of the uncovered issue, recorded for the last subperiod, was due entirely to the emergency measures taken by the government late in 1907. If the observations for 1907 and 1908 are disregarded, the averages compiled for the change in the uncovered issue no longer vary significantly between booms and depressions (Table 3-3). As I show in Chapter 6, the emergency issue of Dominion notes partly neutralized the effect on base-money growth of a seasonal and cyclical contraction in the overall surplus.

3.3. THE RELATIONSHIP BETWEEN THE MONEY STOCK AND THE MONETARY BASE

3.3.1. The Cyclical Attributes of the Money Stock

To determine the cyclical attributes of the Canadian money stock, I rely on a broadly defined aggregate that matches closely the series compiled by Hay (1967). The money stock is assumed to embrace Dominion notes outside the banking system and monetary liabilities of the chartered banks. The later cover demand and notice deposits held by the private non-bank public and the provinces, as well as noted issued by the chartered banks (Tables A-1 and A-2).[13] Notice deposits include funds in savings accounts and time deposits payable on a fixed date. A broadly defined money-stock concept is more attuned to the pre-1914 Canadian institutional environment than a narrow aggregate confined to currency and demand deposits. In Canada, currency and demand deposits were not the sole assets serving as media of exchange. At least a

CHART 3-5

CYCLICAL MOVEMENTS IN THE MONEY STOCK, 1874II-1900IV
(Quarterly Deviations from Growth Trend)

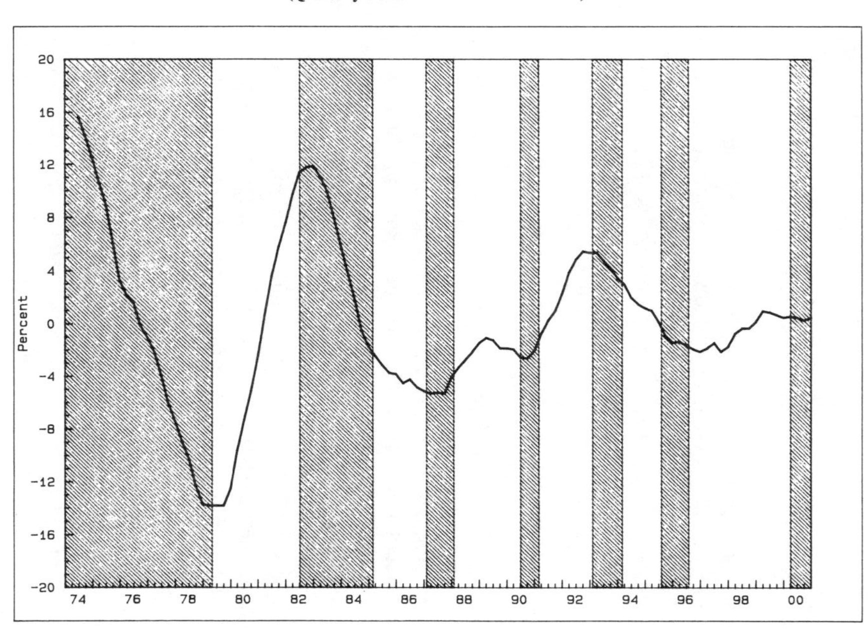

Sources and estimation methods for Chart 3-5

See legend to Table 3-2 for the sources. The data are smoothed by a seven-quarter moving average. The percentage deviations represent the difference between the natural logs of the actual and trend values of the money stock (M). Since the growth in the money stock accelerated considerably with the onset of the wheat boom around 1896, the trend values are determined by two regression equations:

$$\ln M = \underset{(308.9)}{4.34} + \underset{(44.9)}{0.0121}t, \quad R^2 = 0.958, \text{ for 1874II-1896III},$$

$$\ln M = \underset{(888.7)}{5.40} + \underset{(155.0)}{0.0241}t, \quad R^2 = 0.999, \text{ for 1896III-1913I}.$$

portion of savings deposits was endowed with limited chequing privileges (Johnson, 1910, 53), a feature of the Canadian payments system that has been retained to this day. Therefore, notice deposits differed from demand deposits in degree rather than in kind.[14]

In constructing a series for the pre-1914 Canadian money stock, a minor complication arises from deposits on the books of the Canadian banks' foreign branches. It is unclear whether such deposits — which were reported for the first time in July, 1900 — should be part of the Canadian money stock.[15] A case could be made for including them if they had consisted mainly of transactions balances used by foreigners to pay for Canadian exports. Unfortunately, little is known about the nature of these deposits. Therefore, the money stock estimates presented in Tables A-1 and A-2 only take account of deposits booked in Canada. For all practical purposes, however, the conceptual problems posed by deposits booked abroad do not impinge on the subsequent analysis. According to Table 3-2, the cyclical pattern of the Canadian money stock, as estimated in this study, was the same as that of deposits booked abroad. Thus, the cyclical attributes of the money stock would not be altered much if deposits booked abroad were included.[16]

As in the case of exports and imports, the cyclical turning points in the Canadian money stock cannot be timed precisely unless the data are adjusted for trend. Charts 3-5 and 3-6 depict trend-adjusted data, expressed as percentage deviations in the money stock from its growth trend. The evidence indicates that the Canadian money stock moved procyclically during the period under study, except for a short interlude between 1887 and 1895, when its cyclical pattern was irregular.[17] Interestingly enough, the cyclical peaks (troughs) in the trend-adjusted money stock and economic activity tended to coincide, with little evidence of systematic leads or lags between the two variables. Before 1887 and after 1895, there were only two instances of the trend-adjusted money stock failing to rise during a reference-cycle expansion or to fall during a contraction. The expansion of 1885-87 witnessed a drop in the level of the trend-adjusted money stock, but the rate of decline was lower than during the preceding contraction. Conversely, the reference-cycle contraction of 1910-11 was associated with a slowdown in the growth, rather than a reduction in the level, of the trend-adjusted money stock.

During the subperiod 1887-95, the trend-adjusted money stock frequently departed from its normal procyclical pattern. It did not decline during the reference-cycle contraction of 1887-88, nor did it rise after economic activity had passed a cyclical through in 1894. Moreover, the reference-cycle peak of 1890 lagged the corresponding peak in trend-adjusted money by over a year. Interestingly enough, for the entire period under study, including the subperiod 1887-95, the cyclical pattern of the trend-adjusted money stock was similar to that of trend-adjusted imports (Charts 3-2 and 3-3). Like the money stock, imports began to shrink in 1889, well before the reference-cycle expansion of 1888-90 had drawn to a close. Furthermore, after attaining a major peak in 1892, both magnitudes declined continuously until 1895 or 1896, despite a temporary revival of economic activity in 1894.[18] The parallelism of cyclical movements in money and imports during the subperiod 1887-95 may be interpreted in two ways. Either both magnitudes — for common but unknown reasons — did not move in sympathy with economic activity, or the fluctuations in money and imports were consistently procyclical, but masked by flaws in the available reference-cycle series.[19] I do not know which of the two interpretations is correct.

Charts 3-5 and 3-6 do not fully support Hay's (1967) findings as to the cyclical pattern of the Canadian money stock. While the movements were clearly procyclical, my evidence fails to accord with his conclusion that money systematically led economic activity. As I pointed out in Chapter 2, Hay did not compare the *level* of the money stock with the *level* of economic activity, but the *rate of change* in the money stock with the *level* of economic activity. Since the levels of the two variables were closely correlated, it is not surprising that the level of economic activity tended to lag money growth. Moreover, as expected, the lag typically amounted to one-half of the length of the respective reference-cycle expansion or contraction. Chart 3-1 shows that money growth normally reached a peak (trough) halfway between reference-cycle troughs (peaks) and peaks (troughs). A similar pattern would emerge if Chart 3-1 were extended to cover the periods 1874-87 and 1895-1901. The significance tests of Table 3-2 confirm the message of Chart 3-1. Had money growth attained a cyclical peak (trough) near the midpoint of a reference-cycle expansion (contraction), it should have been significantly higher during expansions than during contractions. The null hypothesis that the average rate of growth in the money stock was the same for expansions and contractions is decisively rejected at the 99 percent level of significance, save for the subperiod 1887-95. Thus, contrary to Hay's assertion, the evidence is consistent with the view that there was a close coincidence of cyclical turning points in the money stock and economic activity. These findings suggest that — if applied to Canada — the Friedman-Schwartz procedure of timing the cyclical turning points in the money stock yields highly misleading results.[20]

3.3.2. The Sources of Variation in the Money Stock

The cyclical patterns revealed by Charts 3-1 and 3-6 imply that there was a lag between the cyclical turning points in the money stock and the monetary base. Base-money growth typically peaked near a reference-cycle trough, while money growth reached a cyclical high near the midpoint of the subsequent expansion. A parallel lag pattern obtained for the levels of the two aggregates. In order to time the turning points in the level of the monetary base, I have relied on trend-adjusted data derived in the same way as those for the money stock. According to Chart 3-6, the trend-adjusted monetary base tended to peak near the midpoint of a reference-cycle expansion, while the trend-adjusted money stock — as indicated earlier — attained its highest value near a reference-cycle peak. Thus, the money stock tended to lag the monetary base by one-half of the length of the respective reference-cycle expansion or contraction.

CHART 3-6

CYCLICAL MOVEMENTS IN THE MONEY STOCK AND THE MONETARY BASE, 1900IV-1913I

(Quarterly Deviations from Growth Trend or Rates of Change)

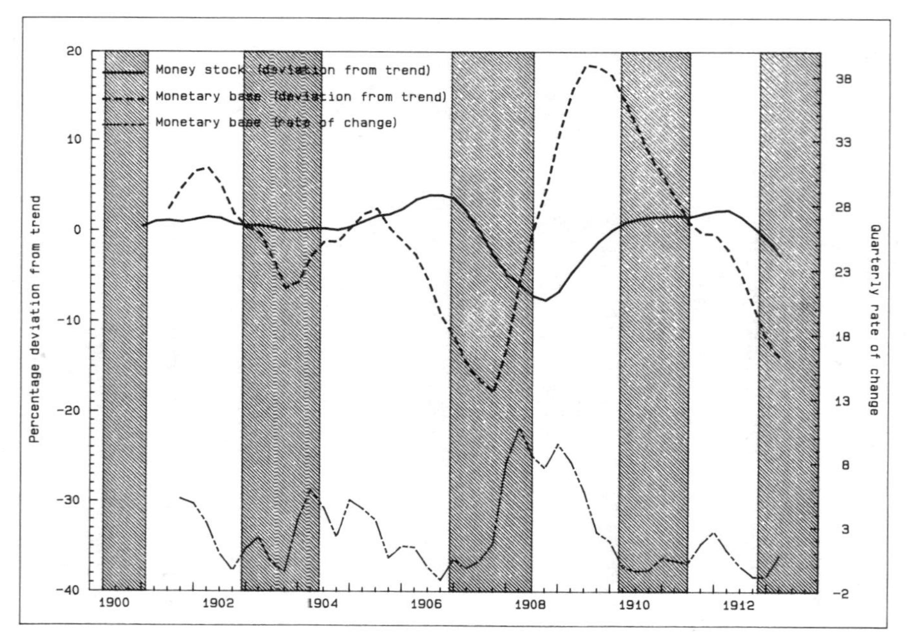

Sources and estimation methods for Chart 3-6

Table A-2. See Chart 3-5 for the regression equation determining the trend values of the money stock. The trend values of the monetary base (H) are determined by the following regression equation:

$$\ln H = \underset{(167.9)}{4.47} + \underset{(29.8)}{0.0281t}, \quad R^2 = 0.95$$

The regression equation is based on data for the period 1901II-1913I. The data are smoothed by a seven-quarter moving average.

Since the two magnitudes were not closely correlated over the business cycle, one must look for other explanations for the procyclical pattern of the money stock. To trace the sources of cyclical variation in the money stock, the following widely-used identities serve as a useful point of departure:

$$M(t) = H(t)[1+\epsilon(t)]/U(t), \tag{3.1}$$

where

$$U(t) = \epsilon(t) + \rho(t). \tag{3.2}$$

Identities (3.1) and (3.2) allow for three possible sources of variation in the money stock (M), that is, changes in the monetary base (H), the currency-liability ratio (ϵ), and the aggregate reserve ratio (ρ). The currency-liability ratio is defined as the ratio of Dominion notes outside the banking system to monetary liabilities of the chartered banks. The aggregate reserve ratio denotes the ratio of cash and secondary reserves to monetary liabilities.[21] All the variables appearing in the two identities are assumed to be functions of time (t).

A technique developed by Friedman and Schwartz (1963, Appendix B) and Cagan (1965) may be employed for determining the relative importance of the three sources of variation in the Canadian money stock. The growth in the money stock is allotted to the three sources by means of equation (3.3):

$$\begin{aligned} d\ \ln M(t)/dt = {} & d\ \ln H(t)/dt - [1/U(t)]d\rho(t)/dt \\ & - [(1-\rho(t))/U(t)(1+\epsilon(t))]d(\epsilon(t)/dt. \end{aligned} \tag{3.3}$$

Equation (3.3) is derived by expressing (3.1) in terms of natural logs, substituting (3.2) into (3.1), and differentiating the resulting expression with respect to time. The left-hand side of (3.3) stands for the growth rate of the money stock, whereas the three terms on the right-hand side show the contributions to money growth of changes in the monetary base, the aggregate reserve ratio, and the currency-liability ratio. Since equation (3.3) is continuous in time, it is not applicable to data that are available only for discrete points in time. Therefore, the contributions to money growth are computed from a discrete-time approximation to equation (3.3):

$$\begin{aligned} \ln M_t - \ln M_{t-1} = {} & \ln H_t - \ln H_{t-1} - (\rho_t - \rho_{t-1})W_{1,t} \\ & - (\epsilon_t - \epsilon_{t-1})W_{2,t} + \eta_t, \end{aligned} \tag{3.4}$$

where

$$W_{1,t} = (1/U_t + 1/U_{t-1})/2 > 0, \tag{3.5}$$

$$W_{2,t} = [(1-\rho_t)/U_t(1+\epsilon_t) + (1-\rho_{t-1})/U_{t-1}(1+\epsilon_{t-1})]/2 > 0 \tag{3.6}$$

and η_t denotes an error term.[22]

According to equations (3.4) through (3.6), the procyclical swings in the money stock could have mirrored procyclical movements in the monetary base or countercyclical movements in either the aggregate reserve or currency-liability ratios. In view of the countercyclical swings in base-money growth,

TABLE 3-5

CHARTERED-BANK RESERVE RATIOS AND CURRENCY-LIABILITY RATIO, 1873-1913 (Percent)

End of Year	Reserve Ratios			Currency-Liability Ratio	Ref. Cycle
	Cash	Secondary	Aggregate		
1873	19.1	9.8	28.9	3.5	P/11
1874	17.5	7.6	25.1	2.5	
1875	18.5	9.2	27.7	3.4	
1876	16.8	6.4	23.2	3.2	
1877	18.2	8.0	26.2	3.3	
1878	16.6	6.5	23.1	2.8	
1879	18.7	27.6	46.3	3.7	T/05
1880	16.0	30.0	46.0	3.6	
1881	14.1	21.0	35.1	4.3	
1882	13.3	8.7	22.0	4.4	P/07
1883	14.8	16.4	31.2	4.4	
1884	15.6	14.1	29.7	4.5	
1885	15.4	15.2	30.6	4.1	T/03
1886	12.8	13.7	26.5	4.7	
1887	12.2	10.6	22.8	4.2	P/02
1887	12.9	15.5	28.4	4.2	
1888	13.2	19.4	32.6	3.9	T/02
1889	10.6	11.8	22.4	3.9	
1890	11.2	6.4	17.6	3.6	P/07
1891	9.9	15.0	24.9	3.3	T/03
1892	10.7	12.5	23.2	3.2	
1893	11.9	9.6	21.5	3.2	P/02
1894	12.4	14.8	27.2	2.9	T/03
1895	13.0	10.8	23.8	3.0	P/08
1896	12.3	10.7	23.0	2.9	T/08
1897	12.0	12.9	24.9	2.7	
1898	10.8	10.5	21.3	2.7	
1899	10.0	9.6	19.6	2.7	
1900	9.9	11.4	21.3	2.6	P/04
1900	9.9	12.4	22.3	2.6	
1901	9.4	15.8	25.2	2.4	T/02
1902	9.7	14.4	24.1	2.3	P/12
1903	11.3	11.7	23.0	2.3	
1904	11.8	15.0	26.8	1.9	T/06
1905	10.9	13.9	24.8	2.0	
1906	10.9	11.3	22.2	1.9	P/12
1907	12.9	8.3	21.2	2.1	
1908	14.6	20.6	35.2	1.9	T/07
1909	12.8	20.0	32.8	1.7	
1910	12.8	13.8	26.6	1.6	P/03
1911	14.1	13.0	27.1	1.8	T/07
1912	12.4	11.6	24.0	2.0	P/11
1913	14.9	12.2	27.1	1.9	

Sources for Table 3-5

Cash reserves: Bank gold [Tables A-1 and A-2, column (3)] and Dominion notes in the hands of the banks, including holdings in the central gold reserves (Curtis, 1931a, 35 and 38).
Secondary reserves: Tables A-1 and A-2, columns (6).
Currency: Difference between aggregate [Tables A-1 and A-2, column (2)] and bank holdings of Dominion notes.
Monetary bank liabilities: difference between the money stock [Tables A-1 and A-2, column (9)] and currency.

the monetary base does not explain the procyclical pattern of the money stock. That leaves the aggregate reserve and currency-liability ratios as possible sources of cyclical variation in the money stock. Table 3-5 and Chart 3-7 describe the cyclical pattern of the two ratios. As indicated by that table, the aggregate reserve ratio exhibited a pronounced countercyclical pattern. Moreover, the quarterly data available for the post-1900 period (Chart 3-7) suggest that the aggregate reserve ratio normally attained a cyclical peak (trough) at or shortly before the midpoint of a reference-cycle expansion (contraction). The decrease (increase) in the aggregate reserve ratio during the second half of a reference-cycle expansion (contraction) explains why the trend-adjusted money stock continued to rise (fall) at that stage of the business cycle, despite a fall (rise) in the trend-adjusted monetary base. In contrast to the aggregate reserve ratio, the currency-liability ratio was insensitive to the business cycle. Thus, the aggregate reserve ratio was largely responsible for the procyclical swings in the Canadian money stock.

Interestingly enough, the aggregate reserve ratio even declined during the unusual reference-cycle expansion of 1896-1900. Although the atypical rise in the overall surplus also caused base-money growth to accelerate, the aggregate reserve ratio did not increase because the money stock expanded even more rapidly than the monetary base. From the end of 1896 to the end of 1900, the two monetary aggregates rose by 50 and 38 percent respectively (Table A-1). The countercyclical pattern of the aggregate reserve ratio, therefore, was virtually flawless.

The paramount importance of the aggregate reserve ratio as a source of cyclical variation in the Canadian money stock is confirmed by Table 3-6, showing the average contributions of the monetary base, the aggregate reserve ratio and the currency-liability ratio to the quarterly growth in the money stock for the post-1900 period. The averages are compiled for the four reference-cycle stages defined in Section 3.2.2. For each cycle stage, the average quarterly growth in the money stock is allocated to the three sources of money growth on the strength of the discrete-time variant of equation (3.2), as well as equations (3.4) through (3.6). The contributions displayed in columns (2), (3) and (4) add up to the average quarterly growth rates of the money stock in column (1), save for minor discrepancies attributables to the error term, η_t, and to rounding.

As indicated by the contributions to average money growth for the post-1900 period as a whole (delineated by the reference-cycle peaks of 1902 and 1912), the trend growth in the money stock was due almost exclusively to base-money growth, while the aggregate reserve and currency-liability ratios did not vary much over the long run. The cyclical movements in the money stock, by contrast, mirrored the joint influence of the monetary base and the aggregate reserve ratio. During expansion I, both the money stock and the monetary base grew at relatively high rates. The rapid increase in the monetary base — that normally exceeded money growth — was explained by the large overall balance of payments surpluses characteristic for this stage of the refer-

CHART 3-7

CHARTERED-BANK RESERVE RATIOS AND CURRENCY-LIABILITY RATIO, 1901II-1913I

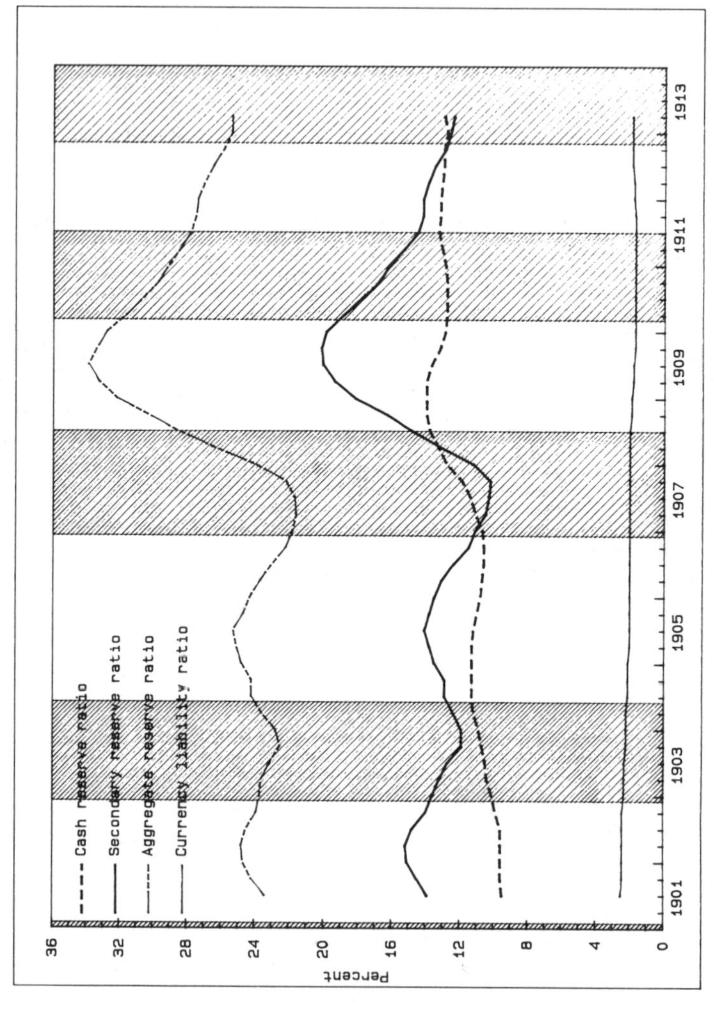

Sources for Chart 3-7

See Table 3-5. The ratios are calculated from data that are smoothed by a seven-quarter moving average.

TABLE 3-6

SOURCES OF VARIATION IN THE CANADIAN MONEY STOCK, 1901III-19013I
(Percent)

Estimation Period	Average Quarterly Rate of Change in Money Stock	Contribution to Rate of Change in Money Stock by		
		Monetary Base	Aggregate Reserve Ratio	Currency-Liability Ratio
	(1)	(2)	(3)	(4)
Expansion I: 1901III-1902I	2.56	4.32	-1.85	0.08
Expansion II: 1902I -1902IV	2.24	1.26	0.94	0.04
Contraction I: 1902IV -1903III	2.23	0.77	1.37	0.09
Contraction II: 1903III-1904II	2.38	3.25	-1.01	0.14
Expansion I: 1904II -1905III	2.67	3.31	-0.71	0.07
Expansion II: 1905III-1906IV	2.73	0.45	2.26	0.02
Contraction I: 1906IV -1907III	0.75	0.72	0.01	0.01
Contraction II: 1907III-1908III	0.92	7.05	-6.16	0.03
Expansion I: 1908III-1909II	3.52	7.46	-4.03	0.09
Expansion II: 1909II -1910I	3.80	2.49	1.23	0.07
Contraction I: 1910I -1910IV	2.80	-0.06	2.87	-0.01
Contraction II: 1910IV -1911III	2.49	0.73	1.81	-0.05
Expansion I: 1911III-1912I	2.67	1.82	0.92	-0.08
Expansion II: 1912I -1912IV	1.60	-0.12	1.80	-0.08
Contraction I: 1912IV -1913I	0.92	-	1.01	-0.09
All Expansions I	2.86	4.26	-1.45	0.05
All Expansions II	2.61	0.95	1.64	0.01
All Contractions I	1.78	0.41	1.36	0.01
All Contractions II	1.85	3.93	-2.12	0.04
Peak to Peak: 1902IV-1912IV	2.37	2.47	-0.13	0.03

Sources and estimation methods for Table 3-6

Data sources

Data on the money stock and the monetary base are available from Table A-2 and are adjusted by a seven-quarter moving average (see Table 3-2 for the adjustment procedure). The data employed for computing the aggregate reserve and currency-liability ratios are also adjusted by a seven-quarter moving average (see legend to Table 3-5 for the sources).

Estimation method

The quarterly growth rates of the money stock and the contributions to money growth are averaged for the various subperiods shown in the table. The subperiods are determined by dividing up the reference cycles into four reference-cycle stages according to Appendix C, procedure 1. For instance, for the first subperiod lasting from 1901III to 1902I, the averages are computed as follows:

Column (1): $\sum_{t=T+1}^{T+3}$

$\ln M_t - \ln M_{t-1})/3 = (\ln M_{T+3} - \ln M_T)/3,$

Column (2): $\sum_{t=T+1}^{T+3}$

$(\ln H_t - \ln H_{t-1})/3 = (\ln H_{T+3} - \ln H_T)/3,$

Column (3): $\sum_{t=T+1}^{T+3}$

$(\rho_t - \rho_{t-1})W_{1,t}/3,$

Column (4): $\sum_{t=T+1}^{T+3} (\epsilon_t - \epsilon_{t-1})W_{2,t}/3,$

where T = 1901II, T+1 = 1901III, ..., T+47 = 1913I. The averages for the other subperiods are calculated analogously.

ence cycle. Inasmuch as the monetary base rose more rapidly than the money stock, the growth differential was offset by an increase in the aggregate reserve ratio. The second half of a reference-cycle expansion invariably saw base-money growth decelerate sharply as the overall balance of payments deteriorated. Despite the slowdown in base-money growth, the money stock continued to expand strongly because of a drop in the aggregate reserve ratio. As the economy passed from expansion II to contraction I, money growth fell. On average, both the monetary base and the aggregate reserve ratio contributed to the decline in money growth. Contraction II once again witnessed an acceleration in base-money growth. However, money growth did not pick up since the increase in base-money growth was absorbed by a pronounced expansion in the aggregate reserve ratio. Consequently, the aggregate reserve ratio acted as a wedge between the money stock and the monetary base. The currency-liability ratio, by contrast, was an insignificant source of cyclical or long-run variation in the money stock.

The evidence is clearly inconsistent with Viner's assertion as to a close link between the Canadian money stock and the balance of payments. There is little doubt that long-run changes in the money stock were due largely to overall balance-of-payments surpluses or deficits. Over the business cycle, however, the two magnitudes were not closely related since the procyclical movements in the money stock mirrored pronounced countercyclical fluctuations in the aggregate reserve ratio of the chartered banks.

3.4. THE RELATIONSHIP BETWEEN THE MONEY STOCK AND INTERNATIONAL GOLD FLOWS

If, as suggested by Viner, the Canadian monetary gold stock had been closely correlated with the chartered banks' monetary liabilities, I would expect that the pattern of net inflows of monetary gold from abroad was procyclical, implying that the cyclical movements in net gold inflows did not parallel those in the overall surplus. Thus, the evidence would conform to Viner's contention that balance-of-payments surpluses or deficits were settled chiefly by flows of secondary reserves, while monetary gold was exported or imported only in response to changes in domestic monetary liabilities. In order to re-examine Viner's thesis about the relationship between the Canadian money stock and international gold flows, I first analyze the role of gold as a means of settling payments imbalances and then turn to the cyclical attributes of monetary gold flows.

3.4.1. Gold Flows as a Means of Settling Payments Imbalances

The role of gold in balance-of-payments adjustment is assessed by regressing monetary gold flows (i.e., first differences in the monetary gold stock) on the overall balance-of-payments surplus and a constant (Table 3-7). The regressions are run not only for aggregate monetary gold (MG) but also for the shares held by the Dominion government (MGG) and the chartered banks (MGB). Equations (3.7) through (3.18) are based on annual data, while for the post-1900 period the parameters are also estimated from quarterly data [equations (3.19) through (3.21)]. Due to the breaks in the data on the overall surplus, the sample period is split up into the subperiods specified earlier. Moreover, the pre-1888 subperiod is subdivided further. Table A-1 suggests that in 1879 and 1880, the composition of international monetary assets shifted substantially in favour of secondary reserves. This shift mirrored a marked increase in the chartered banks' secondary reserves relative to their cash holdings (Table 3-5). In all likelihood, the change in the composition of aggregate bank reserves was a consequence of the United States returning to the gold standard on January 1, 1879. Until the end of 1878, secondary reserves — inasmuch as they were held in the United States — were a poor substitute for gold since they were not convertible into the precious metal at a fixed exchange rate. Therefore, I would expect that the resumption of specie payments in the United States prompted the chartered banks to augment the share of their reserves held in the form of call loans and claims on foreign banks.[23] To allow for the possibility that the resumption of specie payments impinged significantly on the role of gold in balance-of-payments adjustment, the regression equations are estimated separately for the subperiods 1872-1878 and 1881-1888. The observations for 1879 and 1880 are disregarded because the banks do not seem to have adjusted their portfolios instantaneously in response to the resumption of specie payments. The regression analysis yields four noteworthy results.

First, in all the subperiods, aggregate gold inflows tended to be positively correlated with the overall surplus. This piece of evidence suggests that overall surpluses (deficits) were partly settled by inflows (outflows) of monetary gold. For the subperiod 1872-78, the overall surplus explains over 80 percent of the observed variation in ΔMG. In the subperiods 1881-88 and 1901-13, roughly 35-40 percent of the observed variation in ΔMG was due to the overall surplus. Except in the subperiod 1888-1901, the impact of the overall surplus on ΔMG was statistically significant at the 90 percent or higher levels.

Second, though the balance of payments explains a substantial part of the observed variation in aggregate gold inflows, the precious metal was not an important means of settling payments imbalances, except prior to 1879. During the 1870s, gold inflows accounted for roughly 50 percent of the recorded overall surpluses [equation (3.7)]. Upon the return of the United States to the gold standard, they lost much of their significance in balance-of-payments adjustment. From 1881 to 1901, they merely averaged 6-10 percent of the overall surpluses [equations (3.10) and (3.13)]. After the turn of the century, the significance of gold increased once again, with inflows of the precious metal averaging 18-21 percent of the overall surpluses [equations (3.16) and (3.19)]. Thus, the evidence lends support to the view that the resumption of specie payments in the United States strongly impinged on the way payments imbalances were settled in Canada.

TABLE 3-7

RELATIONSHIP BETWEEN MONETARY GOLD FLOWS AND OVERALL BALANCE-OF-PAYMENTS SURPLUS

Sample Period	Dependent Variable a)	Constant	Parameter Estimate of Overall Surplus	$\bar{R}^2$ DW	Equation
1872-1878	ΔMG c)	0.17 (0.62)	0.46 (5.54)	0.83 2.64	(3.7)
1872-1878	ΔMGG c)	0.04 (0.35)	0.15 (4.12)	0.73 2.29	(3.8)
1872-1878	ΔMGB c)	0.13 (0.59)	0.31 (4.76)	0.78 2.50	(3.9)
1881-1888 b)	ΔMG c)	0.47 (1.37)	0.10 (2.28)	0.38 1.55	(3.10)
1881-1888 b)	ΔMGG c)	0.20 (1.21)	0.05 (2.34)	0.39 2.22	(3.11)
1881-1888 b)	ΔMGB c)	0.27 (1.08)	0.05 (1.58)	0.18 1.05	(3.12)
1888-1901	ΔMG c)	1.11 (1.95)	0.06 (1.29)	0.05 2.88	(3.13)
1888-1901	ΔMGG c)	0.68 (1.89)	0.05 (1.81)	0.15 2.72	(3.14)
1888-1901	ΔMGB c)	0.43 (1.44)	0.01 (0.27)	- 3.12	(3.15)
1901-1913	ΔMG c)	7.33 (3.00)	0.18 (2.74)	0.35 1.93	(3.16)
1901-1913	ΔMGG c)	5.02 (2.77)	0.16 (3.35)	0.46 1.37	(3.17)
1901-1913	ΔMGB c)	2.26 (1.97)	0.02 (0.57)	- 2.71	(3.18)
1900IV-13IV	ΔMG d)	1.63 (2.64)	0.20 (5.79)	0.38 1.96	(3.19)
1900IV-13IV	ΔMGG d)	1.33 (2.78)	0.13 (4.67)	0.29 2.07	(3.20)
1900IV-13IV	ΔMGB d)	0.30 (0.70)	0.08 (3.19)	0.15 2.15	(3.21)

a) MG: aggregate monetary gold stock; MGG: government share of MG; MGB: chartered-bank share of MG.
b) The bank-gold series constructed for the period 1871-87 (Table A-1) was extended to 1888.
c) Regressions based on annual first differences in monetary gold and in international monetary assets.
d) Regressions based on quarterly first differences in monetary gold and in international monetary assets.

Sources for Table 3-7

Tables 3-1, A-1 and A-2. The figures in parentheses denote t-values. $\bar{R}^2$ and DW stand for the coefficient of determination, adjusted for degrees of freedom, and the Durbin-Watson statistic respectively.

Third, overall surpluses were associated with flows of gold into both government and bank vaults. During the subperiod 1872-78, bank gold accounted for about two-thirds of the aggregate inflow of precious metal elicited by an overall surplus [equation (3.9)]. The resumption of specie payments in the United States was followed by a gradual decline in the role played by bank gold in balance-of-payments adjustment, while the sensitivity of government-gold flows to overall surpluses rose noticeably. The estimated sensitivity of bank-gold flows, however, is strongly influenced by the periodicity of the data. This is clearly shown by the regression equations estimated for the post-1900 subperiod. Equation (3.18), which is based on annual data, suggests that bank-gold flows were not significantly related to the overall surplus. Equation (3.21), by contrast, points to a highly significant relationship between quarterly inflows of bank gold and the overall surplus. But even on a quarterly basis, flows of government gold were more sensitive to payments imbalances than bank-gold flows.

The disparity between the parameter estimates for the overall surplus in equations (3.18) and (3.21) mirrors the influence of seasonal movements in the overall surplus on the inflow of bank gold. The pre-1914 Canadian balance of payments was subject not only to distinctive cyclical but also to strong seasonal movements. The overall surplus — paradoxically — tended to shrink during the crop-moving season, despite a marked improvement in the balance of payments on current account (see Chapter 6). While bank-gold flows were responsive to seasonal movements in the overall surplus, they did not significantly contribute to balance-of-payments adjustment in the longer run. Cyclical movements in the overall surplus, in particular, did not strongly affect bank-gold flows, especially after 1888.[24]

Fourth, the constants in equations (3.16) and (3.19) are statistically significant at the 95 and 99 percent levels respectively. This piece of evidence points to a marked shift in the composition of international monetary assets in favour of gold after the turn of the century. The existence of a shift is confirmed by Table 3-8, tracing the trend in the share of gold in international monetary assets. To determine that trend, I have compiled averages for five subperiods each covering roughly the full length of a reference cycle (measured from peak to peak). The evidence clearly indicates that after 1900, the share of gold in international monetary assets climbed by roughly 10 percentage points. As a result of a temporary decline between 1873-82 and 1882-86, however, it only increased modestly over the pre-1914 period as a whole.

The causes of the long-run changes in the composition of international monetary assets can be identified with the help of equation (3.22). The share of gold in international monetary assets, by definition, is positively related to the ratio of monetary gold to secondary reserves, f, which can in turn be expressed in terms of five other ratios:

$$f = [\rho_1 + \Omega(\rho_2 + \epsilon)]/\rho_3, \quad (3.22)$$

where

TABLE 3-8

CHANGES IN THE COMPOSITION OF INTERNATIONAL MONETARY ASSETS
(Percent)

	1873-82	1882-86	1887-90	1900III -1902IV	1910II -1912IV
Share of Gold in International Monetary Assets	42.3	36.7	36.9	37.0	47.5
Ratio of Monetary Gold to Secondary Reserves (f)	73.3	57.8	58.6	58.6	90.4
Cash Reserve Ratio ($\rho_1+\rho_2$)	16.6	14.4	12.0	9.6	13.0
Gold Reserve Ratio (ρ_1)	6.9	5.7	5.4	3.9	4.1
Note Reserve Ratio (ρ_2)	9.7	8.7	6.5	5.7	8.9
Secondary Reserve Ratio (ρ_3)	13.8	13.6	13.1	14.3	14.6
Currency-Liability Ratio (ε)	3.5	4.4	3.9	2.4	1.8
Official Reserve Ratio (Ω)	24.1	16.4	21.4	55.1	85.6

Sources and estimation methods for Table 3-8

The data required for calculating the ratios shown in Table 3-8 are averaged for the five subperiods, and the ratios are computed from these averages. The averages for the first three subperiods are based on annual data, those for the other two on quarterly data. The following sources are used:
Monetary gold, secondary reserves and aggregate Dominion notes: Tables A-1 and A-2.
Dominion notes held by banks and non-banks, monetary liabilities of banks: legend to Table 3-5.

ρ_1 : ratio of bank gold to bank monetary liabilities,
ρ_2 : ratio of bank holdings of Dominion notes to bank monetary liabilities,
ρ_3 : secondary reserve ratio,
Ω : ratio of government gold to outstanding Dominion notes.

The currency-liability ratio (ϵ) was defined earlier. The sum of ρ_1 and ρ_2 equals the cash reserve ratio. For the sake of convenience, ρ_1, ρ_2 and Ω are termed the gold reserve ratio, the note reserve ratio and the official reserve ratio respectively.

According to Table 3-6, the decline in f from 1873-82 to 1882-86 was attributable to a decrease in both the cash and official reserve ratios. As indicated earlier, the reduction in the cash reserve ratio reflected the resumption of specie payments in the United States, while the fall in the official reserve ratio was an outgrowth of the Dominion government's experiments with monetary discretion. The rapid expansion in the uncovered stock of Dominion notes during the 1870s and 1880s was associated with a substantial decline in the official reserve ratio (see also Chapter 7, notably Table 7-1).

The subsequent and renewed increase in f stemmed largely from a marked rise in the official reserve ratio following the shift in policy stance of the Dominion government.[25] From 1887-90 to 1910-12, the cash reserve ratio also went up to some extent, but so did the secondary reserve ratio. Moreover, the banks altered the composition of their cash reserves in favour of Dominion notes, as indicated by the inverse movements in the gold and note reserve ratios. The currency-liability ratio, by contrast, declined noticeably over that period. However, the observed movements in the reserve and currency-liability ratios, by themselves, could not have caused f to increase. Had the official reserve ratio remained at its 1887-90 level, the ratio of monetary gold to secondary reserves would have shrunk to 44 percent in 1910-12.

3.4.2. Cyclical Attributes of Monetary Gold Flows

Considering the positive correlation between gold inflows and the overall surplus, I would expect that the cyclical attributes of the two magnitudes were similar. The evidence indeed suggests that gold inflows tended to vary countercyclically. In Charts 3-1 and 3-8, quarterly rates of change in the monetary gold stock are related to the reference-cycle turning points. The data plotted in Chart 3-8 are taken from Curtis since the new estimates of monetary gold presented in Table A-1 are not available quarterly for the pre-1900 period. Owing to various gaps in the Curtis data (see Appendices A and B), it is uncertain whether Chart 3-8 correctly portrays the cyclical swings in the growth rates of the monetary gold stock. However, I doubt that the conclusions drawn from Chart 3-8 would be altered very much if the Curtis data could be adjusted for the missing items.[26]

Inasmuch as any confidence may be placed in the pre-1900 data, the growth in the monetary gold stock tended to be inversely related to the refer-

CHART 3-8
QUARTERLY GROWTH IN THE MONETARY GOLD STOCK, 1872III-1899III

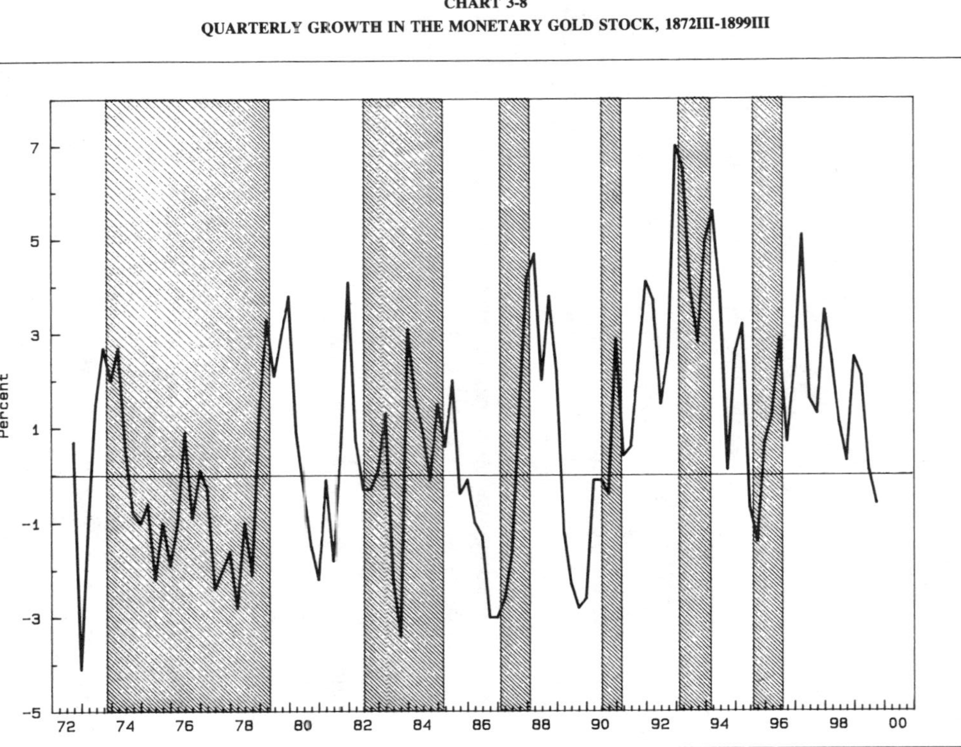

Sources for Chart 3-8
See legend to Table 3-2. The data on the monetary gold stock are smoothed by a seven-quarter moving average.

ence cycle. The countercyclical movements were particularly pronounced after 1885, save for the relatively high growth rates recorded near the reference-cycle peaks of 1893[27] and 1902, as well as a strong increase in 1900 (not shown by Chart 3-8). Beginning in 1904, the growth rates of the monetary gold stock frequently reached a peak (trough) in the second half of a reference-cycle contraction (expansion). This piece of evidence implies that in this subperiod, the monetary gold stock tended to lead secondary reserves and aggregate international monetary assets. Prior to 1885, the growth in the monetary gold stock — like the overall balance-of-payments surplus — was subject to substantial intra-cycle variation. Aside from a bulge in the growth rates coinciding with the trough of 1879, the movements in the monetary gold stock were unrelated to the reference cycle. The conclusions drawn from Charts 3-1 and 3-8 are corroborated by Table 3-2, which reveals a statistically significant countercyclical pattern of the monetary gold stock for both the pre-1900 and post-1900 periods.[28]

As indicated by Chart 3-9, the countercyclical swings in the monetary gold stock reflected parallel movements in the cash reserve ratio of the chartered banks. Notably after 1885, the pattern of bank cash reserves and, hence, the cash reserve ratio was countercyclical, with both bank holdings of monetary gold and Dominion notes inversely related to the reference cycle. The countercyclical movements in bank holdings of Dominion notes, in turn, elicited countercyclical movements in the government gold stock. As I pointed out in Section 3.2, the reliance on an automatic policy regime after 1885 implied a close correlation between the government gold stock and the stock of Dominion notes. Moreover, the cyclical pattern of the aggregate note issue was dominated by the share in the hands of the chartered banks. Dominion notes outside the banking system — like the money stock — varied procyclically, but their cyclical variance was dwarfed by that of bank holdings.[29]

The cyclical patterns of the cash reserve ratio and the monetary gold stock were very similar, except during the first half of the 1880s. Although between 1880 and 1885 the monetary gold stock was unrelated to the reference cycle, the movements in the cash reserve ratio were distinctly countercyclical, due to unusually strong procyclical swings in the money stock recorded over this period (Chart 3-5). According to Chart 3-9, the note and gold reserve ratios, that is, the two constituents of the cash reserve ratio, also varied countercyclically. During the reference-cycle expansion of 1879-82, both ratios declined substantially. However, after 1882, the cyclical amplitude of the gold reserve ratio became significantly smaller than that of the note reserve ratio. Thus, the cyclical movements in the cash reserve ratio reflected chiefly changes in the banks' holdings of Dominion notes relative to their monetary liabilities. The patterns revealed by Chart 3-9 are consistent with the econometric estimates presented in Table 3-7. During much of the period under study, flows of bank gold were not very sensitive to cyclical fluctuations in the overall balance-of-payments surplus. Therefore, it is not surprising that the gold reserve ratio only varied moderately over the business cycle.

CHART 3-9
CHARTERED-BANK CASH RESERVE RATIOS, 1874II-1913I

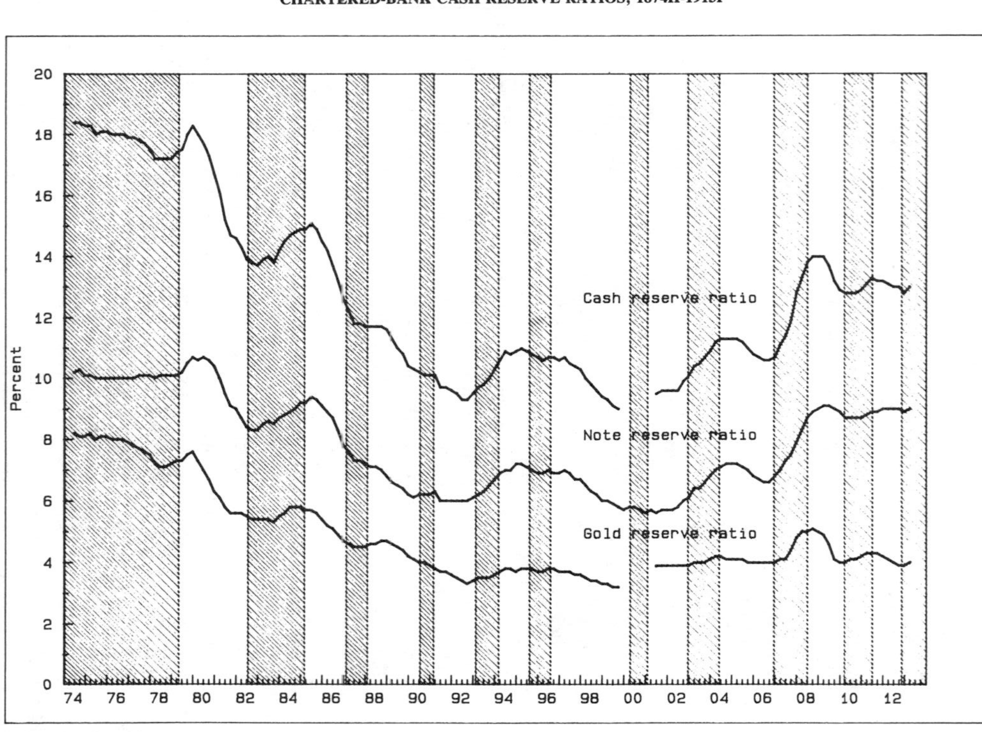

Sources for Chart 3-9
See Table 3-5. The ratios are calculated from data that are smoothed by a seven-quarter moving average.

The evidence presented in this chapter clearly indicates that the cyclical pattern of the monetary gold stock was dominated by the marked countercyclical swings in the cash reserve ratio, rather than by the procyclical movements in the money stock. Thus, over the business cycle, the money stock was not closely related to either the monetary gold stock or international monetary assets. Money growth typically peaked near the midpoint of a reference-cycle expansion, while the growth in the monetary gold stock reached a cyclical high at or immediately before a reference-cycle trough.

In view of the countercyclical swings in Canadian imports of monetary gold, Viner's thesis about the role of gold in balance-of-payments adjustment is not fully borne out by the empirical evidence. There is little doubt that — as suggested by Viner — payments imbalances were settled mainly by flows of secondary reserves. However, gold flows were not completely unresponsive to payments imbalances; as indicated by Table 3-7, overall surpluses gave rise to inflows of both secondary reserves and monetary gold, especially before 1880 and after 1900. Contrary to Viner's assertion, gold inflows were linked directly to the overall surpluses, rather than indirectly by way of changes in the domestic money stock. Had gold inflows been tied closely to the domestic money stock, it would be impossible to explain their countercyclical pattern. Viner failed to realize that distinctive countercyclical movements in the cash reserve ratio drove a wedge between the Canadian stocks of money and monetary gold. In all fairness to Viner, however, I should note that the differences between his results and my own are a matter of emphasis rather than substance. Although Viner (1924, 164-72) stressed the stability of the cash reserve ratio, he was well aware of its countercyclical pattern. But he was not interested in the cyclical aspects of balance-of-payments adjustment and, therefore, overlooked the fact that the cyclical pattern of the monetary gold stock did not match that of the money stock. Viner's emphasis on the stability of the cash reserve ratio, of course, was justified in so far as that ratio did not fluctuate as much as the secondary reserve ratio (Chart 3-7).

3.5 SUMMARY AND FURTHER COMMENTS

Even though money growth was linked closely to the balance of payments in the longer run, the short-run relationship between the two variables was looser than suggested by Viner. The procyclical movements in the pre-1914 Canadian money stock were not attributable to corresponding movements in the monetary base and international monetary assets, but to pronounced countercyclical swings in the cash and secondary reserve ratios of the chartered banks. Thus, bank reserve management offers the key to understanding the procyclical pattern of the pre-1914 Canadian money stock.

Unlike the money stock, the monetary base and international monetary assets displayed a countercyclical pattern. The analysis of Section 3.2 suggests that the balance of payments was the principal source of variation in the monetary base. Discretionary monetary policy, by contrast, did not significantly impinge on the cyclical pattern of the monetary base, except in the period 1867-85. Prior to 1885, discretionary monetary policy was procyclical in the sense that it tended to stimulate to some extent base-money growth during business-cycle expansions.

The countercyclical pattern of international monetary assets and, hence, the overall balance-of-payments surplus mirrored countercyclical swings in inflows of both monetary gold and secondary reserves. The evidence is at variance with Viner's assertion that gold flows were not linked directly to the balance of payments. However, Viner's thesis is valid in so far as secondary reserves played a much more important role in balance-of-payments adjustment than monetary gold.

Until the United States resumed specie payments in 1879, about 50 percent of overall surpluses or deficits were settled by transfers of monetary gold. Thereafter, secondary reserves became a much more important means of settling payments imbalances since the return of the United States to the gold standard rendered them a good substitute for the precious metal. After the turn of the century, the importance of gold in balance-of-payments adjustment increased again. The growing use of monetary gold reflected the Dominion government's shift to an automatic system of monetary policy, which lead to a dramatic increase in the share of Dominion notes backed by gold.

Interestingly, the cyclical pattern of monetary gold and secondary reserves differed fundamentally from that observed for fixed-term loans granted to foreigners by the chartered banks. While monetary gold and secondary reserves varied in a countercyclical fashion, the pattern of fixed-term loans (i.e., other current loans and discounts abroad, as reported by Curtis) was distinctly procyclical (Table 3-2).[30]

The countercyclical pattern of monetary gold suggests that the indirect monetary effects emanating from gold flows between Canada and abroad were destabilizing. During business-cycle expansions, Canada cut her imports of monetary gold and, thus, caused base-money growth in other countries to accelerate. The significance of destabilizing indirect monetary effects is discussed in Chapter 8.

While a close inverse relationship existed between the overall balance-of-payments surplus and the reference cycle, the cyclical patterns of the current-account surplus and residual inflows were less regular. During much of the pre-1914 period, the current-account surplus, like the overall surplus, moved countercyclically. From 1885 to 1895 and after 1900, residual inflows and, hence, capital inflows also varied countercyclically, but otherwise their cyclical pattern was irregular.

The relationship between the Canadian balance of payments and economic activity over the business cycle contrasts sharply with that observed over the long run. A cyclical expansion in Canadian economic activity was normally accompanied by a drop in the overall surplus, while the current account surplus and capital imports frequently shrank too. Over the long run, however, an acceleration of Canadian economic growth — such as the upward shift in the trend growth of Canadian output triggered by the wheat boom — caused the current account to deteriorate and capital imports to rise. Moreover, the surge in capital imports was sufficiently strong to allow for a rise in the overall surplus. Thus, while the overall surplus was negatively correlated with Canadian economic activity over the business cycle, the two magnitudes moved in sympathy over the long run.[31]

The results presented in this chapter are not comparable to those obtained in two previous studies on the sources of variation in the pre-1914 Canadian money stock (Hay, 1968; Macesich and Haulman, 1971) since the concepts of the monetary base underlying these studies differ from my own in two respects. First, Hay and Macesich-Haulman define the monetary base as the sum of the chartered banks' cash reserves, Dominion notes outside the banking system, and aggregate subsidiary coin issued by the Dominion government, but they do not take account of secondary reserves.[32] Second, adopting a concept of the monetary base or "high-powered money" developed by Friedman and Schwartz for the United States, Hay (1968) considers notes issued by the chartered banks to be part of the monetary base. For the period before the Federal Reserve System was established, Friedman and Schwartz (1963b, 50 and Appendix B) subsume in the U.S. monetary base monetary gold and subsidiary coin, as well as notes issued by the U.S. Treasury and U.S. commercial banks. In my opinion, the Friedman-Schwartz concept of the monetary base is not appropriate for Canada. In the United States, bank notes, for all practical purposes, were a government currency in disguise and possessed base-money properties like the notes issued by the U.S. Treasury (see Chapter 1). In Canada, by contrast, bank notes were not an obligation of the government and, therefore, were not fundamentally different from bank deposits.[33]

Endnotes — Chapter 3

1. See Canada, Department of Customs, *Tables of the Trade and Navigation of the Dominion of Canada* for the fiscal years 1896-98.

2. The 1897 peak in the overall surplus lagged the corresponding reference-cycle trough, whose exact timing, however, is uncertain. The 1903 and 1907 troughs in the overall surplus did not significantly lag the corresponding reference-cycle peaks. Note that the latter occurred at the end of 1902 and 1906 respectively.

3. The moving average spans approximately one-half of the median length of a full reference cycle. For the period under study, the median duration of a full reference cycle averaged 13 quarters. Such a moving average eliminates much of the intra-cycle variation in international monetary assets. I also experimented with a seasonally adjusted series, which, however, was still subject to noticeable intra-cycle variation.

4. Except in December, 1902, the leads or lags ranged from zero to two quarters. It is difficult to time precisely the trough in asset growth corresponding to the reference-cycle peak of December, 1902. That trough could have occurred either in 1902III or 1903III. Depending on the timing of the trough, asset growth led the reference cycle by one quarter or lagged it by three quarters.

5. Since the reference-cycle turning points of 1887 and 1888 were recorded in February, the lead observed in these two years might in fact have been very short.

6. It is uncertain whether the current-account surplus in 1907 significantly lagged the reference cycle since the latter peaked at the end of 1906.

7. Table 3-1 possibly overstates the current-account surpluses (and, hence, understates residual or capital inflows) during the Yukon gold rush. There is little doubt that a significant share of Canadian placer gold (see Appendix A, note 16) was mined by foreigners, who transferred part of their incomes to other countries. In October, 1898, only one-fourth of Dawson's population was estimated to be Canadian (see *Monetary Times,* July 23, 1897, 106; Dec. 23, 1898, 831; Aug. 3, 1900, 143). Since such income transfers must be regarded as payments for imported foreign labour services, they should be recorded as a debit item in the non-merchandise trade account. Needless to say, the data required to adjust the non-merchandise trade account are unavailable.

8. Until June, 1871, the government did not hold gold on its own account. Instead, the official reserve consisted of a deposit with the Bank of Montreal (see Chapter 7).

9. Ideally, the monetary base should also cover subsidiary coin held by the Canadian public. Since the chartered banks were required to report specie rather than gold, my estimates of the monetary base include bank holdings of subsidiary coin. However, data on subsidiary coin outside the banking system are unavailable. While annual data exist on aggregate subsidiary coin minted by the Dominion government (Canada, Public Accounts for 1915, xx-xxi), the share absorbed by non-banks is unknown. At the end of 1913, the cumulative value of subsidiary coin issued since 1858 (net of the face value of pieces recoined) equalled $19.0 million, a small sum compared with the aggregate monetary base. U.S. silver coins also circulated widely in Canada (Appendix A).

10. The percentages are calculated from averages of end-of-period values for uncovered Dominion notes and the monetary base (Tables A-1 and A-2).

11. A word of caution is in order. Owing to the volatility of the overall surplus, it is difficult to identify the trend in the monetary base prior to 1888. For this reason, the relative influence of the balance of payments and discretionary monetary policy on the trend growth in the monetary base cannot be determined precisely for that subperiod.

12. Over the period 1872-87, the overall surplus tended to be lower in contraction II than in contraction I (Table 3-4). This departure from the normal cyclical pattern was due mainly to the unusually large overall surplus in 1883. If the value for 1883 is excluded, the average for contraction I falls from $0.8 to $-1.6 million.

13. Coin is excluded from my money-stock estimates since the share held by the non-bank public is unknown (see also note 9). Hay (1967, 264) and Macesich (1970, 260) include in their money-stock series an estimate of aggregate subsidiary coin issued by the Dominion government. The latter, of course, also covers the portion absorbed by the chartered banks. Moreover, Macesich subsumes in the money stock deposits of the Dominion government with the chartered banks.

14. The deposit liabilities of the government and post office savings banks and of other non-bank financial intermediaries are not included in the money stock series presented in this study.

15. See See Curtis (1931a, 31). For the pre-1900 period, only fragmentary unpublished data are available on deposits booked abroad (Appendix B).

16. The simple correlation between the quarterly rates of change in the money stock including and excluding deposits abroad amounts to 0.98. The rates of change are computed from data for the period 1901III-1913I (adjusted by a seven-quarter moving average).

17. The money stock data for the period prior to 1873III exclude provincial government deposits with the chartered banks. Due to the data break in 1873, the smoothed series shown in Chart 3-5 begins with the second quarter of 1874.

18. Also note that during the cyclical downturn of 1910-11, both trend-adjusted money and imports continued to rise, but at a lower rate than during the preceding expansion.

19. Needless to say, one cannot simultaneously plead errors in the reference-cycle series and argue that the overall balance-of-payments surplus displayed a flawless countercyclical pattern from 1887 to 1895.

20. A frequent objection to the use of trend-adjusted data in business-cycle analysis derives from the observation that many time series are described by non-stationary stochastic processes. In this study, I assume that the money stock, the monetary base, international monetary assets, output, prices, interest rates and other variables followed a trend-stationary process. Had these variables been subject to stochastic rather than deterministic trends, the procedure employed in this study for detrending the data would likely overstate the statistical significance of their cyclical variation (see Nelson and Plosser, 1982). To guard against spurious cyclical movements in the levels of these variables, I have also examined the cyclical patterns of first differences. The evidence presented in Chapters 3, 4 and 5 suggests that first differencing does not remove the cyclical variation in these variables. Therefore, the cyclical fluctuations in the levels do not appear to be spurious. However, as Nelson and Plosser point out, first differencing is not an ideal method of trend adjustment either. If a time series follows a non-stationary stochastic process, first differencing does not completely remove the stochastic growth component.

21. Equations (3.1) and (3.2) are derived as follows: Let HR be aggregate bank reserves, HC be Dominion notes outside the banking system, and ML be monetary liabilities of the chartered banks. Then $H = HC + HR$, $M = ML + HC$, and $M/H = (ML+HC)/(HC+HR)$. Divide both the numerator and denominator on the right-hand side of the last equation by ML and obtain $M/H = (1+\epsilon)/(\epsilon+\rho)$ since $\epsilon = HC/ML$ and $\rho = HR/ML$.

22. In deriving equation (3.4), I draw heavily on Cagan (1965, 17-18).

23. As would be expected, the shift in the composition of aggregate bank reserves reflected entirely a sharp increase in the chartered banks' short term claims on countries other than the United Kingdom (Curtis, 1931a, 44-45). Claims on "other" countries consisted mostly of claims on the United States.

24. Had equation (3.21) captured mainly the impact of seasonal fluctuations in the overall surplus on the inflow of bank gold, I would expect that cyclical movements in the two variables were not significantly correlated. This was indeed the case. In order to eliminate intra-cycle variations, the data on international monetary assets and its components are smoothed by a seven-quarter moving average (see also Table 3-2). Re-estimating equation (3.21) from quarterly first differences in the smoothed data on bank gold and international monetary assets, I obtain the following result:

$$\underset{}{\Delta MGB} = \underset{(4.38)}{0.58} + \underset{(0.42)}{0.01}\ OS, \qquad \bar{R}^2 = 0.00,$$

where OS denotes the overall surplus. ΔMG and ΔMGG, by contrast, are significantly related to the overall surplus even if smoothed quarterly data are employed. Using smoothed data, however, is open to criticism since the moving average procedure introduces additional serial correlation in the residuals of the regression equations. For this reason, I also re-estimate equation (3.21) by including three seasonal dummies as independent variables. Due to high multicollinearity between the seasonal dummies and the overall surplus, this approach does not yield meaningful results.

25. As a result of the break in the data on international monetary assets, I do not know to what extent the pre- and post-1888 averages for f, ρ_1 and ρ_3 are comparable.

26. The new series on monetary gold presented in Table A-1 is available on a semi-annual basis for the period 1887IV-1895II [see the sources listed in the legend to Table A-2, column (3)]. The cyclical pattern of the new series (if smoothed by a 1 1/2-year moving average) is similar to that of the Curtis data displayed in Chart 3-8.

27. It is possible that the surge in the monetary gold stock during the second half of 1892 and the early part of 1893 was caused by the disturbances rocketing the U.S. financial system between 1891 and 1897. Agitation over free silver and other difficulties led to a loss of confidence in the willingness or ability of the United States to preserve the gold standard. Repeated speculative attacks on the U.S. dollar triggered outflows of capital and gold. The turmoil in financial markets culminated in the panic of May, 1893. As a result of this panic, a host of banks in the United States was compelled to suspend specie payments (Friedman and Schwartz, 1963b, 104-13). The disturbances in the United States may have prompted Canadian banks to convert temporarily secondary reserves into gold.

28. No statistically significant countercyclical pattern is obtained if the significance test is based on the new data (see note 26) available semi-annually for the period 1887IV-1895II (Rich, 1984, Table 3).

29. In both the subperiods 1888-1901 and 1901-13, the simple correlation between annual first differences in bank holdings of Dominion notes and the government gold stock amounted to 0.89 (calculated from Tables A-1 and A-2, and Curtis, 1931a, 38).

30. As indicated in Chapter 2, secondary reserves include call loans and fixed-term loans maturing in 30 days or less. Other current loans and discounts, as reported by Curtis, cover loans with a term to maturity exceeding 30 days.

31. Note that — over the long run — the relationship between the Canadian balance of payments and economic activity paralleled that observed for the United States. See Williamson, 1964.

32. Macesich and Haulman also include in the monetary base the banks' contributions to the bank circulation redemption fund (see Chapter 1). Although a case may be made for including these contributions, I disregard the problems posed by the bank circulation redemption fund for measuring the monetary base. The estimates of the monetary base presented in this study would not be increased much if the contributions to the fund were added (see Curtis, 1931a, 40, for the latter).

33. I doubt that Friedman and Schwartz would consider their monetary-base concept to be applicable to Canada. They explicitly point out that their procedure of aggregating national bank notes and Treasury currency "is justified only by the special character of the national bank notes and would not be appropriate in general for bank issues of currency" (Friedman and Schwartz, 1963b, 782).

CHAPTER 4

BANK RESERVE MANAGEMENT AND THE CANADIAN BUSINESS CYCLE: A THEORETICAL ANALYSIS

The evidence of marked countercyclical swings in bank reserve ratios suggests that reserve management of the chartered banks was instrumental in generating procyclical movements in the money stock. In this chapter, the causes and effects of the countercyclical movements in bank reserve ratios are analyzed with the help of a simple dynamic macroeconomic model. In accordance with both Keynesian and monetary views of the Canadian business cycle, I assume that cyclical fluctuations in Canadian economic activity were triggered mainly by disturbances imported from abroad. However, the model possesses a distinctive monetarist flavour in that supply and demand conditions on the domestic money market are allowed to impinge on the cycle-transmission process.

To explore the implications of countercyclical movements in bank reserve ratios, a fairly standard open-economy macroeconomic model is modified by taking account explicitly of bank reserve behaviour. Two hypotheses about the causes of the countercyclical swings in bank reserve ratios are specified. Next, I show to what extent the model is able to explain the empirical regularities uncovered in the preceding chapter. The essence of these empirical findings is stated in terms of stylized facts to be explained by the model:

(a) Cyclical movements in Canadian and United States economic activity were positively correlated, with a close coincidence of cyclical turning points in the two series.

(b) The pattern of the nominal Canadian money stock was normally procyclical, while the current-account surplus, the overall balance-of-payments surplus, and international monetary assets, for the most part, varied countercyclically. The cyclical peaks (troughs) in the nominal money stock and the troughs (peaks) in the current-account and overall surplus tended to coincide with peaks (troughs) in Canadian and foreign economic activity.

(c) Like the current-account and overall surplus, capital inflows from abroad frequently varied countercyclically.

(d) The growth in the monetary base was closely linked to the overall balance-of-payments surplus and, hence, the growth in international monetary assets.

(e) The aggregate reserve ratio of the chartered banks moved countercyclically, with cyclical peaks (troughs) normally occurring shortly before the midpoint of a reference-cycle expansion (contraction).

The theoretical analysis also yields interesting propositions about the cyclical patterns of Canadian interest rates. The model suggests that depending on the causes of the countercyclical movements in bank reserve ratios, Canadian interest rates may vary procyclically or countercyclically. Therefore, the causes of the countercyclical movements in bank reserve ratios may be inferred from the observed patterns of Canadian interest rates. Furthermore, the theoretical analysis throws light on the role of interest rates in the cycle-transmission process.

As regards the structure of the model, Canada is treated as a small open economy, with foreign prices, output and interest rates assumed exogenous. The exchange rates between the Canadian dollar and foreign currencies are considered to be fixed, an assumption that is realistic for the post-1879 period. Supply and demand conditions on the domestic money market are assumed to impinge on the cycle-transmission process through changes in domestic interest rates. This assumption implies imperfect international mobility of capital.

The model embraces six markets on which four assets and two goods are traded. The assets considered comprise the Canadian monetary base, the Canadian money stock, as well as domestic and foreign bonds. Bank loans are not explicitly taken into account; instead, the chartered banks are assumed to grant loans exclusively by acquiring bonds from Canadian residents. Furthermore, I assume that only one of the two goods is produced in Canada (home good), while the other one is imported. The home good may be sold either in Canada or abroad. For the moment, I abstract entirely from government expenditure and revenue. The implications of cyclical movements in the budget deficit of the Dominion government are explored in Chapter 7.

The remainder of Chapter 4 is divided into three sections. Section 4.1 specifies the monetary sector of the model. The analysis focusses on the market for base money. For simplicity's sake, cash and secondary reserves are lumped together by treating the various classes of reserve assets as perfect substitutes. In view of the similarity of cyclical movements in the gold, note and secondary reserve ratios, it seems legitimate to aggregate cash and secondary reserves.[1] The real sector of the model is developed in Section 4.2. Section 4.3 examines the consistency of the model with the stylized facts. Moreover, the nature and implications of interest rate movements generated by the model are discussed.

4.1. THE MONETARY SECTOR OF THE MODEL

4.1.1. Demand for Base Money

The monetary sector of the model is specified by demand and supply functions for base money. In order to derive a demand function for base money, I start out from identities (3.1) and (3.2), relating the money stock to the monetary base. Since the currency-liability ratio (ϵ) did not vary over the business cycle, I disregard movements in that ratio by setting $\epsilon = 0$. Thus, the monetary base and the money stock are assumed to match aggregate reserves and monetary liabilities of the chartered banks respectively. Substituting (3.2) into (3.1), and expressing the monetary base and the money stock in real terms, I obtain:

$$h = \rho m, \tag{4.1}$$

where h stands for the real monetary base and m for the money stock. Note that throughout this chapter, nominal values are identified by capital letters, while lower-case letters stand for real values. The real value of a variable corresponds to its nominal value deflated by the price of the home good. Since the model is dynamic, all the variables are assumed to be functions of time.

Equation (4.1) may be viewed as a demand function for bank reserves or base money, provided the determinants of the aggregate reserve ratio (ρ) and the real money stock are specified. As regards the causes of the countercyclical swings in the aggregate reserve ratio, two hypotheses are incorporated in the model. Both hypotheses rest on the assumption that the chartered banks held reserves as a buffer against unexpected cash drains resulting from random movements in their monetary liabilities and from unanticipated shortfalls in debt service payments on their loans. Had reserves played a buffer-stock role, I would expect that the aggregate reserve ratio depended positively on the expected variance of the banks' cash flow relative to their monetary liabilities (EC), and negatively on the opportunity cost of holding reserves. The latter corresponds to the difference between the expected return on the banks' assets, other than reserves (r), and the return on reserves (r_ρ). Since banks are assumed to hold only reserves and domestic bonds, r is equivalent to the domestic bond yield. Thus,

$$\rho = \rho\,(EC,\ r - r_\rho),\ \rho_1 > 0,\ \rho_2 < 0, \tag{4.2}$$

where ρ_i $(i = 1,2)$ denotes the partial derivative of ρ with respect to the ith argument.[2]

Equation (4.2) allows for two possible causes of the countercyclical swings in the aggregate reserve ratio. First, it might be argued that EC varied countercyclically and, thus, produced corresponding movements in the aggregate reserve ratio. A cyclical slump in economic activity was normally accompanied by a deterioration in the financial standing of the banks' debtors. Debt service failures and loan defaults tended to mount, raising the likelihood of reserve losses on the part of the banks. As a result of an increase in EC, the banks were prompted to build up their cash and secondary reserves. Moreover, debt service failures and loan defaults impaired the solvency of the banking system. If the solvency problems were serious enough to open up the prospect of bank failures, financial panics and runs on banks could ensue. The fear of massive deposit withdrawals in turn provided a further incentive to the banks for bolstering their reserves. Although during the period under study Canada did not suffer from financial panics, it is nonetheless possible that business-cycle contractions heightened concerns about runs on banks and prompted the financial institutions to augment their reserve ratios. The public confidence instilled by strong countercyclical movements in reserve ratios might explain — at least in part — the absence of major financial panics in Canada.[3]

These considerations imply an inverse relationship between EC and the Canadian business cycle. The function determining EC rests on the assumption that the banks forecasted the cyclical variance of their cash flow on the strength of the observed deviations of realized Canadian output from its normal (or high-employment) level. Provided economic growth is disregarded and normal output treated as a constant, EC may be determined as follows:

$$EC = g(y),\ g_1 < 0, \qquad (4.3)$$

where y stands for realized Canadian output.

Second, it is conceivable that the countercyclical swings in the aggregate reserve ratio were due to procyclical movements in the opportunity cost of holding reserves. To simplify the analysis, I abstract from interest paid on reserves, that is, I set

$$r_\rho = 0. \qquad (4.4)$$

In Chapter 5, it is shown that the aggregate reserve ratio was insensitive to interest paid on reserves. Therefore, assumption (4.4) appears to be realistic.

The function determining the real money stock rests on the assumption that the banks did not attempt to manage their monetary liabilities by varying deposit rates. Instead, they were prepared to issue any amount of monetary liabilities the non-bank public elected to hold at prevailing interest rates. In all probability, liability management was not an important phenomenon prior to 1914. Bank notes and demand deposits did not yield interest, while the rate on savings deposits was kept constant by price-fixing arrangements during a major part of the period under study (see Chapter 2). Since the deposit rate may be treated as an exogenous variable, it is reasonable to assume that money was entirely demand-determined, that is,

$$m = m(y), m_1 > 0. \tag{4.5}$$

The money-demand function (4.5) only includes domestic output as an argument. It is possible that real money demand also responded to fluctuations in domestic interest rates and other variables. However, the conclusions of this chapter are not altered fundamentally if real demand is assumed to depend on interest rates, as well as output.[4]

Combining equations (4.1) to (4.5), I obtain a demand function for real base money:

$$h = \rho[g(y), r]m(y). \tag{4.6}$$

The subsequent analysis is simplified considerably if equation (4.6) is linearized. To this end, the economy is assumed initially to be in a stationary-state equilibrium, implying that realized output matches its normal level and that both the current and capital accounts are balances. The linear variant of (4.6) is derived by means of a first-order Taylor expansion about the initial stationary-state values of the variables:

$$h = -\alpha_1(r-r') + \alpha_2(y-y') + h', \tag{4.7}$$

where

$$\alpha_1 = -\rho_2 m' > 0, \tag{4.7a}$$

$$\alpha_2 = \rho_1 g_1 m' + m_1 \rho' \gtreqless 0. \tag{4.7b}$$

Primed symbols stand for the initial stationary-state values of the variables. Equation (4.7) differs from standard money-demand functions in that a cyclical increase in output may raise or lower real demand for base money. On the one hand, demand rises because of an increase in the real money stock and — given the aggregate reserve ratio — a need for additional reserves. On the other hand, real demand for base money falls as a result of a drop in the aggregate reserve ratio induced by a cyclical decline in the expected variance of the banks' cash flow.

4.1.2. Supply of Base Money

The nominal supply of base money may be divided up into international monetary assets and uncovered Dominion notes:

$$H = I + UD. \tag{4.8}$$

Equation (4.8) is identical to (2.3). UD is treated as an exogenous variable, while international monetary assets are endogenous and determined by the balance of payments. The subsequent analysis is facilitated by introducing a new variable, termed the cumulative current-account surplus (N), which equals the difference between Canada's international monetary assets and her net non-monetary foreign debt (S):

$$N = I - S. \tag{4.9}$$

Therefore:

$$\dot{N} = Pc, \tag{4.10}$$

where P and c denote the price of the home good and the real current-account surplus respectively. Equation (4.10) is linearized in the same way as (4.6). Since the stationary-state value of the real current-account surplus is zero, it follows that $\dot{N}' = P'c' = O$. If P' is set equal to unity, the linear variant of (4.10) becomes:

$$\dot{N} = c. \tag{4.10a}$$

The current-account surplus and the non-monetary foreign debt are endogenous variables to be determined in Section 4.2.

The specification of the market for base money is completed by an equation relating the nominal to the real value of the monetary base:

$$H = hP. \tag{4.11}$$

The linear variant of (4.11) reads:

$$H = h + h'(P-1), \tag{4.11a}$$

since $P' = 1$ by assumption.

4.2. THE REAL SECTOR OF THE MODEL

4.2.1. The Goods Markets: Principal Assumptions

Following Viner (1924, 227-37), I assume that Canada acted as a price taker on the markets for its imported goods and services, but was able to influence to some extent export prices, notably in areas where domestic production accounted for a large share of world output. Accordingly, import and export prices are treated as exogenous and endogenous variables respectively. Viner's view as to price-setting behaviour in Canadian export markets is supported by empirical evidence on the relationship between real exports and export prices. Had Canada acted as a pure price taker on her export markets, a cyclical increase in foreign economic activity should have impinged on real exports only through a rise in export prices, prompting Canadians to boost production and to cut consumption of exportable goods and services. In these circumstances, I would expect real exports to have lagged export prices since Canadian producers and consumers were unlikely to react instantaneously to price changes.

The cyclical patterns of trend-adjusted Canadian export prices and real exports are depicted by Chart 4-1. Interestingly, there is no evidence to suggest that real exports systematically lagged export prices. On the contrary, the cyclical turning points in real exports normally led those in export prices, especially over the pre-1888 and post-1900 periods.[5] Except during the short reference-cycle contractions of 1890-91 and 1895-96, the pattern of real exports

CHART 4-1

CANADIAN EXPORT PRICES AND REAL EXPORTS
(Deviations from Growth Trend)

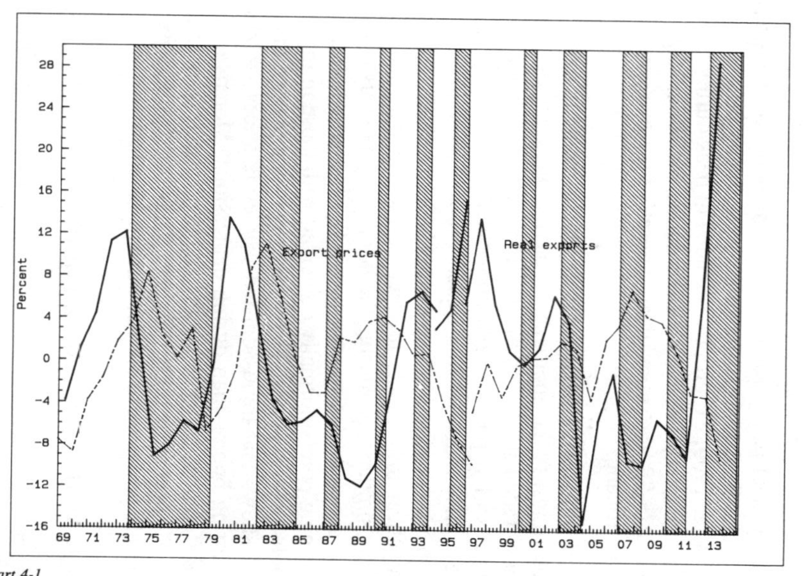

Sources and estimation methods for Chart 4-1

See Chart 4-4 for export prices. In order to estimate real exports, nominal exports [Table A-3, column (1)] are deflated by export prices. Note that data on nominal exports and export prices are available for calendar and fiscal years respectively. Thus, for the purpose of deflating nominal exports, export prices are converted to a calendar-year basis. The conversion procedure rests on the assumption that export prices were changed only upon the termination of a fiscal year. The data shown in Chart 4-1 equal the difference between the natural logs of the actual and trend values of real exports (XMR). The trend values are estimated from the following regression equations:

$$\ln XMR = \underset{(134.8)}{4.245} + \underset{(8.70)}{0.0165t}, \; R^2 = 0.74, \text{ for 1869-96,}$$

$$\ln XMR = \underset{(93.8)}{4.875} + \underset{(8.87)}{0.0425t}, \; R^2 = 0.83, \text{ for 1896-1913.}$$

Nominal exports for 1894 are assumed to be $109.2 million (Table A-3) was distinctly procyclical. For the most part, the cyclical turning points in real exports either led or coincided with the reference-cycle turning points.[6] Export prices also tended to move procyclically, but in contrast to real exports, they frequently lagged the reference cycle. Moreover, their procyclical pattern was not as pronounced as that of real exports. Thus, Chart 4-1 suggests that cyclical movements in export prices were an effect, rather than a cause, of changes in real exports.

The evidence of a lag between export prices and real exports is confirmed by Table 4-1, in which trend-adjusted values of the two variables are averaged for the various reference-cycle stages. Over the period 1873-88, export prices tended to attain a cyclical peak (trough) during the boom (depression) stage of the reference-cycle. Real exports, by contrast, normally peaked during the expansion stage. After 1900, export prices tended to peak during the contraction stage,[7] while real exports reached a high during the boom stage. Except during the period 1873-88, the procyclical patterns of the two variables were not statistically significant.

While there is little doubt about the endogenous nature of export prices, it is more difficult to justify the approach adopted in this study of aggregating exportable and non-traded goods. Aggregation would be legitimate if the cyclical swings in prices of exportable and non-traded goods had been closely correlated. Since a price index for non-traded goods is unavailable, the analysis is confined to a comparison of export to wholesale prices. According to Chart 4-2, the cyclical movements in trend-adjusted export and wholesale prices were broadly similar, save during the last five of six years of the period under study. Both series tended to vary procyclically, but wholesale prices, whose cyclical turning points normally coincided with those in the reference cycle, frequently led export prices. The same conclusion may be drawn from Table 4-1, which shows that trend-adjusted wholesale prices — on average — were higher during booms than during depressions. Moreover, for most subperiods, the differences between booms and depressions were statistically significant at the 90 pecent or higher levels.[8] Thus, the cyclical patterns of export and wholesale prices were similar but not identical.

4.2.2. The Goods Markets: Structural Equations

Canadian output — by assumption — matches production of the home good. The market for the home good, therefore, is in equilibrium if Canadian output equals real aggregate demand:

$$y = b + c. \tag{4.12}$$

Real aggregate demand is broken down into two components: real domestic absorption of home and imported goods (b) and the real current-account surplus (c). Real domestic absorption is assumed to be negatively related to the domestic bond yield and positively related to domestic output:

$$b = -\beta_1 r + \beta_2 y, \ \beta_1, \beta_2 > 0. \tag{4.13}$$

TABLE 4-1

CYCLICAL CHARACTERISTICS OF REAL EXPORTS AND PRICES
(Average Annual Percentage Deviation from Growth Trend)

Estimation Period	Boom Stage	Depression Stage	t-values	Expansion Stage	Contraction Stage	t-values
		Real Exports			Real Exports	
Cal. 1873 - 88	-0.3	-3.1	0.70	2.3	-5.5	2.40
Cal. 1873 - 96	-0.5	-0.6	0.02	0.6	-2.2	0.81
Cal. 1896 - 1913	2.7	-2.7	1.09	0.8	-0.5	0.06
		Export Prices			Export Prices	
Fisc. 1873 - 88	4.1	-0.2	1.89	-0.1	3.1	1.26
Fisc. 1873 - 97	2.2	-0.1	1.15	-0.3	2.2	1.29
Fisc. 1897 - 1914	-0.2	0.4	0.32	0.2	0.6	0.37
		Import Prices			Import Prices	
Fisc. 1873 - 88	3.8	-3.6	3.07	-0.6	0.6	0.36
Fisc. 1873 - 97	2.5	-1.4	1.95	-0.1	1.1	0.55
Fisc. 1897 - 1914	0.4	-0.2	0.22	-0.9	2.1	1.34
		Wholesale Prices			Wholesale Prices	
Cal. 1873 - 88a)	2.9	-4.4	2.60	-0.7	0.2	0.27
Cal. 1873 - 88b)	3.6	-2.0	2.08	1.0	1.2	0.09
Cal. 1873 - 96a)	2.8	-2.9	2.60	0.6	0.1	0.20
Cal. 1873 - 96b	2.7	-2.0	2.13	1.0	0.3	0.26
Cal. 1896 - 1913a)	0.3	-0.4	0.90	0.1	0.1	0.00
Cal. 1896 - 1913b)	0.9	-1.3	1.86	-0.2	0.3	0.34

a) DBS Index
b) Michell Index

Sources and estimation methods for Table 4-1

The averages presented in this table are arithmetic means of trend-adjusted values, as shown in Charts 4-1, 4-2 and 4-4, calculated for the various reference-cycle stages. The annual observations are assigned to the reference-cycle stages according to Appendix C, procedures 3 and 4. See Table 3-2 for the significance test.

CHART 4-2
CANADIAN EXPORT PRICES AND WHOLESALE PRICES
(Deviations from Growth Trend)

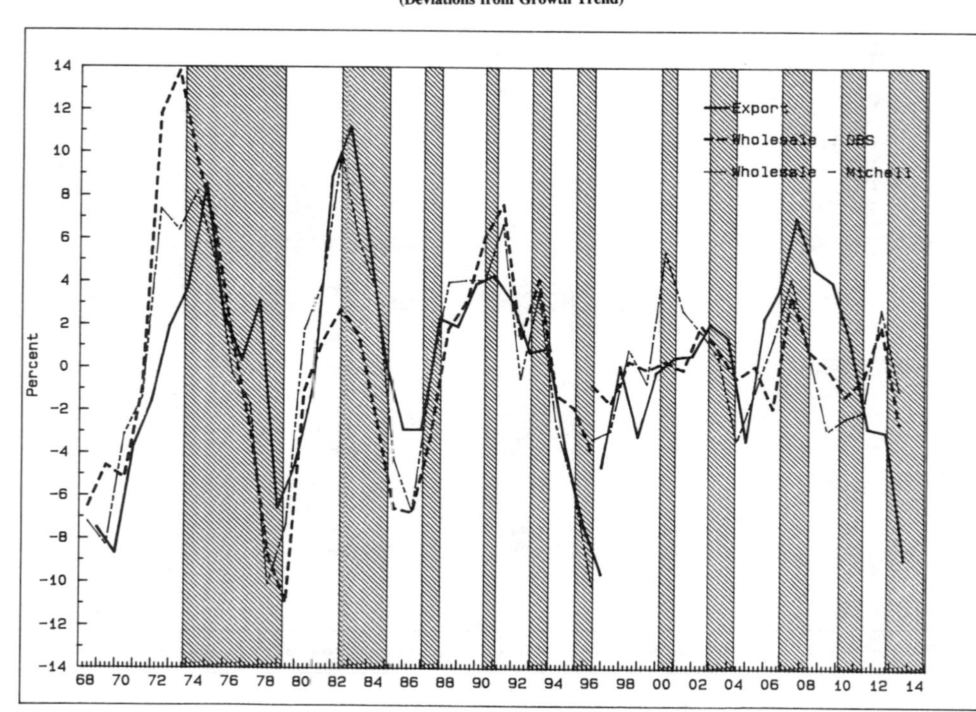

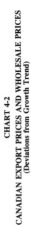

Sources and estimation methods for Chart 4-2
See Chart 4-4.

Although real absorption was liable to respond to changes in real, rather than nominal interest rates, the distinction between real and nominal interest rates is disregarded in this study. Prior to 1914, inflation expectations were unlikely to be sufficiently important to make a significant imprint on nominal interest rates. While Canadian wholesale prices fluctuated considerably from year to year, the inflation trend was negligible by modern standards (see Chapter 1). The neglect of inflation expectations is also justified by Friedman and Schwartz's (1982, ch. 10) empirical findings regarding the relationship between nominal interest rates and inflation expectations in the United States. Their results indicate that up to World War II, nominal interest rates behaved "as if prices were expected to be stable and both inflation and deflation were unanticipated" (1982, 10). Since Canadian price trends were similar to those of the United States, Friedman and Schwartz's conclusions also seem to be valid for Canada.[9]

The real current-account surplus is assumed to depend on the terms of trade, as well as on domestic and foreign output:

$$c = \gamma_1\pi - \gamma_2 y + z, \gamma_1, \gamma_2 > 0, \tag{4.14}$$

where π denotes the relative price of the imported good or the inverse of the terms of trade. The real current-account surplus equals the difference between real foreign demand for Canadian exports and real domestic demand for imports. Real export demand is related to the terms of trade and foreign output, with the variable, z, capturing output-induced changes in real exports. Real import demand is a function of the terms of trade and domestic output. I postulate a positive relationship between c and π, implying that the Marshall-Lerner condition is satisfied.[10]

The relative price of the imported good is defined as follows:

$$\pi = P_f/P. \tag{4.15}$$

The price of the imported good (P_f) is treated as an exogenous variable. Equation (4.15) is linearized in the same way as (4.6), with P'_f and P' set equal to unity:

$$\pi = P_f - P + 1. \tag{4.15a}$$

As far as prices are concerned, the model allows for the possibility that cyclical movements in Canadian output affected the price of the home good. Following Keynes (1936, chs. 20-21, especially pp. 298-303), I assume that the price level reacted rapidly to an exogenous disturbance, while the adjustment in nominal wages was sluggish. A cyclical rise in aggregate demand, therefore, led to a temporary rise in the price level relative to nominal wages, inducing domestic producers to expand output. This implies a relationship between the price of the home good and domestic output:

$$P = \varphi y. \tag{4.16}$$

If the units of output are chosen such as to render $\varphi = 1$, (4.16) may be simplified to read:

$$P = y \tag{4.16a}$$

Equation (4.16a) — which is a standard feature of conventional Keynesian models — may be criticized on the ground that it is inconsistent with the classical postulate of long-run neutrality of money. For example, a monetary disturbance such as a change in the uncovered stock of Dominion notes (UD) may cause realized output to move away permanently from its normal level. Permanent gaps between realized and normal output are implausible since they are likely to trigger wage adjustments that — sooner or later — will cause realized output to return to its normal level. Provided nominal wages responded to gaps between realized and normal output, a Phillips-curve specification of the link between prices and output would be preferable to equation (4.16a). The Phillips curve establishes a positive relationship between first differences in prices and the gap between realized and normal output. In stationary-state equilibrium, realized output, by definition, matches its normal level, that is, long-run neutrality of money is ensured.

Although it would be desirable to equip the model with a mechanism precluding permanent deviations in realized output from its normal level, the subsequent analysis is nevertheless based on equation (4.16a). A Phillips-curve specification of the link between prices and output does not appear to accord with the pre-1914 Canadian evidence. As indicated earlier, Canadian wholesale prices moved in sympathy with the reference cycle, without any evidence of systematic leads or lags between the two variables (Table 4-1, Chart 4-2). Similarly, Chart 4-3 suggests that peaks (troughs) in trend-adjusted real GNP and the GNP deflator tended to coincide with reference-cycle peaks (troughs). However, the two variables did not consistently vary with the reference cycle. Except over the period 1906-13, the GNP deflator was more closely linked to the reference cycle than real GNP. From about the mid-1880s to 1896, in particular, real GNP was unrelated to the reference cycle.[11] Thus, cyclical movements in the levels of the two variables, if related at all, tended to coincide, as suggested by equation (4.16a). The Phillips-curve specification, by contrast, suggests that the price level should have lagged the output level.[12]

The absence on long-run neutrality in the model is not a serious matter if equation (4.16a) is employed exclusively for analyzing the impact of cyclical and other transitory disturbances on the Canadian economy. Aside from a brief discussion of permanent shifts in discretionary monetary policy, presented in Chapter 7 (see also Appendix D), this study does not deal with permanent changes in the exogenous variables. In the event of permanent exogenous disturbances, I assume that a mechanism not explicitly specified ensures equality between realized and normal output in the long run, that is, equation (4.16a) is replaced by (4.16b):

$$y = y'. \tag{4.16b}$$

CHART 4-3

REAL GROSS NATIONAL PRODUCT AND GNP DEFLATOR
(Deviations from Growth Trend)

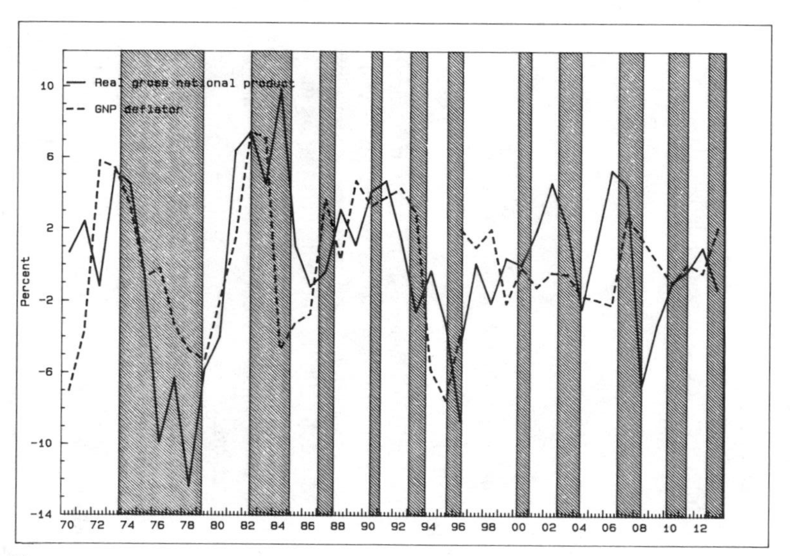

Source and estimation methods for Chart 4-3

Urquhart (1987). The annual observations plotted in Chart 4-3 are centred on June 30. They are expressed as the difference between the natural logs of the actual and trend values. The latter are estimated by regressing the natural logs of real GNP (y) and the GNP deflator (P) on time (t):

$\ln y = \underset{(269.6)}{5.88} + \underset{(19.9)}{0.027t}$, $R^2 = 0.94$, for 1870-96,

$\ln y = \underset{(406.2)}{6.51} + \underset{(41.2)}{0.061t}$, $R^2 = 0.99$, for 1896-1913,

$\ln P = \underset{(254.9)}{4.72} - \underset{(-4.47)}{0.005t}$, $R^2 = 0.44$, for 1870-96,

$\ln P = \underset{(566.0)}{4.50} + \underset{(28.3)}{0.021t}$, $R^2 = 0.98$, for 1896-1913.

4.2.3. Bond Market

By virtue of Walras' Law, one of the six markets covered by the model — domestic bonds — need not be considered explicitly. However, an equation for the non-monetary foreign debt (S) is required to close the model. For simplicity, Canadian residents are not permitted to hold interest-bearing foreign assets other than secondary reserves.[13] Thus, S equals the nominal stock of Canadian bonds in the hands of foreigners. Real foreign demand for Canadian bonds (u) is assumed to depend on domestic and foreign bond yields:

$$u = \delta_1 r - \delta_2 r_f, \ \delta_1, \delta_2 > 0, \qquad (4.17)$$

with r_f denoting the yield on foreign bonds.

To determine u, foreigners are assumed to deflate the nominal value of their bond holdings by P_f. Thus,

$$S = uP_f, \qquad (4.18)$$

with the linear variant of (4.18) given by:[14]

$$S = u + u'(P_f - 1). \qquad (4.18a)$$

Substitution of (4.17) into (4.18a) yields:

$$S = \delta_1 r - \delta_2 r_f + u'(P_f - 1). \qquad (4.19)$$

Equation (4.19) implies that changes in interests rates prompt foreign investors to adjust instantaneously their stocks of foreign assets. Therefore, it differs from the flow specification found in open-economy macromodels cast in the tradition of Mundell (1963). These models rest on the assumption that a change in the *level* of interest rates elicits a shift in capital *inflows* (or in first differences in the non-monetary foreign debt), rather than a once-and-for-all adjustment in asset *stocks*.

4.3. CONSISTENCY OF THE MODEL WITH THE STYLIZED FACTS

4.3.1. Determination of Endogenous Variables

The complete model consists of the eleven equations (4.7), (4.8), (4.9), (4.10a), (4.11a), (4.12), (4.13), (4.14), (4.15a), (4.16a) and (4.19), determining the endogenous variables H, h, I, N, S, P, π, r, y, b and c. Three foreign disturbances are allowed to affect the Canadian economy: output-induced changes in Canadian exports (z), changes in the price of the imported good (P_f) and changes in the foreign bond yield (r_f).

In order to solve for the endogenous variables, the model is reduced to a first-order differential equation in the cumulative current-account surplus (N), while the remaining endogenous variables are expressed in terms of the exogenous variables and N. The solutions for domestic output, the price of the home good and the domestic bond yield may be obtained with the help of the Hicksian IS-LM apparatus. Combining equations (4.14), (4.15a) and (4.16a), I obtain an alternative expression for the current-account surplus:

$$c = -(\gamma_1 + \gamma_2)y + v, \tag{4.20}$$

where

$$v = z + \gamma_1(P_f + 1). \tag{4.21}$$

The new exogenous variable, v, captures foreign-induced changes in the Canadian current-account surplus, that is, changes due to movements in foreign output (z) and the price of the imported good (P_f). According to equation (4.21), an increase in both foreign output and prices, *ceteris paribus,* augments the current-account surplus. To simplify the subsequent analysis, I will only examine changes in v, rather than in z and P_f taken individually, by assuming that cyclical movements in foreign output and prices were closely correlated. This assumption, it should be noted, may not be entirely realistic. As indicated by Chart 4-4 and Table 4-1, import prices, like export prices, were positively correlated with the reference cycle, but tended to lag somewhat economic activity.

Substitution of equations (4.13) and (4.20) into (4.12) yields a locus of domestic output and the domestic bond yield consistent with equilibrium in the goods market:

$$k_1 y + \beta_1 r = v, \tag{4.22}$$

where

$$k_1 = 1 - \beta_2 + \gamma_1 + \gamma_2. \tag{4.23}$$

Equation (4.22) postulates a negative relationship between domestic output and the bond yield provided $k_1 > 0$. This relationship is described by the IS-line shown in Chart 4-5. A sufficient condition for k_1 to be positive and, thus, for the slope of the IS-line to be negative is that the marginal propensity to spend domestic income on the home good $(\beta_2 - \gamma_2)$ be positive and less than unity. This condition is assumed to be satisfied because negative values of k_1 may render the model unstable (see below). Equation (4.22) further indicates that a foreign-induced increase in the current-account surplus (or an increase in v) shifts the IS-line to the right.

Equations (4.7), (4.8), (4.9), (4.11a), (4.16a) and (4.18a) may be reduced to a locus of domestic output and the domestic bond yield consistent with equilibrium in the market for base money:

$$(\alpha_2 + h')y - (\alpha_1 + \delta_1)r = N + w, \tag{4.24}$$

provided UD = 0. Since discretionary monetary policy was not an important source of cyclical variation in the monetary base, I disregard the possibility that Canadian monetary authorities reacted to foreign cyclical disturbances by altering UD.

CHART 4-4
CANADIAN IMPORT PRICES
(Deviations from Growth Trend)

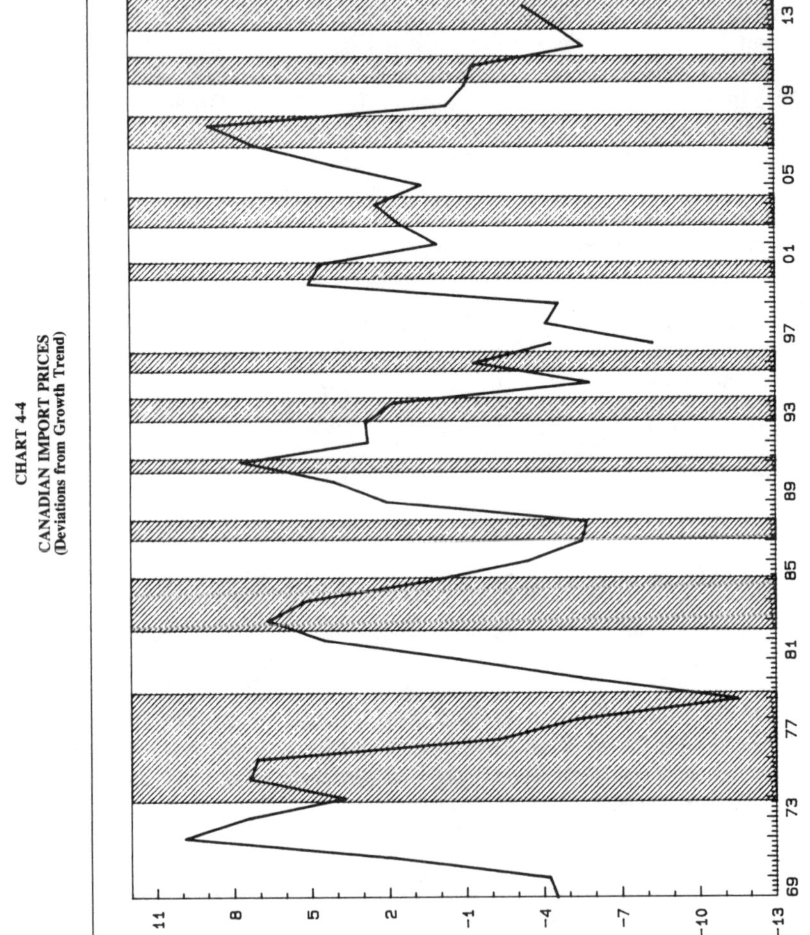

Sources and estimation methods for Charts 4-2 and 4-4

Sources

Export and import prices: Taylor, 1931, 17 and 19. The data compiled by Taylor represent unit values of exports and imports [ratios of nominal exports (imports) to the corresponding real magnitudes valued at 1900 prices]. They are available for fiscal years only.

Wholesale prices:The charts show the indices compiled by Michell (1931, 56), and Canada, Dominion Bureau of Statistics (1954, 14-16). The Michell index is an unweighted geometric mean of the price indices of seventy commodities. For the pre-1890 period, the DBS index, which excludes gold, is compiled in the same way as the Michell index, but the former covers a somewhat wider range of commodities than the latter. For the period starting in 1890, the DBS index is a weighted average of the indices of over 200 commodities. See Asimakopulos in Urquhart and Buckley (1965, 281-87) for a detailed discussion of these price indices.

Estimation methods

The annual price observations plotted in Charts 4-2 and 4-4 are centred on the midpoints of the respective calendar or fiscal years since they are based either on annual merchandise trade flows (import and export prices) or on annual averages of monthly price observations (wholesale prices). The charts show trend-adjusted annual data for the various price indices, expressed as the difference between the natural logs of the actual and trend values. The latter are estimated by regressing the natural logs of the respective price index (P) on time (t):

Michell $\ln P = \underset{(11.8)}{0.270} - \underset{(-9.05)}{0.0120t}$, $R^2 = 0.75$, for 1868-96,

$\ln P = \underset{(18.5)}{-0.864} + \underset{(19.9)}{0.0246t}$, $R^2 = 0.96$, for 1896-1913,

DBS: $\ln P = \underset{(-6.09)}{-0.142} - \underset{(-10.1)}{0.0138t}$, $R^2 = 0.79$, for 1868-96,

$\ln P = \underset{(-49.4)}{-1.29} + \underset{(35.8)}{0.0246t}$, $R^2 = 0.99$, for 1896-1913,

Export: $\ln P = \underset{(-1.71)}{-0.035} + \underset{(1.17)}{0.0014t}$, $R^2 = 0.005$, for fiscal 1869-97,

$\ln P = \underset{(-2.68)}{-0.048} + \underset{(9.79)}{0.0168t}$, $R^2 = 0.86$, for fiscal 1897-1914,

Import: $\ln P = \underset{(14.6)}{0.348} - \underset{(-12.0)}{0.0166t}$, $R^2 = 0.84$, for fiscal 1869-97,

$\ln P = \underset{(-4.23)}{-0.091} + \underset{(6.71)}{0.0138t}$, $R^2 = 0.74$, for fiscal 1897-1914.

The specification of the regression equations for export and import prices is complicated by the fact that the government, in 1907, altered the terminal date of the fiscal year. Until 1906, the fiscal year ended on June 30, but in 1907 the terminal date was advanced to March 31. Therefore, fiscal 1907 only lasted nine months. Since the annual price observations are centred on the midpoints of the fiscal years, the export and import prices, $P_{1897}, P_{1898}, \ldots, P_{1906}, P_{1907}, P_{1908}, \ldots, P_{1914}$, respectively, were regressed on $t = 1, 2, \ldots, 10, 10.875, 11.75, \ldots, 17.75$.

The new exogenous variable, w, measures foreign-induced changes in the Canadian non-monetary debt:

$$w = -\delta_2 r_f + u'(P_f - 1) - \alpha_1 r' + \alpha_2 y'. \tag{4.25}$$

An increase in w — which may reflect a decline in foreign interest rates or a rise in the price of the imported good — augments the Canadian non-monetary foreign debt. A decline in foreign interest rates, *ceteris paribus,* prompts foreign investors to substitute Canadian for foreign assets, while a rise in the price of the imported good induces them to purchase additional Canadian and foreign assets in an effort to preserve the real value of their portfolios.

The locus of domestic output and the domestic bond yield compatible with equilibrium in the market for base money is traced by the LM-line shown in Chart 4-5. Note that the LM-line may be upward or downward sloping, depending on the sign of $\alpha_2 + h'$. The expression $\alpha_2 + h'$ — which plays an important role in the subsequent analysis — will be called the total output sensitivity of nominal base-money demand. It equals the sum of two parameters: the output sensitivity of real base-money demand (α_2) and the sensitivity of nominal base-money demand to changes in the price of the home good (h'). Like real base-money demand, nominal base-money demand and, thus, the domestic bond yield may rise or fall as a result of an increase in domestic output. Since the positive effect of a rise in domestic output on nominal base-money demand is reinforced by an increase in the price of the home good, real base-money demand is less likely to go up than its nominal counterpart. For nominal base-money demand to decline, that is, for the LM-line to be downward sloping, the aggregate reserve ratio must react strongly to cyclical movements in domestic output.

Equations (4.22) and (4.24) may be solved for the price of the home good, domestic output and the domestic bond yield:

$$P = y = [\beta_1(N + w) + (\alpha_1 + \delta_1)v]/k_2, \tag{4.26}$$

$$r = -[k_1(N + w) - (\alpha_2 + h')v]/k_2. \tag{4.27}$$

Substituting equation (4.26) into (4.20), and recalling equation (4.10a), I also obtain a solution for the current-account surplus:

$$c = \dot{N} = -[\beta_1(\gamma_1 + \gamma_2)(N + w) - k_3 v]/k_2, \tag{4.28}$$

where

$$k_2 = k_1(\alpha_1 + \delta_1) + (\alpha_2 + h')\beta_1, \tag{4.29}$$

$$k_3 = (\alpha_1 + \delta_1)(1 - \beta_2) + (\alpha_2 + h')\beta_1. \tag{4.30}$$

As noted earlier, the model may be reduced to a first-order differential equation in the cumulative current-account surplus (N). Current-account surpluses feed back on the supply of base money [equation (4.24)] and, thus, affect the domestic bond yield, output, the price of the home good, and the remaining endogenous variables.

CHART 4-5
SHORT-RUN EFFECTS OF FOREIGN CYCLICAL DISTURBANCE

Total output sensitivity of nominal base-money demand (α_2 + h'):

positive | negative

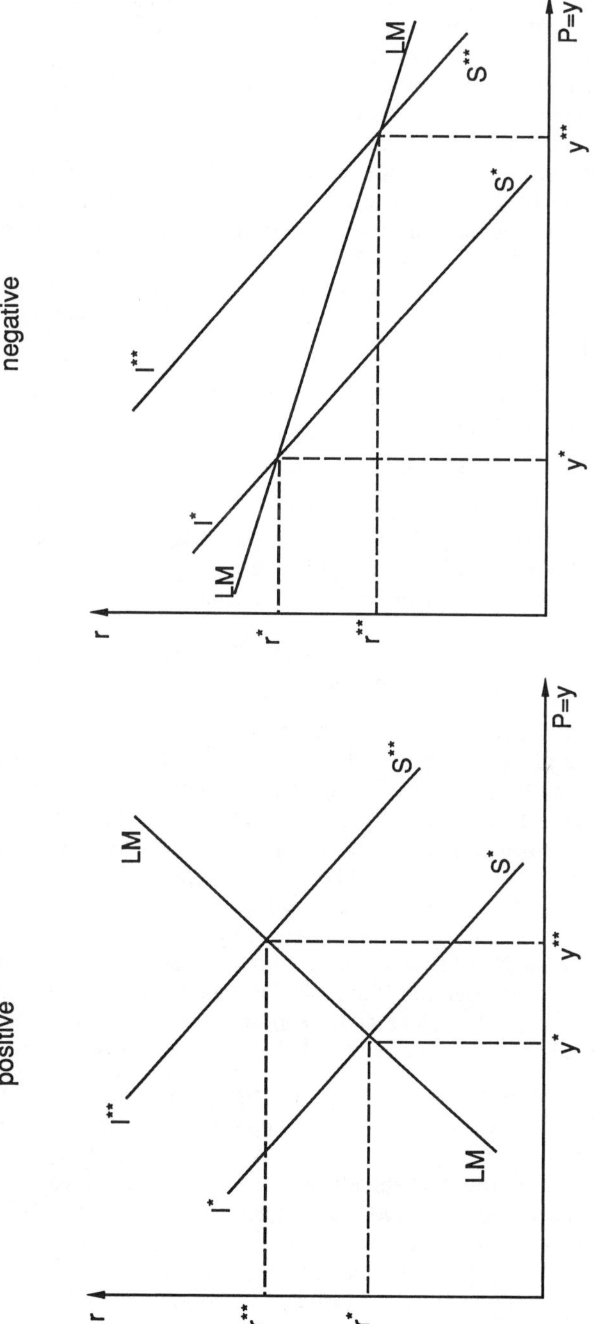

A stable solution to the differential equation (4.28) exists if, given v and w, an increase in N lowers $\dot{N}$. Thus, stability implies $k_2 > 0$ because $\beta_1(\gamma_1+\gamma_2) > 0$. By virtue of Samuelson's correspondence principle, I henceforth rule out negative values of k_2. As may be seen from equation (4.29), k_2 cannot be negative unless k_1 and/or α_2 is negative. Since $k_1>0$ by assumption, the only factor that may render equilibrium unstable is a negative total output sensitivity of nominal base-money demand (α_2+h'). In other words, a strong response of the aggregate reserve ratio to cyclical movements in domestic output may be inconsistent with stability. However, α_2+h' need not be positive; for stability, it is sufficient that $\alpha_2+h' > -[k_1(\alpha_1+\delta_1)/\beta_1]$. In terms of the IS-LM framework, stability implies that the LM-line, if negatively sloped, intersects the IS-line from below. Stable solutions are depicted by Chart 4-5.[15]

Substitution of (4.27) into (4.19) yields a solution for the Canadian non-monetary foreign debt:

$$S = \{-k_1\delta_1 N + (\alpha_2+h')\delta_1 v + [k_1\alpha_1 + (\alpha_2+h')\beta_1]w\}/k_2 + \alpha_1 r' - \alpha_2 y', \tag{4.31}$$

provided equations (4.25) and (4.29) are taken into account. Equations (4.28) and (4.31), combined with (4.8) and (4.9), determine nominal international monetary assets and the nominal monetary base.

4.3.2. Consistency with the Stylized Facts: Short-Run Effects of Foreign Cyclical Disturbances

The model recognizes two channels through which foreign business cycles may impinge on the Canadian economy, that is, foreign-induced changes in the current-account surplus (v) and in the non-monetary foreign debt (w). This chapter deals only with foreign-induced changes in the current-account surplus, while consideration of movements in w is postponed until Chapter 5. The subsequent analysis is based on the assumption that v oscillated continuously over time. For clarity's sake, I distinguish between short- and long-run effects of cyclical fluctuations in v. The short-run effects are determined on the assumption that the cumulative current-account surplus (N) is fixed. As may be seen from equation (4.28), N does not react instantaneously to exogenous disturbances. Therefore, in the short run, changes in the supply of base money induced by current-account imbalances may be disregarded.

In order to determine the short-run effects of a foreign-induced change in the current-account surplus, suppose that v rises as a result of a cyclical expansion in foreign economic activity. From equations (4.23) and (4.26) to (4.31), it follows that an increase in v affects instantaneously domestic output, the price of the home good and the domestic bond yield. Moreover, the change in the domestic bond yield leads to an instantaneous adjustment in Canada's non-monetary foreign debt, international monetary assets and the monetary base. The foreign cyclical disturbance also produces a current-account imbalance that will cause further variations in international monetary assets and the monetary base as time wears on.

According to equation (4.26), domestic output and the price of the home good rise unambiguously. In conjunction with equation (4.5), (4.26) also implies a rise in the real and nominal values of the money stock. Thus, the movements in domestic output, prices and the money stock conform to the stylized facts. Depending on the sign of the total output sensitivity of nominal base-money demand ($\alpha_2 + h'$), the domestic bond yield may rise or fall. If the aggregate reserve ratio decreases strongly in response to the cyclical expansion in domestic output ($\alpha_2 + h' < 0$), demand for base money and, thus, the domestic bond yield will decline.

The short-run effects of an increase in v on domestic output, the price of the home good and the domestic bond yield may also be analyzed with the help of Chart 4-5. A cyclical expansion in v, depicted by a rightward shift in the IS-line (from IS* to IS**), causes the price of the home good and output to rise. If $\alpha_2 + h' > 0$, the domestic bond yield goes up too. Conversely, if $\alpha_2 + h' < 0$, an increase in v lowers the domestic bond yield.

As indicated by Chart 4-5, the higher the output sensitivity of the aggregate reserve ratio, the stronger will be the response of domestic output and prices to a foreign-induced increase in the current-account surplus. For a given shift in the IS-line, the rise in y and P (from y* to y**) will be larger for negative values of $\alpha_2 + h'$ than for positive ones. If $\alpha_2 + h' < 0$, a fall in the domestic bond yield amplifies the effect of a foreign-induced rise in the current-account surplus on domestic output and prices.

Although a cyclical expansion in foreign economic activity, by itself, augments the Canadian current-account surplus, the attendant increase in domestic output and prices may be strong enough to cause the current account to deteriorate. Thus the current-account surplus may rise or fall as a result of a cyclical expansion in v. If the model is to accord with the stylized facts, it must generate countercyclical movements in the current-account surplus, that is, k_3 must be negative [equation (4.28)]. A negative sign for k_3 [equation (4.30)] in turn implies a value of the marginal propensity to absorb home and imported goods in excess of unity ($\beta_2 > 1$) and/or a negative total output sensitivity of nominal base-money demand ($\alpha_2 + h' < 0$). The theoretical analysis, therefore, points to real and monetary causes of the observed countercyclical swings in the current-account surplus. As I showed in Chapter 2, Keynesian students of the Canadian business cycle focus their attention on possible real causes, notably on strong procyclical movements in imports of capital goods induced by corresponding movements in domestic output. If the Keynesian explanation of the observed countercyclical pattern of the current-account surplus were correct, I would expect that the marginal propensity to absorb exceeded unity. However, the factor stressed by Keynesian students of the Canadian business cycle need not have been the only reason for that pattern. Output-induced changes in the aggregate reserve ratio might also explain why the current-account surplus was inversely related to the reference cycle.

The theoretical analysis further suggests that the question as to whether the countercyclical swings in the current-account surplus were due to real or monetary factors may be answered by looking at the cyclical pattern of domestic interest rates. Suppose that the Keynesian explanation of the inverse relationship between the current-account surplus and the reference cycle is valid. Provided $\beta_1 > 1$ and $\alpha_2 + h' > 0$, it follows from equation (4.27) that the domestic bond yield should have moved procyclically. Conversely, if the countercyclical movements in the current-account surplus had been attributable to strong output-induced swings in the aggregate reserve ratio ($\beta_1 < 1$, $\alpha_2 + h' < 0$), the domestic bond yield should have displayed a countercyclical pattern. In this case, the external cyclical disturbance should have been reinforced by countercyclical movements in domestic interest rates, in order to generate swings in domestic economic activity strong enough to cause the current-account surplus to fall (rise) during business-cycle expansions (contractions).

Similarly, the theoretical analysis indicates that the cyclical pattern of domestic interest rates provides information on the causes of the countercyclical movements in the aggregate reserve ratio. According to equation (4.27), a positive relationship between the domestic bond yield and v implies a positive total output sensitivity of nominal base-money demand, that is, a weak response in the aggregate reserve ratio to cyclical fluctuations in domestic output. In this case, countercyclical swings in the aggregate reserve ratio are attributable chiefly to the procyclical movements in domestic interest rates. Conversely, a negative relationship between the domestic bond yield and v implies a strong effect of cyclical fluctuations in domestic output on the aggregate reserve ratio. In this case, the countercyclical pattern of the aggregate reserve ratio is not explained by the domestic bond yield (which also varies countercyclically), but derives entirely from the swings in domestic output.

As regards the Canadian non-monetary debt, the short-run impact of a foreign-induced increase in the current-account surplus is ambiguous. Provided w is treated as a constant, the non-monetary debt is positively correlated with the domestic bond yield [equations (4.19) and (4.25)]. Similarly, the reaction of the monetary base is ambiguous. Since the cumulative current-account surplus is assumed to be fixed in the short run, the monetary base changes by the same amount and in the same direction as the non-monetary debt.

4.3.3. Consistency with the Stylized Facts: Long-Run Effects of Foreign Cyclical Disturbances

The analysis of Section 4.3.2 is incomplete because the current-account imbalances, elicited by fluctuations in v, might have fed back on the endogenous variables. In order to determine the long-run effects of foreign-induced changes in the current-account surplus, I solve the differential equation (4.28) on the assumption that foreign economic activity fluctuated continuously over time, with the oscillations in v described by a sine wave:

$$v = \sin t. \qquad (4.32)$$

For simplicity's sake, I only consider the particular or steady-state solution of equation (4.28). This procedure yields oscillations in the cumulative current-account surplus whose amplitude and frequency are constant. Similar results are obtained for the other endogenous variables. Since the model is solved rigorously in Appendix D, I confine myself to describing and explaining the cyclical movements in the endogenous variables generated by the oscillations in v.

The conclusions drawn from the model are not altered fundamentally if changes in the cumulative current-account surplus are taken into account. The model suggests that both in the short and long run, output, the price of the home good, as well as the real and nominal money stocks are positively correlated with v. Provided $k_3<0$, the model also postulates an inverse relationship between the current-account surplus and v. Furthermore, as in the short-run, the domestic bond yield may be positively or negatively correlated with v. However, the long-run solution differs from its short-run counterpart in that the direction of change in the domestic bond yield no longer depends solely on the sign of the total output sensitivity of nominal base-money demand (α_2+h') as in equation (4.27). Necessary and sufficient conditions as to the direction of change in the domestic bond yield are derived in Appendix D. These conditions are fairly complex and will not be considered in the subsequent analysis. Instead, Table 4-2 presents two alternative sets of conditions that are strikingly simple. Both are based on the assumption of an inverse relationship between the current-account surplus and v ($k_3<0$). The first set of conditions is necessary (but not sufficient), while the second is sufficient (but not necessary).

If the relationship between the domestic bond yield and v is to be positive, the marginal propensity to absorb home and imported goods must exceed unity. The reaction of the aggregate reserve ratio to cyclical swings in output may be strong or weak, but a weak response in that ratio will enhance the likelihood of a positive relationship between the domestic bond yield and v. By contrast, if the domestic bond yield is to be negatively related to v, output-induced movements in the aggregate reserve ratio must be strong (i.e., the total output sensitivity of nominal base-money demand must be negative), while the marginal propensity to absorb may exceed or fall short of unity.

A further difference between the short- and long-run solutions lies in various leads and lags generated by the model if the cumulative current-account surplus is allowed to vary. In particular, the model predicts that domestic output, the price of the home good and the domestic money stock should lead foreign economic activity, with the lead amounting to at most one-quarter of the length of a full v-cycle. Similarly, the cyclical peaks (troughs) in the current-account surplus should lead the corresponding troughs (peaks) in v. The timing of the cyclical turning points in the endogenous variables in relation to the v-cycle is shown in Chart 4-6.

The leads in these endogenous variables derive from the countercyclical movements in the cumulative current-account surplus. In the early stage of a business-cycle expansion, the cumulative current-account surplus rises. Through its effect on the monetary base and the domestic bond yield, the increase in

CHART 4-6

CYCLICAL TURNING POINTS IN THE ENDOGENOUS VARIABLES AND FOREIGN ECONOMIC ACTIVITY*

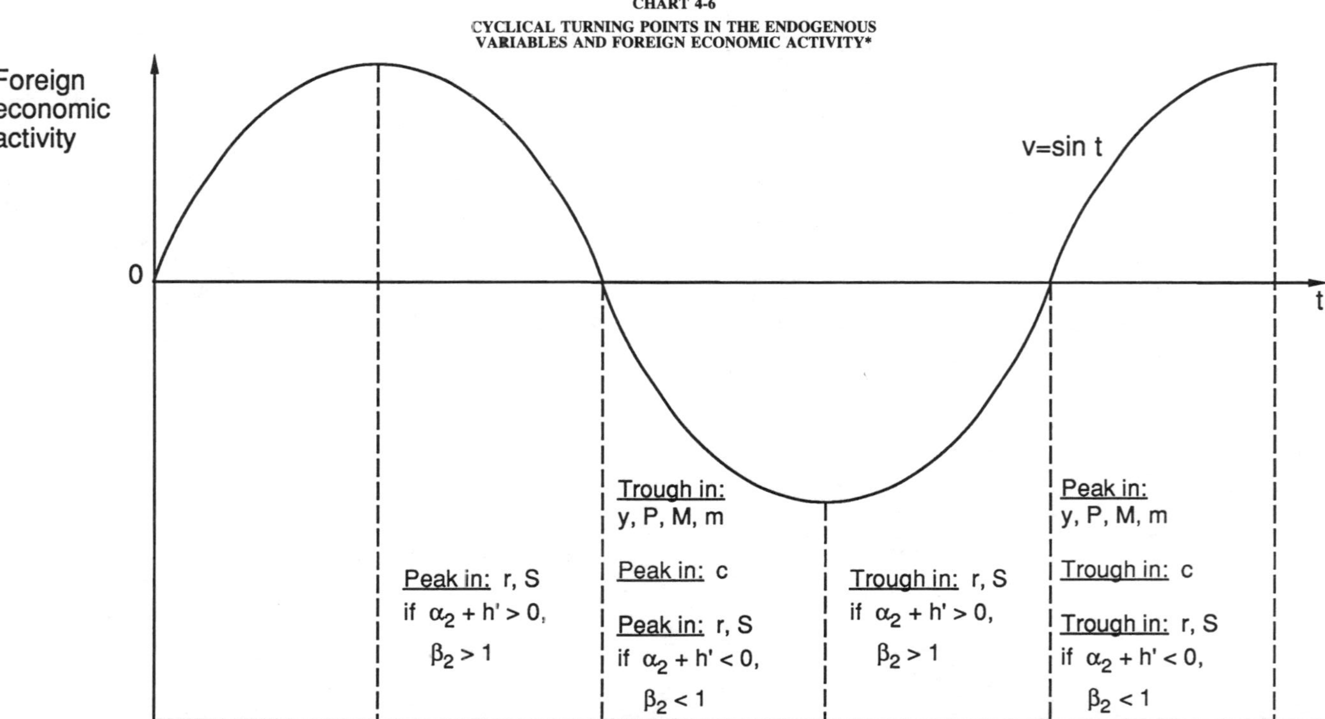

* Foreign cyclical disturbances transmitted through changes in the current-account surplus.

TABLE 4-2
DIRECTION OF CHANGE IN THE DOMESTIC BOND YIELD (r)

Correlation between r and v[a]	Conditions	
	Necessary	Sufficient
Positive	$\beta_2>1$	$\alpha_2+h'>0$ $\beta_2>1$
Negative	$\alpha_2+h'<0$	$\alpha_2+h'<0$ $\beta_2<1$

a) v: foreign-induced changes in the current-account surplus.
Source: Appendix D.

the acumulative current-account surplus stimulates domestic output and, thus, amplifies the impact on domestic output of a surge in v. However, as domestic output continues to expand, the cumulative current-account surplus reaches a cyclical peak. The decline in that surplus during the latter stage of a business-cycle expansion counteracts the effect on domestic output of the rise in v. For this reason, the model suggests that the cyclical turning points in domestic output precede those in v. A similar line of reasoning applies to the price of the home good, the money stock and the current-account balance.

The leads generated between domestic output, the price of the home good, the domestic money stock and the current-account surplus, on the one hand, and v or foreign economic activity, on the other, are inconsistent with the stylized facts enunciated at the outset of this chapter. While the theoretical analysis correctly predicts the direction of change in these endogenous variables, the leads produced by the model require further investigation.

For the domestic bond yield, the model also generates a lead or lag to foreign economic activity. If the movements in the domestic bond yield are procyclical, its turning points lag those in v. In the early stage of a business-cycle expansion, an increase in the cumulative current-account surplus and the monetary base puts downward pressure on the domestic bond yield, counteracting the influence on that yield of the rise in v. By contrast, if the domestic bond yield varies countercyclically, its peaks (troughs) lead the corresponding cyclical troughs (peaks) in v. In this case, the contraction in the cumulative current-account surplus and the monetary base in the latter stage of a business-cycle expansion counteracts the negative impact on the domestic bond yield of a rise in v (Chart 4-6).

Since foreign-induced changes in the Canadian non-monetary debt (w) are ignored at this stage of the analysis, cyclical movements in that debt, as produced by the model, match those in the domestic bond yield. Thus, the non-monetary debt may be positively or negatively correlated with v. The countercyclical pattern of the non-monetary debt, frequently recorded in the pre-1914 period, implies that either Canadian interest rates varied countercyclically or w moved procyclically. Similar results are obtained for international monetary assets and the monetary base, for which the correlations to v are also ambiguous. In contrast to the results for the domestic bond yield, it is impossible to derive simple conditions about the direction of change in international monetary assets and the monetary base. While the theoretical analysis does not preclude countercyclical movements in these two variables, it fails to provide a ready explanation for their almost flawless countercyclical pattern. Thus, the consistency of the model with stylized fact (b) must also be examined further.

4.4. SUMMARY AND CONCLUSIONS

The long-run solutions of the model do not fully conform to the stylized facts. The model successfully accounts for the observed procyclical swings in domestic output, prices and the money stock, as well as for the countercyclical movements in the aggregate reserve ratio. Moreover, it offers two alternative explanations for the observed countercyclical pattern of the current-account surplus. One possible explanation lies in the value of the marginal propensity to absorb domestic and imported goods in excess of unity, as emphasized by Keynesian students of the Canadian business cycle. Another reason might have been strong output-induced movements in the aggregate reserve ratio, a possibility overlooked in the existing literature. While the model correctly predicts the direction of change in these endogenous variables, it is at variance with the evidence in so far as it suggests that domestic output, prices, the money stock and the current-account surplus should have led foreign economic activity. A further shortcoming of the model is its failure to offer a ready explanation for the almost flawless countercyclical pattern of international monetary assets and the monetary base.

An interesting feature of the model is that it yields testable propositions regarding cyclical movements in domestic interest rates. Had Canadian interest rates moved countercyclically, the total output sensitivity of nominal base-money demand should have assumed a negative value, implying a strong response in the aggregate reserve ratio to cyclical swings in domestic output. Thus, econometric tests of equations (4.2) and (4.3) should yield results consistent with the implied output-sensitivity of the aggregate reserve ratio. Conversely, a procyclical pattern of domestic interest rates would imply a value of the marginal propensity to absorb home and imported goods in excess of unity. These testable propositions, as well as the consistency of the model with the stylized facts, are examined further in the following chapter.

Endnotes — Chapter 4

1. A disaggregated analysis of cyclical movements in bank reserve ratios is offered in Chapter 5.

2. Equations such as (4.2) may be derived from stochastic models of bank reserve behaviour, as developed by Edgeworth and later refined by Orr and Mellon. For an excellent discussion of these models, see Niehans (1978).

3. See Friedman and Schwartz (1963b, 449-62) and Morrison (1966, ch. 3) for a similar explanation of cyclical movements in bank reserve ratios.

4. Provided interest rates varied procyclically and exerted a negative influence on money demand, the model may generate countercyclical movements in the real and nominal money stock. This possibility need not be considered in the analysis because it conflicts with stylized fact (b). Since the Urquhart (1987) estimates of Canadian GNP only became available upon completion of this study, I do not present econometric estimates of pre-1914 Canadian money demand. Using the money stock series presented in this study, Dick and Floyd (1987a, 69-77) estimate econometrically money demand equations for the period 1871-1913. They regress the real money stock an real Canadian GNP, the yield on Canadian government bonds, and short-term interest rates in the United States and the United Kingdom. On the whole, the independent variables included in their regression equations are statistically significant and correctly signed. However, Dick and Floyd's results need not imply that equation (4.5) should take account of domestic interest rates as an additional determinant of real money demand. As I show in Chapter 5, the yield on Canadian government bonds was invariant to the business cycle. Therefore, it did not impinge on the cyclical pattern of the Canadian money stock. The statistically significant negative relationship between real money demand and the yield on Canadian government bonds, uncovered by Dick and Floyd, mirrors a secular decline in both the velocity of money (see their chart 4.10) and Canadian interest rates over the period 1871-1913.

5. The available export-price index is based on unit values, which are sensitive to shifts in the composition of exports. Had the composition of exports varied systematically over the business cycle, that index would not trace correctly cyclical movements in export prices. The import-price index analyzed below raises the same difficulty.

6. Real exports lagged the reference cycle only in 1888-89, 1893-94 and 1913. The expansion of 1896-1900 saw real exports reach a high well before the reference-cycle peak, but it is worth noting that the export data presented in Chart 4-1 exclude non-monetary gold. As indicated by Table A-3, exports of non-monetary gold increased enormously between 1897 and 1900. If exports of non-monetary gold are taken into account, the lead-time between real exports and the reference cycle is shortened considerably.

7. Note, however, that the difference between the averages for contractions and expansions was only slightly higher than that for depressions and booms. Although export prices after 1900 normally peaked during the contraction stage of the reference cycle, their pattern was not necessarily countercyclical. In this study, a variable is said to move procyclically if either its level or rate of change reaches a peak near a reference-cycle peak.

8. Trend-adjusted wholesale prices did not vary procyclically in the late 1880s and early 1890s.

9. See Barro (1979) for a model of the gold standard in which inflation expectations are allowed to affect money demand.

10. Real domestic absorption is not assumed to depend on π, that is, I abstract from the Laursen-Metzler (1950) effect. Therefore, changes in π affect the composition but not the level of real absorption.

11. Over the period 1906-13, the GNP deflator was not correlated with wholesale prices (Charts 4-2 and 4-4). The question arises whether the Urquhart estimates offer a correct division of nominal GNP into the price and output components.

12. If first differences in prices move in sympathy with the level of realized output, the price level must lag the output level. It is possible that the sluggish behaviour of nominal wages was due to the existence of implicit or explicit wage contracts, containing — among other provisions — rules for adjusting nominal wages to unanticipated changes in the price level. In a study of wage indexation, Gray (1978) demonstrates that full adjustment in nominal wages to unanticipated changes in the price level (so as to keep real wages constant) would be optimal only if the price level varied as a result of a monetary stochastic disturbance. Should economic agents be unable to distinguish between real and monetary stochastic disturbances, it would not be rational to insist on full adjustment in nominal wages. The preceding analysis rests on the assumption that economic agents were unsure whether the external cyclical disturbances affecting the Canadian economy were real or monetary.

13. This assumption is quite realistic since non-monetary foreign assets were small in relation to liabilities. See Hartland (1960, Tables 5 and 7).

14. The real value of the Canadian non-monetary debt, if deflated by the price of the home good, is given by $S/P = s = u\pi$.

15. For a stable stationary-state equilibrium to exist, the slope of the LM-line must exceed that of the IS-line, that is, $(\alpha_2 + h')/(\alpha_1 + \delta_1) > k_1/\beta_1$. This inequality implies the stability condition $k_2 > 0$.

CHAPTER 5

THE CYCLE-TRANSMISSION PROCESS

The theoretical analysis of the cycle-transmission process yields various propositions that are tested empirically in this chapter. Section 5.1 identifies the cyclical patterns of Canadian short- and long-term interest rates. Furthermore, I attempt to infer from these patterns the causes of the countercyclical swings in the aggregate reserve ratio. In Section 5.2, these causes are investigated directly using regression equations to determine base-money demand and the aggregate reserve ratio. The results of Section 5.2 are in turn compared with those of Section 5.1. The role of bank reserve management in the cycle-transmission process and the consistency of the theoretical analysis with the stylized facts are examined further in Section 5.3. The final Section 5.4 summarizes the monetary view of the cycle-transmission process advanced in this study and provides two additional tests of the importance of money as a destabilizing force.

5.1. THE CYCLICAL ATTRIBUTES OF CANADIAN INTEREST RATES AND THEIR IMPLICATIONS FOR BANK RESERVE BEHAVIOUR

5.1.1. Data Problems

As may be recalled from Chapter 2, data on pre-1914 Canadian interest rates leave much to be desired. In principle, adequate statistical information is available for interest rates on Canadian bank loans and securities issued in Canada. The subsequent analysis focusses on the Montreal call-loan rate, the only Canadian bank loan rate for which monthly or quarterly data are available. Unfortunately, this series — henceforth called MR — does not cover the pre-

1900 period. Moreover, there is some doubt about the reliability of MR as an indicator of borrowing costs in the Montreal call-loan market. According to Chart 2-1, MR did not vary much as compared to call-loan rates in New York and Boston. Notably over the period October, 1906, to April, 1908, MR continuously stuck to a level of 6 percent even though call-loan rates in New York and Boston oscillated violently. The New York call-loan rate, for example, reached a high of 21.00 percent and a low of 1.85 percent in this period.[1] The size of the interest rate differentials recorded between Montreal and its nearest major U.S. cities is puzzling and raises questions about the accuracy of MR as an indicator of borrowing costs in the Montreal call-loan market. A measurement problem may arise from the fact that MR was compiled from rates posted by Montreal banks that may have differed from effective charges to borrowers.[2]

It is difficult to appraise the quality of MR because data on call-loan rates effectively charged by Montreal banks are unavailable. The only piece of evidence suitable for a quality appraisal are unpublished data on the average return on loans booked at the domestic branches of the Bank of Nova Scotia (Table 5-1). This series is available annually for the period 1885-1913 and measures the BNS' effective return on loans. Therefore, it may be compared with MR to identify possible discrepancies between effective and posted rates. Such a comparison, it should be noted, is not entirely legitimate since the BNS series covers aggregate loans, rather than call loans by themselves.[3] Had MR properly reflected borrowing costs in the Montreal call-loan market, I would expect its variance to have exceeded that of the BNS series. Historical experience points to an inverse relationship between the term to maturity of an asset and the variance of its rate of return.[4] Since the average term to maturity for aggregate BNS loans — by definition — was higher than for call loans, MR should have fluctuated more strongly than the BNS series. Thus, if the opposite pattern were to be observed, I would seriously question the accuracy of MR.

As indicated by Table 5-1, there is no evidence of gross inaccuracies in MR. Over the period 1900-13, the variance of MR and the BNS series conformed to the expected pattern. On an annual basis, the minimum and maximum values of MR amounted to 4.21 and 6.26 percent respectively, while the BNS series moved within a range of 5.33 to 5.86 percent. The standard deviations of MR (0.49 percent) and the BNS series (0.14 percent) convey the same message.[5] Thus, depending on the measure of amplitude employed, the fluctuations in MR were three to four times higher than in the BNS series.[6]

Similar statistical problems arise with regard to interest rates on Canadian securities. Annual data exist on the yields of bonds issued by various levels of government (see Neufeld, 1972, Table 15:2), but I am unsure whether they properly reflect borrowing costs in the domestic capital market. The bulk of Canadian government bonds was placed in the London capital market. Moreover, there is some evidence to suggest that the lion's share of these issues was taken up by foreign investors.[7] For these reasons, the yields on Canadian government bonds may have been more responsive to foreign than domestic capital-market conditions.

In an effort to obtain a superior indicator of borrowing costs in the domestic capital market, I compiled quarterly data on the average yield on Canadian corporate bonds (Table E-2), which — unlike securities issued by Canadian governments — were traded on the Montreal stock exchange. An analysis based on corporate bond yields, however, is also fraught with difficulties. Regular price quotations from which corporate bond yields may be estimated are available only for the period 1907I-1913IV. Prior to 1907, bond trading on the Montreal stock exchange was either unimportant or non-existent. Thus, it is impossible to estimate reliably borrowing costs in the domestic capital market for the entire period under study.[8]

5.1.2. Montreal Call-Loan Rate

The cyclical pattern of the Montreal call-loan rate may be analyzed with the help of Chart 5-1. In contrast to Chart 2-1, Chart 5-1 displays seasonally adjusted data that bring out clearly the cyclical patterns of call-loan rates. The evidence suggests that the Montreal call-loan rate displayed a distinctive procyclical pattern, with cyclical peaks (troughs) invariably occurring shortly before or near the midpoint of a reference-cycle contraction (expansion). Note

TABLE 5-1
AVERAGE RETURN ON LOANS BY THE BANK OF NOVA SCOTIA, 1885-1913
(Percent)

	Domestic Branches	Foreign Branches		Domestic Branches	Foreign Branches
1885	6.11	6.57	1900	5.65	5.26
1886	5.92	6.03	1901	5.38	4.90
1887	5.97	6.98	1902	5.47	5.28
1888	5.98	6.78	1903	5.64	5.76
1889	5.86	6.52	1904	5.61	5.15
1890	5.91	6.84	1905	5.47	5.03
1891	5.67	6.68	1906	5.54	5.99
1892	5.92	5.72	1907	5.64	6.49
1893	6.23	8.48	1908	5.79	4.95
1894	5.79	4.68	1909	5.33	4.78
1895	5.89	5.38	1910	5.57	5.68
1896	6.08	6.38	1911	5.62	5.79
1897	5.92	5.05	1912	5.72	5.93
1898	5.84	4.92	1913	5.86	6.01
1899	5.79	4.97			

Source for Table 5-1
BNS Statistics 3. See Appendix B for a description of the source.

that it is impossible to time precisely the cyclical peak in the Montreal call-loan rate corresponding to the reference-cycle contraction of 1907-08. On a seasonally adjusted basis, that rate reached a cyclical peak of 6 percent at the end of the first quarter of 1907 and subsequently remained at that level for half a year.[9] However, despite the uncertainty about the exact timing of this cyclical turning point, there is little doubt that the 1907 peak in the Montreal call-loan rate either coincided with or led the midpoint of the corresponding reference-cycle contraction. Thus, the evidence for 1907 accords with that recorded for the period 1900-13 as a whole. While the Montreal call-loan rate clearly lagged the reference-cycle, its cyclical peaks (troughs) were closer to the midpoints of reference-cycle contractions (expansions) than to the reference-cycle peaks (troughs). Over the period extending from the reference-cycle trough of 1901 to the peak of 1912, the turning points in the Montreal call-loan rate lagged the corresponding turning points in economic activity by an average of 2.5 quarters and led the corresponding midpoints by an average of 0.7 quarters.[10]

The evidence of Chart 5-1 is corroborated by Table 5-2, displaying significance tests for the cyclical patterns of quarterly first differences in the Montreal call-loan rate and other interest rates. These tests are based on first differences, rather than levels, because the Montreal call-loan rate followed a slight upward trend over the period 1900-13. According to Table 5-2, its procyclical pattern was highly significant, with the first differences typically attaining a peak (trough) during the boom (depression) stage of the reference cycle.

Considering the patterns revealed by Chart 5-1 and Table 5-2, one might venture the suggestion that the procyclical movements in the Montreal call-loan rate were attributable mainly to changes in the nominal monetary base. As indicated by Chart 5-2, there was indeed a very close negative correlation between quarterly first differences in that rate and quarterly rates of change in the nominal monetary base.[11] While the latter was inversely related to the reference cycle, first differences in the Montreal call-loan rate attained a cyclical peak (trough) shortly before or near a reference-cycle peak (trough). As would be expected, first differences in that rate tended to lead their levels by a time span equalling one-quarter of the length of a full reference cycle.[12]

From the cyclical patterns exhibited by Chart 5-2, it is possible to draw unambiguous conclusions about the causes of the countercyclical movements in the aggregate reserve ratio. The evidence of a close negative correlation between the Montreal call-loan rate and the nominal monetary base implies that the aggregate reserve ratio reacted *both* to changes in domestic interest rates and cyclical movements in output. In order to prove this proposition, a demand function for nominal base money (H) corresponding to equation (4.7) is derived. Substitution of (4.7) into (4.11a) yields:

$$H = -\alpha_1(r-r') + \alpha_2(y-y') + h'P. \qquad (5.1)$$

Equation (5.1) may be rewritten by setting $P=y$ [equation (4.16a)] and by noting that $H' = h'P' = h'y'$:

CHART 5-1

CALL-LOAN RATES IN MONTREAL, NEW YORK AND BOSTON, 1900III-1913II
(Seasonally Adjusted)

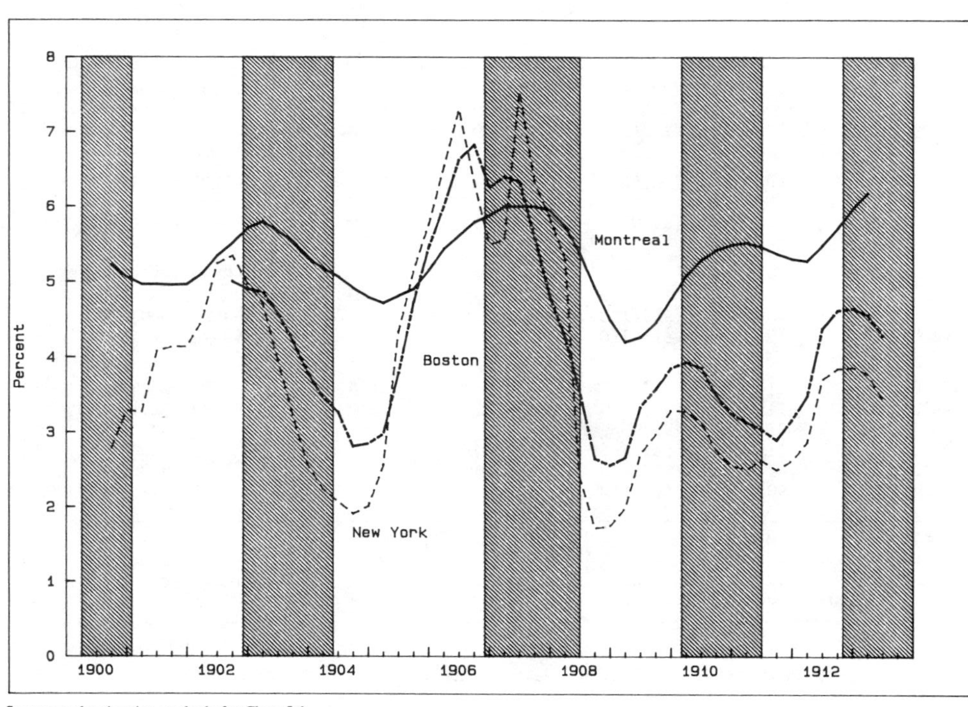

Sources and estimation methods for Chart 5-1

See Chart 2-1. The data are seasonally adjusted by a thirteen-month moving average. The chart shows the Canadian reference-cycle turning points.

TABLE 5-2

CYCLICAL CHARACTERISTICS OF INTEREST RATES: SHORT-TERM ASSETS AND BONDS
(Percent)

Period	Categorie of Assets	Average Quarterly Change in Rate					
		Boom Stage	Depression Stage	t-value	Expansion Stage	Contraction Stage	t-value
1900III-1913I	Montreal Call Loans	0.14	-0.10	6.79(57)	0.05	-0.03	1.47(57)
1900III-1913I	N.Y. Call Loans	-0.02	-0.07	0.24(56)	0.22	-0.26	2.40(57)
1900III-1913I	N.Y. Time Money	0.11	-0.09	1.94(56)	0.17	-0.18	3.25(57)
1900III-1913I	N.Y. Comm. Paper	0.13	-0.08	3.00(56)	0.12	-0.09	2.92(57)
1902IV -1913I	Boston Call Loans	0.03	-0.06	0.70(46)	0.16	-0.24	3.48(46)
1902IV -1913I	Boston Time Money	0.13	-0.10	2.79(46)	0.12	-0.11	2.58(46)
1881II -1900II	Cdn. Municipal Bonds	-	-	0.15(85)	-0.02	-0.03	0.33(86)
1881II -1900II	Cdn. Provincial Bonds	-	-0.02	0.71(85)	-	-0.01	0.20(86)
1881II -1900II	Cdn. Dominion Bonds	-0.01	-0.02	0.22(85)	-0.01	-0.01	0.02(86)
1881II -1900II	U.S. Municipal Bonds	0.01	-0.03	1.45(86)	-0.01	-0.01	0.02(86)
1900III-1913I	Cdn. Provincial Bonds	0.03	0.01	1.26(57)	-	0.03	1.58(57)
1900III-1913I	Cdn. Dominion Bonds	0.03	-	1.43(57)	0.02	0.02	0.18(57)
1900III-1913I	U.S. Municipal Bonds	0.05	-0.01	2.96(56)	0.03	0.02	0.56(57)
1907II -1913IV	Cdn. Corp. Bonds	0.03	-0.03	1.85(29)	-0.05	0.02	2.37(29)
1907II -1913IV	U.S. Railway Bonds	0.04	-0.01	2.43(29)	0.01	0.02	0.69(30)
1900III-1913I	U.S. Railway Bonds	0.04	-	3.84(56)	0.01	0.02	0.63(57)

Sources and estimation methods for Table 5-2

Short-term interest rates are seasonally adjusted by a thirteen-month moving average. The sources mentioned in the legend to Chart 2-1 provide data on call-loan rates, as well as U.S. time-money and commercial-paper rates. For the yields on Canadian bonds, the data sources are described in Appendix E. Data on U.S. bond yields are obtained from Macaulay (1938, Appendix, Tables 10 and 13). The municipal bond yield series for the United States covers only New England and refers to the month immediately following the end of a quarter. As to the railway bond yield, Table 5-2 incorporates the unadjusted variant compiled by Macaulay. Canadian and U.S. interest rates are related to Canadian and U.S. reference cycles respectively. The quarterly changes in interest rates are assigned to the various reference-cycle stages according to Appendix C, procedures 1 and 2.

CHART 5-2

QUARTERLY CHANGE IN THE MONTREAL CALL-LOAN RATE AND MONETARY BASE, 1900IV-1913I

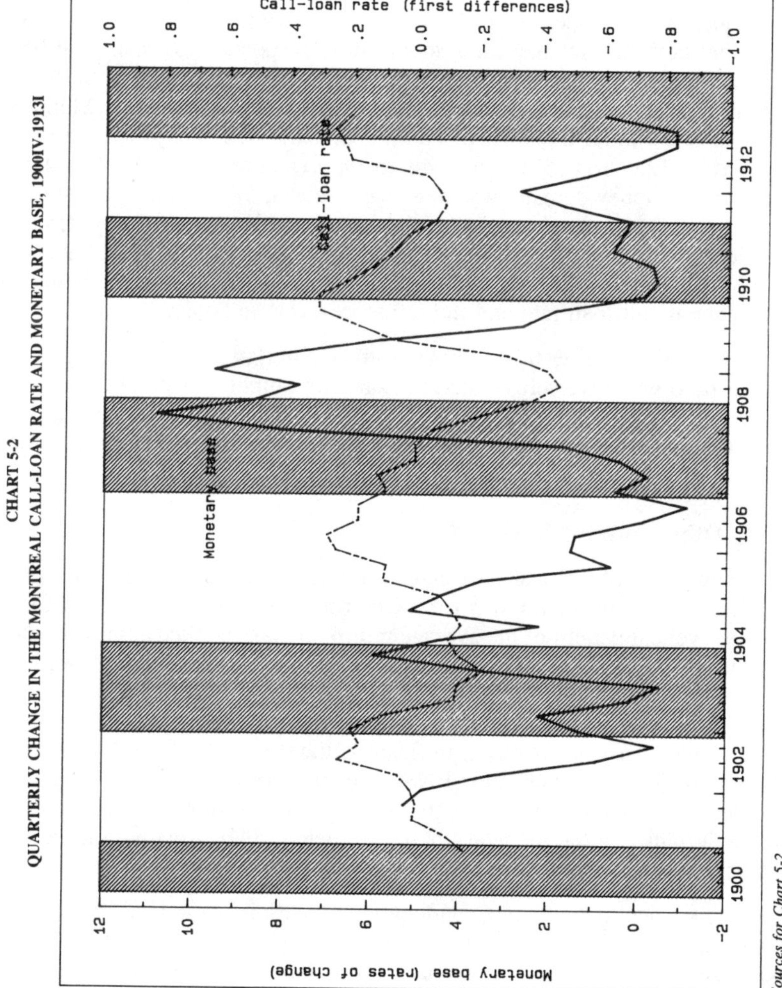

Sources for Chart 5-2
See Charts 3-1 and 5-1.

$$H = -\alpha_1(r-r') + (\alpha_2+h')(y-y') + H'. \qquad (5.1a)$$

As indicated in the preceding chapter, the parameter α_2+h' stands for the total output sensitivity of nominal base-money demand. Equation (5.1a) may also be regarded as a function determining domestic interest rates:

$$r-r' = -(1/\alpha_1)(H-H') + [(\alpha_2+h')/\alpha_1](y-y'). \qquad (5.2)$$

Equation (5.2) does not fully agree with the empirical evidence since it states that domestic interest rates should have responded to changes in both the nominal monetary base and domestic output. Had output and the monetary base influenced cyclical movements in domestic interest rates, the Montreal call-loan rate should have peaked during the first half of a reference-cycle contraction. Equation (5.2) conforms to the evidence only if it is assumed that (a) base-money demand was negatively related to domestic interest rates ($\alpha_1>0$) and (b) the total output sensitivity of nominal base-money demand was close to zero. A positive — but small — value of α_2+h' would account for the frequently observed slight lead between the cyclical turning points in the Montreal call-loan rate and the reference-cycle midpoints.[13]

Provided $\alpha_2+h' \sim 0$, it follows from equation (4.7b) that the aggregate reserve ratio was inversely related to domestic output.[14] Moreover, $\alpha_1 > 0$ implies an inverse relationship between that ratio and domestic interest rates.[15] Thus, the model developed in Chapter 4 appears to rest on realistic assumptions concerning the determinants of the aggregate reserve ratio.

5.1.3. Other Interest Rates

An examination of cyclical movements in other domestic interest rates does not alter the conclusions drawn from Chart 5-2. As may be seen from Chart 5-3, the cyclical pattern of the average return on loans booked at the domestic branches of the Bank of Nova Scotia paralleled that of the Montreal call-loan rate. Both series tended to attain a cyclical peak (trough) during the contraction (expansion) stage of the reference cycle. Moreover, the procyclical pattern of both series was statistically significant at the 99 percent level (Table 5-3). The only major deviations in the BNS series from its procyclical pattern were recorded around 1900 and in 1910-11.[16] It is interesting to recall that the overall surplus and the monetary base also behaved abnormally in these two instances (see Chapter 3).[17]

The cyclical patterns of Canadian bond yields are examined on the basis of new quarterly estimates, rather than the Neufeld (1972) data mentioned above (see Appendix E for the estimation procedure). For the yields on Dominion and provincial government bonds, these estimates cover the entire period under study. I also attempted to estimate yields on Canadian municipal bonds, but the required data were available only from March 31, 1881, to December 31, 1904. Moreover, as indicated earlier, some data exist on Canadian corporate bond yields. Due to the gaps in the municipal bond yield series, Table 5-2 abstracts entirely from the pre-1881 period. If possible, the averages shown

TABLE 5-3
CYCLICAL CHARACTERISTICS OF RETURN ON BANK LOANS
(Percent)

Period	Category of Banks	Average Quarterly Change in Rate					
		Boom Stage	Depression Stage	t-value	Expansion Stage	Contraction Stage	t-value
	Bank of Nova Scotia						
1885/86	Domestic Branches	0.10	-0.09	2.97(26)	-	-0.02	0.14(26)
-1912/13	Foreign Branches	0.29	-0.23	3.91(26)	0.07	-0.13	1.22(26)
	U.S. National Banks						
1888/89	Middle Atlantic[a]	0.42	-0.39	3.69(23)	-0.08	0.11	0.66(23)
-1912/13	Middle Atlantic[b]	0.07	-0.07	1.06(23)	-0.07	0.09	1.21(23)
	New England[a]	0.30	-0.21	1.81(23)	-0.15	0.30	1.53(23)
	New England[b]	0.17	-0.19	2.44(23)	-0.10	0.10	1.21(23)
	Midwest[a]	0.11	-0.22	2.77(23)	-0.15	0.06	1.60(23)
	Midwest[b]	0.03	-0.11	1.08(23)	-0.16	0.14	2.45(23)

a) Reserve city national banks.
b) Non-reserve city national banks.

Sources and estimation methods for Table 5-3

Bank of Nova Scotia: Table 5-1. U.S. national banks: gross return on private earning assets as estimated by Smiley (1975, Tables A-3 and A-4). The average rates of return on loans granted by the domestic and foreign branches of the Bank of Nova Scotia are related to the Canadian reference cycle, while the U.S. returns are compared with the U.S. reference cycle. The annual changes in returns are assigned to the various cycle stages according to Appendix C, procedures 5 and 6.

in Table 5-2 are calculated separately for the periods 1881II-1900II and 1900III-1913I, in order to facilitate a comparison of cyclical movements in bond yields and the Montreal call-loan rate.

From Table 5-2 it is evident that the yields on Canadian government bonds did not exhibit a statistically significant cyclical pattern. However, the average yield on Canadian corporate bonds was sensitive to the reference cycle. In contrast to the Montreal call-loan rate, it moved countercyclically, that is, it tended to fall (rise) during the expansion (contraction) stage of the reference cycle. The evidence of Table 5-2 implies that the average yield on corporate bonds normally reached a peak (trough) near a reference-cycle trough (peak). This is clearly confirmed by Chart 5-4.[18]

Consequently, while Canadian bank-loan rates displayed a statistically significant procyclical pattern, bond yields were not very sensitive to the business cycle. Moreover, if at all, they tended to move countercyclically. This piece of evidence need not contradict the earlier conclusion that the balance of payments was largely responsible for the observed cyclical swings in Canadian interest rates. It is possible that long-term interest rates depended on current and expected short-term rates, as suggested by the expectations hypothesis of the term structure of interest rates. Moreover, expected short-term interest rates may have reacted only gradually to a change in current rates, implying a lag between cyclical movements in long-term and current short-term interest rates.

5.2. BASE-MONEY DEMAND AND RESERVE RATIOS: ECONOMETRIC ESTIMATES

5.2.1. Base-Money Demand

The proposition that the total output sensitivity of nominal base-money demand was near zero may also be tested directly by analyzing the determinants of nominal base-money demand and the aggregate reserve ratio. For the nominal monetary base, I specify a semi-logarithmic variant of the demand function (5.1a):

$$\ln H = \chi_1 + \chi_2 r + \chi_3 \ln y'' + \chi_4 t + \sum_{i=1}^{3} \chi_{4+i} D_i. \qquad (5.3)$$

Equation (5.3) is estimated from quarterly data for the period 1900III-1913I. The coefficient, χ_1, combines the various constant terms included in equation (5.1a). The interest rate, r, is measured by seasonally adjusted end-of-quarter data on the Montreal call-loan rate (see Chart 5-1 for the seasonal adjustment procedure). A difficulty arises from the output variable in equation (5.3). Although Chart 5-2 implies that *cyclical* movements in domestic output and prices did not strongly impinge on base-money demand, trend changes in these two variables were bound to affect desired money balances. To allow for a link between base-money demand and the trend in economic activity,

CHART 5-3

CYCLICAL PATTERN OF AVERAGE RETURN ON LOANS BY THE BANK OF NOVA SCOTIA, 1885-1913

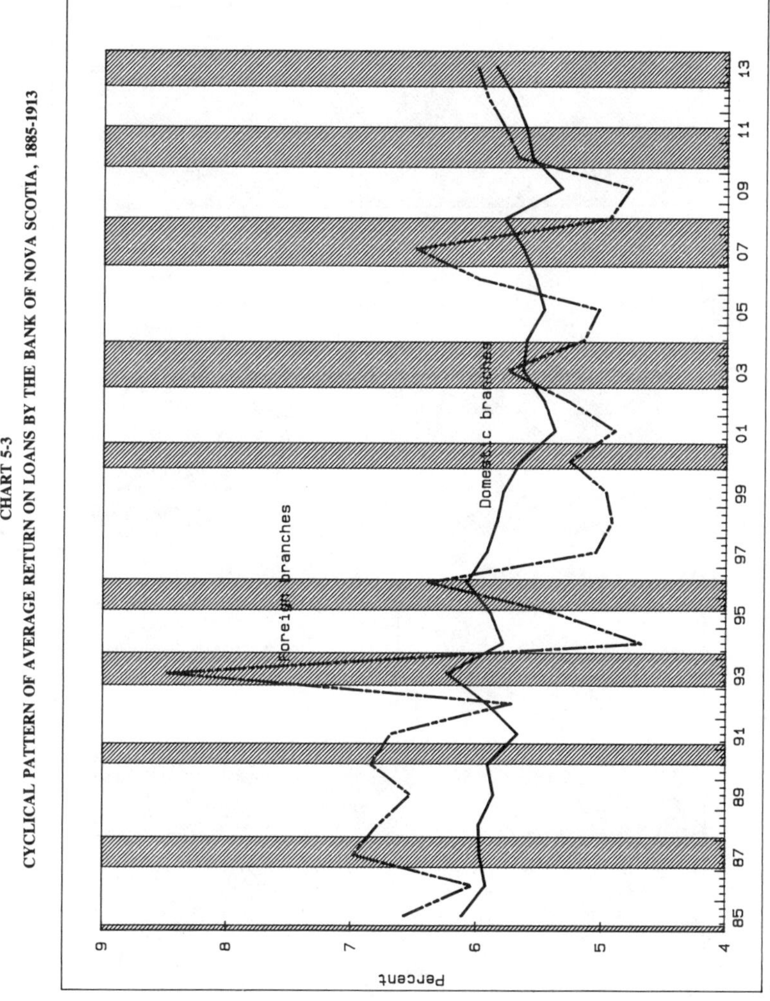

Source for Chart 5-3
Table 5-1.

CHART 5-4
YIELD ON CANADIAN CORPORATE BONDS, 1907I-1913IV

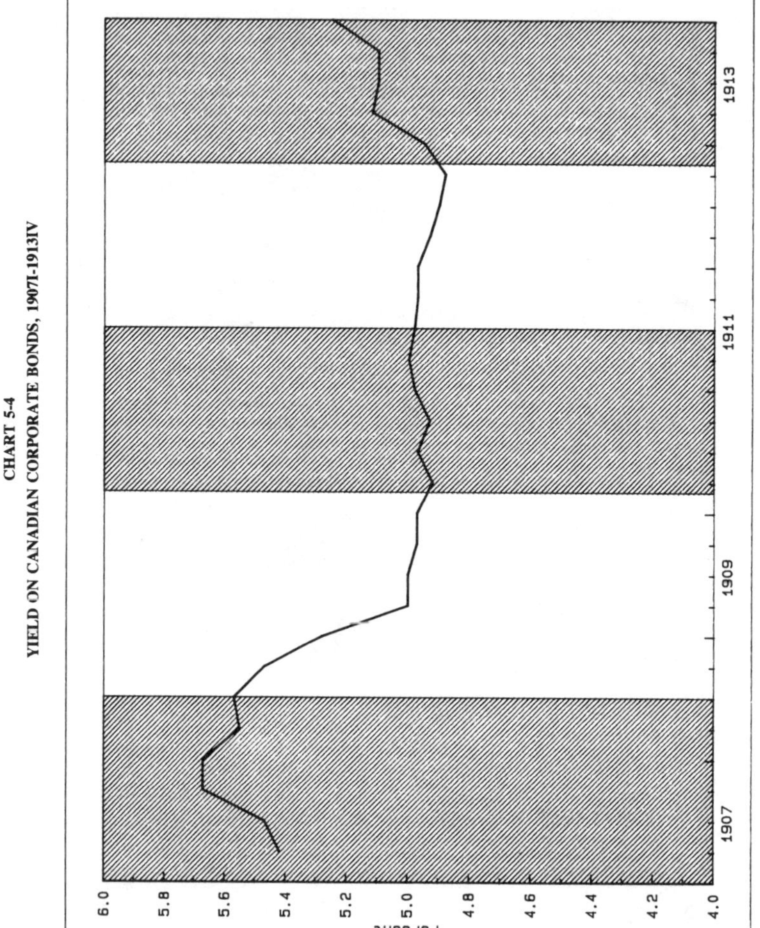

Source for Chart 5-4
Table E-2.

I introduce a new variable, y'', measuring deviations in realized from normal output ($y'' = y - y'$). Output and price trends, as well as other possible determinants of the trend growth in base-money demand are in turn captured by the variable t. Since quarterly data on pre-1914 Canadian GNP are unavailable, y'' is approximated by the percentage deviations in nominal Canadian imports (KM) from their growth trend (KM*):

$$\ln y'' \sim \ln KM - \ln KM^*,$$

where

$$\ln KM^* = \underset{(131.0)}{3.72} + \underset{(26.0)}{0.025}\, t,\ R^2 = 0.93. \quad (5.4)$$

Equation (5.4) is estimated from seasonally adjusted quarterly data for the period 1900III-1913I.[19] The nominal monetary base, by contrast, is not seasonally adjusted. Instead, three seasonal dummies (D_i) are inserted on the right-hand side of equation (5.3).[20]

Econometric tests of equation (5.3) are presented in Table 5-4. Note that OLS estimates yield high serial correlation in the residuals. For this reason equation (5.3) is also estimated with the aid of the Cochrane-Orcutt (CO) procedure. The results are clearly consistent with the conclusion of the preceding section. Provided $\alpha_2 + h' \sim 0$, I would expect that H was not significantly related to y''. This is indeed confirmed by equations (5.5) and (5.6). Regardless of the estimation procedure employed, it is impossible to reject the null hypothesis that χ_3 equalled zero. By contrast, base-money demand was highly responsive to changes in the Montreal call-loan rate, with χ_2 displaying the expected negative sign. Interestingly, the estimates of χ_2 are not sensitive to the choice of specification and estimation procedure. Both the OLS and CO estimates suggest that a rise in the Montreal call-loan rate by one percentage point caused base-money demand to decline by roughly 20 percent.

5.2.2. Reserve Ratios

Similar conclusions may be drawn from regression equations determining the aggregate reserve ratio (ρ). From equations (4.2), (4.3) and (4.4), the following relationship may be derived:

$$\ln \rho = \tilde{\chi} + \tilde{\chi}_1 r + \tilde{\chi}_3 \ln y'' + \tilde{\chi}_4 t + \sum_{i=1}^{3} \tilde{\chi}_{4+i} D_i. \quad (5.8)$$

Equation (5.8) is also specified in semi-logarithmic form, with allowance made for a time trend and seasonal fluctuations in the aggregate reserve ratio. The results of Section 5.1 imply that the aggregate reserve ratio — unlike the monetary base — should have been negatively related to cyclical fluctuations in output. While the estimates of $\tilde{\chi}_3$ are indeed negatively signed, there is considerable doubt about their statistical significance [equations (5.9) to (5.12) in Table 5-5]. If estimated by OLS, $\tilde{\chi}_3$ is statistically significant at the 95

TABLE 5-4
DETERMINANTS OF CANADIAN DEMAND FOR BASE MONEY, 1900III-1913I

Dependent	Const.	r	ln y"	t	D_1	D_2	D_3	$\bar{R}^2$	SEE	DW	Estimation Procedure	Equ. No.
ln H	5.48 (31.3)	-0.22 (-6.50)	0.08 (0.50)	0.03 (39.4)	0.06 (2.08)	0.01 (0.44)	-0.04 (-1.20)	0.97	0.076	0.69	OLS	(5.5)
ln H	5.49 (21.9)	-0.22 (-4.69)	0.15 (0.63)	0.03 (21.3)	0.07 (4.05)	0.02 (0.88)	-0.03 (-1.98)	0.95	0.058	1.75	CO	(5.6)
ln H	5.39 (28.7)	-0.20 (-5.73)		0.03 (21.6)	0.07 (4.05)	0.02 (1.00)	-0.03 (-1.92)	0.95	0.057	1.76	CO	(5.7)

Sources for Table 5-4
Monetary base (H): Table A-2. Montreal call-loan rate (r): legend to Chart 2-1.

percent level, but application of the Cochrane-Orcutt procedure lowers the t-values of $\tilde{\chi}_3$ to 0.9 and less. As would be expected, there was a statistically significant and negative relationship between the aggregate reserve ratio and the Montreal call-loan rate. Thus, the results weakly support the conclusions of Section 5.1.

Besides the independent variables included in equation (5.8), changes in the rates of return on reserves may have influenced the aggregate reserve ratio, a possibility disregarded up to now [equation (4.5)]. For this reason, the New York ($r_{\rho N}$) and London ($r_{\rho L}$) call-loan rates are introduced as additional independent variables. According to equations (5.11) and (5.12), there is no evidence to suggest that the aggregate reserve ratio was sensitive to changes in these two rates.[21]

Table 5-5 also offers evidence on the determinants of the cash reserve ratio, that is, the sum of the gold (ρ_1) and note (ρ_2) reserve ratios. Equations (5.13) and (5.14) show that the cash reserve ratio was not determined in the same way as the aggregate reserve ratio. While a highly significant inverse relationship existed between the cash reserve ratio and cyclical movements in domestic output, the Montreal call-loan rate was not significant. If the New York and London call-loan rates are also taken into account, the Montreal call-loan rate shows up as a statistically significant variable, but with wrong sign [equation (5.15)]. Thus, I doubt that the cash reserve ratio was sensitive to changes in the Montreal call-loan rate. The New York call-loan rate, by contrast, exerted a highly significant negative influence on the cash reserve ratio.[22]

The differences in interest sensitivities revealed by equations (5.12) and (5.15) help to explain why the cyclical movements in the aggregate and secondary reserve ratios frequently lagged those in the cash reserve ratio (see Chart 3-7). The reason for this lag becomes obvious if one considers the cyclical pattern of the New York call-loan rate. According to Chart 5-1, that rate tended to vary procyclically, with a peak (trough) typically attained near a reference-cycle peak (trough).[23] Therefore, the Montreal call-loan rate — which normally started to rise (fall) near the midpoint of a reference-cycle expansion (contraction) — tended to lag its New York counterpart. The lagged response in the Montreal call-loan rate in turn produced an analogous lag between the aggregate and cash reserve ratios. Since the cash reserve ratio reacted strongly to cyclical movements in the New York call-loan rate and Canadian output, it tended to rise (fall) during reference-cycle contractions (expansions). Due to the lagged response in the Montreal call-loan rate, the aggregate and secondary reserve ratios, by contrast, did not start to decline until the Canadian economy approached the midpoint of a cyclical expansion.

As a result of procyclical movements in the New York call-loan rate and Canadian output, the gold and note reserve ratios — the two constituents of the cash reserve ratio — also varied countercyclically. However, as I pointed out in Chapter 3, the gold reserve ratio did not fluctuate as much as the note

TABLE 5-5

DETERMINANTS OF CHARTERED-BANK RESERVE RATIOS, 1900III-1913I

Dependent Variable	Const.	r	$r_{\rho N}$	$r_{\rho L}$	ln y"	t	D_1	D_2	D_3	$\bar{R}^2$	SEE·	DW	Estim. Proce-dure	Equ. No.
ln ρ	-0.52	-0.19			-0.32	0.01	0.05	0.02	-0.02	0.79	0.071	0.72	OLS	(5.9)
	(-3.14)	(-6.19)			(-2.20)	(9.14)	(1.72)	(0.54)	(-0.63)					
ln ρ	-0.48	-0.20			-0.20	0.01	0.05	0.02	-0.02	0.83	0.055	1.80	CO	(5.10)
	(-2.02)	(-4.50)			(-0.90)	(5.37)	(3.29)	(0.86)	(-1.17)					
ln ρ	-0.51	-0.20	-0.007	0.04	-0.40	0.01	0.04	0.02	-0.02	0.78	0.072	0.76	OLS	(5.11)
	(-2.83)	(-4.62)	(-0.72)	(0.82)	(-2.32)	(6.36)	(1.51)	(0.52)	(-0.64)					
ln ρ	-0.51	-0.19	0.004	-0.04	-0.11	0.01	0.06	0.01	-0.02	0.82	0.056	1.81	CO	(5.12)
	(-1.99)	(-3.16)	(-0.29)	(-0.70)	(-0.40)	(4.78)	(3.33)	(0.71)	(-1.22)					
ln $(\rho_1+\rho_2)$	-2.36	-0.002			-0.60	0.01	0.01	0.03	-0.0003	0.84	0.056	0.91	OLS	(5.13)
	(-18.3)	(-0.07)			(-5.26)	(14.0)	(0.59)	(1.21)	(-0.01)					
ln $(\rho_1+\rho_2)$	-2.25	-0.02			-0.49	0.01	0.01	0.02	-0.004	0.91	0.047	2.02	CO	(5.14)
	(-12.0)	(-0.59)			(-2.89)	(8.08)	(0.75)	(1.38)	(-0.27)					
ln $(\rho_1+\rho_2)$	-2.53	0.07	-0.02	-0.05	-0.52	0.01	0.01	0.01	-0.01	0.91	0.041	2.03	CO	(5.15)
	(-19.0)	(2.29)	(-3.45)	(-1.34)	(4.09)	(10.7)	(0.41)	(0.80)	(-0.77)					

Sources for Table 5-5

Aggregate (ρ) and cash reserve $(\rho_1 + \rho_2)$ ratios: legend to Table 3-5. Montreal (r) and New York $(r_{\rho N})$ call-loan rates: legend to Chart 2-1. London call-loan rate $(r_{\rho L})$: Chart 5-5.

reserve ratio. The chartered banks' gold stock served mainly as a buffer for absorbing normal drains of precious metal.[24] In order to cope with cyclical fluctuations in inflows and outflows of gold, the banks tended to vary their holdings of Dominion notes. In this way, they were able to economize on the cost of storing gold. Needless to say, Dominion notes were not an adequate hedge against drains of precious metal unless they were fully convertible into gold. As I show in Chapter 7, the convertibility of Dominion notes was not always assured under the pre-1914 gold standard. Until the mid-1880s, in particular, the government maintained various restrictions on the covertibility of its notes. The existence of such restrictions may explain why the cyclical variance of the gold reserve ratio was still substantial in the period up to 1885, but declined markedly relative to that of the note reserve ratio in subsequent years (Chart 3-9).

5.3. BANK RESERVE MANAGEMENT AND THE CYCLE-TRANSMISSION PROCESS

For expositional convenience, the role of bank reserve management in the cycle-transmission process is examined in three steps. First, as in Chapter 4, I simplify the analysis by disregarding foreign-induced changes in the Canadian non-monetary debt (w). Second, I complicate the analysis by allowing for foreign cyclical disturbances to be transmitted to the Canadian economy through both the balance of payments on current and capital accounts. Third, I examine further the consistency of the model with the stylized facts listed at the beginning of Chapter 4.

5.3.1. The Cycle-Transmission Process: A Simplified Analysis

Suppose again that there was a cyclical expansion in United States economic activity. The resulting foreign-induced increase in the Canadian current-account surplus (increase in v), in the short-run, caused Canadian output, the price of the home good, and nominal demand for money to rise. The chartered banks in turn accommodated the expansion in money demand by a corresponding increase in supply. Despite the rise in the money stock, an increase in v, in the short run, did not affect nominal demand for base money since the total output sensitivity of that demand was close to zero. The rise in base-money demand, associated with the expansion in the money stock, was offset by an output-induced cut in the aggregate reserve ratio. Thus, in the short run, domestic interest rates were invariant to a rise in v. This may be proved formally if the model of Chapter 4 is modified by setting $\alpha_2 + h' \sim 0$. Rewriting equations (4.27) and (4.29) accordingly and substituting the latter into the former, I obtain:

$$r = -(N + w)/(\alpha_1 + \delta_1). \tag{5.16}$$

Clearly, domestic interest rates no longer react instantaneously to foreign-induced changes in the current-account surplus.

Since the cyclical expansion in domestic economic activity normally caused the current account to deteriorate, the long-run effect of a rise in v was to augment domestic interest rates through a contraction in the supply of base money. As long as domestic economic activity continued to expand, the nominal demand for money also increased. Because of an output- and interest-induced decline in the aggregate reserve ratio, the banks were able to accommodate the cyclical rise in nominal money demand despite a drop in the supply of base money.

According to the theoretical analysis of Chapter 4, the cyclical rise in the domestic interest rate should have fed back on domestic output, the price of the home good, and the current-account balance. However, as I showed earlier, the model does not appear to account properly for these feedback effects. Before examining further this issue, I turn to the implications of non-monetary capital flows for the cycle-transmission process.

5.3.2. The Cycle-Transmission Process: Implications of Non-Monetary Capital Flows

Besides the balance of payments on current account, the non-monetary foreign debt could have linked Canadian and foreign business cycles. As may be recalled from equation (4.25), foreign-induced changes in the Canadian non-monetary debt are captured by the exogenous variable w, which is assumed to be negatively and positively related to foreign interest rates (r_f) and the price of the imported good (P_f) respectively. In principle, the pattern of w could have been procyclical or countercyclical. As far as r_f is concerned, I already pointed out that the New York call-loan rate varied procyclically. As I show later, the movements of other foreign interest rates were also procyclical. Since P_f was positively correlated with the business cycle too, the question arises whether r_f or P_f dominated the cyclical movements in w.

Considering the cyclical pattern of the Canadian non-monetary debt, one cannot help concluding that the influence of foreign interest rates was dominant. Had w borne a positive relationship to the reference cycle, it would be difficult to explain the countercyclical pattern of the Canadian non-monetary debt recorded during a major part of the period under study. This may readily be seen if equation (4.19) is modified to take account of definition (4.25):

$$S = \delta_1 r + w + \alpha_1 r' - \alpha_2 y'. \qquad (5.17)$$

Since the pattern of domestic interest rates tended to be procyclical, the Canadian non-monetary debt (S) could have moved countercyclically only if w had been negatively correlated with the reference cycle.[25] Furthermore, the procyclical movements in foreign interest rates should have been strong enough to outweigh the influence of domestic interest rates and foreign prices on the non-monetary debt. Provided the sensitivities of that debt to domestic and foreign interest rates were of the same order of magnitude, I would expect that the cyclical variance of foreign interest rates was larger than that of comparable domestic rates.[26]

The evidence indeed suggests that interest rate differentials between Canada and abroad varied countercyclically. As far as call-loan rates are concerned, there is little doubt that their cyclical fluctuations were less pronounced in Montreal than in the United States. As may be seen from Chart 5-1, the Montreal call-loan rate — over the business cycle — was very stable as compared to its New York counterpart. However, because of New York's role as a lender of last resort to other parts of the United States, the volatility of call-loan rates in that city may have been atypical. Therefore, Chart 5-1 also shows the cyclical movements of call-loan rates in Boston, the U.S. financial centre nearest to Montreal. The evidence clearly indicates that the cyclical variance of call-loan rates was far smaller in Montreal than in either of the two U.S. cities. On the whole, the New York and Boston rates were more closely correlated with one another than with their Montreal counterpart. Interestingly, the cyclical turning points in both U.S. rates tended to coincide closely with the reference-cycle turning points. In interpreting the evidence of Chart 5-1, it should be remembered that call-loan rates ruling in Montreal and the two U.S. cities are related to the Canadian — rather than the United States — reference cycle. However, it does not matter much which of the two reference-cycle series is employed. The close coincidence of cyclical turning points in U.S. call-loan rates and the reference cycle remains if U.S. reference-cycle turning points are substituted for their Canadian equivalents in Chart 5-1.[27] Since the Montreal call-loan rate, by contrast, lagged the reference cycle, there was a corresponding lag between that rate and call-loan rates in New York and Boston. As indicated by Table 5-6, the lag between call-loan rates ruling in Montreal and the United States averaged roughly two quarters.

The message of Chart 5-1 is strongly corroborated by significance tests presented in Table 5-2. In contrast to Chart 5-1, Table 5-2 relates cyclical movements in U.S. interest rates to the United States — rather than Canadian — reference cycle. Both the New York and Boston call-loan rates exhibited a statistically significant procyclical pattern, with the maximum (minimum) quarterly first differences typically recorded during the expansion (contraction) stage of the reference cycle. As indicated earlier, first differences in the Montreal call-loan rate also displayed a statistically significant procyclical pattern but tended to peak during reference-cycle booms. Thus, Table 5-2 confirms the existence of a lag between call-loan rates in Montreal and the United States.

Further evidence on the relative stability of Canadian interest rates is provided by an analysis of cyclical movements in the average rates of return on Canadian and U.S. bank loans. Table 5-3 identifies the cyclical attributes of the average return on loans booked at the domestic branches of the BNS and at national banks located in the northeastern and midwestern regions of the United States. The U.S. data were estimated by Smiley (1975) and appear to be comparable to the BNS series.[28] Note that for four out of the six categories of national banks covered by Table 5-3, the average return on loans displayed a statistically significant procyclical pattern.[29] For the other two categories, the average return was either invariant to the reference cycle (middle atlantic non-reserve city banks) or moved countercyclically (midwestern non-

TABLE 5-6

MONTREAL CALL-LOAN RATE: LAGS TO U.S. RATES

New York Call-Loan Rate: Turning Points (End of Quarter)	Boston Call-Loan Rate: Turning Points (End of Quarter)	Montreal Call-Loan Rate		
		Turning Points (End of Quarter)	Lag to New York Call-Loan Rate (Quarters)	Lag to Boston Call-Loan Rate (Quarters)
(1)	(2)	(3)	(4)	(5)
T/I 01	n.a.	T/III 01	2	n.a.
P/III 02	P/III 02	P/I 03	2	2
T/III 04	T/III 04	T/I 05	2	2
P/II 07[a)]	P/III 06	P/II 07[b)]	-	3
T/III 08	T/IV 08	T/I 09	2	1
P/IV 09	P/I 10	P/I 11	5	4
T/III 11[a)]	T/III 11	T/I 12	2	2
P/IV 12	P/IV 12	n.a.	n.a.	n.a.

a) It is difficult to time these cyclical turning points. The (seasonally adjusted) New York call-loan rate already reached a high of 7.31 percent at the end 1906II. Subsequently, it fell temporarily and surged again to 7.55 percent at the end of 1907II. In 1911, it fell to a low of 2.51 percent at the end of the first quarter. After a temporary increase, it declined again to 2.50 percent at the end of the third quarter.

b) On a seasonally adjusted basis, the Montreal call-loan rate stood at 6 percent from the end of 1907I to the end of 1907III. I assume that the peak occurred at the end of 1907II.

Sources and estimation methods for Table 5-6

The cyclical turning points in call-loan rates are timed on the basis of the seasonally adjusted data shown in Chart 5-1.

reserve city banks). Furthermore, provided the pattern was procyclical, first differences in the average return on U.S. loans tended to reach a peak (trough) during the boom (depression) stage of the reference cycle. This piece of evidence implies that in the United States, interest rates on fixed-term loans normally lagged call-loan rates. As indicated by Table 5-2, U.S. interest rates on such fixed-term assets as time money and commercial paper also lagged call-loan rates.[30] Thus, while a lag existed between call-loan rates in Montreal and the northeastern United States, the BNS series tended to move in sympathy with the average return on U.S. bank loans.

Despite this parallelism of cyclical movements, the amplitude of the BNS series was not as large as that of the average return on U.S. bank loans. For reserve city banks in the U.S. Northeast and Midwest, the cyclical amplitudes of the average return on loans (as measured by the difference between the averages for booms and depressions in Table 5-3) were 1.5 to 2.5 times larger than for the domestic branches of the BNS. For non-reserve city banks, the amplitudes were similar to that of the BNS series, but I doubt that loan rates charged by these institutions significantly impinged on international capital flows.

A comparison of cyclical movements in the average return on loans booked at the domestic and foreign branches of the BNS also testifies to the relative stability of Canadian interest rates. As may be seen from Table 5-3, the cyclical amplitude of the average return at the BNS' foreign branches was almost three times higher than at home. The evidence for the BNS, however, is liable to overstate the difference in the cyclical amplitude of Canadian and foreign interest rates because the composition of loans booked in Canada and abroad was not the same. A large share of the assets booked abroad consisted of call loans, for which interest rates were more variable than for other types of loans.

Similar results are obtained from an analysis of cyclical movements in Canadian and U.S. bond yields. As far as the United States is concerned, pre-1914 data are available for yields on municipal and railway bonds.[31] While Canadian bond yields did not vary much over the business cycle, the yields on both U.S. municipal and railway bonds moved procyclically. Furthermore, over the period 1900III-1913I, their procyclical pattern was statistically significant at the 99 percent level, with the quarterly first differences in U.S. bond yields attaining a peak (trough) in the boom (depression) stage of the reference cycle (Table 5-2). Thus, the cyclical pattern of U.S. bond yields resembled that of the average return on loans booked at northeastern and midwestern reserve city banks.[32]

In contrast to the patterns revealed by Chart 5-1, the cyclical amplitudes of the London and Montreal call-loan rates were virtually identical (Chart 5-5). Moreover, there was a striking coincidence in their cyclical turning points.[33] Thus, interest rate differentials between Canada and the United Kingdom varied little over the business cycle. However, the close coincidence of cycl-

CHART 5-5

CALL-LOAN RATES IN MONTREAL AND LONDON, 1900II-1913I

(Seasonally Adjusted)

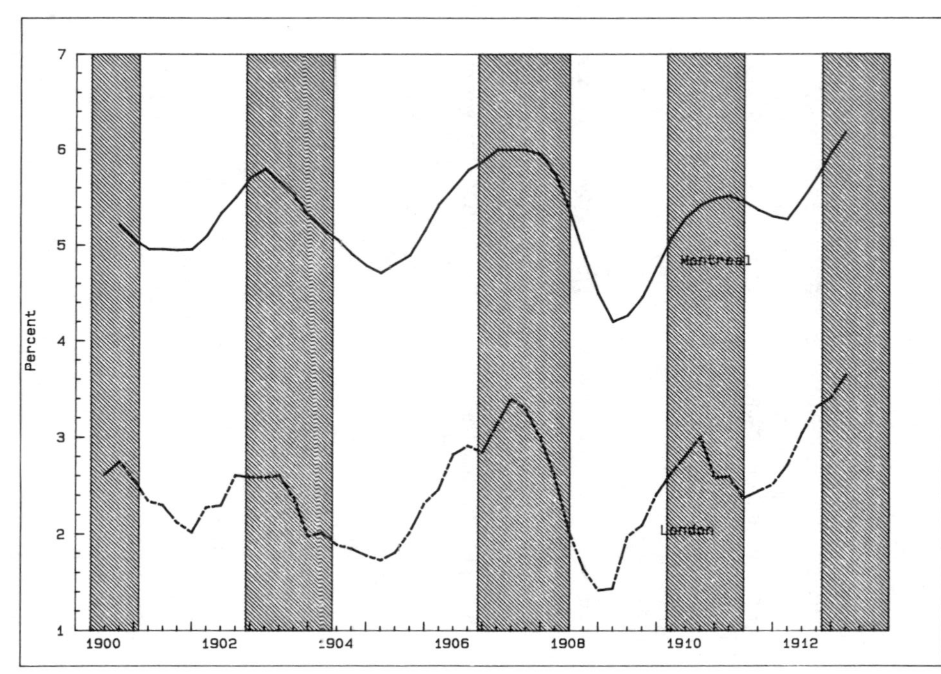

Sources for Chart 5-5

Montreal call-loan rate: Chart 2-1. London call-loan rate: Peake, 1926, Appendix I. The London rate represents the interest rate on floating money for the first Friday following the end of a quarter. The data are seasonally adjusted by a thirteen-month moving average.

ical turning points in the Montreal and London call-loan rates should not be interpreted to imply that arbitrage served to link tightly call-loan markets in the two cities. The Montreal rate invariably exceeded its London counterpart by roughly 2.5 to 3 percentage points.

The cyclical patterns of interest rates and capital flows suggest that the Canadian economy was influenced not only by disturbances transmitted through the current account but also by countercyclical swings in the Canadian non-monetary debt, induced by procyclical movements in foreign interest rates. A cyclical expansion in U.S. economic activity was normally accompanied by an increase in U.S. call-loan rates. The rise in these rates, by itself, did not impinge on the Canadian non-monetary debt because there is no evidence to suggest that non-banks arbitrated funds between Canadian and U.S. call-loan markets.[34] However, as the business-cycle expansion proceeded, interest rates on U.S. fixed-term bank loans, bonds and other fixed-term assets began to rise, eliciting a decrease in foreign demand for Canadian non-monetary assets and an increase in interest rates on Canadian bank loans.[35] Thus, the rise in interest rates on U.S. fixed-term assets amplified the effect on domestic loan rates of the deterioration in the Canadian current-account balance, typically associated with a cyclical expansion in foreign and domestic economic activity. In terms of equation (5.16), both a decrease in the cumulative current-account surplus (N) and a foreign-induced decline in the Canadian non-monetary debt (decline in w) were responsible for the increase in Canadian loan rates typically observed during reference-cycle booms.

Since interest rate differentials between Canada and the United States (other than those involving U.S. call-loans), reached a trough near the midpoint of a reference-cycle contraction, the Canadian non-monetary debt also tended to attain a low at that stage of the business cycle. First differences in the non-monetary debt or capital inflows in turn tended to reach a trough near a reference-cycle peak. Thus, movements in U.S. and Canadian interest rates appear to account for the observed countercyclical pattern of Canadian capital inflows.

Although Canadian and U.S. financial markets were connected through capital flows, international arbitrage was not strong enough to tie closely Canadian to U.S. interest rates. The responsiveness of Canadian to U.S. interest rates was tempered substantially by reserve management of the Canadian chartered banks, that is, by a strong sensitivity of the aggregate reserve ratio to changes in domestic interest rates. This conclusion also follows from equation (5.16). A high interest sensitivity of base-money demand (α_1) moderated the effect of procyclical movements in U.S. interest rates (or of countercyclical movements in w) on borrowing costs in domestic money and capital markets (r). Prior to World War I, risks and information costs associated with capital flows apparently were still sufficiently high to prevent arbitrage from equalizing interest rates across national borders or even within countries.

5.3.3. Consistency of the Model with the Stylized Facts: Significance of Feed-Back Effects

A problem still to be resolved lies in the leads generated by the model between such endogenous variables as domestic output, prices, the money stock and the current-account surplus, on the one hand, and cyclical movements in foreign economic activity on the other. One way of reconciling the model fully with the stylized facts is to assume that (a) cyclical and other transitory changes in domestic interest rates exerted a smaller impact on domestic aggregate demand than permanent ones and (b) the observed cyclical movements in domestic interest rates were not sufficiently large to impinge significantly on domestic absorption, that is, β_1 was close to zoro. Provided $\beta_1 = \alpha_2 + h' \sim 0$, equations (4.26) and (4.28) may be modified to read:

$$P = y = v/k_1, \tag{5.18}$$

$$c = \dot{N} = (1-\beta_2)\ v/k_1, \tag{5.19}$$

since $k_2 = k_1(\alpha_1+\delta_1)$ and $k_3 = (\alpha_1+\delta_1)(1-\beta_2)$. Obviously, a zero value of β_1 implies that foreign-induced changes in the Canadian current-account surplus (changes in v) led to an instantaneous adjustment in domestic output (y), the price of the home good (P), the current-account surplus (c), and the domestic money stock. Therefore, the model now allows for a perfect coincidence of the cyclical turning points in these four endogenous variables with those in v and foreign economic activity. However, foreign cyclical disturbances still elicited a gradual adjustment in domestic interest rates by way of changes in the cumulative current-account surplus (N), that is, equation (5.16) remains valid if β_1 is set equal to zero. The model of Chapter 4 reduces to a system of differential equations consisting of (4.16a), (5.16), (5.18), (5.19) and a modified variant of (4.31), determining the price of the home good, output, the current-account surplus, the domestic bond yield and the Canadian non-monctary debt (S). The solution is derived in Appendix D.

If β_1 — for all practical purposes — had equalled zero, the preceding analysis would lend strong support to the Keynesian view of the cycle-transmission process. As is readily apparent from equation (4.24), the parameter $1/k_1$, linking domestic output to v, represents nothing else than a variant of the Keynesian export multiplier.[36] Furthermore, according to equation (5.19), countercyclical movements in the current-account surplus imply $1-\beta_2<0$, that is, the marginal propensity to absorb home and imported goods should have exceeded unity. As suggested by Keynesian students of the Canadian business cycle, the analysis presented in this study leads to the conclusion that induced investment was instrumental in generating the observed countercyclical swings in the current-account surplus.[37] Output-induced fluctuations in the aggregate reserve ratio — though present — were not strong enough to generate countercyclical movements in domestic interest rates and, therefore, do not explain the countercyclical pattern of the current account surplus.

While these conclusions, at first sight, seem consistent with the Keynesian standpoint, the view of the cycle-transmission process espoused in this study should not be regarded as an apology of Keynesian business-cycle analysis. The preceding discussion need not imply that money was an unimportant driving force behind the pre-1914 Canadian business cycle. On the contrary, through an increase in the domestic money stock, the chartered banks' ability to accommodate a cyclical expansion in economic activity strengthened the impact of foreign cyclical disturbances on the Canadian economy. Notably during the second half of a business-cycle expansion, the chartered banks continued to expand the money stock relative to its growth trend, despite a deterioration in the Canadian balance of payments and an attendant contraction in the domestic monetary base. Although the cyclical decline in the monetary base caused Canadian short-term interest rates to rise, the increase in borrowing costs was not large enough to curb significantly the cyclical expansion in economic activity. By keeping domestic interest rates relatively stable, the chartered banks exposed the Canadian economy to the full force of the Keynesian export multiplier. Thus, I do not negate the role of money in the Canadian business cycle but attempt to demonstrate how bank reserve management created an environment highly favourable to the operation of a Keynesian cycle-transmission process.

5.4. A MONETARY VIEW OF THE CYCLE-TRANSMISSION PROCESS: SUMMARY AND FURTHER COMMENTS

5.4.1. Summary

The analysis presented in this study lends strong support to the view that accommodative reserve management by the chartered banks enhanced the sensitivity of the Canadian economy to foreign cyclical disturbances. As a result of pronounced interest- and output-induced countercyclical swings in the aggregate reserve ratio and corresponding procyclical movements in the money stock, the chartered banks managed to keep the cyclical variance of domestic interest rates within narrow bounds. Movements in domestic interest rates — though procyclical — were not strong enough to dampen significantly the effect of foreign cyclical disturbances on Canadian economic activity. Thus, money played an important role in the transmission of foreign cyclical disturbances.

The monetary view of the cycle-transmission process advanced in this study may be summarized as follows. A cyclical expansion in foreign economic activity was transmitted to Canada by way of an increase in real exports and possibly import prices.[38] These disturbances caused output, the price level and nominal money demand in Canada to rise. Through an output-induced reduction in the aggregate reserve ratio, the chartered banks in turn accommodated the cyclical increase in money demand by a parallel adjustment in supply. Since equilibrium in the market for base money was not disturbed, domestic interest rates, at least in the short run, remained unchanged. However, as the business-cycle expansion proceeded, domestic interest rates rose to some extent, because of a cyclical contraction in the supply of base money triggered by a deterioration in the balance of payments on current account. Trend-adjusted international monetary assets and the monetary base typically did not start to decline until the cyclical expansion in Canadian economic activity had reached its midpoint. Domestic interest rates, therefore, followed economic activity with a time lag amounting to one half of the length of the respective reference-cycle expansion or contraction.

The procyclical swings in domestic interest rates were frequently reinforced by corresponding movements in United States interest rates. A cyclical expansion in U.S. economic activity invariably saw a rise in call-loan rates in such financial centres as New York and Boston. The increase in U.S. call-loan rates, by itself, did not affect demand for Canadian non-monetary assets, but prompted the chartered banks to substitute foreign call loans for cash and, thus, to alter the composition of their reserves. Coupled with an output-induced decline in the cash reserve ratio, the shift in the composition of bank reserves caused the (trend-adjusted) Canadian monetary gold stock to fall soon after economic activity had passed its cyclical trough. For these reasons, the monetary gold stock tended to lead the monetary base, notably over the post-1900 period.

As the business-cycle expansion progressed, interest rates on U.S. fixed-term assets also began to rise. Average rates of return on loans of U.S. national banks and U.S. bond yields, in particular, started to increase near the midpoint of a reference-cycle expansion and continued their upward course during the first half of the subsequent contraction. The surge in interest rates on U.S. fixed-term bank loans and bonds in turn lowered demand for Canadian non-monetary assets, pushing up further domestic interest rates. However, domestic interest rates did not rise as much as their U.S. counterparts. The evidence is consistent with the assumption underlying equation (4.19) as to a quick reaction in the Canadian non-monetary debt to shifts in foreign and domestic interest rates. A quick response implies that the non-monetary debt — like the differential between Canadian interest rates and those on U.S. fixed-term assets — reached a cyclical trough near the midpoint of a business-cycle contraction, while capital inflows (or first differences in the non-monetary debt) attained a corresponding low near a reference-cycle peak.

5.4.2. Further Comments

Although money appears to have played a significant destabilizing role, this study does not prove conclusively that cyclical movements in the Canadian money stock exerted strong direct effects on economic activity. For this reason, two further tests of the monetary view advanced in this study are presented. First, I compare the cyclical performance of the Canadian and United States gold standards by analyzing the cyclical amplitudes of the two countries' nominal GNP and money stocks. Second, I attempt to trace directly the channels through which foreign cyclical disturbances were transmitted to Canada.

The results of the preceding analysis imply that the monetary sector would have acted as an automatic stabilizer of the Canadian business cycle if the chartered banks had not been prepared to accommodate cyclical movements in money demand as readily as they did. A less accommodative stance would have served to moderate cyclical fluctuations in Canadian economic activity by enhancing the cyclical amplitude of domestic interest rates and by quickening their response to foreign cyclical disturbances.

Considering the cyclical patterns of Canadian and U.S. interest rates, one might venture the suggestion that the destabilizing effect on economic activity of procyclical movements in the money stock was less pronounced in the United States than in Canada. In his study of the Canadian cycle-transmission process, Rosenbluth (1957, 489-94) provides some empirical support for this conjecture. Prior to World War I, he concludes, Canadian output fluctuations exceeded those in the United States. Rosenbluth's results, however, must be interpreted with care because his investigation was hampered by an absence of annual data on pre-1914 Canadian output. He bypassed this difficulty by relying on railway ton-miles as a proxy for output. If the recently released Urquhart (1987) estimates of Canadian GNP are employed, Rosenbluth's conclusion no longer seems to conform to the empirical evidence.

The cyclical amplitudes of Canadian and U.S. GNP growth may be analyzed with the help of Table 5-7. Two measures of amplitude are presented. The table shows, on the one hand, average annual GNP growth for reference-cycle expansions and contractions, with the difference between these two averages used as a measure of amplitude [column (3)],[38] as well as the standard deviation of the annual growth rates on the other [column (4)]. The last column displays the simple correlation between the growth in Canadian and U.S. GNP. The evidence suggests that Canadian GNP growth, until the 1890s, tended to lag somewhat its U.S. counterpart. While the swings in the two countries' GNP deflators typically coincided, Canadian real GNP frequently reacted with a lag of about a year to corresponding movements in the United States. The delayed response in Canadian real GNP is consistent with the lag uncovered in Chapter 4 between the Canadian reference-cycle and real exports. For this reason, the data presented in Table 5-7 are compiled separately for two subperiods, delineated by the onset of the wheat boom in Canada. For the subperiod 1870/71-95/96, the number in column (5) represents the simple correlation between Canadian GNP growth and its U.S. equivalent lagged by one year.[39] For the second subperiod, the contemporaneous correlation between the two countries' growth rates is shown. Although the correlation between the growth in Canadian and U.S. GNP, not surprisingly, was fairly strong, it was not as high as might be expected on the strength of the reference-cycle analysis presented in Chapter 2.[40]

While the correlation patterns seem to have shifted in the 1890s, the measures of cyclical amplitude displayed in columns (3) and (4) yield rather similar results for the two subperiods. Both measures of amplitude suggest

TABLE 5-7

CYCLICAL AMPLITUDE OF GNP AND THE MONEY STOCK IN CANADA AND THE UNITED STATES
(Percent)

	Annual Rates of Change				
	Average Rate of Change			Standard Deviation	Correlation between Canadian and U.S. Variables
	Expansions	Contractions	Difference		
	(1)	(2)	(3)=(1)-(2)	(4)	(5)
1870/71 - 95/96					
Canada: Nominal GNP	5.5	-1.3	6.9	6.2	0.56[a)]
United States: Nominal GNP	6.2	-1.8	8.0	7.5	
Canada: Money Stock[b)]	8.2	0.8	7.4	6.1	0.69
United States: Money Stock[b)]	8.3	1.3	7.5	6.6	
1896/97 - 1912/13					
Canada: Nominal GNP	10.7	6.1	4.6	4.4	0.68
United States: Nominal GNP	9.2	3.3	5.9	6.7	
Canada: Money Stock	12.1	6.8	5.3	4.5	0.64
United States: Money Stock	9.5	5.6	3.9	4.0	

a) Correlation between Canadian nominal GNP growth for the period 1870/71-1895/96 and the corresponding U.S. values lagged by one year.
b) 1874/75-95/96

Sources for Table 5-7

See Urquhart (1987, Table 9) and Friedman and Schwartz (1982, Table 4.8) for annual data on Canadian and U.S. GNP respectively. Data on the U.S. money stock — which represent annual averages of quarterly or monthly observations — are also obtained from that source. The data on the Canadian money stock are annual averages of quarterly observations (see Table A-2 and legend to that table). The Canadian and U.S. data, respectively, are assigned to Canadian and U.S. reference-cycle expansions or contractions according to Appendix C, procedures 5 and 6.

that over the business cycle, Canadian GNP fluctuated less than its U.S. counterpart. The same results are obtained if cyclical fluctuations in real, rather than nominal, GNP are analyzed.[41] Thus, in contrast to Rosenbluth's conclusions, Canada experienced less pronounced cyclical fluctuations in nominal and real GNP than the United States. Despite the relative stability of Canadian interest rates, the cyclical performance of the Canadian economy was better than that of the United States.

The preceding analysis, it might be argued, is incomplete because accommodative behaviour of the chartered banks need not have played a destabilizing role in all circumstances. Had the banks' willingness to accommodate changes in money demand served as a prophylactic against financial crises, bank reserve behaviour would have fostered cyclical stability. Canadian and U.S. data offer some support to this view. In the wake of the financial panic of 1893, U.S. nominal GNP dropped by 11.9 percent (from 1893 to 1894), while Canadian GNP declined by merely 4.5 percent. Similarly, the panic of 1907 elicited a fall in U.S. and Canadian GNP by 11.0 and 4.3 percent respectively (from 1907 to 1908). However, even if the observations for a full reference-cycle following each of the two panics are excluded, the cyclical amplitudes of the growth in Canadian and U.S. GNP still fail to conform to the pattern postulated by Rosenbluth.[42] Thus, no matter whether periods of financial panics are disregarded, it cannot be argued that cyclical fluctuations in Canadian GNP exceeded those in the United States.

In contrast to the patterns observed for nominal GNP, there is some evidence to suggest that the Canadian money stock fluctuated more strongly than its U.S. counterpart. While the cyclical amplitudes of the two countries' money stocks were virtually identical in the first subperiod, Canadian money growth was more variable after 1896 (Table 5-7). Thus, in the second subperiod, accommodative bank behaviour in Canada not only produced stabler interest rates but also more variable money growth than in the United States. In both subperiods, there was a fairly close contemporaneous correlation between Canadian and U.S. money growth.

While the case for the monetary view advanced in this study is not strengthened by a comparison of the growth patterns in Canadian and U.S. GNP, additional support may be gained by analyzing directly the various transmission channels. Table 5-8 seeks to determine the relative importance of the key transmission channels that were liable to link Canadian to U.S. nominal GNP. The analysis focusses on two transmission channels, that is, Canadian merchandise exports and the money stock, both expressed in nominal terms. Thus, both a real and a monetary transmission channel are considered in the analysis.[43] The adjusted coefficients of determination ($\bar{R}^2$) presented in Table 5-8 are derived from regression equations relating the dependent to the independent variables shown in the respective rows. As suggested by the coefficients of determination in row (1), in the subperiods 1874/75-1895/96 and 1896/97-1912/13 respectively, roughly one-third and one-half of the observed variation in Canadian GNP was explained by movements in U.S. GNP. If regressions of Canadian GNP on merchandise exports [row (2)], on the one hand, and of merchandise exports on U.S. GNP [row (3)], on the other, yielded coefficients of determination equalling or exceeding those exhibited in row (1), I would accept the real view of the cycle-transmission process. An analogous procedure is employed for assessing the role of money in linking Canadian to U.S. GNP [rows (4) and (5)].

For the first subperiod, both the real and the monetary views perform equally well, but, taken by themselves, they do not fully account for the observed relationship between Canadian and U.S. GNP. Canadian GNP was more closely linked to its U.S. equivalent than either Canadian merchandise exports or money. For the second subperiod, by contrast, the monetary view clearly wins the day. The coefficients of determination in rows (2) and (3) indicate that neither Canadian nor U.S. GNP was closely correlated with merchandise exports. As may be recalled from Chapter 2, Rosenbluth reached exactly the same conclusion. But inspite of its superior performance, even the monetary view does not fully explain the observed link between Canadian and U.S. GNP. In particular, Canadian GNP was not strongly related to the

TABLE 5-8
REAL AND MONETARY TRANSMISSION CHANNELS

Dependent Variable (Annual Growth Rates)	Independent Variables (Annual Growth Rates)	Coefficient of Determination (R^2)		Row
		1874/75 - 95/96	1896/97 - 1912/13	
Cdn. GNP	U.S. GNP	0.31[a)]	0.46	(1)
Cdn. GNP	Cdn. Exports	0.36	0.16	(2)
Cdn. Exports	U.S. GNP	0.24[a)]	0.14	(3)
Cdn. GNP	Cdn. Money	0.45	0.21	(4)
Cdn. Money	U.S. GNP	0.23[a)]	0.45	(5)
Cdn. GNP	Cdn. Exports and Money		0.43	(6)

a) U.S. GNP lagged by one year.

Sources for Table 5-8

See Table 5-7 for GNP and Canadian money stock. Canadian merchandise exports: Table A-3, column (1).

domestic money stock [row (4)]. However, provided Canadian GNP is regressed on both merchandise exports and the money stock, the resulting coefficient of determination roughly matches the value shown in row (1). Thus, the evidence of Table 5-8 lends support to the view advanced in this study that the cycle-transmission process cannot be understood unless the role of money is taken into account. In all likelihood, both monetary and real channels were instrumental in transmitting foreign cyclical disturbances to the Canadian economy.[44]

Endnotes — Chapter 5

1. Chart 2-1 likely understates the variability of U.S. call-loan rates. The U.S. data represent monthly averages of daily rates, while the Montreal data are reported for the first day of each month. Averaging of daily rates tends to reduce the variability of a time series. See also Chapter 6, note 1.

2. I am indebted to Peter Temin (1984) for drawing my attention to possible discrepancies between posted and effective rates.

3. The data source (BNS Statistics 3) does not specify how that series was calculated.

4. See Kessel (1965, ch. 4). Both seasonal and cyclical movements in the rate of return on an asset tend to increase as its term to maturity decreases.

5. This comparison is based on annual averages of MR, as shown in Canada, Board of Inquiry (1915, 739).

6. The quality test performed here, of course, does not rule out the possibility that the effective fluctuations in the Montreal call-loan rate exceeded those in MR. The same results are obtained if the fluctuations in MR are compared with those in interest rates on Canadian fixed-term loans, as compiled by Coats (Canada, Board of Inquiry, 1915, 720-34). The cyclical amplitudes of the Coats data on fixed-term loans and of the BNS series were similar. The variance of MR was also larger than that of an annual mortgage rate series compiled by Neufeld (1972, Table 15:2). Over the period 1900-12, the latter attained maximum and minimum values of 7.48 and 6.00 percent respectively.

7. The evidence refers to domestic holdings of Dominion government bonds. See Section 7.2.

8. Despite the paucity of price quotations, an active Canadian bond market already existed before 1907 (see Appendix E, note 1).

9. On a seasonally unadjusted basis, the Montreal call-loan rate stayed constant even longer (see Section 5.1.1).

10. In order to estimate the length of these leads or lags, the following procedure is adopted. A reference-cycle turning point or midpoint that fell into the middle month of a quarter is assigned to the 15th day of that month. If it fell into the initial and terminal months of a quarter, it is assigned to the first and last day of that quarter respectively. The turning points in the Montreal call-loan rate are timed on the basis of seasonally adjusted end-of-quarter data (see Chart 5-1 for the adjustment procedure).

11. Chart 5-2 shows growth rates, rather than first differences, in the monetary base because H was subject to a log-linear trend.

12. Table 5-2 conveys the same message.

13. The slight lead revealed by Chart 5-2 between the Montreal call-loan rate and the monetary base could also be explained in this way.

14. The partial derivative of the aggregate reserve ratio with respect to domestic output is given by $\rho_1 g_1$ [equations (4.2) and (4.3)]. According to (4.7b), $\rho_1 g_1 = -m_1\rho'/m' + \alpha_2/m' < 0$, provided $\alpha_2 + h' \sim 0$.

15. The partial derivative of the aggregate reserve ratio with respect to the domestic interest rate is given by ρ_2 [equation (4.2)], which must be negative if $\alpha_1>0$ [equation (4.7a)].

16. In the first instance, the BNS series decreased during a reference-cycle boom, while in the second instance it increased during a depression, albeit at a lower rate than during the preceding boom. Note that the Montreal call-loan rate only fell slightly during the reference-cycle depression of 1910-11.

17. Other deviations from the normal pattern occurred in 1888 and 1909, when cyclical peaks in the BNS series coincided with reference-cycle troughs. Moreover, in 1890, a cyclical peak in the BNS series coincided with a reference-cycle peak. Some of these deviations may be spurious because it is difficult to determine precisely the length of leads or lags to economic activity in periods in which reference-cycle expansions and contractions were very short.

18. In one instance (1907-08), a peak in the average yield on corporate bonds led the corresponding reference-cycle trough.

19. KM is compiled from unrevised monthly statements of imports entered for consumption. Sources: for 1900-02, Canada, *Monthly Reports of the Department of Trade and Commerce,* fiscal year 1909; for 1903-13, Canada, Department of Customs, *Trade and Navigation,* various issues. The data are seasonally adjusted by a 5-quarter moving average.

20. The quarterly seasonal dummies included in equation (5.3) assume the following values: D_1 = 0,0,1,0; D_2 = 0,0,0,1; D_3 = 1,0,0,0.

21. Similar results are obtained if call-loan rates in New York and London are introduced separately.

22. In a study of bank reserve behaviour over the period 1900-14, Clark and Bond (1972) also detect a significant negative relationship between the cash reserve ratio and the New York call-loan rate. Furthermore, their research indicates that the cash reserve ratio was influenced by changes in the ratio of demand deposits plus bank notes to aggregate bank liabilities. They do not investigate the link between the cash reserve ratio and domestic output.

23. Chart 5-1 relates the New York call-loan rate to the Canadian reference-cycle turning points. The conclusions about the cyclical pattern of that rate would not be altered if Chart 5-1 showed U.S. turning points (see also below).

24. Cash drains to domestic residents typically assumed the form of outflows of Dominion notes, but in the event of drains to foreigners the chartered banks were frequently asked to pay out gold.

25. It is possible that the countercyclical pattern of the non-monetary debt was due to factors not considered in equations (4.19) or (5.17). Specifically, foreign demand for domestic bonds might have depended positively on domestic output. See H.G. Johnson (1972, ch. 6) for an analysis of this case. However, adding domestic output on the right-hand side of equation (5.17) does not help to explain the countercyclical pattern of the non-monetary debt. Only an inverse relationship between that debt and foreign output could account for the observed pattern.

26. Provided $\delta_1=\delta_2$, equation (4.19) is modified as follows: $S = \delta_1(r-r_f) + u'(P_f-1)$. Clearly, countercyclical movements in the interest differential, $r-r_f$, are a necessary — but not sufficient — condition for the pattern of S to be countercyclical.

27. Over the period covered by Chart 5-1, only the Canadian reference-cycle peak of December, 1906, and the trough of July, 1911, were significantly out of phase with the corresponding U.S. turning points (Table 2-1).

28. Smiley estimated the average return on the national banks' private earning assets, covering securities in addition to loans. The BNS series does not appear to embrace securities.

29. For reserve city national banks in New England, the procyclical pattern was significant only at the 90 percent level.

30. The average lag (quarters) between the U.S. short-term interest rates covered by Table 5-2 and the U.S. reference cycle was as follows (numbers in parentheses indicate the maximum range of variation in these lags): New York call: 0.1 (−1.0/1.0); Boston call: 0.0 (−2.5/1.0); New York time: 0.9 (−1.0/2.0); Boston time: 1.1 (−1.0/2.0); New York commercial paper: 1.3 (−1.0/3.0). These calculations are based on seasonally adjusted end-of-quarter data for the

period September 30, 1902 to June 30, 1913 (see Chart 5-1 for the adjustment procedure). U.S. reference-cycle turning points are assigned to the nearest available quarter by the procedure outlined in note 10.

31. Yields on bonds issued by the U.S. federal government — for which data are also available — are disregarded since they were distorted by the requirement that notes circulated by national banks be backed by such bonds (see Chapter 1).

32. The cyclical fluctuations in the yields on Canadian corporate and U.S. railway bonds were of similar order of magnitude (Table 5-2). However, I doubt whether these yields are comparable because the risk characteristics of Canadian corporate and U.S. railway bonds were unlikely to be identical.

33. Quarterly first differences in the seasonally adjusted London call-loan rate averaged 0.15 and −0.09 percent for *Canadian* booms and depressions respectively. Thus, the cyclical amplitudes of the London and Montreal call-loan rates were identical (see Table 5-2). While the Montreal call-loan rate lagged the Canadian reference cycle, cyclical peaks (troughs) in the London call-loan rate tended to coincide with U.K. reference-cycle peaks (troughs). Nonetheless, the Montreal call-loan rate moved in sympathy with its London counterpart since the U.K. reference-cycle turning points, over the period 1900-13, normally lagged the corresponding North American turning points (see Hay, 1966).

34. Existing studies of the pre-1914 Canadian and U.S. financial systems do not contain any statements about arbitrage activities by non-banks in call-loan markets.

35. See Chapter 6 for a discussion of the relationship between the Canadian non-monetary debt and seasonal movements in U.S. interest rates.

36. In contrast to the traditional Keynesian export multiplier [given by $1/(1-\beta_2+\delta_2)$], $1/k_1$ also allows for terms-of-trade effects on the current-account balance.

37. As may be seen from equations (4.28) and (4.30), this conclusion would be valid even if base-money demand had been highly sensitive to changes in domestic interest rates (high value of β_1), provided $\alpha_2 + h' \sim 0$.

38. Both U.S. and Canadian GNP growth tended to attain a cyclical peak (trough) in the expansion (contraction stage of the reference cycle.

39. Over this subperiod, the contemporaneous correlation between the growth in Canadian and U.S. nominal GNP amounted to 0.43. The corresponding correlation for real GNP was −0.05.

40. While in the United States GNP tended to vary with the reference cycle, that relationship was less pronounced in Canada, especially in the latter part of the first subperiod (see also Chart 4-3). A useful topic for future research would be to appraise the quality of the available reference-cycle series and the Urquhart GNP estimates as indicators of cyclical movements in Canadian economic activity.

41. The cyclical behaviour of the GNP deflator was curious. Over the first subperiod, its cyclical amplitude was larger in Canada than in the United States. After 1896, its cyclical variability in both countries was small. As indicated in Chapter 4, the Canadian GNP deflator was unrelated to the reference cycle for a major part of the second subperiod (Chart 4-3). See also note 43.

42. But the cyclical amplitudes become virtually identical. If the observations for 1893/94 and 1894/95 are excluded, average GNP growth in the first subperiod assumes the following values (expansions/contractions): Canada (6.3/−1.0); United States (5.9/−0.9). The corresponding averages for the second subperiod, excluding the observations for 1907/08 to 1909/10, are: Canada (10.8/7.8); United States (8.7/5.7).

43. No attempt is made to examine separately the transmission channels for Canadian output and prices. The behaviour of the Canadian GNP deflator defies explanation. Therefore, all the variables are expressed in nominal terms.

44. Dick and Floyd (1987a, 119-20) also find a positive and contemporaneous correlation between the Canadian money stock and foreign prices (or real income). However, their interpretation of this evidence differs from my own.

CHAPTER 6

THE CRISIS OF 1907*

An important feature of the pre-1914 Canadian gold standard was its ability to operate with a minimum of government intervention on the money and foreign exchange markets. As I pointed out in Chapters 2 and 3, the government followed — for the most part — a passive monetary policy stance. Save for the debt-management experiments conducted until the mid-1880s, monetary policy meant little else than to alter the supply of Dominion notes passively in response to fluctuations in the official gold reserve. The emergency measures taken by the government during the financial crisis of October and November, 1907, however, constitute an important departure from its laissez-faire approach.

The crisis of 1907 has received considerable attention in the existing literature since it prompted the Canadian government to assume, for the first time, the role of lender of last resort to the banking system. The emergency measures foreshadowed the fundamental reorientation of Canadian monetary policy that was to result from the passage of the Finance Act of 1914.

Although various — mostly contemporary — accounts of the crisis of 1907 are available, little is known about the causes of the financial stringency. In as much as the causes of the crisis are discussed at all, existing studies (especially Johnson, 1910) tend to stress various internal factors. A re-examination of the evidence, however, casts serious doubt on the validity of existing interpretations of the crisis. In this chapter, an alternative view is offered. I show that the monetary analysis of the Canadian business cycle developed in the preceding chapters sheds light on the causes of the crisis, provided that analysis is extended to take account of seasonal movements in the Canadian balance of payments. The main thesis advanced in this chapter is that the 1907 crisis was attributable to the coincidence of a cyclical trough in Canadian international monetary assets and bank reserves with an unusually severe seasonal deterioration in the balance of payments, rather than to purely internal factors. The remainder of this chapter is organized as follows. In Section 6.1, I chronicle the events that led up to the crisis. Section 6.2 demonstrates that existing studies have not correctly traced the causes of the financial stringency. Section 6.3 is devoted to an analysis of the seasonal pattern of the pre-1914 Canadian balance of payments, while the causes of the crisis are examined in Section 6.4.

6.1. A CHRONICLE OF THE CRISIS

The financial crisis started in the United States. As a result of a strong cyclical expansion in economic activity, U.S. money markets tightened considerably, with a severe financial squeeze appearing in the summer of 1907. On October 22, the monetary stringency culminated in a veritable panic, due to the collapse of the Knickerbocker Trust Company of New York. The failure of that institution triggered massive deposit withdrawals from banks throughout the United States. Numerous institutions were compelled to suspend specie payments and bank failures were an everyday occurrence. The scramble for liquidity caused interest rates in New York and other parts of the United States to surge to record levels (Chart 2-1).[1] The financial panic ushered in a drastic slump in U.S. economic activity. Although the recession was short-lived, the repercussions of the crisis were far-reaching. The panic greatly stimulated the debate on banking reform and led to the establishment of the U.S. National Monetary Commission, whose deliberations resulted in the creation of the Federal Reserve System.

In his path-breaking study of the New York money market, Goodhart (1969, 29) argues that the severity of the U.S. financial crisis was attributable to a coincidence of cyclical and seasonal peaks in money demand.[2] The evidence suggests that U.S. economic activity attained a cyclical peak in May, 1907 (Table 2-1). Furthermore, U.S. money demand tended to rise in the autumn, when the crops were moved from the interior to the seaboard and to overseas destinations. Since New York banks were heavily engaged in financing agricultural trade, the seasonal fluctuations in U.S. money demand were associated with corresponding movements in short-term interest rates in New York and other U.S. financial centres. The New York call-loan rate, for example, typically reached a seasonal peak in December and a trough in the summer (Chart 2-1). When — as in the autumn of 1907 — the seasonal bulge in money demand came on top of a cyclical peak, the New York money market tightened to such an extent that short-term interest rates were pushed up to very high levels.

The U.S. financial stringency quickly developed into an international crisis. The New York crash was followed by a drastic tightening of Canadian and European money markets. As in the United States, money demand in Canada invariably peaked during the crop-moving season. Owing to the strained financial conditions, the chartered banks in Canada strove to cut back their lending even though the wheat crop was just about to be shipped to the East. Western farmers' associations and grain dealers complained that the chartered banks were unwilling to loan the funds needed to move the crop. The difficulties were compounded by the fact that, due to poor weather, the grain was harvested later than usual. Moreover, a large part of the crop was damaged by frost and could not be stored over the winter. In order to minimize the losses from storage, it was imperative to ship the crop as quickly as possible. In response to Western anxieties, the government, on November 20, 1907, decided to ease the credit squeeze and undertook to offer advances to chartered banks involved in financing the grain trade. The advances were made through the Bank of Montreal against the collateral of high-grade securities.[3] The government provided the funds required to finance the advances in the form of Dominion notes deposited with the Bank. The additional notes were issued on an uncovered basis.[4] Although the government was authorized to circulate $10 million worth of additional notes, the banks only chose to borrow $5.3 million under the emergency scheme. The advances were supplied between November 20, 1907, and January 2, 1908, and were fully repaid by the end of April, 1908 (Jamieson, 1955, 38). Interestingly, the request for emergency assistance originated entirely with Western agricultural interests, whereas the chartered banks were reluctant to participate in the scheme. Despite the disturbed financial conditions, the chartered banks did not need government help. No Canadian bank was forced to suspend specie payments, nor did any bank failures take place.

Since the Canadian crisis reached its climax shortly after the New York crash, one would expect that the turbulence in the United States was a major cause of the Canadian credit squeeze. Nevertheless, existing studies of the 1907 crisis, surprisingly, do not attach much importance to the external causes of the Canadian difficulties, but tend to stress internal factors that allegedly were responsible for the credit squeeze. In the following section, I examine various possible internal and external causes of the crisis.

6.2. INTERNAL AND EXTERNAL CAUSES OF THE CRISIS

6.2.1. Internal Causes

The Canadian crisis — like the New York crash — occurred at the end of a vigorous business-cycle expansion that caused a marked tightening of the domestic money market. In Canada, economic activity began to pick up in June, 1904, and attained a cyclical peak in December, 1906, about half a year earlier than in the United States (Table 2-1). As was concluded in the preceding chapter, a cyclical upturn in Canadian economic activity was normally accompanied by a rise in short-term interest rates, prompted by a deterioration in the balance of payments and an attendant contraction of bank reserves (relative to trend). That increase in short-term interest rates typically set in near the midpoint of a business-cycle expansion and continued until the midpoint of the subsequent contraction. For this reason, the Montreal call-loan rate began to rise in the second half of 1905 and climbed by about 1.5 percentage points to a level of 6 percent, which was considered high by the standards of the pre-1914 period. As may be seen from Chart 2-1, it remained at that level throughout 1907 and the first quarter of 1908. Although interest rates were high, the cyclical tightening of the money market, by itself, does not explain why that business-cycle expansion developed into a financial crisis, since Canadian banks up to that moment had never encountered major difficulties in absorbing cyclical losses of reserves. What was unusual about the situation in 1907 was not the monetary tightness as such, but the severity of the squeeze.

As far as the severity of the financial stringency is concerned, most contemporary observers believed that the source of the difficulties resided mainly in a decline in the seasonal elasticity of the bank-note circulation, besides the problems caused by poor weather. Canadian demand for bank notes invariably rose during the crop-moving season, attaining a seasonal peak in October or November (Curtis, 1931a, 21). The chartered banks, in turn, accommodated the seasonal swings in note demand by corresponding changes in supply. The banks' ability to adapt their note issue to fluctuations in demand, however, was not unlimited. As I showed in Chapter 1, the Canadian Bank Act stipulated that a bank's note issue was not to exceed its paid-up capital. For a long time, the statutory ceiling imposed by the Bank Act did not constrain the supply of bank notes, for the note issue remained well below paid-up capital. But around the middle of the 1890s, the note issue began to rise relative to paid-up capital and gradually approached the statutory ceiling in the early 1900s (Curtis, 1931a, 20, 33).

In a study prepared for the U.S. National Monetary Commission, Johnson (1910, ch. 8) analyzed the 1907 crisis in detail and argued that the statutory ceiling was a major cause of the difficulties. In his opinion, the banks were reluctant to expand lending during the last three months of 1907. They were concerned that the demand for bank notes would rise above the ceiling if they were too generous in accommodating the seasonal increase in activity. Since the penalty attached to excess issues was prohibitive,[5] the banks took pains to keep their note circulation within the limits of the Bank Act. Of course, they could have met the additional currency demand by paying out Dominion notes in lieu of their own notes, but this would have depleted their cash reserves and diminished their ability to accommodate the seasonal rise in activity. In Johnson's (1910, 118-19) own words,

> the banks dared not make large advances to the buyers of grain lest the depletion of their reserves or an excessive issue of notes should result ... [N]o bank felt that it could authorize its branches to increase the issue of notes; the risk of being called upon to pay the penalty for excessive issue was too great.

The government apparently shared the views espoused by Johnson. In his budget speech of March 17, 1908 (see note 3), Finance Minister Fielding outlined the emergency measures and ventured the opinion that the seasonal elasticity of the bank-note issue should be enhanced if similar crises were to be avoided in the future. To this end, Parliament, in 1908, passed an amendment to the Bank Act, known as the crop-moving provisions (see Chapter 1).

Although the statutory ceiling, sooner or later, was bound to impinge on the banks' lending behaviour, I doubt that the 1907 crisis was attributable to a decline in the seasonal elasticity of currency supply. The bank-note issue began to push against the statutory ceiling for the first time in October, 1902, when it climbed to a seasonal high of 95 percent of paid-up capital. In the period 1903 through 1906, the autumnal peaks in the note issue remained near the ceiling, reaching a level of 91 to 94 percent of paid-up capital. The high of 93 percent attained in November, 1907, was not exceptionally large as compared with the seasonal maxima recorded between 1902 and 1906.[6] Considering the patterns of the note issue and paid-up capital, I fail to see how the Johnson thesis accounts for the timing of the crisis.[7] Of course, the statutory ceiling, if at all, may not have constrained the banks' ability to accommodate the autumnal surge is the demand for credit and currency until 1907. In this event, the seasonal amplitude of the bank-note issue should have shrunk significantly in that year.

The seasonal amplitude of the note issue may be estimated from data on the largest amount of bank notes in circulation at any time during the month, with the spread between the months showing the largest and smallest amount of notes in circulation employed as a measure of seasonal amplitude. Between 1896 and 1906, that spread varied from 20 to 32 percent of the average annual note circulation. No significant reduction in the spread was recorded in 1907. That year's 21 percent figure was relatively low, but still within the normal range of fluctuations.[8]

Had the statutory ceiling served as a binding constraint, I would further expect that the banks were forced to pay out Dominion notes in lieu of their own notes to meet the seasonal increase in currency demand. However, as will be shown later, the fourth quarter of 1907 did not witness an unusual rise in the circulation of Dominion notes outside the banking system. All in all, it is hard to see how concern about the statutory ceiling could have precipitated the crisis of 1907.

6.2.2. External Causes

While the seasonal elasticity of the bank-note issue attracted a great deal of attention, possible external causes of the crisis went largely unnoticed. In particular, most contemporary observers failed to realize that immediately after the New York crash, the exceptionally high interest rates in New York caused the Montreal price of New York exchange to rise above the gold export point. The premium on New York exchange provided an incentive to move gold to New York. On November 30, 1907, the *Monetary Times* (p. 871) reported that $2 million worth of gold had been shipped from Montreal to New York. It also pointed out that the government was worried about the gold drain and had taken steps to stem the flow of precious metal to New York.[9] Since a gold outflow tended to diminish bank cash reserves, it is possible that as a result of the New York crash, Canadian banks were compelled to curtail their lending to safeguard their liquidity position. Apart from a few financial journalists, contemporary observers did not believe that gold was exported from Canada in the wake of the New York crash. On the contrary, they claimed that international gold flows had served to moderate the Canadian monetary stringency. For example, Johnson (1910, 117) noticed that during October and November, 1907, the Canadian banks had cut drastically their call loans to foreigners and had increased simultaneously their cash reserves. In his opinion, the chartered banks reacted to the New York crash by withdrawing gold from U.S. banks. Johnson's view is shared by Goodhart (1969, 152), who argues that the difficulties in New York prompted the Canadian banks to convert foreign call loans into gold.

The belief that international gold flows tended to assuage the Canadian monetary stringency rests on the traditional view as to how the Canadian banks responded to seasonal fluctuations in money demand. Johnson (1910, 94-99) succinctly summarized the traditional view. In his opinion, the banks satisfied the additional money demand during the crop-moving season by augmenting their domestic loans and liabilities. Moreover,

> as their liabilities increase ...on account of expanding deposits and note circulation, they reduce their call loans in New York City, and so add a few million to their cash reserves (1910, 95).

Consequently, the seasonal expansion in credit and deposits was sustained by a gold inflow from New York. Similar views were expressed by Finance Minister Fielding (Canada, *Debates,* 1907-08, 4307), contemporary financial journalists (see *Monetary Times,* November 30, 1907, 865) and by Denison (1967, 295). In essence, the Canadian banks were thought to regard New York as a lender of last resort that could always be relied upon as a source of cash when money was scarce. New York's alleged lender-of-last resort function led Viner (1924, 182) to reason that the Canadian banks, in periods of financial sringency, frequently compounded the liquidity problems of New York banks. If the traditional view of the seasonal adjustment mechanism were valid, it would not be sensible to trace the Canadian crisis to the New York crash. Rather, one would have to argue that liquidity management of the Canadian banks was one of many factors responsible for the monetary squeeze in New York.

Needless to say, there is nothing specifically Canadian about the views enunciated by Johnson. The same kind of adjustment mechanism was thought to operate within the United States. According to the traditional view as applied to the United States, the crop-moving season saw substantial flows of cash from New York to the interior in response to an increase in money demand by the agricultural sector, while during the slack season cash was returned to New York. The traditional view, however, has been challenged by Goodhart

(1969). In his opinion, cash tended to flow from the interior to New York in the crop-moving season. Whatever the merit of Goodhart's assault on the traditional view as applied to the United States, a re-examination of the Canadian evidence suggests that Johnson's account of the adjustment mechanism is inconsistent with the facts. If the nature of that mechanism is properly understood, the severity of the 1907 crisis may be readily explained. An analysis of seasonal movements in the Canadian balance of payments provides the key to understanding the 1907 crisis.

6.3. SEASONAL MOVEMENTS IN THE CANADIAN BALANCE OF PAYMENTS

6.3.1. The Seasonal Adjustment Mechanism: The Evidence

Tables 6-1 to 6-3 help to explain the relationship between seasonal movements in the Canadian money stock and the balance of payments. The analysis is confined to the period 1900-13 because reliable quarterly data on international monetary assets are unavailable for earlier years. Table 6-1 clearly indicates that the money stock and international monetary assets were subject to pronounced seasonal fluctuations. Moreover, there was a fairly close positive correlation between the seasonal swings in the two aggregates. The growth in both the money stock and international monetary assets typically started to accelerate in the spring and attained a seasonal peak in the second or third quarter. From October to December, the money stock normally increased further, but at a much lower rate than during the preceding quarter. The growth in international monetary assets also slowed down; the fourth quarter frequently saw them decline in absolute terms. Finally, in the first quarter, the money stock did not change much, while international monetary assets typically continued to shrink.

In Table 6-2, an attempt is made to determine and compare the seasonal amplitudes of international monetary assets and the money stock. To this end, the trend and cyclical fluctuations are eliminated from the data. The series, thus adjusted, will be termed adjusted international monetary assets (AI) and the adjusted money stock (AM). They capture mainly the seasonal swings in the data and, therefore, can be used for estimating the seasonal amplitudes of the two aggregates. Table 6-2 shows the end-of-quarter averages of AI and AM for the years 1901 to 1912. The evidence suggests that AI fluctuated more strongly than AM, but the difference in the seasonal amplitudes of the two aggregates was small. Thus, the seasonal swings in the Canadian money stock were matched by corresponding swings in international monetary assets. The similarity of seasonal movements in the two aggregates is confirmed by the following regression equation:

$$\underset{}{AM} = \underset{(0.25)}{0.79} + \underset{(9.06)}{0.78}\,AI, \quad \bar{R}^2 = 0.65,\ DW = 1.97, \qquad (6.1)$$

sample period: 1901IV-1912IV.

Equation (6.1) is estimated using the Cochrane-Orcutt technique since the corresponding OLS estimates are marred by strong serial correlation in the residuals.[10] However, both estimation procedures yield virtually identical parameter estimates for AI. Equation (6.1) corroborates my earlier result that the seasonal variance of AI was slightly higher than that of AM.

Unlike AI and AM, bank loans to domestic borrowers, surprisingly, did not fluctuate much over the year. As indicated by Table 6-2, adjusted domestic bank loans tended to decline somewhat during the harvest and crop-moving season, but it should be noted that their seasonal pattern was less regular than that of the adjusted money stock. Considering the importance attached by

TABLE 6-1
QUARTERLY CHANGES IN CANADIAN INTERNATIONAL MONETARY ASSETS AND THE MONEY STOCK
(Millions of Dollars)

	Int. Monetary Assets (1)	Money Stock (2)		Int. Monetary Assets (1)	Money Stock (2)
			1907 I	-21.6	-11.3
			II	14.9	17.7
			III	9.2	1.4
1900 IV	9.1	7.2	IV	-19.6	-36.4
1901 I	3.1	5.5	1908 I	13.8	-11.9
II	5.0	15.4	II	25.1	12.5
III	15.6	15.9	III	63.6	42.4
IV	-3.8	4.3	IV	15.7	34.7
1902 I	-7.0	-0.3	1909 I	-	9.8
II	11.3	9.8	II	5.7	35.3
III	7.5	20.6	III	21.9	41.8
IV	-5.1	8.0	IV	0.5	45.9
1903 I	-12.2	2.1	1910 I	-5.4	11.6
II	6.5	6.6	II	9.3	31.9
III	10.1	18.7	III	6.7	30.1
IV	-0.6	4.4	IV	-40.1	-3.6
1904 I	-3.2	7.8	1911 I	0.8	6.5
II	1.7	16.2	II	25.1	42.7
III	25.7	21.0	III	17.9	34.7
IV	7.2	10.8	IV	-8.6	20.5
1905 I	-3.2	0.9	1912 I	5.1	18.2
II	-7.3	11.9	II	34.9	69.1
III	22.1	31.7	III	-19.1	2.6
IV	-7.8	16.1	IV	-27.4	-12.3
1906 I	-5.4	18.0	1913 I	-0.5	-11.4
II	-2.8	10.5	II	-2.2	0.4
III	17.1	28.0	III	-9.9	17.3
IV	-8.0	24.6	IV	39.7	-10.6

Source: Table A-2

contemporary observers to seasonal movements in the demand for credit, I am puzzled by the evidence of Table 6-2. Apparently, contemporary observers were mistaken in their belief that the credit needs of the agricultural sector caused the demand for domestic bank loans to surge in the autumn.[11] During the harvest and crop-moving season, the chartered banks were called upon mainly to augment the money supply, but not to provide additional loans to domestic borrowers. The seasonal expansion in the money supply, in turn, was backed entirely by a rise in Canadian holdings of international monetary assets. Clearly, financing agricultural trade was a money problem, not a credit problem.

Table 6-3 shows how the various components of the Canadian balance of payments contributed to the seasonal movements in international monetary assets. It offers quarterly data on the overall balance-of-payments surplus (or quarterly first differences in international monetary assets), the merchandise trade surplus (deficit) and extended residual inflows (ER). In contrast to resid-

TABLE 6-2
SEASONAL MOVEMENTS IN INTERNATIONAL MONETARY ASSETS, THE MONEY STOCK AND DOMESTIC BANK LOANS, 1901-12
(Millions of Dollars)

Average Stock at End of Quarter	International Monetary Assets (Adjusted) (1)	Money Stock (Adjusted) (2)	Domestic Bank Loans (Adjusted) (3)
<u>1901-11</u>			
IV	-	2.8	-2.1
<u>1902-12</u>			
I	-8.9	-9.8	1.4
II	-1.3	-0.8	1.4
III	12.9	9.4	-2.6
IV	-1.1	3.2	-0.5

Sources and estimation methods for Table 6-2

Sources

Columns (1) and (2): Table A-2.
Column (3): Total loans in Canada (Curtis, 1931a, 50). This series covers loans to domestic borrowers and appears to be reasonably homogenous (Curtis, 1931a, 12). It includes the following items: current loans in Canada; call and short loans in Canada; loans to the Dominion government; loans to provincial governments; and from July, 1913, onwards loans to cities, towns, municipalities and school districts. Before July, 1913, the last item was subsumed in "current loans in Canada."

Estimation methods

The data shown in the table are averages of end-of-quarter differences between the actual and smoothed values of the respective aggregate. The data are smoothed by a seven-quarter moving average. See Table 3-2 for the smoothing procedure.

ual inflows as shown in Table 3-1, ER cover the non-merchandise trade surplus and capital inflows, and are estimated by taking the difference between the overall and merchandise trade surplus. Since the requisite quarterly data are unavailable, it is impossible to separate capital inflows from the non-merchandise trade surplus. Note that the quarterly data on the merchandise trade surplus employed in this chapter differ somewhat from the annual data presented in Table A-3. Furthermore, the overall surplus is split up into inflows of monetary gold and secondary reserves.

The thirteen-year averages presented in the top four rows of Table 6-3 clearly reveal the seasonal attributes of the Canadian balance of payments. As would be expected, the merchandise trade surplus increased strongly during the second half of the year and reached a seasonal peak in the fourth quarter.[12] Interestingly enough, the seasonal movements in the overall surplus did not parallel those in the trade surplus. The seasonal increase in the overall surplus from the first to the second quarter was due mainly to an acceleration of ER. The further expansion from the second to the third quarter, by contrast, reflected the improvement in the trade balance setting in after the start of the harvest season. However, the overall surplus did not rise as much as the trade surplus since the seasonal improvement in the trade balance was largely offset by a decline in ER. The movements in the overall surplus between the third and fourth quarter, once again, were dominated by ER. Paradoxically, the overall surplus declined sharply, despite a massive rise in the trade surplus. Thus, except for the changes between the second and third quarter, the seasonal fluctuations in the overall surplus were dominated by extended residual inflows.

Table 6-3 further indicates that the seasonal swings in the overall surplus were settled both by flows of monetary gold and secondary reserves. Much like the overall surplus, the growth of the monetary gold stock and secondary reserves tended to accelerate between the first and second quarter and to slow down between the third and fourth quarter. However, the seasonal amplitude of secondary reserves was much stronger than that of monetary gold. During the fourth quarter, secondary reserves normally declined absolutely, while the monetary gold stock continued to grow, albeit at a slower rate than during the preceding quarter.

6.3.2. The Seasonal Adjustment Mechanism: An Interpretation

A re-examination of the seasonal adjustment mechanism suggests that extended residual inflows were instrumental in generating seasonal fluctuations in Canadian international monetary assets and the money stock. Thus, if the working of the adjustment mechanism is to be understood, one must explain the seasonal movements in ER. In all probability, these movements mirrored strong seasonal swings in Canadian net imports of short-term capital, for it is hard to see how non-merchandise trade could have accounted for the sharp temporary drop in ER normally recorded in the fourth quarter.[13] Moreover, the seasonal movements in ER were likely due to shifts in short-term foreign borrowing or lending by Canadian non-bank residents. Aside from secondary reserves, the

TABLE 6-3

SEASONAL MOVEMENTS IN BALANCE OF PAYMENTS AND MONETARY BASE, 1901-13
(Millions of Dollars)

	Balance of Payments					Δ Uncovered	Δ Monetary Base		
Quarter	Merchandise Trade balance[a]	Extended Residual Inflows[b]	Overall Surplus			Dominion Notes	Total	of which	
			Total	Δ Monetary Gold	ΔSecondary Reserves			Bank Cash Reserves	Dominion Notes Outside Banks
	(1)	(2)	(3)=(1)+(2)	(4)	(5)	(6)	(7)=(3)+(6) =(5)+(8)+(9)	(8)	(9)
Average									
1901-1913									
I	-36.0	33.3	-2.7	-0.9	-1.8	-0.3	-3.0	-0.7	-0.4
II	-33.8	43.6	9.8	3.9	5.9	-	9.8	2.9	1.0
III	-19.0	33.5	14.5	5.2	9.3	-	14.5	4.1	1.0
IV	1.3	-5.8	-4.5	2.0	-6.5	0.5	-4.0	3.2	-0.7
Year									
1907									
I	-41.7	20.1	-21.6	-1.7	-20.1	-0.6	-22.2	-2.1	-
II	-46.9	61.8	14.9	5.0	10.0	-	14.9	4.4	0.6
III	-11.5	20.7	9.2	3.5	5.8	-0.3	8.9	2.7	0.4
IV	-11.7	-7.9	-19.6	-2.4	-17.3	6.0	-13.5	4.2	-0.5

a) Merchandise exports minus imports. The latter do not include imports for re-export, for which monthly data are not available for the entire period 1901-13.
b) Overall surplus minus merchandise trade balance.

Sources for Table 6-3

Column (1): 1901-02: Canada, *Monthly Reports*, fiscal 1909. 1903-13: Canada, Department of Customs, *Trade and Navigation. Unrevised Monthly Statements*, 1905-13. These sources contain monthly data on merchandise exports and imports entered for consumption. The export and import data exclude trade in coin and bullion.
Column (3): Overall surplus equals quarterly first differences in international monetary assets (See Table 6-1).
Columns (4), (5), (7) and (9): Table A-2 or legend to that table.
Column (6): Chart 3-4.
Column (8): See legend to Table 3-5.

Canadian banks' foreign assets and liabilities did not fluctuate much over the year and, therefore, do not account for the observed seasonal pattern of extended residual inflows.[14]

The significant role non-bank borrowing or lending appears to have played in the adjustment mechanism is surprising since existing research suggests that foreign short-term assets and liabilities of Canadian non-bank residents were negligible (Cairncross, 1968, 169-70). It is probably true that Canadian non-banks did not hold foreign bank deposits and did not raise loans from foreign banks to any great extent. However, they might have lent funds to foreigners through leads and lags in export finance, a possibility overlooked in existing studies of Canadian capital flows. In my opinion, leads and lags were likely to be an important phenomenon since existing accounts of pre-1914 Canadian export finance do not make sense unless it is assumed that Canadian producers normally were paid for exports well after goods shipped to other countries had crossed the Canadian border.

According to contemporary observers, Canadian banks typically financed exports of grain up to the point at which the shipments reached the eastern seaports. After the harvest, western farmers transported their grain to a nearby elevator or to Winnipeg, where it was purchased by milling companies or large dealers. The farmers were paid in bank notes, which the buyers of the grain obtained by raising loans from the chartered banks.[15] Grain destined for export to Europe was then shipped along the Great Lakes route to the eastern seaports. With the assistance of the chartered banks, Canadian dealers drew "inland" drafts on New York and other export houses charged with shipping the grain. These export houses in turn negotiated sterling or continental bills of exchange on behalf of their Canadian customers, who sold these bills in the New York money market, probably with the help of Canadian banks.[16] Thus, upon arrival of the grain at the eastern seaports, Canadian dealers received cash, which they used to repay their loans from the chartered banks.

This account of Canadian export finance possesses two features that are at variance with the empirical evidence. First, had Canadian grain dealers cashed their sterling or continental bills of exchange upon arrival of their shipments at the eastern seaports, I would expect that seasonal peaks in the overall balance-of-payments surplus coincided with, or lagged somewhat, the corresponding peaks in the merchandise trade surplus. As indicated above, the overall surplus normally peaked roughly one or two quarters earlier than the merchandise trade surplus. Second, seasonal peaks in the money stock should have lead, rather than coincided with, seasonal peaks in international monetary assets.

The above analysis may be reconciled with the empirical evidence if it is assumed that Canadian export credit was sensitive to (a) the merchandise trade balance, (b) New York money market rates and (c) changes in the transactions demand for domestic money induced by seasonal movements in Canadian economic activity. The autumnal surge in the trade surplus might have been counteracted, at least in part, by a rise in export credit growth and, hence, by a decline in ER. Moreover, the sharp increase in New York money market rates toward the end of the year might have lowered ER further by prompting Canadian exporters to postpone cashing their sterling or continental bills of exchange. For these reasons, export receipts might have lagged exports. Finally, it is possible that Canadian exporters took account of their needs for transactions balances in timing their sales of bills of exchange. They might have met a seasonal rise in demand for transactions balances by substituting domestic money for export credit, thereby reducing the lag between export receipts and exports. Similarly, they might have accommodated a seasonal drop in money demand by lengthening that lag.

The relationship between ER and these three factors is explored in two steps because it is difficult to construct a satisfactory indicator of seasonal fluctuations in pre-1914 Canadian economic activity. In a first step, only factors (a) and (b) are considered. For this reason, ER are regressed on the merchandise trade surplus (TS) and quarterly first differences in the New York call-loan rate ($r_{\rho N}$). The latter is employed as a measure of borrowing costs in the New York money market. The analysis rests on the assumption that levels of interest rates determined stocks, rather than flows, of foreign capital. Due to a marked increase in ER over the sample period, the regression equation also includes a linear time trend. OLS estimates for the period 1901I-1913IV point to a highly significant inverse relationship between ER and TS:

$$\begin{aligned} ER &= \underset{(0.07)}{0.37} - \underset{(-0.99)}{0.61}\, \Delta r_{\rho N} - \underset{(-6.77)}{0.78}\, TS + \underset{(1.40)}{0.30}\, t, \qquad (6.2) \\ \bar{R}^2 &= 0.70,\ DW = 1.91. \end{aligned}$$

The size of the estimated TS parameter suggests that movements in the trade balance — at least in the short run — were largely offset by capital flows. As a matter of fact, the null hypothesis that the TS parameter equalled unity can be rejected only at the 90 percent and lower levels of significance. As would be expected, ER were also inversely related to first differences in the New York call-loan rate, but the latter variable was not statistically significant. This result, however, need not imply that ER were insensitive to changes in New York money market rates because of multicollinearity between $\Delta r_{\rho N}$ and TS (r = 0.28). If TS is dropped from equation (6.2), $\Delta r_{\rho N}$ shows up as statistically significant variable (almost at the 99 percent level) with negative sign.[17]

The observed relationship between ER and TS implies that the overall balance-of-payments surplus and the growth in the domestic money stock were virtually invariant to seasonal movements in the trade balance. Over the period 1901I-1913IV, the simple correlation between first differences in the money stock and the trade balance was indeed very small (r = 0.04). However, it appears that international monetary assets and the money stock responded to seasonal movements in domestic economic activity and New York money market rates. In Table 6-4, the seasonal pattern of the money stock is compared to that of quarterly merchandise exports, with the latter employed as an (probably imperfect) indicator of seasonal swings in domestic economic activity. The data presented in Table 6-4 are adjusted in the same way as those in Table 6-2. Since the money stock data represent end-of-quarter stocks, quarterly export flows are centred at the last month of the quarter in order to guard against spurious leads or lags between the two variables. For example, centred exports for the second quarter embrace the flows recorded for May, June and July. Table 6-4 points to a fairly close correlation between seasonal movements in the *level* of the money stock and the *level* of centred exports, even though *first differences* in the money stock were unresponsive to changes in

TABLE 6-4
SEASONAL MOVEMENTS IN THE MONEY STOCK AND EXPORTS
(Millions of Dollars)

Average at End of Quarter	Money Stock (Adjusted)			Centred Exports (Adjusted)
	Total	Notes[a)]	Deposits	
1901-11				
IV	2.8	2.4	0.4	9.6
1902-12				
I	-9.8	-4.6	-5.2	-26.0
II	-0.8	-2.7	1.9	1.2
III	9.4	4.4	5.0	14.3
IV	3.2	3.0	0.2	9.9
1903-13				
I	-10.1	-4.6	-5.5	-26.3
1907				
I	3.4	-0.4	3.8	-28.8
II	19.4	-0.4	19.8	3.6
III	21.3	5.3	16.0	20.1
IV	-17.2	3.0	-20.2	7.7
1908				
I	-37.7	-6.2	-31.5	-24.1

a) Bank notes are not adjusted for float. Notes and cheques on other banks — which were not reported separately — are deducted from deposits.

Sources and estimation methods for Table 6-4

The procedure for calculating the adjusted money stock is described in Table 6-2. The data on the two components of the money stock and on centred merchandise exports are adjusted accordingly. See Table 6-3 for the export data sources.

the *level* of exports (or of the trade surplus). The levels of both variables tended to reach a seasonal trough near the end of the first quarter and a peak near the end of the third quarter.[18]

Further insights into the seasonal adjustment mechanism are gained if the relationship between centred exports and the two principal components of the domestic money stock, that is, notes (Dominion and bank notes) and deposits, is examined. As indicated by Table 6-4, during the crop-moving season, notes were more closely correlated with centred exports than deposits. Both notes and centred exports only decreased slightly in the fourth quarter, but fell strongly in the subsequent three months.[19] Deposits, by contrast, decreased at a steady pace during both the fourth and the first quarter. A plausible explanation for the relatively strong fourth-quarter decrease in deposits — which occurred at the height of the crop-moving season — was the autumnal surge in New York money market rates, inducing Canadian exporters to substitute export credit for domestic deposits. Thus, while notes moved in sympathy with domestic economic activity, it is likely that deposits were responsive to seasonal movements in both domestic economic activity and New York money market rates.[20] As a result of timing their export receipts in accordance with seasonal movements in domestic economic activity and New York money market rates, Canadian exporters were largely responsible for the seasonal gyrations in international monetary assets and the money stock.

In contrast to Canadian exporters, the Canadian government and the chartered banks, for the most part, played a passive role in the seasonal adjustment mechanism. According to Table 6-3, the seasonal swings in international monetary assets were mirrored by corresponding fluctuations in the monetary base. Unlike the balance of payments, uncovered Dominion notes were only a minor source of seasonal variation in the monetary base. Moreover, the seasonal swings in the monetary base mirrored mostly fluctuations in bank cash and secondary reserves. On the whole, a seasonal increase (decrease) in the money stock was balanced by an increase (decrease) in bank reserves of the same order of magnitude.

The similarity of seasonal movements in bank reserves and the money stock implies that the aggregate reserve ratio of the chartered banks normally reached a seasonal peak at the end of the third quarter, as shown by the gap between the actual and smoothed values shown in Chart 6-1.[21] The banks did not react to the increase in their reserve ratios by augmenting their loan supply. They knew that their reserve ratios would go up only temporarily and, therefore, did not see fit to expand lending. Since neither the supply of nor the demand for bank loans was significantly affected by the seasonal rise in Canadian economic activity, Canadian bank loan rates did not vary much over the year. The stability of the Montreal call-loan rate, in particular, was remarkable in the face of the sharp seasonal swings in U.S. short-term interest rates. Even in London, the call-loan rate fluctuated more than in Montreal (Table 6-5).

TABLE 6-5
SEASONAL MOVEMENTS IN CANADIAN, UNITED STATES AND BRITISH SHORT-TERM INTEREST RATES
(Percent)

Averages of End-of-Quarter Rates during Period 1902-13	Quarter I	Quarter II	Quarter III	Quarter IV
Montreal Call Loans	5.3	5.3	5.4	5.6
New York Call Loans	3.5	2.5	3.9	7.2
New York Time Money	4.1	3.4	4.8	5.5
New York Commercial Paper	4.8	4.4	5.3	5.5
Boston Call Loans	4.2	3.3	4.0	5.9
Boston Time Money	4.8	4.4	5.2	5.7
Chicago Commercial Paper	4.9	4.8	5.4	5.6
London Call Loans	2.7	1.7	2.2	2.8

Sources for Table 6-5
Montreal, New York, Boston: Chart 2-1.
Chicago: Goodhart, 1969, Table 14. No quotation is available for the June, 1909, Chicago commercial paper rate. I assume that rate to have amounted to 4 percent (equivalent to the quotations for May and July). Like the other U.S. rates, the Chicago commercial paper rate is an average for the last month of the quarter.
London: Chart 5-5.

In summary, the traditional account of the seasonal adjustment mechanism must be modified in three respects. First, the seasonal movements in the money stock were backed by corresponding movements in international monetary assets, rather than by changes in domestic bank loans. The seasonal swings in the two monetary aggregates were generated by Canadian exporters varying the lags in export finance in response to changes in domestic economic activity and New York money market rates. Second, although the beginning of the harvest season normally saw Canadian imports of monetary gold accelerate, the seasonal advance in gold imports, contrary to Johnson's assertion, did not result from a shift in the composition of bank reserves, but went hand in hand with a sharp rise in inflows of secondary reserves. Third, it is too simplistic to argue that in periods of tight money Canada stepped up her gold imports from New York and, thus, compounded the liquidity problems of banks in that city. Only in the third quarter did a seasonal acceleration of gold imports (Table 6-3) coincide with a rise in short-term interest rates in New York (Table 6-5). In the fourth quarter — when the seasonal stringency in the New York money market reached a climax — Canada tended to curtail substantially her gold imports and, thus, alleviated the liquidity problems of New York banks. In other words, in periods of severe financial strain, Canada typically acted as a lender to the New York money market. Considering the relative size of the Canadian and United States economies, however, I doubt that the fourth-quarter decline in Canadian gold imports was large enough to make a strong imprint on the New York money market.

6.4. THE CAUSES OF THE 1907 CRISIS

As I pointed out in Section 6.1, the 1907 crisis broke out shortly after Canadian economic activity had passed a cyclical peak. International monetary assets, the monetary base, and aggregate reserves of the chartered banks normally reached a cyclical low near the midpoint of a business-cycle contraction. During the contraction of 1907-08, which lasted from December, 1906, to July, 1908, that trough was recorded in the autumn of 1907 (Chart 3-6). As may be seen from the smoothed line in Chart 6-1, the aggregate reserve ratio — whose cyclical movements were dominated by bank reserves — attained a cyclical low at about the same time. Thus, when the crisis erupted, the Canadian banks' liquidity position had already deteriorated as a result of a cyclical expansion in economic activity and the attendant decline in the overall balance-of-payments surplus.

The cyclical decline in the aggregate reserve ratio was reinforced by an exceptionally large seasonal drop in international monetary assets recorded in the fourth quarter of 1907. Therefore, adjusted international monetary assets, expressed as a percentage of the corresponding smoothed values, plunged to a record low (Chart 6-2). As a result of the outflow of monetary gold and secondary reserves, the aggregate reserve ratio of the chartered banks, at the end of 1907, amounted to only 21.1 percent, as compared with an end-of-year average of 26.2 percent for the period 1901-13 as a whole (see note 21). This ratio would have been even lower without the emergency measures adopted by the government. As indicated by Table 6-3, the loss of monetary gold in the fourth quarter of 1907 roughly corresponded to the figure quoted by the *Monetary Times* (see p. 167). Thanks to the emergency issue of Dominion notes, the banks were able to augment their cash reserves by $4.2 million despite the gold outflow (Table 6-3). This increase in cash reserves mirrored not only an expansion in the banks' holdings of Dominion notes but also a rise in their monetary gold stock. The banks apparently boosted their gold holdings by redeeming a portion of the additional Dominion notes issued by the government. The rise in bank holdings of gold recorded in the fourth quarter of 1907 explains why Johnson and Goodhart thought that Canada had imported gold after the New York crash. They overlooked the fact that the increase in these holdings was more than offset by a loss of government gold (Table A-2).

An obvious explanation for the massive contraction in adjusted international monetary assets in the last quarter of 1907 was the surge in New York money market rates elicited by the October crash. As I showed in Section 6.3, it was normal for Canadian capital imports to shrink during the crop-moving season. Part of this decline was due to the improvement in the merchandise trade balance characteristic for this time of the year. The extent

CHART 6-1

AGGREATE RESERVE RATIO OF CHARTERED BANKS, 1900III-1913IV

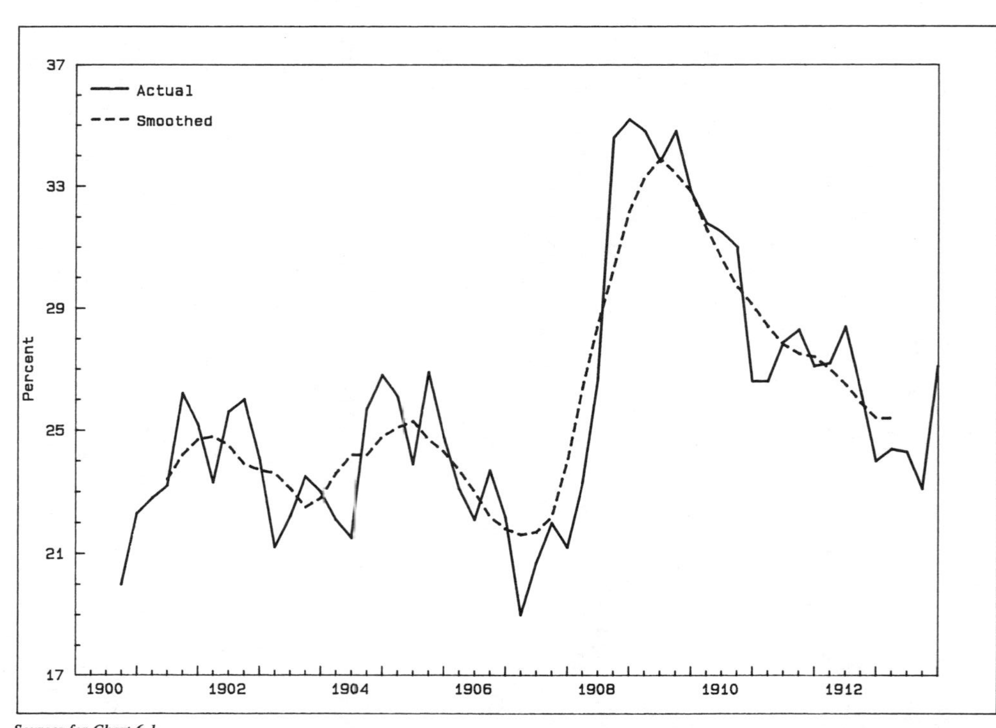

Sources for Chart 6-1

Legend to Table 3-5. To derive the broken line, both aggregate reserves and monetary liabilities are smoothed by a seven-quarter moving average.

CHART 6-2

SEASONAL MOVEMENTS IN INTERNATIONAL MONETARY ASSETS, 1901IV-1912IV
(Deviations from Smoothed Values)

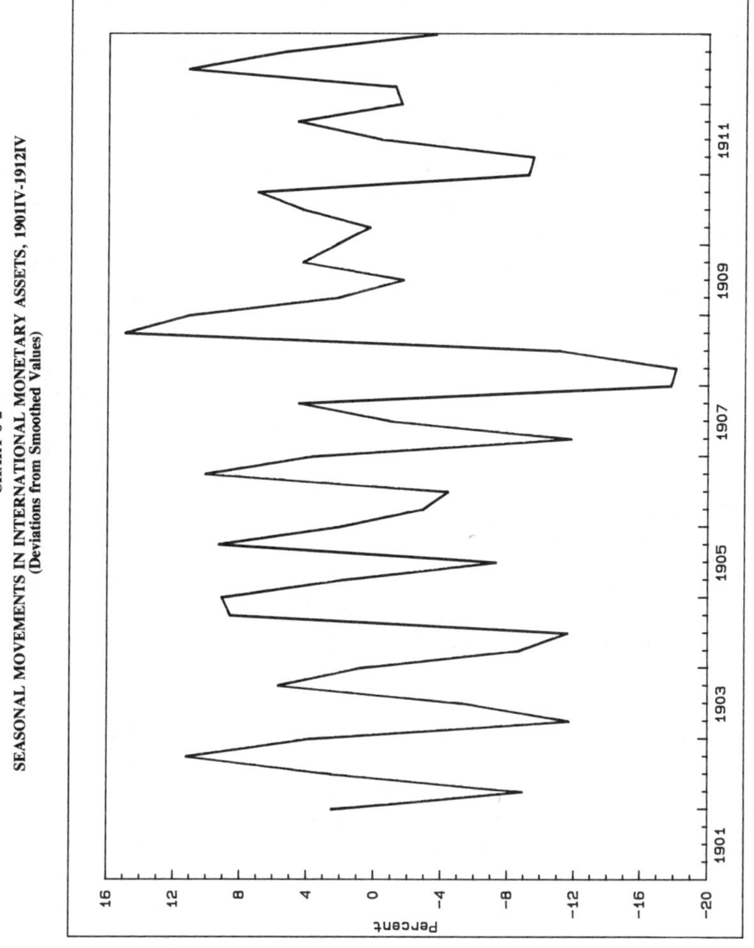

Sources for Chart 6-2
Table A-2. Percentage deviations in international monetary assets from values smoothed by a seven-quarter moving average.

of the 1907 autumnal reduction in capital imports, however, was unusual. In contrast to the patterns typically observed for the period under study, the trade balance did not improve from the third to the fourth quarter. Nevertheless, extended residual inflows fell sharply (Table 6-3). In view of money market conditions in New York, this decline is not surprising. As a result of the October crash, the discount at which bills of exchange could be sold in New York was far greater than usual, inducing Canadian exporters to expand export credit. In November, 1907, the financial press reported that it was practically impossible to sell sterling bills of exchange in New York (see *Monetary Times*, Nov. 16, 1907, 794). In order to finance the additional trade credit, Canadian exporters ran down their domestic money holdings. For this reason, the drop in adjusted international monetary assets during the fourth quarter of 1907 was matched by an equally massive contraction in the adjusted money stock. This decrease in the money stock mirrored largely a fall in deposits, while the behaviour of notes conformed closely to the pattern observed for the period 1901-13 as a whole (Table 6-4). Thus, the evidence is consistent with the view that Canadian exporters substituted trade credit for deposits in the wake of the New York crash.

Through an expansion in trade credit, Canadian exporters assumed the role of lenders to the hard-pressed New York money market. The consequence of that role was the sharp reduction in bank reserves reported for the fourth quarter of 1907. While the drop in Canadian banks' secondary reserves did not make additional cash available to the New York money market, the gold outflow from Canada contributed somewhat to easing the financial squeeze in New York.[22] In view of the precarious state of their liquidity, it is not surprising that the chartered banks took steps to cut back their lending.

Although the government passed its emergency measures with a view to enhancing the seasonal elasticity of the Canadian currency supply, their effect was to neutralize part of the reserve drain triggered by the New York crisis. As may be seen from Table 6-3, the drop in the Canadian monetary base in the fourth quarter of 1907 was much smaller than the overall balance-of-payments deficit because of the temporary expansion in the uncovered stock of Dominion notes. Thus, through the emergency issue of Dominion notes, the government eased the banks' liquidity problems. Normally, the banks managed to absorb the fourth-quarter cash drain to New York without being forced to curtail their lending. However, it appears that in times of financial distress, the ability of a laissez-faire banking system to supply cash to the New York money market was severely overtaxed unless the public was prepared to tolerate a significant reduction in domestic bank lending.

In contrast to Dominion notes in the hands of the chartered banks, non-bank holdings of government money decreased slightly in the fourth quarter of 1907, as was typical for the period under study. [Table 6-3, column (9)]. Since neither bank notes nor Dominion notes outside the banking system behaved abnormally in the autumn of 1907, it is unlikely that the statutory ceiling on the bank-note issue was the source of the difficulties.

6.5. SUMMARY AND CONCLUSIONS

In this chapter I have shown that in periods of severe financial strain Canada acted as a lender to the New York money market. Prior to 1914, money markets in New York and other financial centres typically tightened during the crop-moving season, with short-term interest rates attaining a seasonal peak in December. Contrary to the traditional view of the seasonal adjustment mechanism, Canada did not step up her gold imports when the financial stringency in New York reached its seasonal climax. Instead, the seasonal movements in Canadian gold imports were closely correlated with seasonal movements in the Canadian money stock. Canadian money demand normally peaked at the end of the third quarter, well before New York interest rates attained their seasonal highs. In this chapter I argued that Canadian exporters responded to the autumnal surge in New York money market rates by lengthening the lag between export receipts and exports, thus, increasing their trade credit to foreigners. They financed the additional trade credit by running down their domestic money balances. Since this caused the Canadian money stock, bank reserves and monetary gold holdings to shrink (relative to their trends), gold flows between Canada and the United States contributed to softening the autumnal financial squeeze in New York. Canadian banks in turn did not attempt to stem the reserve loss by raising domestic interest rates, but simply allowed their reserve ratios to decline. Thus, in contrast to Viner's suggestion, Canadian banks, in periods of financial distress, did not compound the liquidity problems in New York.

The role played by Canadian exporters as lenders to the New York money market was particularly pronounced after the 1907 crash. As a result of soaring short-term interest rates in New York, Canadian capital imports shrank drastically, resulting in a massive balance-of-payments deficit, gold outflows and reserve losses by the Canadian banks. The reserve drain triggered by the New York crash occurred at a time when a strong cyclical expansion in economic activity had already led to a substantial deterioration in the banks' liquidity position. To shore up their liquidity, the banks took steps to curtail their lending. The prospect of a credit squeeze prompted the government to provide liquidity assistance to the banks. Thus, the causes of the Canadian crisis were attributable directly to the New York crash. Most contemporary observers offered an alternative explanation of the crisis and argued that it was due to a decline in the seasonal elasticity of the Canadian bank-note issue. In this chapter I have shown that the elasticity of the bank-note issue was unlikely to be the source of the difficulties.

The analysis presented in this chapter suggests that seasonal movements in Canadian international monetary assets and capital flows are best explained by a variant of the monetary approach to balance-of-payments analysis. Seasonal movements in the trade balance did not significantly affect international monetary assets but were largely offset by capital flows. Instead, the seasonal swings in international monetary assets were attributable mainly to changes in domestic money demand, caused by seasonal fluctuation in domestic economic activity and New York interest rates. Trade credit by Canadian exporters to foreigners played a crucial role in generating seasonal movements in Canadian international monetary assets and the money stock.

Endnotes — Chapter 6

1. Chart 2-1 understates the extent of the increase in the New York call-loan rate immediately after the crash. In the fourth week of October, 1907, that rate reached a high of 125 percent (Goodhart, 1969, 133).

2. See Friedman and Schwartz (1963, 156-68) and Goodhart (1969, ch. 4) for excellent discussions of the New York panic.

3. The Bank of Montreal was charged by the government with setting the interest rate on the advances. The Bank also administered the collateral and collected the interest on behalf of the government. For a more detailed discussion of the emergency measures, see the budget speech of March 17, 1908 (Canada, *Debates,* 1907-08, 5151-58), Johnson (1910, 199-222), and Jamieson (1955, 37-40).

4. As a result of the increase in the uncovered note issue, the government failed to meet the minimum gold reserve requirement. In 1908, Parliament sanctioned retroactively the temporary breach of the Dominion Notes Act (Jamieson, 1955, 38-39). The emergency measures were authorized by an Order in Council, rather than by an act of Parliament.

5. The penalty depended upon the size of the excess issue. The maximum penalty, which was applicable to excess issues of over $200,000, amounted to $100,000 (Canada, *Statutes,* 53 Vict. Cap. 31, Section 51).

6. The seasonal peak values of the bank-note issue are expressed as a percentage of paid-up capital at the beginning and end of the month in which a seasonal peak occurred. They are derived from monthly data on the largest amount of bank notes in circulation at any time during the month. These data were collected for the first time in July, 1891 (Curtis, 1931a, 21 and 33).

7. During the crop-moving season of 1906, some banks already complained that the statutory ceiling impeded their ability to meet the increase in currency demand (Beckhart, 1929, 382-83).

8. See note 6 for the data source. From 1892 to 1895, the spread was consistently smaller than 20 percent.

9. Normal practice was to redeem the Dominion notes in U.S. eagles. In an effort to curb the gold drain, the government decided to pay out sovereigns in lieu of eagles. See Chapter 7 of this technique of restricting gold outflows.

10. The numbers in parentheses stand for t-values.

11. The evidence of Table 6-2, of course, need not imply that credit demand by the agricultural sector failed to rise during the harvest and crop-moving season. It is possible that the increase in agricultural credit demand was offset by a reduction in credit demand by other sectors of the economy.

12. In 1907, the seasonal peak in the merchandise trade surplus fell into the third quarter. However, the value for 1907III was virtually the same as that for 1907IV.

13. Freight, tourism and non-commercial remittances were the components of non-merchandise trade most likely to display seasonal fluctuations. I doubt that payments and receipts on account of freight and tourism were responsible for the fourth-quarter drop in ER. From 1901 to 1913, payments and receipts on account of the two components of non-merchandise trade were approximately balanced. Moreover, for both tourism and freight, payments and receipts probably displayed the same seasonal patterns, that is, net receipts did not vary significantly over the year. It is possible that Canadian non-commercial remittances to foreigners peaked in the fourth quarter since during the crop-moving season farmers and merchants possessed ample funds for making such payments. However, for this item to explain the fourth-quarter drop in residual inflows, one would have to assume that the funds were remitted exclusively between October and Decem-

ber. Over the period 1901-13, non-commercial remittances to foreigners averaged $40.3 million per year, a sum that roughly equalled the drop in ER between the third and fourth quarter (Table 6-3). It seems implausible to assume that non-commercial remittances were made exclusively in the fourth quarter. See Hartland (1955, Table XXXI) for annual data on the various components on non-merchandise trade.

14. In addition to secondary reserves, the banks showed on their books other current loans to and deposits from foreigners (Curtis, 1931a, 21, 52). These two balance-sheet items did not fluctuate much over the year. For example, in the third and fourth quarter of 1907, net imports of capital by the banks, other than in the form of net reductions in secondary reserves, amounted to $ − 0.3 and $ − 4.0 million respectively (Δ deposits abroad minus Δ other current loans abroad). The variable ER, by contrast, shrank from $20.7 to $ − 7.9 million (Table 6-3). Thus, banks only accounted for 13 percent of the reduction in ER between the second and third quarter of 1907.

15. For a good discussion of Canadian export finance, see the interview granted by Finance Minister Fielding to the *Monetary Times,* Nov. 16, 1907, 796-98. From that interview it is not entirely clear how the additional bank notes were brought into circulation. Fielding merely stated that the notes were "loaned" to the farmers.

16. Fielding did not explain in detail how the bills of exchange were sold in New York.

17. First differences in the Montreal call-loan rate (r), if introduced in the estimated equations as an additional independent variable, always appear with a wrong sign. Moreover, the explanatory power of the equations is not improved much if ER is regressed on the differential, $\Delta r\text{-}\Delta r_{\rho N}$. This piece of evidence — confirming the message of Table 6-2 — suggests that the autumnal increase in export credit was not financed by raising additional loans from the chartered banks.

18. Over the period 1901IV-1912IV, the simple correlation between the adjusted money stock and adjusted centred exports amounted to 0.5. A similar result is obtained for the correlation between first differences in the unadjusted values of the two variables.

19. As was the case for bank notes, merchandise exports tended to peak in October or November.

20. In the spring and summer, notes were less closely correlated with exports than deposits. However, exports may not have been a reliable indicator of seasonal movements in economic activity at that time of the year.

21. For the period 1901-13, the end-of-quarter averages of the aggregate reserve ratio assumed the following values (percent): Quarter I: 25.0, II: 25.5, III: 27.1, IV: 26.2.

22. According to Friedman and Schwartz (1963, 162), New York banks in November and December, 1907, imported over $130 million worth of gold. Inflows from Canada (of slightly over $2 million) only accounted for a small part of aggregate imports.

CHAPTER 7

MONETARY, BUDGETARY AND DEBT MANAGEMENT POLICIES OF THE DOMINION GOVERNMENT

Aside from the emergency measures discussed in the preceding chapter, government management of the monetary base did not reflect a desire to influence bank lending, but was almost entirely an outgrowth of the Dominion's budgetary and debt management policies. Although prior to 1914, Dominion government expenditures only accounted for 5 to 6 percent of GNP,[1] the public sector was a significant source of variation in the monetary base. The budgetary and debt management policies of the Dominion government impinged on the monetary base in two ways. First, as we saw in Chapter 3, the government influenced the monetary base through discretionary monetary policy or variations in the uncovered stock of Dominion notes. Second, the government financed a large part of its budget deficits by issuing debt abroad. Like capital imports by the private sector, government borrowing abroad augmented the monetary base since the government normally deposited with the domestic banks the foreign exchange acquired through debt issues and, thus, boosted the banks' cash or secondary reserves. Moreover, as the government spent the proceeds from the debt issues, bank deposits of the Canadian public and, hence, the money stock rose.[2]

Since the existing literature throws little light on the monetary implications of pre-1914 budgetary and debt management policies, this chapter draws extensively on the unpublished records of the Finance Department and other primary sources.[3] In Section 7.1, I examine further the monetary policy experiments of the 1870s and 1880s. An attempt is made to explain the cyclical pattern of the uncovered stock of Dominion notes, as well as the shift to an automatic policy stance in the mid-1880s. Section 7.2 traces the effects of the government budget on international capital flows. In particular, I determine the cyclical characteristics of the budget deficit and foreign borrowing by the government. Furthermore, the significance of the budget as a source of cyclical variation in the monetary base is investigated.

Before I turn to the discussion of monetary policy, it is necessary to describe briefly the key features of pre-1914 debt management. Prior to 1914, the debt management operations of the Dominion government were handled largely by domestic and foreign banks. These institutions were instrumental in underwriting and servicing government bonds. Moreover, banks served as important sources of short-term government finance since Canada lacked a well-developed money market. The bulk of the debt management operations was entrusted to the government's fiscal agents. A large part of the government's domestic and foreign business was conducted by the Bank of Montreal. In Canada, the Bank served as the government's exclusive fiscal agent. In London, it shared that task with the venerable banking houses of Baring Brothers and Glyn, Mills & Currie (henceforth called the London agents), but in 1893 it took over the government's entire London business (Denison, 1967, 253-56).

While the fiscal agents administered the funded debt, they did not serve as the sole source of temporary finance. As regards cash-flow management, the government took pains not to become too dependent upon its fiscal agents. To keep them at bay, it deposited surplus cash with and obtained temporary loans from a wide range of domestic and foreign banks.[4] As I show below, the fiscal agents were only too eager to take advantage of the government if they were placed in a monopoly position.

7.1. MONETARY POLICY

7.1.1. Antecedents

Although proposals for a government bank of issue had been discussed intermittently since the 1840s, the chartered banks were able to resist government encroachment on their note issue until 1866, when the Province of Canada (Ontario and Quebec) was empowered to circulate notes, which were convertible into gold and subject to a minimum gold reserve requirement.[5] As I pointed out in Chapter 2, government intrusion into the monetary sector was motivated by a desire to lighten the interest burden of the public debt. As a result of misguided railway ventures, the Province of Canada acquired a poor credit rating on the London capital market and was forced to offer interest rates on its bonds that exceeded substantially the yield on British consols.[6] The provincial notes were intended to supplant the existing bank money, but the government largely failed to dislodge the chartered banks as the traditional suppliers of media of exchange. On the contrary, to put the notes into circulation, the government was forced to negotiate with its domestic fiscal agent a costly arrangement, which remained in effect after Confederation and was terminated at the end of June, 1871.[7] Under this arrangement, the Bank of Montreal relinquished its own circulation and assumed responsibility for the issue and redemption of provincial or Dominion notes. Since the Bank redeemed the notes on behalf of the government, the latter saw no need to maintain a gold reserve. In order to "comply" with the minimum reserve requirement, the government earmarked as gold a portion of its deposits with the Bank of

TABLE 7-1

OFFICIAL GOLD STOCK AND STOCK OF OUTSTANDING DOMINION NOTES, 1867III-1886IV
(Thousands of Dollars)

End of Quarter	Gold Stock[a)] (1)	Aggregate Dominion Notes (2)	Uncovered Dominion Notes (3) = (2) - (1)	Excess Gold Reserve[b)] (4)	Official Reserve Ratio[c)] (5) = (1) ÷ (2)	Minimum Reserve Requirement (6)
1867 III	764	3,560	2,796	52	21	20% on $0-5 m;
IV	870	4,265	3,395	17	20	25% on $5-8 m;
						Ceiling on issue:
1868 I	850	3,764	2,824	97	23	$8 m (Aug. 15,
II	800	3,795	2,995	41	21	1866)
III	1,030	4,603	3,573	109	22	
IV	959	4,318	3,359	95	22	
1869 I	918	3,885	2,967	141	24	
II	1,175	4,792	3,617	217	25	
III	1,020	5,050	4,040	7	20	
IV	n.a.	5,834	n.a.	n.a.	n.a.	
1870 I	n.a.	n.a.	n.a.	n.a.	n.a.	
II	1,694	7,294	5,600	0	23	20% on authorized
III	1,713	7,313	5,600	0	23	issue; 100% on
IV	1,808	7,408	5,600	0	24	remainder;
						authorized issue =
1871 I	1,778	7,378	5,600	0	24	$7 m (May 12, 1870)
II	1,644	7,244	5,600	0	23	
III	2,758	9,164	6,406	-6	30	Authorized issue
						= $ 8 m.
IV	4,114	11,167	7,053	147	37	Authorized issue
						= $ 9 m.
1872 I	3,795	11,015	7,220	-20	34	
II	2,390	10,321	7,931	128	23	20% on $0-9 m;
III	2,345	10,788	8,443	-81	22	35% on remainder.
IV	2,980	11,588	8,608	274	26	(June 14, 1872)
1873 I	2,464	11,398	8,934	-175	22	
II	2,526	11,314	8,788	-84	22	
III	2,808	10,830	8,022	367	26	
IV	3,254	12,095	8,841	371	27	
1874 I	3,475	12,292	8,817	523	28	
II	3,308	12,176	8,868	396	27	
III	3,394	12,428	9,034	394	27	
IV	3,374	12,040	8,666	510	28	
1875 I	2,981	10,607	7,626	619	28	
II	2,789	10,780	7,991	99	26	20% on $0-9 m;
III	2,819	11,023	8,204	7	26	50% on $9-12 m;
IV	2,997	11,373	8,376	10	26	100% on remainder
						(April 8, 1875)
1876 I	2,916	11,221	8,305	6	26	
II	3,033	11,535	8,502	-34	26	
III	2,971	11,413	8,442	-35	26	
IV	2,898	11,124	8,226	36	26	

Table 7-1 continued

End of Quarter		Gold Stock[a)] (1)	Aggregate Dominion Notes (2)	Uncovered Dominion Notes (3) = (2) - (1)	Excess Gold Reserve[b)] (4)	Official Reserve Ratio[c)] (5) = (1)÷(2)	Minimum Reserve Requirement (6)
1877	I	2,911	11,065	8,154	78	26	
	II	2,705	10,680	7,975	65	25	
	III	3,223	11,396	8,173	225	28	
	IV	3,211	11,584	8,373	119	28	
1878	I	2,614	10,714	8,100	-43	24	
	II	2,520	10,435	7,915	2	24	
	III	2,574	10,619	8,045	-35	24	
	IV	2,575	10,501	7,926	24	25	
1879	I	2,594	10,591	7,997	-1	24	
	II	2,860	10,790	7,930	165	26	
	III	3,368	11,356	7,988	390	30	
	IV	3,648	12,311	8,663	37	30	
1880	I	n.a.	12,473	n.a.	n.a.	n.a.	
	II	2,755	13,566	10,811	720	20	15% on $0-20 m; ceiling on issue = $20 m. (May 7, 1880)
	III	3,328	14,364	11,036	1,173	23	
	IV	3,147	14,234	11,087	1,012	22	
1881	I	2,897	14,195	11,298	768	20	
	II	3,059	14,540	11,481	878	21	
	III	3,129	15,140	12,011	858	21	
	IV	2,833	14,999	12,166	583	19	
1882	I	2,149	14,315	12,166	2	15	
	II	3,710	15,797	12,087	1,340	23	
	III	4,216	17,047	12,831	1,659	25	
	IV	2,471	16,115	13,644	54	15	
1883	I	2,381	15,802	13,421	11	15	
	II	2,592	16,005	13,413	191	16	
	III	2,425	16,152	13,727	2	15	
	IV	2,572	16,775	14,203	56	15	
1884	I	2,549	16,901	14,352	14	15	
	II	2,874	15,344	12,470	572	19	
	III	3,405	16,727	13,322	896	20	
	IV	2,524	16,399	13,875	64	15	
1885	I	2,346	15,600	13,254	6	15	
	II	2,477	15,423	12,946	164	16	
	III	4,012	17,836	13,824	1,337	22	
	IV	3,188	17,791	14,603	519	18	
1886	I	4,060	16,859	12,799	1,531	24	
	II	3,937	16,289	12,352	1,494	24	
	III	3,733	16,230	12,497	1,298	23	
	IV	2,740	15,251	12,511	452	18	

a) From 1867III to 1871II, funds held in the specie reserve account with the Bank of Montreal.
b) Required reserve compiled by applying the minimum reserve requirement, as shown in column (6), to the data in column (2). Excess reserve = gold stock [column (1)] minus required reserve.
c) Percent.

Sources for Table 7-1

Columns (1) and (2): Curtis (1931a, 92-93) and the periodic returns on the government gold stock and outstanding Dominion notes, published in the *Canada Gazette*. The Curtis data were checked against the periodic returns and various errors were corrected. In particular, they were adjusted for predating of gold by the government. For window-dressing purposes, the government, at the end of 1876I and III, 1878I-III, and 1879I-II, did not show gold actually held on the respective reporting date, but added precious metal received during the subsequent three or four days. Since the periodic returns were published roughly one week after the reporting date, the government was able to "doctor" them to some extent.

Column (6): For the minimum reserve requirement, see the respective provision of the Dominion Notes Act, i.e.,
1866: *Statutes of the Province of Canada,* 29-30 Vict. Cap. 10, pp. 51-55. Re-enacted after Confederation (*Statutes of Canada,* 31 Vict. Cap. 46, pp. 118-23).
1870: 33 Vict. Cap. 10, pp. 41-42, and Rich (1977).
1872: 35 Vict. Cap. 7, p. 30.
1875: 38 Vict. Cap. 5, p. 36.
1880: 43 Vict. Cap. 13, pp. 50-52.
Further modifications of the reserve requirement on July 23, 1894 (ceiling on issue repealed, 100 percent on issue in excess of $20 million; 58-59 Vict. Cap. 16, p. 71) and on August 13, 1903 (15 percent on $0-30 million, 100 percent on issue in excess of $30 million, 10 percent on deposits in government and post office savings banks; 3 Edw. VII, Cap. 43, pp. 213-14, and Cap. 62, p. 435).

Montreal. The earmarked deposits either slightly exceeded or exactly equalled the required reserve. This may be seen from Table 7-1, which presents data on the official gold stock, aggregate and uncovered Dominion notes, excess gold reserves, as well as the official reserve ratio.[8]

Owing to the dismal state of provincial finances, the government found itself in a weak bargaining position vis-à-vis its domestic fiscal agent. For this reason, it is not surprising that the compensation extracted by the Bank for its services was such as to erode all the gains the government expected to derive from the note issue.[9] The government benefited from its monetary experiments only insofar as the arrangement with the Bank paved the way towards public acceptance of new notes.

After Confederation the government once again attempted to monetize a portion of the public debt. To this end, the ruling Conservatives under Sir John A. Macdonald sought to substitute Dominion notes for the notes issued by the chartered banks. These plans encountered strong resistance because of a widespread concern that the government would use the note issue privilege irresponsibly. The Liberal opposition, in particular, failed to see the need for a government money. After a series of protracted negotiations, the government, under the tenure of Sir Francis Hincks as Finance Minister, managed to extend its scope for discretionary monetary action in two directions. First, through monetary and banking legislation passed in 1870, the government was able to secure a permanent place for its notes in the Canadian financial system. In order to stimulate demand for the government money, the Dominion was awarded the exclusive right for issuing small-denomination notes. Furthermore, the chartered banks were required to hold at least one-third of their cash reserves in the form of Dominion notes (Breckenridge, 219-63; Shortt, 1904a; b). Second, Hincks shrewdly exploited a substantial improvement in the financial standing of the Dominion to extricate the government from the arrangement with the Bank of Montreal.[10] Subsequently, the government took on exclusive responsibility for administering the Dominion note system. The issue and redemption of the notes was entrusted to Assistant Receivers General (ARGs) located in the various provincial capitals.

7.1.2. Discretionary Monetary Policy and the Constraints of the Gold Standard

The discretionary powers won in 1870 were immediately employed by the government to boost the uncovered stock of Dominion notes. However, its scope for monetizing the interest-bearing public debt was not unlimited since the gold standard severely restricted its freedom of action. If the significance of these constraints is recognized, it is possible to explain the procyclical movements in the uncovered issue up to the mid-1880s and the subsequent shift to an automatic system of monetary policy. I submit that the choice of an appropriate policy stance involved a rational decision by a government eager to minimize the interest burden of the public debt within the constraints of the gold standard.

Any government intent on monetizing part of the public debt could not be oblivious to the fact that the balance of payments seriously restricted its room for manoeuvre. Discretionary management of the note issue, by itself, was not sufficient to ensure that the government would succeed in boosting permanently the aggregate stock of Dominion notes. In the long run, a discretionary expansion in the note issue, *ceteris paribus,* was offset by an automatic contraction and an attendant loss of official gold. In the short-run, an increase in the uncovered issue caused domestic interest rates to fall, and the domestic monetary aggregates, including the aggregate stock of Dominion notes, as well as prices and output to rise. The drop in domestic interest rates in turn elicited a decline in the Canadian non-monetary debt. The ensuing contraction in international monetary assets and the monetary base was reinforced by current-account deficits resulting from the rise in domestic economic activity. Thus, the expansion in the uncovered issue released a price-specie-flow process that caused interest rates, the monetary aggregates, prices and output to return to their initial levels. In the long run, the sole effect of the government's discretionary action was to change the composition of the monetary base in favour of uncovered Dominion notes (see Appendix D, Section D.2 for a proof of this proposition).[11]

Since the aggregate stock of Dominion notes, in the long run, remained unchanged, the fall in the official gold reserve, elicited by the expansion in the uncovered issue, was associated with a decline in the official reserve ratio. Policy-induced changes in the official reserve ratio, of course, severely limited the scope for expanding the uncovered issue. The government could not allow the official gold stock to fall below the required level. If an increase in the uncovered issue and the subsequent loss of official gold resulted in a reserve deficiency, the government could not help abandoning its expansionary monetary policy. To make up for the reserve deficiency, it was compelled to purchase — on a discretionary basis — gold abroad and, thus, to reverse the initial increase in the uncovered issue.

Considering these constraints on debt management, the government could not be certain that an increase in the uncovered issue would be permanent. A policy of boosting the uncovered issue was likely to be successful as long as the government confined itself to accommodating passively the expansion in the demand for Dominion notes stemming from the trend growth in Canadian output. However, the government was not content with following a purely passive policy course. To increase the chance of a successful outcome, it attempted to underpin its expansionary monetary policy by legislation designed to stimulate the demand for Dominion notes. Although Conservative governments repeatedly sought to introduce such legislation, they were not overly successful in obtaining Parliamentary support for their debt-management ventures. Aside from the legislation enacted in 1870, Parliament was not prepared to pass further measures designed to widen the market for the Dominion notes, save for a number of minor regulations introduced in 1880.[12] The notes proved to be popular with the banks since they could usefully be employed for the purpose of settling domestic clearing-house balances,[13] but holdings by non-banks were confined to the small denominations issued exclusively by the government.

Another obstacle to monetizing the public debt were substantial random fluctuations in the notes issue, resulting in unexpected losses of official gold. Unanticipated note redemptions would not have caused major difficulties if the government had been prepared to hold adequate excess reserves of gold. However, large excess reserves reduced the usefulness of the Dominion notes as a fiscal expedient. For this reason, Conservative and Liberal governments alike attempted to keep excess reserves as small as possible. This objective was achieved with the help of discretionary purchases and sales of gold. Finance ministers frequently deposited excess reserves with domestic banks and met reserve deficiencies by withdrawing gold from domestic banks or by purchasing sovereigns in London. Table 7-1 clearly reveals the extent to which governments — up to the mid-1880s — sought to minimize excess reserves.[14]

Due to the low level of excess reserves, the government repeatedly encountered difficulties in complying with the redemption and minimum reserve requirements. Despite these difficulties, it was not prepared to raise excess reserves. Instead, it adopted two sets of measures designed to take the sting out of these requirements.

First, the government made every effort to emasculate the minimum reserve requirement. To this end, it relied on a variety of dodges, ranging from ambiguous wording of the reserve requirement (Rich, 1977), failure to meet the requirement, to concocting misleading gold statistics for window-dressing purposes.[15] Furthermore, the government occasionally suppressed the returns on the official gold reserve and outstanding Dominion notes, which it was required to publish regularly, in order to conceal a reserve deficiency.[16]

Second, the government devised ingenious techniques for discouraging the banks from converting Dominion notes into gold.[17] Since the government held deposits with virtually all the chartered banks,[18] it frequently "punished," through gold withdrawals, institutions intending to redeem substantial amounts of Dominion notes. Another technique was to raise the Canadian gold export point vis-à-vis New York by redeeming the Dominion notes in sovereigns rather than eagles. Paying out sovereigns augmented the cost of exchanging Canadian for U.S. funds because British gold coins were not accepted at par in New York.[19] In response to complaints by the banks, the government stated categorically that it was not required to redeem its notes in any particular kind of gold coin.[20] Not surprisingly, the banks very much resented the restrictions placed on convertibility.[21]

7.1.3. Cyclical Movements in the Uncovered Stock: An Interpretation

The procyclical movements in the uncovered issue, recorded up to the mid-1880s, appear to be attributable to two factors. The sharp division of opinion between Conservatives and Liberals about the wisdom of discretionary monetary policy accounts for a large part of the cyclical fluctuations in the uncovered issue. The surge in the uncovered issue during the business-cycle expansion ending in 1873 and during the expansion of 1879-82 coincided with the tenure of Conservative governments. As indicated earlier, the Conservatives were strongly in favour of an expansionary policy stance. Much of the business-cycle contraction of 1873-79, by contrast, overlapped with the Liberal regime of Prime Minister Alexander MacKenzie. The Liberals were opposed, in principle, to the system of government money and, therefore, did not attempt to boost the uncovered issue.

While the differences in policy attitudes between the two parties were an important reason for the shifts in policy stance recorded before the mid-1880s, they do not fully explain the procyclical pattern of the uncovered issue. As I pointed out earlier, an expansion-minded government could not necessarily assume that its policies would be successful. Due to the constraints of the gold standard, the uncovered issue was unlikely to rise much unless the economic environment was conducive to an expansionary monetary policy. Early in the 1870s and early in the 1880s, the government benefited from an economic environment that sustained strongly its expansionary policy stance. However, the situation changed drastically during the business-cycle contraction of 1882-85, when the Conservatives got caught in a serious conflict between their expansionary policies and the dictates of the gold standard. The government's inability to boost the uncovered issue after 1882 was an important reason for the shift to an automatic system of monetary policy. A survey of the discretionary monetary policies pursued from 1871 to the mid-1880s clearly shows how policy attitudes and the economic environment interacted to produce procyclical swings in the uncovered stock of Dominion notes.

After the arrangement with the Bank of Montreal had been terminated at the end of June, 1871, the uncovered issue surged from $5.6 million to almost $9 million at the end of March, 1873 (Table 7-1). In all probability, the government relied on note deposit policy to engineer this marked expansion in the uncovered issue. Hincks explicitly stated that small-denomination notes were normally circulated in this way.[22] The surge in the uncovered issue coincided with the latter stage of a cyclical expansion in economic activity. As was normal for that stage of the business cycle, the balance of payments tended to deteriorate. Although a large overall balance of payments deficit was recorded in 1872 (Table 3-1), the government stuck to its expansionary policy course. As indicated by Tables A-1 and 7-1, the uncovered issue continued to creep up throughout 1872, despite the fact that both the aggregate and official stocks of monetary gold fell as a result of the deficit. Thus, the expansion in the uncovered issue neutralized to some extent the impact of the deficit on the monetary base. However, due to the loss of gold, the expansionary monetary policy began to conflict with the minimum reserve requirement. In 1872 and the first half of 1873, the official gold stock frequently dropped below the required level (Table 7-1). To get around this difficulty, Hincks, in 1872, requested that the reserve requirement be relaxed so he could continue to issue small-denomination notes on an uncovered basis (Canada, *Parliamentary Debates,* 1872, 117-18, 677).

Aside from the modification of the minimum reserve requirement, a strong increase in bank and non-bank demand for Dominion notes enabled the government to boost the uncovered issue despite the balance-of-payments deficit. The rise in demand was due to the legislation of 1870 and to a substantial shift in the composition of bank reserves towards the government money.[23] This shift mirrored the growing significance of the notes as a means of settling domestic clearing-house balances.

In 1874, the Conservatives were replaced by the Liberal MacKenzie government. In view of Liberal attitudes towards the Dominion notes, it is not surprising that the MacKenzie government put monetary discretion on the back burner. During the four years of Liberal tenure, the uncovered issue did not grow at all. Though the Liberals showed little interest in discretionary monetary policy, they did not attempt to abolish the system of government money. Finance Minister Cartwright felt certain measures could not be altered once they had been introduced. As a token concession to their ideological position, the Liberals, in 1875, tightened the minimum reserve requirement (Canada, *Debates,* 1875, 305).

After the Conservatives had returned to power in 1878, monetary policy switched back to an expansionary stance. For fiscal reasons (Shortt, 1906, 15), the new government was determined to boost once again the uncovered issue even though it was thoroughly in the dark as to how this goal was to be achieved. At first, the drastic improvement in the balance of payments, recorded in 1879, exonerated the government from the need to think about new expedients for augmenting the uncovered issue. The huge overall surplus in that year swelled the official gold stock and allowed the government to increase the uncovered issue through discretionary sales of gold. Under a fractional-reserve system of government money, an automatic increase in the official gold stock necessarily generated excess gold reserves. In order to augment the uncovered issue, the government simply deposited the excess gold with the domestic banks. As a result, the uncovered issue rose by $0.7 million during the fourth quarter of 1879 (Table 7-1).[24]

The following year, the official gold stock ceased to grow although the balance of payments still showed a modest surplus. Therefore, the government was no longer able to augment the uncovered issue through discretionary sales of gold. Since it was determined to stick to its expansionary policy course, it had little choice but to rely on note deposit policy for achieving its aims. Its policy of issuing additional uncovered Dominion notes, however, ran up against a serious obstacle. Towards the end of 1879, the aggregate stock of Dominion notes passed the level of $12 million, beyond which a gold reserve of 100 percent was required (Table 7-1). To make room for a further increase in the uncovered issue, the government asked Parliament once again to relax the minimum reserve requirement. The Liberal opposition expressed serious misgivings about the government's proposed course of action and doubted that the public would be willing to take up voluntarily the additional notes. Despite repeated questioning by the opposition, Finance Minister Tilley refused to give precise information about the size of the planned uncovered issue, the mode of issuing the notes, and the measures the government intended to take to keep the notes in circulation, aside from the curious statement that in the future, the Indians in the Northwest and British Columbia would receive their annuities in the form of one-dollar notes (Canada, *Debates,* 1724-27).[25] In all probability, the government deposited with the chartered banks $2 million worth of Dominion notes immediately after the minimum reserve requirement had been adjusted.[26] This figure roughly corresponds to the change in the uncovered issue recorded for 1880 (Table 7-1).

In 1881 and 1882, the government continued to augment the uncovered issue, but the Finance Department records fail to reveal how that increase came about. The expansionary policy was supported to some extent by changes in banking legislation designed to enhance further bank and non-bank demand for Dominion notes (see note 12). All in all, the period 1878IV-1882IV, which largely coincided with a reference-cycle expansion, saw the uncovered issue rise by over $5 million or by roughly one-half of aggregate Dominion notes outstanding at the end of 1879. As was typical for business-cycle expansions, the balance-of-payments surpluses recorded near the trough of 1879 gradually gave way to deficits. Thus, over that period, discretionary monetary policy at first amplified, and later partly neutralized, the impact of the balance of payments on base-money growth.

7.1.4. The Transition to an Automatic System

As the policy makers gained experience with monetary discretion, they increasingly came to realize that the uncovered issue could not be greatly expanded unless the convertibility of the Dominion notes was restricted to some extent. There is little doubt that official gold losses repeatedly played havoc with discretionary monetary policy. On February 23, 1875, for example, Finance Minister Cartwright complained that over the past six or seven weeks he had been forced to redeem over $2 million worth of notes (Canada, *Debates,* 1875, 305). This sum equalled roughly 60 percent of the official gold stock at the end of 1874. As indicated by Table 7-1, the first quarter of 1875 indeed witnessed a substantial contraction in the aggregate stock of Dominion notes. Yet, the official gold stock only fell slightly. Evidently, the government could not help contracting the uncovered issue in order to forestall a reserve deficiency. The problem, I suspect, was resolved by means of discretionary gold purchases.

From the standpoint of debt management, restrictions on convertibility were a mixed blessing. On the one hand, such restrictions allowed the government to thwart unwanted contractions in the uncovered issue and, thus, to increase the fiscal benefits of the Dominion-note system. On the other hand, the expedients introduced for protecting the official gold stock were not costless. The banks could be kept in line only so long as the government was prepared to purchase sovereigns in Britain and to tie up substantial resources in the form of demand deposits. Table 7-2 offers indirect evidence suggesting that the cost of these protective devices must have been substantial. From 1872 to 1882, government claims on the domestic banks — which to a large extent consisted of demand deposits — increased intermittently with the uncovered stock of Dominion notes. The marked growth in government deposits implies that prior to 1883, the benefits from the note issue were reaped solely in the form of interest on time deposits since the money "created" by the government was not allotted to the retirement of interest-bearing debt.

Would it have been possible to pursue an effective discretionary monetary policy without maintaining such large deposits at domestic banks? The answer to this question was provided in the period 1883-85, when the government's budgetary situation deteriorated drastically as a result of its involvement in the construction of the Canadian Pacific Railway. This episode proved conclusively that a drastic reduction in government claims on the domestic banks compounded considerably the note redemption problems.

As is well known, the government assisted the railway company through a variety of subsidies and loans. Towards the end of 1882, the government unexpectedly ran into cash-flow problems directly attributable to CPR finance. Between November, 1882, and September, 1883, it gradually withdrew time deposits from a wide range of banks (Table 7-2).[27] Throughout 1883, CPR finances continued to deteriorate. In response to a request for emergency assistance, the government, the following year, agreed to extend to the company a loan of $22.5 million. The CPR request reached Ottawa at a most inopportune moment. In addition to the mounting budget deficits, the government was faced with $30 million worth of bonds due to mature in 1884 (Canada, Public Accounts for 1915, part I, 31). Since British investors did not look favourably upon a major new Dominion loan,[28] the government, late in 1884 and early 1885, decided to borrow heavily from foreign and domestic banks. At the end of June, 1885, temporary loans obtained from British and Canadian financial institutions reached $14.6 and $4.4 million respectively (Table 7-3). With deposits amounting to $5.6 million (Table 7.2), net government claims on the domestic banks dropped to a low of $1.2 million.

Owing to its budgetary problems, the government lost the protective shield of its claims on the domestic banks and was no longer able to restrict informally the convertibility of its notes. The Finance Department records suggest that the Bank of Montreal took advantage of the government's vulnerability and returned temporarily for redemption any notes it was not legally required to hold.[29] In December, 1884, the Deputy Minister of Finance complained that the Bank, during the past month, had endeavoured to drive the government "in a corner" by redeeming more than $1 million worth of notes,

> forcing us to bring in another $500,000 of gold as if the CPR financing was not enough in all considered.[30]

TABLE 7-2
GOVERNMENT DEPOSITS AT THE CHARTERED BANKS AND UNCOVERED DOMINION NOTES
(Millions of Dollars)

June 30	Deposits (domestic banks only)			Uncovered Notes
	Time	Demand	Total	
1872	0.8	3.9	4.7	7.9
1873	4.3	4.7	9.0	8.8
1874	5.0	4.4	9.4	8.7
1875	4.7	6.0	10.7	8.0
1876	2.7	4.8	7.5	8.5
1877	1.6	4.8	6.4	8.0
1878	1.4	5.2	6.6	7.9
1879	0.6	5.6	6.2	7.9
1880	2.1	7.3	9.4	10.8
1881	2.5	7.2	9.7	11.5
1882	6.9	7.6	14.5	12.1
1883	3.0	3.4	6.4	13.4
1884	0.4	5.2	5.6	12.5
1885	0.1	5.5	5.6	12.9
1886	0.1	7.8	7.9	12.4
1887	0.1	5.1	5.2	12.3
1888	5.0	5.2	10.2	12.4
1889	3.8	4.4	8.2	12.2
1890	-	2.9	2.9	12.1

Sources: Tables 7-1 and 7-3.

TABLE 7-3

GOVERNMENT CLAIMS ON AND LIABILITIES TO DOMESTIC AND FOREIGN BANKS
(Millions of Dollars)

	Claims			Liabilities		
	Time Deposits		Domestic Demand	Temporary Loans		London Agents
June 30	Domestic (1)	Foreign (2)	Deposits (3)	Domestic (4)	Foreign (5)	(Net) (6)
1867	-	-	0.7	2.2	-	1.2
1868	0.6	-	1.6	2.5	-	1.3
1869	0.1	-	3.9	-	-	-1.1
1870	-	-	3.5	2.0	-	0.1
1871	-	-	3.8	1.2	-	-0.5
1872	0.8	0.1	3.9	0.5	-	-0.8
1873	4.3	0.1	4.7	-	-	2.7
1874	5.0	-	4.4	-	-	-0.1
1875	4.7	1.1	6.0	-	-	1.5
1876	2.7	3.6	4.8	-	-	-0.9
1877	1.6	3.2	4.8	-	-	-1.1
1878	1.4	0.1	5.2	-	-	4.1
1879	0.6	0.1	5.6	-	-	-0.3
1880	2.1	-	7.3	-	-	-0.8
1881	2.5	-	7.2	-	-	-1.3
1882	6.9	-	7.6	-	-	-0.9
1883	3.0	-	3.4	-	-	-0.6
1884	0.4	4.1	5.2	-	-	-0.3
1885	0.1	-	5.5	4.4	14.6	0.2
1886	0.1	-	7.8	1.3	-	-2.0
1887	0.1	-	5.1	-	1.2	-0.3
1888	5.0	-	5.2	-	5.7	1.7
1889	3.8	-	4.4	-	-	-0.2
1890	-	-	2.9	-	1.9	-0.2
1891	-	-	2.5	-	7.8	-0.3
1892	-	-	2.8	-	-	2.2
1893	-	-	3.1	-	1.5	0.1
1894	-	-	2.8	-	2.4	-0.3
1895	-	-	3.9	-	-	0.2
1896	-	-	2.6	-	1.9	0.1
1897	-	-	1.8	-	4.9	-0.4
1898	-	-	1.8	-	-	-1.1
1899	-	-	2.3	-	3.9	0.2
1900	-	-	1.1	-	-	0.2
1901	-	-	0.3	-	-	3.3
1902	-	-	1.5	-	-	6.6
1903	-	-	1.6	-	-	-2.7
1904	5.8	-	0.8	-	4.9	-0.3
1905	6.4	-	4.2	-	2.9	2.2
1906	16.3	-	0.7	-	2.9	0.2
March 31						
1907	6.7	-	3.2	-	1.2	0.4
1908	4.2	-	6.9	-	9.3	-5.0
1909	1.3	-	4.5	-	13.6	-19.7
1910	6.0	-	6.7	-	17.0	-0.3

1911	8.2	-	1.1	-	-	-2.5
1912	-	-	1.7	-	-	-15.5
1913	-	-	1.2	-	-	-1.9
1914	-	-	4.8	-	8.3	-13.2

Sources and estimation methods for Table 7-3

The bulk of the data shown in this table is obtained from Canada, Public Accounts for 1915, part I, *Sessional Paper* No. 2, 22-91. Numbers in parentheses denote the respective pages in that sessional paper.

Columns (1) and (2): Cover interest-bearing bank deposits. For the period up to June 30, 1903, I draw on Table VI (41-42), while for the subsequent fiscal years the data must be pieced together from the general statement of assets, where time deposits are reported under the headings of "investments" or "miscellaneous accounts" (Canada, Public Accounts for 1868-1914). For the period June 30, 1904, onwards my estimates of time deposits cover special deposits and funds deposited with the banks in connection with loans granted for railway construction (especially Canadian Northern and Grand Trunk Pacific). The Public Accounts do not separate time deposits with domestic banks from those with foreign banks. However, it is possible to estimate the shares held in Canada and abroad since the Public Accounts indicate the names of banks receiving government deposits. Deposits with the London branches of the Bank of Montreal are considered foreign. As regards deposits with the Bank of Montreal, the Public Accounts do not always state explicitly whether the funds were placed in Canada or London. In case of doubt, I assume that the value of a deposit in London normally amounted to a round sterling number. If the Canadian-dollar value, divided by $4.86 2/3, yields a round number, the deposit is treated as foreign. The data reported under "balance of Dominion loan account" (41) and "sinking fund special inscription account" (58) are included in foreign time deposits, but it is unclear whether the latter account was held with a foreign bank. "Bank of Montreal silver debentures" (42) and the "special circulation account" (58) are subsumed in domestic time deposits.

Column (3): Covers "cash," as reported in the Public Accounts. For the period up to June 30, 1903, see (43). For the subsequent period, see Canada, Public Accounts for 1904-14, statement of assets. For the period up to June 30, 1871, the data also include funds in the issue account, which equals the difference between the specie reserve, as shown in (45), and the actual specie reserve of the government. For the latter, see legend to Table 7-5, column (6).

Column (4) and (5): Loans obtained from the Bank of Montreal (36) and temporary loans (39). If the Public Accounts do not explicitly state whether a loan is domestic or foreign, the procedure described under columns (1) and (2) is employed. Note that there are large discrepancies between the data in column (4) and the corresponding series obtained from the monthly bank returns (Curtis, 1931a, 56).

Column (6): Net liabilities to Baring Brothers, Glyn, Mills and Currie, and the London branches of the Bank of Montreal, except time deposits and temporary loans. Minor accounts with such London institutions as the Crown Agents for the Colonies, the Bank of England, the Colonial Office, Morton and Rose, and Sir John Rose, as well as an account held on behalf of the government's London emigration agent, are also included. See Canada, Public Accounts for 1868-1914, "miscellaneous (banking) accounts."

Table 7-3 does not cover numerous minor accounts held by the government in connection with various public works projects. It is impossible to compile a homogeneous series encompassing the entire gamut of government accounts. Also note that liabilities include neither Dominion government bonds held by domestic and foreign banks, nor the contributions by the chartered banks to the circulation redemption fund. The latter is reported under "trust funds" (29). See Ch. 1 for the circulation redemption fund.

The Bank clearly had an incentive to engage in such activities as it provided the lion's share of the domestic temporary loans.[31] The note redemptions augmented the government's borrowing requirements and allowed the Bank to put pressure on the government with a view to extracting a high return on the temporary loans.

The turbulent events of 1884-85 clearly revealed the heel of Achilles in the Dominion note system. Effective management of the uncovered issue was impossible unless the government was prepared to tie up substantial resources in bank balances, notably demand deposits with the domestic banks. These balances enabled the government to keep the redemption problems within bounds but simultaneously reduced the fiscal benefits from the note issue. The CPR crisis apparently prompted the government to reconsider the wisdom of discretionary monetary policy. Towards the end of 1885, the Deputy Minister of Finance ventured the suggestion that against any future increase in the note circulation, the government should hold "dollar for dollar in coin."[32] As indicated in Chapter 3, the government accepted the advice of the Deputy Minister. Around 1885, monetary discretion was abandoned in favour of an automatic system. Interestingly enough, the government did not think it advisable to inform the public about the policy shift. On the contrary, it made every effort to hush up the matter. The policy shift was not officially acknowledged until 1894, when the Liberal opposition — in the context of a debate on the Dominion Notes Act — conjectured with considerable satisfaction that the two parties no longer disagreed on the wisdom of monetary discretion. This assessment of the situation was not contested by the government (Canada, *Debates,* 1894, 6030-31). Therefore, the shift from a discretionary to an automatic policy stance went largely unnoticed.

Considering the obstacles to discretionary monetary policy under the gold standard, a rational government could not help concluding that the Dominion notes were a dubious fiscal expedient. The CPR crisis showed that the fiscal benefits from the note issue were much smaller than the government had originally anticipated. A gradual decline in the yield on Canadian government bonds (Table 7-4), as well as in the interest earned by the government on time deposits,[33] provided a further incentive for abandoning monetary discretion. Much of the decrease in the bond yield reflected an improvement in the credit rating of the Canadian government in London, as manifested by the fact that the yield differential between Dominion government bonds and British consols dropped from 2.2 percentage points in 1870 (see note 6) to 0.7 in 1890.

After the switch to an automatic system of monetary policy, the government was able gradually to accumulate excess gold reserves.[34] Ample excess

TABLE 7-4
AVERAGE YIELD ON DOMINION GOVERNMENT BONDS
(Percent)

	Yield		Yield		
1868	5.7	1880	4.2	1900	3.0
1869	5.5	1881	3.9	1901	3.1
		1882	3.8	1902	3.1
1870	5.4	1883	3.8	1903	3.2
1871	5.0	1884	3.8	1904	3.3
1872	4.9	1885	3.8	1905	3.2
1873	4.9	1886	3.6	1906	3.2
1874	4.6	1887	3.5	1907	3.3
1875	4.6	1888	3.3	1908	3.3
1876	4.5	1889	3.2	1909	3.5
1877	4.4				
1878	4.4	1890	3.4	1910	3.5
1879	4.3	1891	3.4	1911	3.5
		1892	3.4	1912	3.6
		1893	3.3	1913	4.0
		1894	3.2		
		1895	3.0		
		1896	2.9		
		1897	2.8		
		1898	3.0		
		1899	3.0		

Source for Table 7-4

See Appendix E. The data shown in the table are annual averages of end-of-quarter data.

reserves eased considerably the note redemption problems and obviated the need for large deposits with domestic banks. From 1890 to 1903, government holdings of demand deposits typically stayed below $3 million. Moreover, the government did not maintain any time deposits at domestic or foreign banks. After 1903, government deposits once again varied substantially (Table 7-3), but there is no evidence to suggest that these fluctuations were related to monetary policy. As far as may be judged from the available published and unpublished records, the government, on the whole, ceased to restrict the convertibility of the Dominion notes after it had accumulated sufficient excess reserves. However, exceptions did occur. During the financial crisis of 1907 (see Chapter 6), the government once again refused to redeem Dominion notes in eagles in order to stem a drain of gold to New York (*Monetary Times*, Nov. 30, 1907, 871).

7.2. IMPACT OF THE DOMINION GOVERNMENT BUDGET DEFICIT ON THE BALANCE OF PAYMENTS AND THE MONETARY BASE

7.2.1. The Budget Deficit and Borrowing: The Data

Table 7-5 presents data on government expenditure and revenue, the budget deficit and government borrowing. Expenditure comprises purchases of goods and services, outlays on public works, subsidies, and interest payments on the public debt. Revenue covers receipts from all sources, except interest earned on government investments. The latter is deducted from both aggregate expenditure and revenue.[35] As may be gleaned from Table 7-5, customs duties accounted for approximately 60 percent of total revenue. Another important source of revenue were excise taxes. Income taxes, by contrast, were unknown prior to 1914.

As regards the budget deficit, two variants are estimated. The first one, termed the ordinary deficit, equals the difference between expenditure and revenue. It roughly corresponds to the modern national-income concept of the deficit, except that it also embraces subsidies to the provinces and railway companies. The second variant is an estimate of the cash deficit and measures the government's borrowing requirements. It differs from the ordinary deficit in that it includes payments and receipts on account of Dominion government loans to provinces, municipalities, railways and other enterprises.

The cash deficit is estimated from data on government liabilities and assets as reported in the Public Accounts. From among the various liabilities and assets, I attempt to single out those items that served mainly a financing purpose:

Financing liabilities (LF)
= Loans from domestic and foreign banks,
+ bonds issued in Canada and abroad,
+ deposit liabilities of government and post office savings banks,

TABLE 7-5

DOMINION GOVERNMENT BUDGET DEFICIT AND FOREIGN BORROWING
(Millions of Dollars)

Fiscal Year Ended June 30	Expenditure	Revenue		Budget Deficit		Domestic Borrowing		Foreign Borrowing	Canadian Reference Cycle
		Total	of which Customs	Ordinary	Cash	Total	of which uncovered Dominion Notes		
	(1)	(2)	(3)	(4)=(1)-(2)	(5)=(6)+(8)	(6)	(7)	(8)	(9)
1868	13.5	13.5	8.6	-	1.2	1.7	0.6	-0.5	
1869	13.1	13.0	8.3	0.1	4.3	-1.9	0.7	6.2	
1870	17.5	15.1	9.3	2.4	7.2	6.1	1.8	1.1	
1871	18.3	18.8	11.8	-0.5	-0.5	-0.1	-0.3	-0.4	
1872	23.0	20.2	12.8	2.8	1.0	1.6	2.3	-0.6	
1873	24.3	20.5	13.0	3.8	0.1	-2.9	0.7	3.0	
1874	25.3	23.6	14.3	1.7	6.1	1.6	0.1	4.5	P/11/73
1875	31.1	23.7	15.4	7.4	11.1	-2.7	-0.9	13.8	
1876	29.0	21.8	12.8	7.2	8.5	3.4	0.5	5.1	
1877	30.9	22.2	12.5	8.7	10.9	1.4	-0.5	9.5	
1878	28.1	21.6	12.8	6.5	6.8	1.9	-	4.9	
1879	28.1	26.4	12.9	1.7	2.6	2.3	-	0.3	T/05/79
1880	32.0	22.6	14.1	9.4	10.3	3.0	2.9	7.3	
1881	31.8	28.8	18.4	3.0	2.1	5.1	0.7	-3.0	
1882	32.4	34.2	21.6	-1.8	-3.2	1.4	0.6	-4.6	
1883	40.5	35.7	23.0	4.8	6.5	9.2	1.3	-2.7	P/07/82
1884	45.8	31.8	20.0	14.0	34.7	21.8	-0.5	12.9	
1885	45.1	31.2	18.9	13.9	24.5	6.4	0.2	18.1	T/03/85
1886	54.4	31.0	19.4	23.4	-1.9	0.3	-0.8	-2.2	
1887	38.9	34.8	22.4	4.1	4.1	2.3	-0.1	1.8	P/02/87
1888	42.1	34.9	22.1	7.2	4.0	-6.3	0.1	10.3	T/02/88
1889	39.1	37.4	23.7	1.7	2.4	5.3	-0.2	-2.9	

(Table 7-5 continued)

Fiscal Year Ended June 30	Expenditure	Revenue		Budget Deficit		Domestic Borrowing		Foreign Borrowing	Canadian Reference Cycle
		Total	of which Customs	Ordinary	Cash	Total	of which uncovered Dominion Notes		
	(1)	(2)	(3)	(4)=(1)-(2)	(5)=(6)+(8)	(6)	(7)	(8)	(9)
1890	38.7	38.7	23.9	-	1.7	3.8	-0.1	-2.1	P/07/90[b)]
1891	37.6	37.4	23.3	0.2	1.4	-6.6	0.2	8.0	T/03/91
1892	37.9	35.7	20.4	2.2	1.5	-2.3	-0.1	3.8	
1893	37.3	36.9	20.9	0.4	0.6	1.5	-0.2	-0.9	P/02/93
1894	39.1	35.0	19.1	4.1	4.6	0.5	-0.2	4.1	T/03/94
1895	39.1	32.6	17.6	6.5	6.7	-0.4	-	7.1	
1896	40.6	35.2	19.8	5.4	6.2	6.5	-0.1	-0.3	P/08/95
1897	39.4	36.3	19.4	3.1	2.9	2.6	-	0.3	T/08/96
1898	40.3	38.9	21.6	1.4	1.7	2.3	-0.2	-0.6	
1899	47.0	44.9	25.2	2.1	2.2	-0.3	-0.2	2.5	
1900	48.5	49.2	28.2	-0.7	0.4	7.1	2.4	-6.7	P/04/00
1901	53.7	50.7	28.3	3.0	4.1	4.7	-0.5	-0.6	T/02/01
1902	59.4	56.1	31.9	3.3	3.5	2.6	0.8	0.9	
1903	56.9	63.6	36.7	-6.9	-11.0	-1.0	-0.8	-10.0	P/12/02
1904	62.1	68.4	40.5	-6.3	-8.3	-1.4	-0.9	-6.9	T/06/04
1905	74.4	69.1	41.4	5.3	-1.6	-2.2	-0.1	0.6	
1906	78.6	77.8	46.1	0.8	-1.6	5.2	2.9	-6.8	
Fiscal Year Ended March 31[a)]									
1907	63.1	66.5	39.7	-3.4	0.1	-3.8	2.2	3.9	P/12/05
1908	107.7	94.1	57.2	13.6	15.0	0.9	1.6	14.1	
1909	127.4	83.2	47.1	44.2	45.3	-0.8	-1.3	46.1	T/07/08
1910	109.5	98.8	59.8	10.7	22.7	-9.3	-0.5	32.0	P/03/10
1911	118.6	116.1	71.8	2.5	-1.0	1.3	-1.5	-2.3	
1912	133.5	134.7	85.1	-1.2	2.9	7.0	-1.3	-4.1	T/07/11
1913	141.3	166.9	111.8	-25.6	-14.6	-4.0	-0.8	-10.6	P/11/12
1914	180.3	161.0	104.7	19.3	40.3	-2.8	3.1	43.1	

a) Fiscal 1907 lasted from July 1, 1906, to March 31, 1907.
b) Both the reference-cycle peak of 1890 and the trough of 1891 fall into fiscal 1891.

Sources and estimation methods for Table 7-5

The bulk of the data shown in this table is obtained from Canada, Public Accounts for 1915, part I, *Sessional Paper* No. 2, 22-91. Numbers in parentheses denote the respective pages in that sessional paper.

Column (1): Aggregate expenditures, as shown in the Public Accounts, are adjusted in a number of respects. From total disbursements (22), the following items are deducted:

— Allocations to the sinking funds (67). The contributions to the sinking funds, which were used to retire outstanding bonds, must be regarded as a fictitious expenditure item. The government included these contributions in total disbursements but deducted them again when it calculated the budget deficit.

— Discount on loans (89). For accounting purposes, the government valued bond issues at par, no matter whether the securities were in fact sold at par. The premium (discount) on the par value of bond issues, in turn, was treated as an expenditure (revenue) item. If the discount (premium) is deducted from aggregate expenditure (revenue), the increase in the value of outstanding bonds, as shown in the Public Accounts, must be adjusted accordingly, that is, the increase must be valued at the market price rather than at par.

— Allowances to the provinces (89). Upon Confederation, the Dominion government took over the entire provincial debt. Each province was awarded a debt allowance. If a province transferred debt in excess of the allowance, it was required to pay to the Dominion government interest of 5 percent on the difference. Conversely, if debt transferred fell short of the allowance, the provinces received interest of 5 percent on the difference. After Confederation, the debt allowance was raised several times. The increase in the allowance was recorded in the Public Accounts as a reduction in the net claims of the Dominion government on the provinces, even though the transaction did not entail a sale of assets. The drop in net claims, in turn, was balanced by a fictitious expenditure item with the caption "allowances to provinces." This item is excluded from aggregate expenditure as it grossly distorts the data. For the changes in the debt allowance, see *Statutes of Canada,* 36 Vict. Cap. 30; 47 Vict. Cap. 4; 48-49 Vict. Cap. 50; and 49 Vict. Cap. 8.

— A reduction in net claims on Ontario and Quebec by $5.4 million in fiscal 1904, balanced by a fictitious expenditure item under "consolidated fund transfers" (88). The adjustment in net claims on the two provinces was based on 47 Vict. Cap. 4 (see Public Accounts for 1904, part I, 14).

— Interest receipts by the government (62). A substantial proportion of interest receipts was revenue on account of the sinking funds, which consisted almost exclusively of the government's own bonds. Revenue arising from the premium or discount on the exchange rate (65) is treated in the same way as interest receipts.

Column (2): From total receipts (23), the following items are deducted:

— Premium on loans (91). See column (1), discount on loans.

— Interest receipts, and revenue arising from the premium or discount on the exchange rate. See column (1).

— An increase in net claims on Ontario and Quebec by $3.3 million in fiscal 1903, balanced by a fictitious revenue item under "consolidated fund transfers" (90). This adjustment constitutes a debt settlement between the Dominion and the two provinces arising out of Confederation (Canada, Public Accounts for 1903, xi-xii).

Column (3): (60).

Column (6): Equals the net increase in the following items:

— Liabilities to minus claims on domestic banks, as shown in Table 7-3 [columns (4) − (1) − (3)].

— Funded debt (bonds) payable in Canada (28), deposit liabilities of the government and post office savings banks (28), and trust funds (29). I assume that bonds payable in Canada were held only by Canadian residents. This assumption seems reasonable as the Finance Department records in the Public Archives include numerous letters written by Department officials to holders of such bonds. The vast majority of these letters were sent to addresses in Canada (vols. 2750, 2771-88). Apparently, these bonds could be purchased only at the post office savings banks (see letter by Courtney, May 9, 1883, vol. 2785).

— Government bonds payable in London, held by the domestic insurance companies [Table 7-6, column (1)]. Bond holdings at the end of the fiscal years are determined by straight-line interpolation. The holdings at the end of fiscal 1914 are assumed to equal those at the end of calendar 1913.

— An estimate of government bonds payable in London, held by the chartered banks. The increase (decrease) in these holdings is estimated to have amounted to +4.0, −1.5, −1.0 and +2.0 million dollars in fiscal 1886, 1887, 1888 and 1898 respectively. For an explanation of the estimation procedure, see Appendix F.

— Uncovered Dominion notes, i.e., aggregate notes (28) minus the official specie reserve (45). Aggregate notes include a small amount of provincial notes (28) remaining in circulation after Confederation. For the period up to June 30, 1871, the data on the specie reserve, recorded in (45), include funds held in the issue account. Funds in that account are deducted from the specie reserve since they are already included in claims on domestic banks. Data on the specie reserve, net of funds in the issue account, were reported in Canada, Public Accounts for 1868-71, under the heading of "banking accounts."

Column (7): See column (6).

Column (8): Equals the net increase in the following items:

— Liabilities to minus claims on foreign banks, as shown in Table 7-3 [columns (5) + (6) − (2)].

— Funded debt (bonds) payable in London (28), minus the following government assets: bonds held by the government in sinking funds (30), miscellaneous consolidated fund investments (46), India bonds (45), sterling debentures (59), and a small amount of foreign assets extracted from the category "miscellaneous accounts," as reported in Canada, Public Accounts for 1868-1914. Like the sinking funds, miscellaneous consolidated fund investments consisted largely of Dominion government bonds payable in London (see Canada, Public Accounts for 1868-1914, statement of "interest on investments"). Outstanding bonds payable in London exclude holdings by domestic insurance companies and the chartered banks [see column (6)]. Moreover, they are adjusted for the premium (91) and discount (89) on loans [see column (1)].

+ uncovered Dominion notes,
+ miscellaneous minor liabilities.

Financing assets (AF)
= Deposits with domestic and foreign banks,
+ bonds held by the government in sinking funds.
+ miscellaneous minor assets.

The cash deficit (CD), as estimated in this study, equals the change in net financing liabilities, that is,

$CD = \Delta LF - \Delta AF$.[36]

In order to finance cash deficits, the government relied on both foreign and domestic sources of funds. Bond issues in the London capital market constituted the principal means of raising foreign funds.[37] The government also frequently tapped the resources of foreign banks. Inasmuch as the government conducted business with foreign banks, it dealt almost exclusively with British institutions, including the London branches of the Bank of Montreal.[38] During the period under study, it never borrowed funds from or made deposits with U.S. banks.[39]

The bulk of the funds borrowed by the government domestically was obtained through the government and post office savings banks. The chartered banks also served as important sources of domestic finance. Domestic bond issues, by contrast, were not used much to cover cash deficits, except during the budgetary crisis of 1884-85. However, a small share of the bonds issued in London was acquired by Canadian residents, notably by chartered banks and insurance companies (Table 7-6). For this reason, the estimates of domestic borrowing take account, as far as possible, of changes in domestic holdings of government bonds payable in London (see Appendix F for the estimation problems posed by bank holdings of bonds).

The cash deficits incurred by the government were financed, in large measure, by foreign borrowing. Domestic borrowing, by contrast, was important only up to the mid-1880s. Over the period fiscal 1868-86, domestic borrowing averaged no less than 45 percent of the cumulative cash deficit. However, from fiscal 1886 onwards, the share of domestic borrowing shrank rapidly to an average of less than 10 percent. In my opinion, the sharp decline in that share was due to a marked shift in the interest cost of domestic debt as compared with the average yield on government bonds issued in London. From 1867 to the end of the 1880s, the yield on bonds issued in London fell steadily relative to the deposit rate offered by the government and post office savings banks (Tables 2-2 and 7-4).[40] Thus, while savings deposits were a highly attractive source of finance until the 1880s, they gradually lost their glamour as time wore on.[41] Evidently, the move away from domestic borrowing was motivated by similar considerations as the shift to an automatic system of monetary policy.

TABLE 7-6

DOMINION GOVERNMENT BONDS HELD BY INSURANCE COMPANIES
(Millions of Dollars)

End of Calendar Year	Payable in London	Total	End of Calendar Year	Payable in London	Total
1868	n.a	n.a	1890	5.3	6.5
1869	n.a	n.a	1891	2.3	3.3
			1892	2.2	3.4
1870	n.a	n.a	1893	4.1	5.8
1871	n.a	n.a	1894	2.4	3.4
1872	n.a	n.a	1895	2.7	4.0
1873	n.a	n.a	1896	2.9	3.8
1874	n.a	n.a	1897	3.0	4.0
1875	0.3	1.4	1898	1.9	4.0
1876	0.4	1.5	1899	3.3	4.2
1877	0.6	3.1			
1878	1.3	3.1	1900	2.6	3.8
1879	0.9	2.5	1901	5.8	6.9
			1902	2.2	3.6
1880	1.0	3.1	1903	1.9	2.8
1881	0.6	2.9	1904	1.8	3.1
1882	1.6	1.9	1905	1.6	2.9
1883	1.2	1.7	1906	1.5	2.9
1884	6.4	7.0	1907	1.2	2.5
1885	1.4	1.9	1908	2.9	3.4
1886	2.0	2.7	1909	2.6	3.7
1887	2.2	3.1			
1888	2.4	3.3	1910	1.4	2.9
1889	9.9	11.1	1911	1.2	2.7
			1912	0.6	1.8
			1913	0.8	1.5

Sources and estimation methods for Table 7-6

Canada, *Annual Report of the Superintendent of Insurance*, 1875-1913. The *Report* provides data on bonds held by each insurance company, broken down by type of security. In case of doubt as to whether a particular bond was payable in London or Canada, I resort to the procedure described in the legend to Table 7-3, columns (1) and (2). The data are based on the par values of bonds and cover life, fire and casualty insurance companies.

7.2.2. Cyclical Characteristics of the Budget Deficit and Foreign Borrowing

As indicated by Chart 7-1, the ordinary and cash deficits, as well as foreign borrowing by the government were closely correlated.[42] A change in the ordinary budget deficit was normally associated with a corresponding change in the cash deficit, which in turn was financed, for the most part, by foreign borrowing. From 1868 to the reference-cycle peak of 1879, the three magnitudes varied procyclically, but thereafter their patterns were distinctly countercyclical. The budget deficits and foreign borrowing typically reached their cyclical troughs (peaks) near reference-cycle peaks (troughs). A few deviations from the countercyclical pattern recorded after 1879, however, did occur. From 1887 to 1892, the cash deficit did not display a discernible cyclical pattern. Moreover, over a short period lasting from 1894 to 1896, both the ordinary and cash deficits moved procyclically.

Despite the occasional departures of the budget deficits from their normal cyclical patterns, the countercyclical swings in foreign borrowing, after 1879, were almost flawless. Notably from 1887 to 1896, foreign borrowing continued to move countercyclically even though the variations in the cash deficit, if at all, were procyclical. However, the countercyclical swings in foreign borrowing should not be taken to imply that the government systematically altered the composition of its debt in response to cyclical movements in economic activity. Only between 1888 and 1890 does it seem that the government managed its debt in this way. In fiscal 1888, which coincided with a reference-cycle trough, the government temporarily raised additional loans from foreign banks and invested the proceeds in domestic time deposits (Table 7-3). The surge in foreign borrowing recorded near the reference-cycle trough of 1891, by contrast, was not induced by the government, but mirrored chiefly a decline in the share of London bonds absorbed by Canadian insurance companies (Table 7-6).[43] Thus, a variety of reasons existed for the compensating movements in domestic and foreign borrowing between 1887 and 1896.

The countercyclical movements in the budget deficits were due mainly to pronounced procyclical swings in customs revenue (Table 7-5). As I showed in Chapter 3, the movements in merchandise imports were distinctly procyclical. Therefore, customs revenue — not surprisingly — tended to increase during business-cycle expansions and decrease during contractions. Government expenditure frequently varied procyclically too, but its fluctuations were not strong enough to swamp the movements in revenue, except during the pre-1879 period. Until the end of the 1870s, expenditure displayed marked procyclical swings, attributable mainly to the vast public works projects initiated by the government after Confederation (e.g., the construction of the Intercolonial Railway linking Central Canada with the Maritime provinces). Much of the spending on these projects coincided with the reference-cycle expansion ending in 1873. Although revenue, on the whole, was also positively correlated with the reference cycle,[44] the cyclical patterns of the budget deficits were dominated by the movements in expenditure. During the 1880s,

CHART 7-1
DOMINION GOVERNMENT BUDGET DEFICIT AND FOREIGN BORROWING, FISCAL 1868-1914

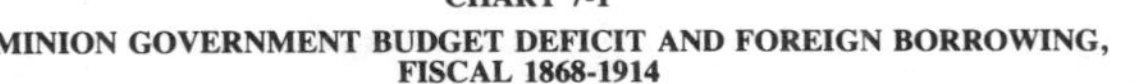

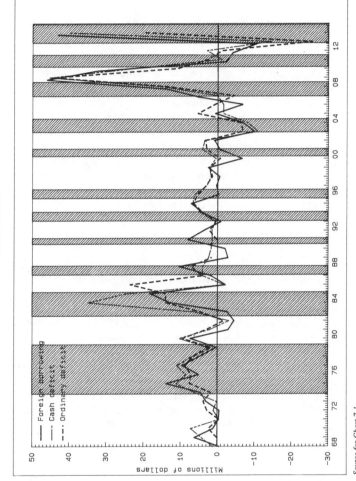

Source for Chart 7-1
Table 7-5. Data for fiscal 1907 are annualized.

spending on public works projects once again made a strong imprint on the budget. The massive deficits incurred in fiscal 1884-86 arose largely from the sharp expansion in government assistance to the CPR. However, in contrast to infrastructure spending in the late 1860s and early 1870s, the bulk of the funds provided to the CPR was expended during a depression. Thus, in the 1880s, government expenditure amplified the countercyclical swings in the ordinary and cash deficits.

7.2.3. Significance of Foreign Borrowing as a Source of Cyclical Variation in the Monetary Base

The evidence offered by Chart 7-1 suggests that foreign borrowing by the government, during much of the period under study, displayed the same cyclical pattern as the overall balance-of-payments surplus and base-money growth. Owing to the similarity of cyclical patterns, it is likely that government borrowing was a significant cause of the countercyclical swings in base-money growth. The size of the cyclical movements in foreign borrowing was certainly large enough to make a noticeable imprint on base-money growth. As far as may be judged from the available evidence, the cyclical amplitudes of the two variables were of similar order of magnitude. In order to compare the size of the cyclical movements in the two variables, I regress fiscal-year first differences in the monetary base (ΔH) on foreign borrowing (FB) for the period fiscal 1902-14:[45]

$$\Delta H = \underset{(1.28)}{8.45} + \underset{(3.95)}{1.26}\, FB, \quad \bar{R}^2 = 0.55, \quad DW = 2.51. \qquad (7.1)$$

Obviously, a fairly close positive correlation existed between base-money growth and foreign borrowing. Since during the sample period, ΔH and FB did not follow a statistically significant upward trend, the parameter estimate of FB indicates by how much base-money growth tended to fluctuate over the business cycle as compared with foreign borrowing. Equation (7.1) suggests that the cyclical amplitude of base-money growth was roughly 25 percent higher than that of foreign borrowing. A similar message is conveyed by the standard deviations of the two variables. During the sample period, the standard deviations from the fiscal-year means amounted to $31.7 and $19.2 million for ΔH and FB respectively. Consequently, foreign borrowing was likely to be a significant source of variation in base-money growth.[46]

7.3. SUMMARY AND CONCLUSIONS

The evidence presented in this chapter suggests that the Dominion government, during much of the period under study, pursued policies that tended to moderate cyclical fluctuations in Canadian economic activity. From the late 1870s onwards, the government typically stepped up foreign borrowing during business-cycle contractions and, thus, contributed significantly to the improvement in the overall balance of payments and the acceleration of base-money growth normally taking place in that phase of the cycle. Conversely, during business-cycle expansions, the government tended to curb foreign borrowing. However, the government did not consciously attempt to moderate cyclical fluctuations in economic activity, for countercyclical stabilization policies were practically unknown before World War I. The stabilizing role of foreign borrowing was largely automatic and derived from the fact that the government did not attempt to balance the budget when cyclical swings in customs revenue generated surpluses or deficits. Since budget deficits were financed, for the most part, through bond issues in London and loans from British banks, foreign borrowing, like the budget deficit, was inversely related to the business cycle.

Prior to 1879, the government's influence on the economy was largely destabilizing. Due to strong procyclical swings in government expenditure, the movements in the budget deficit and foreign borrowing were positively correlated with the business cycle. Monetary policy also played a destabilizing role in the infant years of the Dominion. Until the mid-1880s, Conservative governments, for fiscal reasons, experimented extensively with discretionary monetary policy. These experiments caused the uncovered Dominion note issue to rise substantially during the business-cycle expansion ending in 1873 and during the subsequent expansion of 1879-82. In the late 1860s and early 1870s, discretionary monetary policy reinforced the expansionary effect of foreign borrowing on the monetary base. The expansion of 1879-82, by contrast, saw foreign borrowing decline, while the uncovered issue increased once again. However, the surge in the uncovered issue was not large enough to nullify the stabilizing effect of foreign borrowing. If the sum of foreign borrowing and changes in the uncovered stock of Dominion notes is employed as a measure for the joint effect of budgetary and monetary policies on the monetary base, the behaviour of the government was clearly stabilizing after 1879 (Table 7-5).

Through an expansion of the uncovered issue, Conservative governments endeavoured to lighten the interest burden of the public debt. However, the government largely failed to monetize a portion of the public debt because of its inability to reconcile discretionary management of the note issue with the dictates of the gold standard. The government could not manage the note issue without restricting the convertibility of the Dominion notes by means of costly devices that tended to erode the fiscal benefits of its monetary experiments. The budgetary crisis of 1884-85 laid bare the defects of discretionary monetary policy and pursuaded the government to abandon discretion in favour of a predominantly automatic system. After renouncing monetary discretion, the government adhered to the gold standard "rules of the game" in an exemplary manner, notwithstanding the aberration from the path of virtue during the crisis of 1907. Thus, from the mid-1880s onwards, monetary policy ceased to counteract the stabilizing movements in foreign borrowing. The pre-1914 policy experience brings home a clear-cut message: the stabilizing influence of the public sector was strongest when the government refrained from pursuing an activist policy course.

Endnotes — Chapter 7

1. Over the periods 1872-74 and 1911-13, Dominion government expenditures amounted to 5.4 and 6.0 percent of Canadian GNP respectively (calculated from Table 7-5 and Urquhart, 1987, Table 9). Fiscal-year data are converted to a calendar-year basis according to the procedure described in Appendix A. For both periods, the middle year includes a reference-cycle peak.

2. The budgetary policies of the Dominion government could have influenced Canadian economic activity through a variety of channels. In this study, I only deal with the budgetary impulses transmitted by way of changes in the monetary base. Note that foreign borrowing did not affect the monetary base if the government spent the proceeds from the loans on foreign goods and services. The problems arising from expenditure (revenue) by the Dominion government in (from) other countries are disregarded. We do not know to what extent expenditure and revenue gave rise to money flows between Canada and abroad. Data are available only on interest payments on the government's net foreign-currency debt. This expenditure item was cyclically stable and, therefore, did not contribute to the countercyclical movements in the monetary base (see also Appendix A, note 15).

3. The unpublished records of the Finance Department are kept at the Public Archives. They are identified by the file number RG 19, followed by a volume number. Subsequently, I only quote the volume numbers.

4. During the budgetary crisis of 1884-85, the Deputy Minister of Finance explicitly made this point. Courtney to Bolitho (banker in Penzance, England), Dec. 4, 1884, vol. 2997. The episode of 1884-85 is discussed below.

5. See the Provincial Notes Act of 1866 for the regulations governing the note issue. After Confederation this piece of legislation was re-enacted in the form of the Dominion Notes Act of 1868.

6. The new Dominion government inherited the Province's poor credit rating. In 1870, Dominion government bonds traded in London and 3-percent British consols commanded yields of 5.4 and 3.2 percent respectively (Table 7-4; Homer, 1963, Table 19).

7. Statement by Finance Minister Hincks, June 5, 1871, vol. 3378.

8. Although the earmarked deposits were frequently characterized as specie deposited with the Bank of Montreal (e.g., Canada, *Parliamentary Debates,* 1870, 659; *Monetary Times,* Nov. 14, 1867), they were not meant to delineate government claims on the gold stock of the Bank. Finance Minister Hincks took pains to point out that — in principle — all government demand deposits with the Bank, not only the earmarked share, served as a security for the note issue (Canada, *Parliamentary Debates,* 1870, 222). As long as the agreement with the Bank was in effect, the government, within certain limits, could determine arbitrarily the size of the official gold reserve. Needless to say, as regards the security of the note issue, the size of deposits earmarked as gold was not particularly relevant. What really mattered was the size of the Bank's gold stock.

9. This point is convincingly made by Shortt (1904a). For a detailed discussion of the terms of the arrangement, see that source and Denison (1967, 146-47). In 1864, the government had already accepted two other restrictive conditions in order to obtain financial assistance from the Bank of Montreal. The Finance Minister was required to keep with the Bank a minimum balance of $0.4 or $0.5 million and was not permitted to deposit funds with any other domestic banks (Hincks to Treasury Board, Dec. 14, 1869, vol. 3377).

10. Under the terms of Confederation, the government was entitled to place in the London market a loan, guaranteed by Britain, for the purpose of constructing the Intercolonial Railway. The bonds were issued successfully in 1868 and generated substantial liquid funds. In addition, a cyclical increase in revenue further alleviated the budgetary problems of the Dominion (Perry, 1955, 51-58). The arrangement with the Bank of Montreal was renegotiated early in 1870 before it was terminated. The government also declared that it was not longer bound by the restrictions on deposits (see preceding note), after the Bank had declined to accept, at interest rates Hincks and his predecessor considered satisfactory, the funds arising from the Intercolonial loan. Finally, Hincks suspected that the Bank abused its position as the government's exclusive foreign-exchange

broker, a role it had assumed on the basis of an informal agreement between the two parties. For this reason, he initiated a system under which all the domestic banks were invited to submit tenders when the government wished to purchase or sell foreign exchange. For a more detailed discussion of these points, see Rich (1976, 21-23).

11. According to equations (D.18), (D.19) and (D.20), an increase in the uncovered stock of Dominion notes, in the long run, does not affect the nominal and real values of the monetary base, but only lowers international monetary assets.

12. The share of cash the chartered banks were required to hold in the form of Dominion notes was raised from 33-1/3 to 40 percent. Moreover, the banks were obliged to issue their own notes in denominations of $5 or multiples thereof and to pay out on demand up to $50 in $1 and $2 notes (Canada, *Debates,* 1880, 1724).

13. The proportion of the aggregate issue absorbed by the banks fluctuated widely, but from 1873 to 1886 it averaged about two-thirds. Calculated from Table 7-1 and Curtis (1931a, 38).

14. Hincks stated explicitly that an objective of discretion was to keep the official gold stock as small as possible (Rich, 1977).

15. See the legend to Table 7-1.

16. Prior to 1880, excess reserves were frequently negative (Table 7-1). The returns were not published late in 1869, early 1870 and July, 1871. From February to May, 1880, the government, though publishing the returns, did not report its actual gold holdings. Instead, all the returns for that period show the gold stock held early in February. Curtis (1931a, 92) did not notice this problem and reproduced the misleading statistics supplied by the government. Unpublished data suggest that the government suffered from a reserve deficiency of $0.5 million at the end of 1880I (vol. 2489). It is unclear why the government failed to publish the returns late in 1869 and early 1870 since no gold was held at that time.

17. For a critical discussion of these techniques, see *Monetary Times,* April 11, 1873, 890-91; June 6, 1884, 1369-70.

18. The government began to diversify its deposits soon after the removal of the restrictions imposed by the Bank of Montreal.

19. See Officer (1986, 1048-49) for an estimate of transactions costs associated with selling sovereigns in New York.

20. Courtney to ARG in Toronto, June 10, 1879, vol. 2772.

21. See the exchange between the *Monetary Times* and Hincks, reprinted in Neufeld (1964, 183-91).

22. Hincks to Thomas (banker), Jan. 29, 1873, vol. 3378.

23. In July, 1871, Dominion notes accounted for 37 percent of aggregate bank cash reserves (earliest available figure). By the end of 1872, this percentage had risen to 56 and fluctuated about that level from 1873I to 1879IV. As a result of the change in the legal provision on the composition of bank cash reserves (see note 12), the share of Dominion notes increased once again in 1880 and averaged 62 percent over the period 1880II-1886IV (average stock of Dominion notes as a percentage of average cash reserves held during the respective period, with averages calculated from quarterly data as reported by Curtis (1931a, 36 and 38).

24. For 1879, the Finance Department records offer numerous examples of gold sales to domestic banks (e.g., various transactions in September and October, vol. 2774; Courtney to ARG, Toronto, Nov. 24, 1879, vol. 2775).

25. Cartwright sarcastically expressed the hope that the Indians would not be blessed with notes redeemable in Halifax, Montreal or Toronto (Canada, *Debates,* 1880, 1728).

26. In a letter to the ARGs, Courtney pointed out that the government had sanctioned a special issue of Dominion notes amounting to $2 million. He further inquired "as to means that might be employed to circulate these notes ... in a manner of course that would not attract too great attention on the part of the Public and which at the same time would not be undignified"

(May 19, 1880, vol. 2776). The notes presumably were deposited in the usual manner since other "dignified" means were not available.

27. For the deposit withdrawals, see vols. 2784-87. In November, 1882, the Deputy Minister of Finance advised the General Manager of the Bank of Montreal that the government would be compelled to withdraw time deposits because "the Canadian Pacific Railway upsets our calculations" (Courtney to Buchanan, Nov. 24, 1882, vol. 2784). The CPR was authorized to issue bonds secured by a land grant from the government. Any proceeds from the bond issue were to be deposited with the government, which agreed to disburse the funds to the company as the construction project progressed. The government overestimated the deposits that would be made by the CPR on account of the bond sale. Due to the dismal state of the company's finances, investors were reluctant to take up the issue (Innis, 1923, 104, 108; McDougall, 1968, 53).

28. Tilley to Macdonald, June 12, 1884 (quoted in Berton, 1971, 322-23). The government floated in the London market $24 million worth of bonds. Additional bond issues were placed in 1885, 1886 and 1888 (Canada, Public Accounts for 1915, part I, 33).

29. Courtney to Tupper, Dec. 18, 1884, vol. 2997. The monthly bank returns *(Canada Gazette)* indicate that the Bank of Montreal was the only institution causing difficulties for the government. In November and December, 1884, the Bank reduced its holdings of Dominion notes to slightly over 40 percent of aggregate cash reserves, the minimum required by law. Early in 1885, it restored its holdings to the October, 1884, level. The other banks did not vary significantly their holdings of Dominion notes.

30. Courtney to Rose, Dec. 4, 1884, vol. 2997. The note-redemption problems were compounded by the fact that the Bank of Montreal acted as the government's agent for the import of sovereigns. The Bank, therefore, had an incentive to maximize the flow of gold out of official vaults. Needless to say, this arrangement was modified in 1885 (Courtney to Cartwright, Dec. 7, 1885, vol. 2997).

31. Out of the total of $4.4 million, the Bank of Montreal and the Montreal City and District Savings Bank contributed $2.0 and $1.2 million respectively (Canada, Public Accounts for 1885, *Sessional Paper,* No. 2, 1886, xxix). The latter institution was controlled by the Bank of Montreal (Naylor, 1975, vol. 1, 86).

32. Courtney to Cartwright, Dec. 7, 1885, vol. 2997.

33. The following percentages may be calculated for the average return on the government's time deposits (averages of annual rates): fiscal 1872-74: 4.7; 1881-83: 3.7; 1889: 2.5. Since it is impossible to compile separately the average return on time deposits at domestic and foreign banks, I selected years in which the share held with foreign banks was small (see Canada, Public Accounts for 1915, part I, 41-42).

34. Table 7-1 does not cover the post-1886 period. From 1892 onwards, excess reserves seldom dropped below $3 million (Rich, 1976, Table 1). However, at the end of 1907, the government failed to meet the reserve requirement (see Chapter 6).

35. See the legend to Table 7-5, column (1), for a justification of this procedure.

36. The change in net *aggregate* liabilities, as shown in the Public Accounts, equals the ordinary deficit.

37. The estimates of Dominion government bonds issued in London, as presented in this study, differ sharply from those compiled by Simon (1970). See Appendix F for a comparison of the two sets of estimates.

38. Prior to 1914, there was only one instance of the government raising loans from banks outside Canada and the United Kingdom. In fiscal 1909, the government borrowed temporarily $3.9 million from French banks.

39. During the budgetary crisis of 1884-85, Finance Department officials explored the possibility of raising a temporary bank loan in New York. However, neither New York banks nor the New York branches of the Canadian banks were able to offer attractive terms (Courtney to Rose, Dec. 4, 1884; Courtney to Tupper, April 9, 1885, vol. 2997).

40. Bonds issued in Canada commanded similar yields as those issued in London (Canada, Public Accounts for 1915, part I, 35-37; and Table 7-4), but it should be remembered that the former were an unimportant source of finance.

41. From the end of fiscal 1872 to the end of fiscal 1886, deposits at the government and post office savings banks grew more rapidly than the chartered banks' notice deposits, that is, at average annual rates of 15 and 6 percent respectively. Thereafter, the growth patterns were reversed, with the annual increases averaging 1.5 and slightly less than 10 percent for the remainder of the pre-1914 period (calculated from Canada, Public Accounts for 1915, part I, 28; Curtis, 1931a, 23). Naylor's (1975, vol. 1, 85-95) predilection for conspiracy theories of banking leads him to argue that the chartered banks — starting in 1880 — undertook to force the government out of the savings deposit business. In my opinion, the government was not a victim of greedy commercial bankers, but lost interest in its savings banks after cheaper sources of finance had become available.

42. For the subperiods fiscal 1868-86 and 1887-1914, the simple correlation between foreign borrowing and the cash deficit amounted to 0.82 and 0.96 respectively.

43. On the whole, the stock of London bonds held by insurance companies did not fluctuate much (Table 7-6).

44. The temporary surge in revenue in 1879 was caused by the Halifax fishery award of $4.5 million.

45. Data sources: Tables A-2 and 7-5. The monetary base at the end of 1914I is estimated in the same way as the values for 1913III and IV. The data for fiscal 1907, which lasted nine months, are not annualized.

46. I do not mean to imply that equation (7.1) may be used to determine the impact of a change in foreign borrowing by the government on base-money growth. In order to simulate the effect on the monetary base of alternative budgetary strategies pursued by the government, a full-fledged macroeconometric model of the Canadian economy would be required. The gaps in the available data preclude the construction of such a model.

CHAPTER 8

EPILOGUE

8.1. THE OPERATION OF THE CANADIAN GOLD STANDARD: SUMMARY AND CONCLUSIONS

Advocates of the gold standard tend to argue that the fetters on pre-1914 discretionary monetary management compelled monetary authorities and commercial banks to behave in a stabilizing manner. By the standards of the 1970s and 1980s, pre-1914 inflation trends were indeed very modest. But as a cyclical stabilizer, the performance of the pre-1914 gold standard was less satisfactory, as indicated by substantial short-run swings in price level and output. In spite of the fetters imposed by the gold standard, money supplies tended to move procyclically. Evidence marshalled by Hay (1967) and Macesich (1970) suggests that the pattern of the Canadian money stock was procyclical, both before and after World War I. Furthermore, these authors find a consistent lag between Canadian economic activity and money. They take the lag to imply that money was an important source of cyclical instability in Canada. Thus, the gold standard did not preclude destabilizing movements in the Canadian money stock.

In this study, I explored the stabilizing or destabilizing powers of the gold standard in the light of Canadian experience. To this end, I examined the causes and effects of the observed procyclical movements in the Canadian money stock. The principal results may be summed up as follows:

(i) While this study corroborates Hay and Macesich's findings as to marked procyclical swings in the Canadian money stock, there is no evidence of a systematic lag between economic activity and money. On the contrary, the cyclical turning points in money coincided closely with those in economic activity. The procyclical pattern of the money stock reflected pronounced countercyclical movements in the aggregate reserve ratio of the chartered banks, induced by procyclical swings in domestic output and interest rates. The monetary base and the currency-liability ratio, by contrast, did not account for the procyclical pattern of the money stock. The monetary base varied countercyclically, while the currency-liability ratio was unrelated to the business cycle.

(ii) The countercyclical movements in the monetary base were attributable entirely to the balance of payments. The overall balance-of-payments surplus and, hence, base-money growth were negatively correlated with economic activity, with cyclical peaks (troughs) in the overall surplus and base-money growth coinciding closely with cyclical troughs (peaks) in economic activity. The pattern of the current-account surplus also tended to be countercyclical because of strong procyclical swings in imports. The analysis suggests that over the business cycle, the marginal propensity to absorb home and imported goods exceeded unity. During a major part of the period under study, net capital inflows to Canada also varied countercyclically. In all probability, this pattern is explained by countercyclical movements in interest rate differentials between Canada and the United States. Interest rates in both countries tended to vary procyclically, but in Canada their amplitude was much smaller than in the United States.

(iii) Unlike the balance of payments, discretionary monetary policy was only a minor source of cyclical variation in the monetary base. In the first twenty years following Confederation, the government actively employed discretionary monetary policy for debt management purposes. In an effort to lighten the interest burden of the public debt, the government attempted to issue uncovered Dominion notes. During this period, discretionary monetary policy was an important determinant of the growth trend of the monetary base. Moreover, the uncovered stock of Dominion notes varied procyclically, but these movements were not strong enough to impinge significantly on the countercyclical pattern of the monetary base. From the mid-1880s onwards, monetary policy became largely automatic, with the supply of Dominion notes varying passively in response to changes in the official gold reserve. The shift to an automatic system was motivated by the fact that the fetters of the gold standard precluded effective management of the note issue for debt management purposes. In particular, the government was at a loss to keep the uncovered Dominion notes in circulation without adopting costly devices designed to restrict their convertibility into gold. These devices eroded the seigniorage the government expected to reap from the Dominion note issues.

Foreign borrowing was another channel through which government policy affected the monetary base. Except in the 1870s, the budget deficit of the Dominion government varied countercyclically as a result of pronounced procyclical swings in revenue, notably in the form of income from customs duties. Since a large share of the deficit was financed by raising funds in the London capital market, foreign borrowing by the government was inversely related to the business cycle too. Thus, government borrowing abroad amplified the countercyclical movements in the monetary base during a major part of the period under study.

The cyclical patterns of uncovered Dominion notes and foreign borrowing suggest that the behaviour of the government was largely stabilizing. The source of the procyclical movements in the money stock did not reside in Dominion government monetary and budgetary policies but in reserve management of the chartered banks.

(iv) The main contribution of this study was to develop and test a monetary model of the Canadian business cycle that explicitly allows for destabilizing reserve behaviour on the part of the chartered banks. In line with previous research, I assumed that cyclical movements in Canadian economic activity were triggered by disturbances imported from the United States and other foreign countries. A cyclical expansion in U.S. economic activity, for example, elicited a rise in Canadian output, prices and nominal money demand by way of an increase in exports and possibly import prices. Owing to an output-induced decline in the aggregate reserve ratio, the chartered banks accommodated higher nominal money demand by a corresponding rise in supply. As a result of accommodative behaviour of the chartered banks, the cyclical expansion in money demand did not lead to an instantaneous rise in Canadian interest rates. Short-term interest rates began to rise only near the midpoint of a business-cycle expansion, in response to a deterioration in the balance of payments and an attendant contraction (relative to trend) in the monetary base. Long-term interest rates, if at all, reacted with an even longer lag to the cyclical expansion in Canadian economic activity. As indicated earlier, the deterioration in the balance of payments typically reflected a fall in both the current-account surplus and net capital inflows.

Because of a high interest-sensitivity of the aggregate reserve ratio, the cyclical rise in Canadian interest rates, prompted by the deterioration in the balance of payments, was very modest as compared with the frequently substantial cyclical surge in U.S. rates. The available evidence lends at least indirect support to the view that the cyclical movements in Canadian interest rates were not strong enough to impinge significantly on the cyclical pattern of Canadian economic activity. For this reason, a variant of the Keynesian export multiplier model appears to account best for the observed cyclical swings in Canadian economic activity.

The consistency of the results with the Keynesian viewpoint, however, need not imply that the Canadian business cycle was invariant to changes in the Canadian money stock. On the contrary, the principal thesis advanced in this study is that money did matter. Accommodative reserve management by the chartered banks weakened the stabilizing powers of the gold standard and exposed the Canadian economy to the full force of the Keynesian export multiplier. However, this study did not prove conclusively that money was an important cause of cyclical instability in Canadian economic activity. In particular, it is impossible to say to what extent a less accommodative stance by the Canadian chartered banks would have dampened the cyclical swings in Canadian economic activity.

(v) The importance of accommodative reserve management by the chartered banks further implies that the price-specie-flow mechanism — though operative in the longer run — did not function properly in the short run. As far as the cyclical aspects of balance-of-payments adjustment are concerned, the evidence presented in this study only lends partial support to Viner's (1924) assertion that the mode of operation of the pre-1914 Canadian adjustment-mechanism closely conformed to the classical theory of the gold standard. As suggested by that theory, a cyclical increase in Canadian prices and output caused the Canadian balance-of-payments surplus and base-money growth to shrink. A cyclical decline in the balance-of-payments surplus was also accompanied by a slowdown in inflows of monetary gold to Canada. Contrary to the classical theory of the gold standard, however, a cyclical decline in the balance-of-payments surplus did not curb the growth in Canadian money stock, nor did it moderate to any significant extent the rise in Canadian prices and output.

Had the money stock borne a close relationship to the monetary base, the price-specie-flow mechanism would have acted as an automatic stabilizer of cyclical fluctuations in Canadian economic activity. Countercyclical movements in the Canadian money stock would have enhanced the procyclical swings in domestic interest rates and, thus, dampened the Canadian business cycle. In this context, it is interesting to note that my conclusions about the short-run stabilizing powers of the classical adjustment mechanism closely resemble views expressed by Hawtrey (1928; 1947) a long time ago. Hawtrey (1947, 33-44 and 86-91) clearly recognized the destabilizing role of countercyclical movements in bank reserve ratios under the gold standard. A cyclical expansion in economic activity, he maintained, was at first accommodated by an increase in the supply of commercial-bank credit and money. The credit expansion continued until economic activity had grown sufficiently to generate substantial current-account deficits and losses of bank reserves. The reserve drains from the banking system in turn placed a brake on credit growth. The slowdown in credit growth — in due course — was followed by a cyclical contraction in economic activity.[1]

Hawtrey's analysis implies that the price-specie-flow mechanism was operative in the long run, but did not work quickly enough to quell procyclical movements in credit, money and economic activity. In his view, the business

> cycle is a *credit* cycle, and is traceable to a defect in the gold standard as a regulator of credit. Conformity to the gold standard sooner or later keeps credit movement within bounds, but *not soon enough*. The credit cycle occurs because it takes years for the restrictive influence of gold to make itself felt. (Hawtrey, 1947, 88).

Although this study takes issues with various aspects of Viner's analysis, it does not follow McCloskey and Zecher's suggestion for discarding entirely the classical price-specie-flow model. The McCloskey-Zecher perfect-arbitrage framework for analyzing the classical adjustment mechanism does not appear to accord with pre-1914 Canadian evidence. In particular, the McCloskey-Zecher framework does not account for the observed cyclical pattern of Canadian interest rates. Interest rates in Canada were not linked rigidly to those in the United States and other countries through perfect arbitrage, but responded distinctly to shifts in demand for and supply of domestic base money.[2] Therefore, the Canadian cycle-transmission process must be investigated within the framework of the traditional price-specie-flow model that allows for direct effects of changes in the domestic money stock on domestic economic activity.

(vi) The monetary analysis presented in this study also offers new insights into the causes of the 1907 crisis. This episode in Canadian monetary history has attracted considerable attention in the existing literature because it manifested itself in a serious credit squeeze that prompted the Canadian government to assume, for the first time, the role of lender of last resort to the chartered banks. Students of the 1907 crisis have almost unanimously stressed such international causes as an alleged inability of the chartered banks to meet a seasonal rise in the demand for bank notes as a result of a statutory ceiling on the note issue. This emphasis on internal causes is surprising since the crisis broke out in New York and sent shock waves throughout the gold-standard world. Therefore, I would expect that the difficulties in New York were a major cause of the Canadian credit squeeze.

In this study, I have argued that the external causes of the 1907 crisis were indeed much more important than has previously been believed. The crisis occurred in the autumn of 1907, near the midpoint of a business-cycle contraction. As was typical for that stage of the business cycle, the monetary base and aggregate reserves of the chartered banks were at a cyclical trough. However, the cyclical drop in bank reserves was unlikely to be the sole cause of the crisis because the chartered banks normally did not encounter major problems in absorbing cyclical losses of reserves. The factor that distinguished this episode from other business-cycle contractions was an unusually severe seasonal fall in bank reserves. Interestingly, the Canadian monetary base and bank reserves invariably fell (relative to their trends) during the crop-moving season in the autumn, despite a massive seasonal rise in exports of agricultural products and a corresponding improvement in the balance of payments on current account, because the increase in exports was more than offset by a decline in net capital inflows from abroad. Among other factors, a sharp temporary surge in U.S. short-term interest rates typically recorded during the crop-moving season was responsible for the autumnal decrease in net capital inflows. In the autumn of 1907, the financial crisis in New York caused short-term interest rates to soar to record levels, triggering an unusually large drop in net capital inflows. Thus, the credit squeeze in Canada resulted from an exceedingly large interest-induced seasonal loss of bank reserves that came on top of a normal cyclical contraction.

The autumnal fall in the overall balance-of-payments surplus was associated with outflows of both monetary gold and secondary reserves. The evidence of a marked decline in the Canadian stock of monetary gold during the crop-moving season contrasts sharply with traditional views about the mechanics of seasonal adjustment. Most contemporary observers believed that in periods of financial stringency the Canadian banks compounded the liquidity problems in New York by withdrawing monetary gold from financial institutions in that city. In view of the autumnal decline in the Canadian stock of monetary gold, the Canadian banks clearly did not behave in this way but contributed to alleviating liquidity problems in New York. The role played by the Canadian banks as suppliers of liquidity to the New York market was particularly evident in the aftermath of the 1907 crash.

(vii) The Canadian stock of monetary gold not only responded to seasonal movements in U.S. interest rates. A cyclical rise in these rates also led to a decline in the Canadian stock of monetary gold, mainly as a result of the chartered banks altering the composition of their reserves by substituting call loans for cash. Thus, the pattern of the Canadian stock of monetary gold was countercyclical. Since the overall balance-of-payments surplus also varied countercyclically, this piece of evidence implies that Canadian payments imbalances were settled by flows of both secondary reserves and gold. Therefore, the observed cyclical pattern of the overall surplus and its components is inconsistent with Viner's view that monetary gold flows were related to the growth in the domestic money stock rather than the state of the balance of payments. However, Viner's conclusions are valid in the sense that secondary reserves played the dominant role in cyclical balance-of-payments adjustment, notably after 1879.

The evidence of countercyclical swings in the monetary gold stock suggests that the destabilizing effects of procyclical movements in the Canadian money stock passed through both direct and indirect channels. Since national business cycles were closely synchronized, the countercyclical pattern of the Canadian stock of monetary gold accentuated procyclical fluctuations in foreign money stocks and, thus, contributed to instability abroad. Increased instability abroad in turn fed back on domestic economic activity.

Needless to say, indirect monetary effects emanating from Canada, by themselves, were unlikely to be sufficiently strong to make a substantial imprint on world economic activity. Nonetheless, an analysis of indirect monetary effects is interesting because it appears that they were an important source of cyclical instability in the gold-standard world as a whole. Countercyclical movements in monetary gold flows did not arise exclusively in Canada, but were widespread under the pre-1914 gold standard. A brief — and somewhat cryptic — comparison of Canadian experience with that of other major gold-standard countries helps to illuminate the destabilizing role of countercyclical monetary gold flows. Furthermore, it shows that the failure of the price-specie-flow mechanism to act as a cyclical stabilizer was not a uniquely Canadian phenomenon, but enhanced cyclical instability elsewhere in the world too.

8.2. COMPARISON WITH OTHER COUNTRIES

Students of the gold standard have long recognized the defects of the classical adjustment mechanism as a cyclical stabilizer. They point to a number of factors, to be discussed here, that tended to weaken the stabilizing powers of that mechanism: destabilizing capital flows, failure to adhere to the gold standard "rules of the game," and destabilizing movements in the money multiplier.

8.2.1. Destabilizing Capital Flows

The problems arising from destabilizing capital flows were analyzed as early as in the 1920s by Taussig and his disciples. They noticed that contrary to the predictions of the traditional price-specie-flow model, some countries tended to speed up their imports of monetary gold during the expansion phase of the business cycle, despite a deterioration in the current-account balance induced by rising prices and output. They traced the source of the conflict with the traditional doctrine to procyclical or destabilizing movements in net capital inflows from abroad.

The explanation offered by Taussig (1927, 207-09) for the occurrence of destabilizing capital flows is akin to arguments put forward by H.G. Johnson (1973) almost fifty years later under the heading of the monetary approach to balance-of-payments theory. A cyclical expansion in economic activity in a particular country, Taussig argued, was associated with an increase in domestic money demand and interest rates. As a result of the rise in interest rates, the country was able to attract additional capital and monetary gold from abroad. Thus, the cyclical increase in domestic money demand was sustained by an expansion in supply arising from the inflow of monetary gold. Because the decline in the current-account surplus was more than offset by a rise in net capital inflows from abroad, the classical adjustment mechanism failed to act as a cyclical stabilizer even though the behaviour of the current account conformed to the classical doctrine.

While in Canada capital flows, on the whole, played a stabilizing role, they appear to have served as a major destabilizing force in the United Kingdom (see Beach, 1935; Ford, 1962, ch. 3; Goodhart, 1972, chs. 14-15; McCloskey and Zecher, 1976). Although during business-cycle expansions the combined balance-of-payments on current and long-term capital accounts tended to deteriorate,[3] the United Kingdom typically stepped up her imports of monetary gold from abroad by means of destabilizing short-term capital flows. In the early stage of a business-cycle expansion, the Bank of England was faced with a drain of gold into general circulation as U.K. money demand increased. Moreover, the deterioration in the combined balance-of-payments on current and long-term capital accounts initially led to outflows of gold from the United Kingdom. In an effort to replenish its dwindling gold reserve, the Bank hiked its discount rate and, thus, was able to attract additional short-term capital and monetary gold from abroad.[4] Through frequent variations in its discount rate, the Bank managed to safeguard the convertibility of its liabilities without having to maintain an excessively large gold reserve. Consequently, destabilizing capital flows allowed the Bank to accommodate procyclical movements in U.K. money demand.[5]

Andrew (1907), Beach (1935, Appendix A), as well as McCloskey and Zecher (1976, 369) claim that in the United States, inflows of monetary gold were also positively correlated with the business cycle. This view has been contested by Goodhart (1969, 28), who fails to detect a statistically significant difference between average net U.S. imports of gold coin for the expansion and contraction stages of the reference cycle. A re-examination of the evidence indeed suggests that the pattern of net U.S. imports of gold coin was not consistently procyclical.[6] Thus, in the United States, gold flows do not appear to have accounted to any significant extent for the observed procyclical pattern in the money stock.[7]

The United Kingdom would not have managed to accommodate cyclical expansions in domestic money demand by additional imports of monetary gold unless other countries had been prepared to release precious metal. There is no reason to believe that the world stock of monetary gold varied procyclically.[8] I already showed that Canada was one of those countries curbing her net imports of monetary gold during business-cycle expansions. Further examples of countries whose net inflows of monetary gold moved countercyclically are Germany and France. In the case of these two countries, the countercyclical pattern of net gold inflows reflected largely a failure of the respective central banks to comply with the gold-standard rules of the game.

8.2.2. Adherence to the Gold-Standard Rules of the Game

In a pioneering study of monetary policy under the pre-1914 gold standard, Bloomfield (1959) shows that Continental European central banks frequently violated the rules of the game. Monetary policy was considered to be consistent with the rules of the game so long as monetary authorities did not attempt to neutralize the effects of international gold flows on the domestic monetary base. Therefore, adherence to the rules of the game implies a close positive correlation between a country's monetary gold stock and its monetary base.[9]

Chart 8-1 illustrates the cyclical patterns of German net inflows of monetary gold, as well as of the growth in the German monetary base and money stock M_1. Net inflows of monetary gold are assumed to match first differences in the German stock of monetary gold, covering the holdings of the Reichsbank and gold coin in general circulation. A small amount of monetary gold held by the imperial government and private banks of issue is not taken into account. The German monetary base comprises monetary gold, subsidiary coin and imperial government notes outside the Reichsbank and the private banks of issue, as well as notes and deposits outstanding at the Reichsbank and the private banks of issue. In Germany, the bulk of notes was issued by the Reichsbank and the imperial government, while the private banks of issue —

CHART 8-1

NET GOLD INFLOWS, GROWTH IN THE MONETARY BASE AND MONEY STOCK M_1: GERMANY, 1892-1913

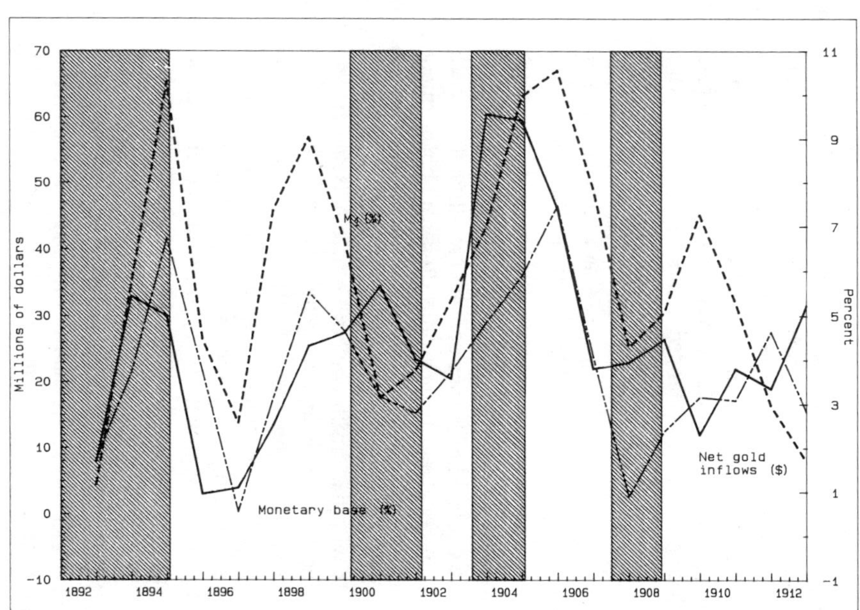

Sources and estimation methods for Chart 8-1

To reduce intra-cycle variation, the first differences or growth rates plotted in Chart 8-1 are calculated from end-of-year data that are smoothed by a two-year moving average. First differences or growth rates based on the averages for, say, 1891/92 and 1892/93 are centred on December 31, 1892. Net inflows of monetary gold equal first differences in end-of-year data on the German stock of monetary gold, encompassing (a) holdings of the Reichsbank and (b) gold outside the Reichsbank, the imperial government, and the private banks of issue (Germany, Bundesbank, 1976, 14 and 329). Item (b) includes gold coin minted in Germany and absorbed by foreigners or domestic non-monetary users, and excludes foreign gold coin circulating in Germany. The monetary base covers item (b), subsidiary coin outside the Reichsbank and the private banks of issue, notes issued by the imperial government, the Reichsbank and the private banks of issue, as well as deposits with the Reichsbank and the private banks of issue (Germany, Bundesbank, 14 and 16). Data on the money stock M_1 are taken from Tilly (1973, 346). The data are converted to dollar values at the mint par value of $0.238 per Reichsmark. See Morgenstern (1959, 41) for the dates of German reference-cycle turning points.

which gradually lost ground after the establishment of the Reichsbank in 1876 — only played a minor role as suppliers of base money (see Seeger, 1968, 19-22). The aggregate M_1 embraces currency and demand deposits in the hands of non-banks, as estimated by Tilly (1973, 346). Chart 8-1 only covers the period 1892-1913 because of gaps in the data for earlier years.[10]

The evidence clearly indicates that German net inflows of monetary gold varied countercyclically, with a cyclical peak (trough) normally attained during the contraction (expansion) stage of the reference cycle. The countercyclical pattern of gold inflows is also revealed by Table 8-1.[11] The cyclical pattern of base-money growth, by contrast, was less regular than that of gold imports. In the 1890s, base-money growth moved countercyclically, while over the period 1900-13 its pattern was largely procyclical, with a peak (trough) normally recorded during the expansion (contraction) phase of the reference cycle. Only in one instance (1903-04), did base-money growth fail to decrease during a contraction. The money stock M_1 tended to move in sympathy with the monetary base, that is, its pattern was also largely procyclical.[12] However, the procyclical fluctuations in M_1 were more pronounced than those in the monetary base, due to mild countercyclical movements in the cash reserve ratio of commercial banks.[13] The currency-deposit ratio was invariant to the reference cycle.[14]

Similar conclusions may be drawn from French experience. Chart 8-2 depicts net inflows of gold to France and the growth in the French monetary base. Note that the available French gold flow data cover imports of both monetary and non-monetary gold. The French monetary base is assumed to embrace notes and monetary gold outside the Bank of France, as well as demand deposits with that institution. In France, only the central bank was authorized to issue notes. Although the cyclical patterns of the series displayed in Chart 8-2 were not very regular, net inflows of gold tended to be higher during reference-cycle contractions than during expansions. The countercyclical pattern of French gold inflows is also brought out clearly by Table 8-1.[15] French base-money growth, by contrast, moved procyclically. Except in the 1890s, base-money growth during reference-cycle expansions typically exceeded the corresponding values during contractions.

The patterns revealed by Charts 8-1 and 8-2 suggest that the Reichsbank and the Bank of France — like the Bank of England — accommodated procyclical movements in domestic money demand. However, in contrast to the Bank of England, the two Continental European central banks did not sustain a cyclical rise in the domestic money stock by importing additional gold from abroad; they expanded instead their holdings of domestic assets. A fact commonly known to contemporary observers was that both the Reichsbank and the Bank of France attempted to keep their discount rates as stable as possible. The Bank of France, in particular, repeatedly asserted that large interest rate movements were harmful to commerce and industry (Morgenstern, 1959, 379). During business-cycle expansions, when German and French market interest rates typically rose,[16] the two central banks adjusted only sluggishly their own discount rates (Morgenstern, 1959, 407-08). As market rates increased relative to official discount rates, the private sector was prompted to borrow additional funds from the two central banks. Thus, the Reichsbank and the Bank of France accommodated the business-cycle expansion through an increase in the supply of base money. The cyclical upswing in economic activity in turn caused the balance of payments to deteriorate and net inflows of monetary gold to decline.[17] The resulting external loss of monetary gold by the two central banks was reinforced by a drain of precious metal into internal circulation. If the reserve drain persisted, the Reichsbank and Bank of France were forced to react by raising their discount rates.

In general, the Bank of France was more successful in shielding the domestic monetary base from international gold flows than the Reichsbank. By international standards, the Bank of France maintained a very high gold reserve relative to its liabilities and, therefore, was able to absorb large reserve drains.[18] Moreover, in contrast to the Reichsbank and the Bank of England, the Bank of France was not subject to minimum reserve requirements. The Bank of France showed greater willingness than the Reichsbank to restrict outflows of gold by manipulating the gold export point (White, 1933, 182-88; Morgenstern, 1959, 441). The relative immunity of the Bank of France to foreign shocks was brought into sharp relief during the crisis of 1907. While the Bank of France weathered the crisis without much difficulty, the Reichsbank was confronted with a massive outflow of monetary gold. The size of its reserve drain was such that it was powerless to avert an equally

TABLE 8-1
CYCLICAL AMPLITUDE OF NET INFLOWS OF MONETARY GOLD TO CANADA, GERMANY AND FRANCE, 1900-13
(Millions of Dollars)

Country	Expansion Stage	Contraction Stage
Canada	4.1	15.4
Germany	20.9	50.3
France	51.0	89.3

Sources and estimation methods for Table 8-1

See Table A-2, Charts 8-1 and 8-2 for the data sources. Annual data on net inflows of monetary gold are assigned to the expansion and contraction stages of the respective country's reference cycle. For Canada, I employ the assignment procedure 3 in Appendix C. For the other countries, an analogous assignment procedure is used:
Expansions in Germany: 95-99, 02-03, 05-07, 09-12
Expansions in France: 80-81, 88-90, 95-99, 05-07, 09-12.

CHART 8-2

NET GOLD INFLOWS AND GROWTH IN THE MONETARY BASE: FRANCE, 1880-1913

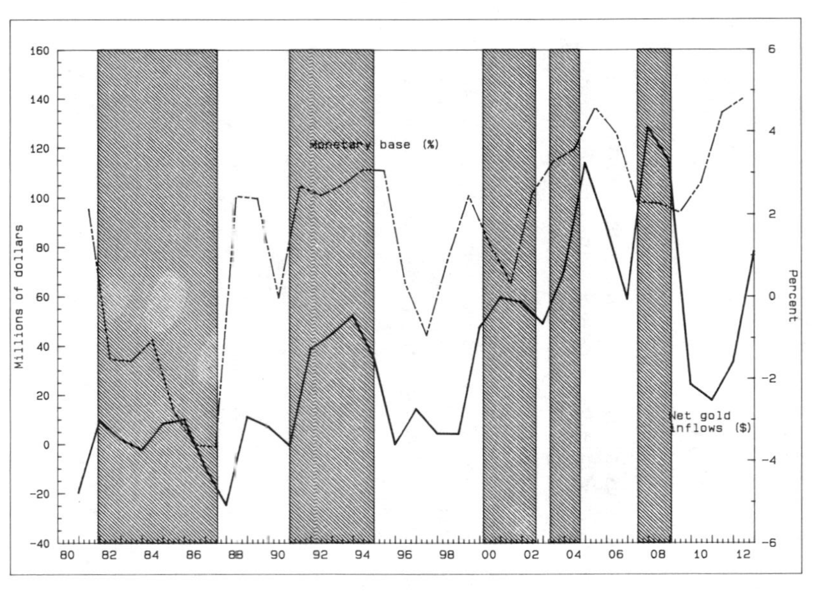

Sources and estimation methods for Chart 8-2

Annual data on net inflows of monetary gold are taken from White (1933, Table 29). They cover trade in gold coins and bullion, but do not separate monetary from non-monetary gold. In contrast to the German data shown in Chart 8-1, they are derived from French trade statistics. The French monetary base covers (a) bank notes and gold outside the Bank of France, and (b) demand deposits with the Bank of France. Item (a): White (1933, Table 35 and 208-10). White estimated the gold component of item (a) from data on the specie circulation in 1903. From that bench-mark figure, he added or subtracted cumulative monthly net imports of gold coin, gold bullion and silver coin for the other years, in order to obtain a complete set of data for the period 1880-1913 as a whole. This procedure yielded a series on the aggregate stock of specie. He then adjusted that aggregate for the holdings of the Bank of France and for gold transferred to non-monetary use. Item (b): White (1933, Table 30). The data on the monetary base represent annual averages of monthly values. They are smoothed by a two-year moving average and are converted to dollar values at the mint par value of $0.193 per franc. Therefore, the growth rate in that aggregate from, say, 1880/81 to 1881/82 is centred on June 30, 1881. Net gold inflows are centred in the same way as the observations in Chart 8-1. See Morgenstern (1959, 41) for the dates of French reference-cycle turning points.

drastic contraction in base-money growth (Chart 8-1). A contemporary observer of that episode complained that "the president of the Reichsbank is no longer master of the currency but its slave" (Seeger, 1968, 36, translation mine). Even so, it is remarkable to what extent pre-1914 central banks were able to divorce the domestic monetary base from international gold flows despite the fetters of the gold standard.

Among the three European central banks examined in this study, the Bank of England maintained the least accommodative policy stance. Econometric evidence suggests that it adjusted its discount rate more speedily to reserve losses than either of the two Continental European central banks (Neuburger and Stokes, 1979). For this reason, market interest rates in Germany and France fluctuated less strongly than in the United Kingdom (Morgenstern, 1959, 78-79). The relative stability of French interest rates, in particular, received much attention by contemporary observers of financial markets (e.g., Taussig, 1927, 210-12). The emphasis of central banks on stable interest rates implies that monetary policy before and after 1914 was more similar than has often been believed. Goodhart's assessment of the Bank of England's behaviour prior to World War I appears even more valid if applied to the Reichsbank and the Bank of France:

> Milton Friedman has regularly complained that the preference of central banks for setting interest rates rather than the monetary base imparts a procyclical bias to monetary changes. It is interesting to find that this may have been the same in the United Kingdom under the gold standard, as subsequently (1984, 224).

An analysis of Continental European experience leads to the surprising conclusion that the decentralized laissez-faire financial system of Canada functioned in a very similar way as the centralized systems of Germany and France. The absence of a central bank need not have strengthened the stabilizing powers of the gold standard. Under both the Canadian and the two Continental European systems, there was sufficient slack in the money-supply process to allow for accommodative behaviour on the part of commercial or central banks. Accommodative behaviour resulted in stable interest rates, impairing the effectiveness of the gold standard as a stabilizer of cyclical fluctuations in economic activity.[19] Moreover, a common feature of both types of systems was a tendency to generate countercyclical movements in net inflows of monetary gold and, thus, of producing instability through indirect monetary effects.

The indirect monetary effects emanating from Canada were smaller than those originating in Germany and France, but the differences between Canada and the two Continental European countries were not as large as might be expected at first sight. Over the period 1900-13, reference-cycle expansions saw Canada cut her annual net imports of monetary gold by an average of about $10 million, as compared with $30 million for Germany and $40 million for France (Table 8-1). Canada's importance as a supplier of gold during business-cycle expansions derived from a relatively high cyclical amplitude of her monetary gold flows. While the cyclical amplitude (as shown in Table 8-1) of Canadian monetary gold flows amounted to one-third and one-fourth of that recorded for Germany and France, the Canadian stock of monetary gold at the end of 1913 equalled only one-sixth and one-fourteenth of German and French holdings respectively.[20] Thus, accommodative reserve behaviour of the Canadian chartered banks was one among other reasons for the ability of such countries as the United Kingdom to accelerate her imports of monetary gold during reference-cycle expansions.[21]

8.2.3. Destabilizing Movements in the Money Multiplier

Various students of the gold standard have pointed to the money multiplier as another possible source of cyclical instability.[22] As I concluded in this study, procyclical movements in the money multiplier were an important destabilizing force in Canada. In the United States, this factor also accounts for the observed procyclical pattern of the pre-1914 money stock. However, Canadian and United States experiences differ sharply as to the causes of the procyclical swings in the money multiplier. In the United States, these swings were dominated by countercyclical movements in the currency-deposit ratio. U.S. bank reserve ratios also varied countercyclically, but their influence on the money stock was minor compared with that of the currency-deposit ratio (Cagan, 1965).

Another difference between pre-1914 Canadian and U.S. experiences lay in the stability of Canadian interest rates as compared with the frequently violent fluctuations in the United States. The cyclical patterns of Canadian and U.S. interest rates suggest that accommodative bank behaviour was more pronounced in Canada than in the United States. The superior ability or willingness of Canadian chartered banks to accommodate cyclical or seasonal movements in money demand may have impinged on the business cycle in two ways. On the one hand, the relatively small cyclical variance of Canadian interest rates implies that in Canada the gold standard was likely to be a less powerful cyclical stabilizer than in the United States. On the other hand, the extent of accommodative behaviour in Canada helps to explain why Canada was spared major liquidity crises and waves of bank failures. The absence of financial panics imparted an element of stability to the Canadian banking system that may have spilled over to the real sector of the economy. Depending on the circumstances, therefore, the effect of accommodative behaviour could have been stabilizing or destabilizing. Whether the Canadian gold standard, on balance, was a less effective stabilizer than its U.S. equivalent is clearly a complex issue requiring further investigation. Cryptic evidence presented in Chapter 5 suggests that in Canada, nominal GNP tended to fluctuate less strongly than in the United States.

Equally unresolved is the question why accommodative behaviour was more prevalent in Canada than in the United States. A distinguishing feature of the Canadian financial system was the oligopolistic structure of the banking industry, as well as the dominance of branch banking and the attendant high degree of centralization of reserve management. It should not be forgotten that a large share of aggregate Canadian reserves was administered by a single institution, the Bank of Montreal, that came close to assuming the role of a central bank. Another difference resided in the Canadian and United States approaches of issuing bank notes. While the Canadian banks were able to adjust the supply of notes to seasonal and cyclical fluctuations in demand, the rigid U.S. system offered little scope for accommodative behaviour (see Chapter 1).

8.2.4. Concluding Remark

Detailed studies of individual countries' experiences are essential for understanding the monetary sources of cyclical instability under the pre-1914 gold standard. Nonetheless, an analysis of the stabilizing powers of the gold standard cannot be confined to a series of individual-country studies. Even if one is not prepared to endorse fully the McCloskey-Zecher hypothesis of perfect arbitrage across the gold-standard world, one must admit that pre-1914 business cycles were not purely national phenomena. International influences on domestic economic activity were important, in the case of many countries, even dominant. Individual-country studies are useful for identifying the domestic sources of monetary instability. They may also demonstrate how the domestic financial sector impinged on the transmission of foreign cyclical disturbances to the domestic economy. But they do not show whether and to what extent monetary forces accounted for cyclical instability in the gold-standard world as a whole. A full monetary analysis of business cycles clearly must transgress the confines of individual countries. It must demonstrate how procyclical movements in the various countries' money stocks interacted to produce cyclical instability at the global level. I dared not embark on such an ambitious endeavour, but I hope that my study will prove a useful building block for a global analysis of the stabilizing powers of the gold standard.

Endnotes — Chapter 8

1. Hawtrey also analyzed a simultaneous credit expansion in all gold-standard countries. In this case, credit growth was restrained by drains of bank reserves into currency held by domestic non-banks, rather than by balance-of-payments deficits.

2. In their most recent study, McCloskey and Zecher (1984) do not address the question of arbitrage in financial markets. It is unclear whether they consider their hypothesis to be valid for financial markets as well.

3. Outflows of long-term capital from the United Kingdom varied procyclically (Ford, 1962, 74), while the pattern of the merchandise trade surplus was complex. Mintz (1969) found that the merchandise trade surplus — on the whole — was positively correlated with the business cycle. Goodhart (1972, 199-200), by contrast, uncovered a weak inverse relationship between the merchandise trade surplus and economic activity.

4. Econometric evidence suggests that there was a statistically significant negative relationship between the Bank's discount rate and its liquidity position (level of gold reserve or ratio of gold reserve to liabilities). See Goodhart, 1972, 207, and Dutton, 1984, Tables 3.3 and 3.5. Dutton argues that the Bank also varied its discount rate in response to changes in the unem-

ployment rate. Furthermore, Goodhart (1972, 201-02) finds a statistically significant positive relationship between net inflows of short-term capital to the U.K. and the differentials between interest rates ruling in London, on the one hand, and in Paris and New York on the other.

5. Movements in the U.K. money stock were positively correlated with the level of economic activity (Goodhart, 1972, 219). Performing Granger-Sims causality tests on pre-World War I data for the U.K. money stock and national income, Mills and Wood (1979) also conclude that causality ran from economic activity to money.

6. The data on U.S. monetary gold flows employed in these studies are taken from Beach (1935). They cover only imports and exports of gold coin passing through New York, but this city handled the bulk of U.S. international gold transactions. A comparison of the Beach data with the reference cycle does not reveal a consistent procyclical pattern. Note that the U.S. merchandise trade surplus — as its Canadian counterpart — varied countercyclically (Mintz, 1959).

7. As Williamson (1964) has shown, in the long run, an increase in U.S. money demand, elicited by an expansion in U.S. economic activity, gave rise to inflows of monetary gold unless the rise in money demand could be accommodated by an increase in gold supply from domestic sources (e.g., new discoveries). This pattern clearly emerges if long swings in U.S. economic activity are analyzed. Interestingly, Williamson (1964, 161) argues that it "seems particularly important to discard the usual classical specie-flow model, which is more applicable for short-term analysis." This study indicates that even in the short run, the adjustment mechanism did not always operate in the way suggested by the classical theory of the gold standard.

8. The growth in the world stock of monetary gold was determined by (a) new gold production and (b) consumption of gold for non-monetary purposes. Except for a marked procyclical pattern recorded in the period 1895-1901, gold production was unrelated to the business cycles of major gold-standard countries (see U.S. Commission, 1982, 188-89, for data on world gold production). Furthermore, I would expect non-monetary consumption of gold to have moved procyclically.

9. If neutralization was only partial, the correlation between net inflows of monetary gold and base-money growth remained positive, but the latter varied less than the former. Suppose that as a result of a balance-of-payments deficit, a central bank incurred a loss of monetary gold. Provided it did not vary its domestic assets (securities, bills, advances to commercial banks), the drop in its gold reserve was matched by a decline in its liabilities and, hence, the monetary base. The monetary base also fell if the central bank partly neutralized the gold loss by an increase in its domestic assets. For the monetary base to expand, the central bank had to increase its domestic assets by more than the loss of monetary gold.

10. See McGouldrick (1984) for a discussion of the institutional environment governing pre-1914 German monetary policy.

11. The Reichsbank held a small share of its reserves in the form of foreign assets (see Germany, Bundesbank, 1976, 329). The cyclical pattern of first differences in these assets was similar to that of net inflows of monetary gold.

12. Over the period 1892-1913, the average annual rate of growth in the monetary base amounted to 4.1 percent for reference-cycle expansions and 2.7 percent for contractions. For M_1 growth, the respective figures were 6.5 and 4.1 percent. See the legend to Table 8-1 for assigning the annual observations in base-money and M_1 growth to reference-cycle expansions and contractions.

13. During reference-cycle expansions and contractions, the ratio of cash reserves to demand deposits fell by an average of 0.6 and 0.1 percentage points per year respectively (calculated from Tilly, 1973, 346). See also McGouldrick (1984, Table 7.14).

14. These results are at variance with McGouldrick's (1984) assessment of pre-1914 German monetary policy. He argues that the German monetary base varied countercyclically, while gold inflows to Germany did not exhibit a cyclical pattern. This conflict, I believe, is explained by the fact that McGouldrick constructed his data on gold inflows and the monetary base from estimates of gold imports, net of exports, supplied by Hoffman and the U.S. National Monetary

Commission (see McGouldrick, 1984, Tables 7.5 and 7.6 for these sources). I have employed more recent estimates by the German Bundesbank. Interestingly, it does not make much difference whether net inflows of monetary gold are estimated from data on the German monetary gold stock, as in Chart 8-1 and Table 8-1, or whether merchandise trade data on gold imports and exports are used, which also cover trade in non-monetary gold. The series on net imports of monetary gold shown in Chart 8-1 is closely correlated (r = 0.96) with the corresponding series drawn from the merchandise trade account, as reported in Germany, Bundesbank (1976, 324). A full analysis of the reliability of the various German data sources is beyond the scope of this study.

15. The countercyclical pattern of net inflows of gold to France has been noticed in existing studies (see Bloomfield, 1959, 39).

16. In Germany, France and the United Kingdom, short-term market rates of interest prior to 1914 were positively correlated with the respective reference cycles (Morgenstern, 1959, 95).

17. I do not know how the countercyclical swings in net inflows of monetary gold were generated since the mechanics of cyclical adjustment in the pre-1914 German and French balance of payments has not been investigated. However, the German merchandise trade surplus varied countercyclically (McGouldrick, 1984, 332-33).

18. Over the period 1891-1913, the ratio of gold to total liabilities (notes and deposits) of the Bank of France typically exceeded 60 percent (White, 1933, 183). In the case of the Reichsbank, that ratio was normally less than 40 percent (calculated from Germany, Bundesbank, 1976, 36-37).

19. Bloomfield (1959) characterized the behaviour of pre-1914 central banks as stabilizing since they varied their discount rates in a procyclical manner. However, their behaviour was destabilizing in the sense that their accommodative monetary policies resulted in procyclical movements in the money stock. Steady growth in the money stock could have been achieved only by widening the cyclical amplitude of official discount rates.

20. See the legends to Table 8-1 and Chart 8-2 for data on the German and French stocks of monetary gold. Data on Canadian holdings of monetary gold are obtained from Table A-2. The available French data represent annual averages of monthly figures.

21. Beach emphasizes the role of the Bank of France as a supplier of gold to the Bank of England. He suggests that the Bank of France, to some extent, became "the central bank for England, as well as France, and [was] permitting the use of [its] bullion stock because the English system was not competent or willing to take care of seasonal and other needs" (1935, 150).

22. On the whole, these students focus attention on the countercyclical movements in bank reserve ratios. Aside from Hawtrey, Taussig (1927, ch. 17) and Beach (1935, ch. 2), discuss extensively instability arising from this source.

APPENDIX A

REVISED ESTIMATES OF THE PRE-1914 CANADIAN BALANCE OF PAYMENTS

A thorough investigation of cyclical movements in the pre-1914 Canadian balance of payments is greatly hampered by various deficiencies and gaps in the existing data. The government did not publish balance-of-payments statistics prior to World War I, but various unofficial estimates are available for the pre-1914 period. The best-known estimates are those presented by Viner (1924) in his study of the classical adjustment mechanism. His statistical investigation, covering the period 1900-13, constitutes one of the first Canadian ventures into the thorny field of balance-of-payments accounting.[1] Hartland (1955; 1960) later supplemented the Viner data with estimates for the period 1868-99.[2] To investigate the cyclical patterns of the Canadian balance of payments, it is necessary to modify the Viner-Hartland estimates in two respects.

First, Viner and Hartland did not separate monetary from non-monetary balance-of-payments flows. Therefore, monetary flows must be discerned from the Viner-Hartland estimates. In line with standard principles of balance-of-payments accounting, I distinguish between the balance of payments on current and capital accounts, as well as monetary flows or the overall surplus (or deficit).

Second, the Viner-Hartland estimates are marred by numerous errors and omissions. The estimates of monetary flows, as discerned from Viner and Hartland, are especially unreliable. For this reason, this study presents new estimates of the pre-1914 Canadian balance of payments. Drawing on new published and unpublished evidence, I try to rectify — as far as possible —

the defects in the Viner-Hartland estimates. The new series on monetary flows differs significantly from that implicit in the Viner and Hartland studies, while for the other components of the Canadian balance of payments, the data revisions only result in minor adjustments to the Viner-Hartland estimates.

A.1. MONETARY FLOWS: GOLD

In principle, pre-1914 monetary gold flows may be estimated in direct and indirect ways. The direct estimates are based on data for gold exports and imports compiled by the Department of Customs within the context of the Canadian merchandise trade statistics. This source offers statistical information on various categories of gold flows. After 1900, the Customs Department distinguished between exports and imports of unrefined gold, refined gold bullion and gold coin. Before 1900, the statistics were less detailed. Exports of gold, silver and copper coin were reported under a single heading. Moreover, until 1889, the Customs Department lumped together trade in coin and bullion.[3]

Although the Customs Department differentiated between flows of unrefined gold, gold bullion and gold coin, rather than between monetary and non-monetary flows, it is possible to estimate monetary gold flows from the Customs Department trade statistics for at least part of the period under study. Inasmuch as any conclusions may be drawn from the available evidence, monetary gold flows, for all practical purposes, corresponded to imports and exports of gold coin. Prior to 1914, the bulk of Canadian monetary gold was held in the form of coin, that is, U.S. eagles and British sovereigns, while the stock of monetary bullion was negligible.[4] Moreover, only a very small share of imports of gold coin was absorbed by the non-monetary sector of the Canadian economy.[5]

The indirect approach for estimating monetary gold flows rests on the observation that any increase (decrease) in the Canadian stock of monetary gold mirrored either imports (exports) of the precious metal or shifts of gold from domestic non-monetary (monetary) to monetary (non-monetary) use. Prior to 1914, most of these shifts were attributable to the coinage of the Ottawa Mint.[6] Monetary gold flows, therefore, may be estimated by adjusting the Canadian monetary gold stock for coin minted in Canada and for other known shifts of gold between non-monetary and monetary use.

Data on the Canadian monetary gold stock are available from two sources. On the one hand, the chartered banks were required to file with the government monthly returns on their assets and liabilities. These returns yield data on the banks' specie holdings, that is, gold and Canadian subsidiary coin. For all practical purposes, specie was synonymous to gold since subsidiary coin probably only accounted for a small share of specie.[7] On the other hand, the government was obliged to complete periodic returns on the official gold reserve and the outstanding stock of Dominion notes. Both the bank and government returns were published in the *Canada Gazette*. Thanks to the useful compendium of Canadian monetary and banking statistics assembled by Curtis (1931a), the data contained in these returns (Curtis data) are now easily accessible.

Since monetary gold flows may be estimated in direct and indirect ways, the question arises as to which of the two estimation procedures should be chosen. The answer hinges on the relative accuracy of the Customs Department and Curtis data. If the trade statistics proved a more reliable source of information than the Curtis compendium, the direct procedure would be the most appropriate. As regards the quality of the trade statistics, there is virtually unanimous agreement among existing researchers that the Customs Department committed huge errors in measuring gold exports and imports (see U.S. Bureau of the Mint, 1900, 41; Canada, Board of Inquiry, 1915, 848; Viner, 1924, Table II; Hartland, 1955, ch. 1; Morgenstern, 1955, 25). The shortcomings of the Customs Department gold-flow statistics prompted Viner to rely on the indirect method for estimating net imports of gold coin. Hartland also found that source to be wanting but nonetheless opted for the direct approach.[8]

While the inadequacies of the Customs Department gold-flow statistics are generally recognized, existing researchers have overlooked the fact that the Curtis data on monetary gold are not flawless either. Notably for bank holdings of monetary gold, the Curtis compendium is not an entirely satisfactory source of information. The defects in the Curtis data on bank gold derive mainly from the reporting problems posed by the foreign branches of the Canadian banks. As I show in Appendix B, the chartered banks relied extensively on their foreign branches for managing their cash and secondary reserves. A substantial part of the banks' gold stock was carried on the books of the foreign branches. At the end of 1913, bank gold held abroad amounted to no less than 42 percent of the total.[9] Furthermore, the bulk of the funds the banks placed in foreign call-loan markets passed through their foreign branches, especially those in New York and London.

Although the foreign branches were an important constituent of the banks' overall operations, the monthly returns for a long time did not cover assets and liabilities booked abroad. While the monthly returns, from the beginning, embraced claims and liabilities vis-à-vis foreign correspondent banks, the chartered banks — up to June, 1900 — were not obliged to report loans to and deposits from other foreigners. Since foreign loans and deposits were typically managed by the banks' foreign branches, much of the assets and liabilities booked abroad went unreported. In an effort to plug these data gaps, the government revised the monthly returns in July, 1900, with a view to capturing fully the banks' foreign branches. The chartered banks were henceforth required to report their call loans, fixed-term loans and deposits abroad.

Gold on the books of the foreign branches caused similar reporting problems. Before July, 1900, the banks did not uniformly include in their reported gold holdings the shares carried at their foreign branches. After the 1900 revision of the monthly returns, most banks adopted the practice of reporting their entire gold stock, no matter whether it was held in Canada or abroad. A major exception was the Bank of Montreal that continued to omit part of the gold booked at its foreign branches.

In Tables A-1 and A-2 an attempt is made to fill the gaps in the Curtis data. The new estimates of bank gold shown in column (3) are adjusted — as far as possible — for underreporting of gold carried at the banks' foreign branches. For the subperiod starting on September 30, 1900, the new estimates are available quarterly and appear to cover fully gold held abroad. For 1913III and IV, Table A-2 incorporates the Curtis data because the practice of underreporting bank gold disappeared entirely in July, 1913, when the government began to ask for a breakdown between gold booked domestically and abroad. The annual estimates for the subperiod 1887-99, in all probability, also capture most of the gold carried at the banks' foreign branches. Thus, the post-1887 estimates of bank gold are reasonably complete. A comparison of the new estimates with the corresponding Curtis data leaves little doubt as to the significance of the omissions in the monthly returns. For the subperiods 1887-99 and 1900III-1913II the new estimates surpass the Curtis data by averages of 36 and 24 percent respectively.[10]

In contrast to the new estimates for the post-1887 period, those for 1886 and earlier years are neither complete nor entirely homogeneous (see legend to Table A-2). In particular, they exclude gold carried by the Bank of Montreal at its foreign branches, for which data are unavailable prior to 1887. As a result, they do not exceed much the Curtis data on bank gold (Appendix B).

Tables A-1 and A-2 also exhibit new estimates of monetary gold in the hands of the Dominion government. They depart from the corresponding Curtis data in a number of respects, but most of the deviations are minor. The sum of bank and government gold, as shown in the two tables, is equivalent to the Canadian stock of monetary gold.

Considering the high quality of the new estimates of Canadian monetary gold, I regard the indirect approach as the most suitable method for estimating monetary gold flows. In accordance with standard principles of balance-of-payments accounting, however, monetary gold flows, as estimated in this study, do not correspond to actual exports and imports of monetary gold. Instead, I treat any increase (decrease) in the Canadian monetary gold stock as an import (export) of monetary gold. This procedure implies that domestic non-monetary gold transferred to monetary use is treated as a simultaneous export of non-monetary and import of monetary gold.[11] In other words, monetary gold flows are assumed to equal the first differences in the Canadian monetary gold stock. Shifts of gold between non-monetary and monetary use are in turn recorded in the current account as exports or imports of non-monetary gold.

No attempt is made to estimate monetary flows of silver and other precious metals. One cannot rule out the possibility that exports and imports of U.S.

TABLE A-1

CANADIAN INTERNATIONAL MONETARY ASSETS, MONETARY BASE AND MONEY STOCK, 1871-1900
(Millions of Dollars)

End of Year	Dominion Government		Chartered Banks				International Monetary Assets	Monetary Base	Money Stock
				Secondary Reserves					
	Gold	Dominion Notes	Gold	Call Loans Abroad	Net Claims on Foreign Banks	Total			
	(1)	(2)	(3)	(4)	(5)	(6) = (4)+(5)	(7) = (1)+(3)+(6)	(8) = (2)+(3)+(6)	(9)
1871	4.1	11.2	8.8			13.4	26.3	33.4	76.0 a)
1872	3.0	11.6	6.3			9.1	18.3	27.0	80.6 a)
1873	3.3	12.1	7.2			8.4	18.9	27.7	88.5
1874	3.4	12.0	7.5			7.5	18.4	27.0	100.3
1875	3.0	11.4	6.9			7.7	17.6	25.9	86.2
1876	2.9	11.1	6.2			5.5	14.6	22.8	89.0
1877	3.2	11.6	6.1			6.6	15.9	24.3	85.1
1878	2.6	10.5	5.9			5.5	14.0	21.9	86.8
1879	3.6	12.3	7.1			23.9	34.7	43.3	89.9
1880	3.1	14.2	6.2			31.3	40.6	51.7	108.0
1881	2.8	15.0	6.8			24.8	34.4	46.6	123.3
1882	2.5	16.1	6.7			11.2	20.4	34.0	133.5
1883	2.6	16.8	7.5			20.7	30.7	44.9	131.7
1884	2.5	16.4	7.8			17.1	27.4	41.3	126.1
1885	3.2	17.8	7.5			19.5	30.1	44.8	134.2
1886	2.7	15.3	6.4			17.0	26.1	38.6	129.7
1887	3.1	15.7	6.5			14.3	23.9	36.5	141.1
1887	3.1	15.7	7.5	12.1	8.8	20.9	31.6	44.2	141.1
1888	4.3	16.6	9.3	15.5	13.8	29.3	42.9	55.3	156.9
1889	2.8	15.1	7.3	12.0	6.2	18.2	28.3	40.6	160.7
1890	3.3	15.6	8.7	4.5	6.1	10.6	22.5	34.8	169.3
1891	3.6	16.2	7.9	12.8	14.5	27.3	38.8	51.4	188.1
1892	6.6	18.8	9.1	17.3	7.7	25.0	40.7	52.9	207.1
1893	7.8	19.8	10.5	8.7	10.4	19.1	37.4	49.3	206.0
1894	9.5	21.2	10.5	16.6	14.2	30.8	50.9	62.6	214.1
1895	10.7	22.4	11.7	8.2	14.9	23.1	45.4	57.2	219.3
1896	10.1	21.7	12.2	8.4	15.5	23.9	46.2	57.9	229.5
1897	13.0	24.6	12.4	3.4	29.0	32.4	57.8	69.4	257.3
1898	13.2	24.6	13.1	5.1	24.2	29.3	55.6	66.9	287.5
1899	12.4	26.4	13.1	11.5	18.3	29.8	55.4	69.4	317.8
1900	14.9	28.4	13.4	25.9	12.2	38.1	66.4	79.8	343.8

a) Excludes provincial government deposits

Sources and estimation methods: See Table A-2

TABLE A-2

CANADIAN INTERNATIONAL MONETARY ASSETS, MONETARY BASE AND MONEY STOCK, 1900-13

(Millions of Dollars)

End of Quarter	Dominion Government		Chartered Banks				International Monetary Assets	Monetary Base	Money Stock
	Gold	Dominion Notes	Gold	Secondary Reserves: Call Loans Abroad	Secondary Reserves: Net Claims on Foreign Banks	Secondary Reserves: Total			
	(1)	(2)	(3)	(4)	(5)	(6) = (4)+(5)	(7) = (1)+(3)+(6)	(8) = (2)+(3)+(6)	(9)
1900 III	13.9	27.5	13.4	20.7	12.6	33.3	60.7	74.3	336.6
IV	14.9	28.4	13.4	29.3	12.2	41.5	69.8	83.3	343.8
1901 I	15.2	28.5	12.7	37.7	7.3	45.0	72.9	86.2	349.3
II	14.6	27.9	13.9	43.3	6.1	49.4	77.9	91.2	364.7
III	16.3	29.4	14.9	46.5	15.8	62.3	93.5	106.6	380.6
IV	16.2	30.3	14.0	45.9	13.5	59.4	89.7	103.8	384.9
1902 I	15.9	29.9	14.4	44.9	7.4	52.3	82.7	96.6	384.6
II	18.9	32.8	15.3	46.4	13.4	59.8	94.0	107.9	394.4
III	19.3	32.9	16.2	49.9	16.1	66.0	101.5	115.1	415.0
IV	21.3	34.4	15.5	43.7	15.9	59.6	96.4	109.6	423.0
1903 I	20.7	33.8	15.8	39.8	7.9	47.7	84.2	97.3	425.1
II	25.9	39.0	17.5	39.5	7.7	47.2	90.7	103.8	431.7
III	27.8	40.6	17.6	36.5	18.9	55.4	100.8	113.6	450.4
IV	28.7	41.1	19.3	35.0	17.3	52.3	100.2	112.6	454.8
1904 I	27.4	39.8	18.6	41.0	10.0	51.0	97.0	109.4	462.6
II	29.4	41.6	19.7	37.0	12.5	49.5	98.7	110.8	478.8
III	34.5	46.6	20.8	49.4	19.8	69.2	124.4	136.6	499.8
IV	35.7	47.8	20.9	48.8	26.2	75.0	131.6	143.7	510.6
1905 I	35.8	47.8	20.0	46.0	26.5	72.5	128.4	140.4	511.5
II	35.3	47.3	20.2	43.1	22.5	65.6	121.1	133.1	523.4
III	35.9	50.6	21.7	58.6	27.1	85.7	143.2	158.0	555.1
IV	34.3	49.0	23.1	61.0	17.0	78.0	135.4	150.1	571.2

Table A-2 continued

End of Quarter		Dominion Government		Chartered Banks						
					Secondary Reserves					
		Gold (1)	Dominion Notes (2)	Gold (3)	Call Loans Abroad (4)	Net Claims on Foreign Banks (5)	Total (6) = (4)+(5)	International Monetary Assets (7) = (1)+(3)+(6)	Monetary Base (8) = (2)+(3)+(6)	Money Stock (9)
1906	I	32.6	47.2	23.5	55.3	18.5	73.8	130.0	144.5	589.2
	II	35.0	49.9	22.5	53.5	16.2	69.7	127.2	142.1	599.7
	III	37.4	51.9	24.3	63.8	18.9	82.7	144.3	158.8	627.7
	IV	38.7	56.5	25.3	59.0	13.4	72.4	136.3	154.1	652.3
1907	I	37.6	54.8	24.7	51.3	1.0	52.3	114.7	131.9	641.0
	II	41.1	58.3	26.2	55.3	7.0	62.3	129.6	146.8	658.7
	III	45.0	61.9	25.8	63.2	4.9	68.1	138.8	155.7	660.1
	IV	39.7	62.6	28.7	43.5	7.3	50.8	119.2	142.2	623.7
1908	I	41.7	60.5	26.0	52.5	12.8	65.3	133.0	151.7	611.8
	II	45.3	63.1	34.8	52.3	25.8	78.1	158.1	175.9	624.3
	III	58.6	76.4	46.7	59.8	56.5	116.3	221.7	239.4	666.7
	IV	61.7	79.4	34.2	97.1	44.4	141.5	237.4	255.2	701.4
1909	I	61.6	79.4	30.7	117.9	27.3	145.2	237.4	255.2	711.2
	II	61.2	79.0	31.5	115.3	35.2	150.5	243.1	260.9	746.5
	III	62.8	80.5	33.5	131.6	37.1	168.7	265.0	282.7	788.3
	IV	69.5	87.0	31.6	138.5	25.8	164.3	265.5	282.9	834.2
1910	I	69.7	87.1	31.4	130.2	28.7	158.9	260.1	277.5	845.8
	II	72.1	89.3	31.9	130.2	35.3	165.5	269.4	286.6	877.7
	III	75.6	92.1	36.8	103.5	60.2	163.7	276.1	292.6	907.8
	IV	74.8	90.7	38.1	90.7	32.4	123.1	236.0	251.9	904.2
1911	I	74.2	90.0	41.4	85.3	36.0	121.3	236.8	252.6	910.7
	II	83.7	99.3	42.9	97.9	37.3	135.2	261.9	277.4	953.4
	III	88.3	103.4	43.9	93.5	54.0	147.5	279.8	294.8	988.1
	IV	100.6	115.1	41.9	92.1	36.6	128.7	271.2	285.7	1,008.6

Table A-2 continued

End of Quarter	Dominion Government		Chartered Banks				International Monetary Assets	Monetary Base	Money Stock
				Secondary Reserves					
	Gold (1)	Dominion Notes (2)	Gold (3)	Call Loans Abroad (4)	Net Claims on Foreign Banks (5)	Total (6) = (4)+(5)	(7) = (1)+(3)+(6)	(8) = (2)+(3)+(6)	(9)
1912 I	98.9	113.4	40.4	94.7	42.4	137.1	276.3	290.8	1,026.8
II	98.1	111.9	42.6	120.6	49.8	170.4	311.2	324.9	1,095.9
III	103.0	116.0	42.0	112.8	34.3	147.1	292.1	305.1	1,098.5
IV	104.1	115.8	37.4	106.0	17.3	123.3	264.7	276.4	1,086.2
1913 I	98.5	112.1	42.5	109.2	14.0	123.2	264.2	277.8	1,074.8
II	100.4	116.4	42.5	89.4	29.7	119.1	262.0	277.9	1,075.2
III	99.0	115.5	42.8	86.6	23.7	110.3	252.1	268.6	1,092.5
IV	115.4	131.2	46.6	116.0	13.8	129.8	291.8	307.6	1,081.9

Sources and estimation methods for Tables A-1 and A-2

Columns (1) and (2): For 1871-86, see Table 7-1. For 1887 and subsequent years, see Curtis (1931a, 92-93), and the periodic returns on the government gold stock and outstanding Dominion notes published in the *Canada Gazette*. For the period August 31, 1903, to December 31, 1913, the Curtis data on the government gold stock are incorrect. After August 13, 1903, the government was required to earmark a certain amount of gold as a reserve against deposits at the government and post office savings banks. Although this requirement did not alter the government gold stock, Curtis excluded the earmarked portion from the total. The data in column (1) show the entire stock, including the earmarked portion.

Column (3): Covers bank gold, as reported by Curtis (1931a, 36), and gold held in the central gold reserves (Curtis, 1931a, 35), plus the following two items: (a) For 1887IV-1913II, gold not reported by the Bank of Montreal [difference between columns (2) and (1) in Table B-2]. (b) For the period up to 1899, currency and coin at the San Francisco branches of the BNA and the BBC. The Canadian Bank Act was not applied to the BBC before 1885. Therefore, the Curtis data cover the assets and liabilities of the BBC only from 1885 onwards (Ross, 1920, vol. 1, 330). Considering this change in coverage, I include currency and coin held by the BNA and the BBC for 1878-99 and 1885-99 respectively (Table B-4). For 1895-99, currency and coin in San Francisco is estimated as follows:

end of 1895: average of observations for 1895II and 1896II;
1896: observation for June, 1896;
1897: assumed $1.2 million;
1898: assumed $1.2 million;
1899: average of observations for 1899II and 1900II.

Column (4): For 1887-1900, see Table B-6, column (3). For 1900II-1913IV, see Curtis (1931a, 52). The Curtis data are adjusted for an error in the monthly returns of the Bank of Montreal. From 1900IV to 1902I, the Bank showed on its books a special loan to the Newfoundland government. A clerk in Ottawa apparently believed that the Bank had erroneously included the special loan in its reported call loans abroad and adjusted them accordingly. However, the special loan was not included (see GML, Section B-2.1).

Column (5): For 1887-99, see Table B-7, column (3). For 1900II-1913IV: difference between balances due from and balances due to banks and banking correspondents in the United Kingdom, and elsewhere than in Canada and the United Kingdom, as reported by Curtis (1931a, 30-31 and 44-45).

Column (6): For 1871-87, the series covers net claims on foreign correspondent banks, as reported by Curtis [see column (5)]. For the years 1871-74, the BNA's liabilities to foreign correspondent banks are disregarded since they suffer from an anomaly that grossly distorts aggregate net claims (see Curtis, 1931a, 8, for the source of the problem). When reported correctly, BNA liabilities to foreign banks were negligible.

Column (9): Covers Dominion notes outside the banking system, that is, the difference between aggregate Dominion notes [column (2)] and the share held by the banks in their vaults or in the central gold reserves (Curtis, 1931a, 35 and 38), bank notes, as well as demand and notice deposits held by the private non-bank public and the provinces (Curtis, 1931a, 20, 24-25). An attempt is made to adjust the money stock for float by deducting from aggregate bank liabilities notes and cheques on other banks (Curtis, 1931a, 40-41). This adjustment is dubious since notes and cheques on other banks include foreign currencies, which were not reported separately until 1923.

silver coin, in particular, accounted for a significant share of aggregate monetary flows. Before World War I, U.S. silver coin and occasionally U.S. silver certificates were used widely as media of exchange in Canada. Unfortunately, reliable estimates of flows of silver coin do not exist. The Customs Department trade statistics offer some data on exports and imports of silver coin (see Section A.4), but it is likely that much of the trade in silver coin went unreported.[12]

A.2. MONETARY FLOWS: SECONDARY RESERVES

In addition to data on monetary gold, Tables A-1 and A-2 display new estimates of the chartered banks' secondary reserves, that is, call loans to foreigners and net claims on (claims on minus liabilities to) foreign correspondent banks. Owing to various shifts in reporting procedures, it is impossible to extract from the monthly returns homogeneous and reliable estimates of secondary reserves for the entire period under study. The principal difficulty arises once again from the 1900 revision of the monthly returns. As indicated earlier, the banks were not required to report call loans abroad prior to that revision. Moreover, at least one bank — the Bank of Montreal — altered substantially its procedure for reporting claims on foreign correspondent banks. Until June, 1900, the Bank of Montreal treated its foreign branches — for reporting purposes — like foreign correspondent banks. Since the bulk of the funds the foreign branches received from head office were invested in gold and call loans, the pre-1900 movements in the Bank's reported foreign banking claims mirrored largely movements in monetary gold and call loans booked abroad. Upon the 1900 revision of the monthly returns, the Bank deleted from reported banking claims positions vis-à-vis its foreign branches. As a result, the Bank's reported net banking claims shrank drastically from June to July, 1900. Because of the Bank's dominant position in the Canadian financial system, aggregate net banking claims also fell sharply when the monthly returns were modified. As regards the reporting procedures followed by the other chartered banks, I doubt that their reported net banking claims embraced head-office positions vis-à-vis their foreign branches at any time during the period under study (Appendix B).

In Tables A-1 and A-2, I attempt to rid the Curtis data on secondary reserves of the distortions introduced by the 1900 revision of the monthly returns. These adjustments to the Curtis data yield a homogeneous series for the period 1887-1913. The quarterly data shown in Table A-2, column (6), correspond to those compiled by Curtis, except that they are adjusted for an error in the monthly returns of the Bank of Montreal. For the period 1887-99, my estimates of secondary reserves differ from the Curtis data in two major respects. First, the estimates of call loans abroad presented in Table A-1, column (4), are based on unpublished information rather than the monthly returns. Second, net claims on foreign correspondent banks, as reported by Curtis, are adjusted for head-office positions of the Bank of Montreal vis-à-vis its foreign branches [column (5)]. Without this adjustment, the pre-1900 estimates of international monetary assets would be distorted since gold and call loans on the books of the Bank's foreign branches would be counted twice, that is, directly under the respective headings in Table A-1, and indirectly under net claims on foreign correspondent banks. While the estimates of secondary reserves for 1887-99 are comparable to those for the subsequent period, they are not as reliable as the post-1900 data (Appendix B).

For want of a better alternative, the pre-1887 estimates of secondary reserves displayed in Table A-1 are based entirely on the monthly returns and equal the difference between claims on and liabilities to foreign correspondent banks as tabulated by Curtis. Therefore, they are not free of the distortions caused by the 1900 revision of the monthly returns. In particular, they do not embrace call loans abroad, save for the share extended by the Bank of Montreal, which is captured in a roundabout and highly imperfect manner. Moreover, they include head-office claims on gold carried at the foreign branches of the Bank of Montreal, an item that ideally should be part of bank gold as shown in column (3).

A.3. BALANCE OF PAYMENTS: CURRENT ACCOUNT, OVERALL SURPLUS AND RESIDUAL INFLOWS

The estimates of the current account shown in Table A-3 are based on a variety of sources. For data on merchandise exports and imports, I draw mainly on the Customs Department trade statistics. However, the Customs Department data cannot be incorporated in Table A-3 without modification. As indicated earlier, they include monetary flows in the form of coin and bullion, items already covered by the overall surplus. Moreover, the Customs Department is an unreliable source of information on either monetary or non-monetary gold flows. For these reasons, non-monetary flows of precious metals must be estimated or re-estimated.

Merchandise exports and imports, as shown in columns (1) and (2), correspond to the respective Customs Department aggregates, save for trade in coin and bullion. In lieu of the Customs Department data on trade in coin and bullion, new estimates of net exports of non-monetary gold are inserted in column (3), embracing net exports of unrefined gold and refined gold bullion, as well as net shifts of gold from domestic non-monetary to monetary use. Since trade in coin and bullion encompasses both gold and silver, Table A-3 also presents new estimates of net exports of non-monetary refined silver, covering net exports of silver bullion and Dominion-government imports of British-produced Canadian subsidiary coin. The procedures employed for estimating net exports of non-monetary gold and silver are discussed in Sections A.4. and A.5.

Data on non-merchandise trade are derived from Hartland's (1955; 1960) studies of the Canadian balance of payments. Hartland revised Viner's (1924, chs. 3 and 4) estimates of non-merchandise trade for the post-1900 period and generated new data for the period 1868-99. The non-merchandise trade

TABLE A-3

BALANCE OF PAYMENTS ON CURRENT ACCOUNT, 1868-1913
(Millions of Dollars)

	Merchandise Trade					Non-Merchandise Surplus	Current Account Surplus
	Exports (excl.Gold, etc.)	Imports (excl.Gold, etc.)	Net Exports of Non-Monetary Gold	Net Exports of Non-Monetary Refined Silver	Surplus		
	(1)	(2)	(3)	(4)	(5)=(1)-(2) +(3)+(4)	(6)	(7)=(5)+(6)
1868	54.4	66.4	0.4	-	-11.6	3.4	-8.2
1869	60.8	67.3	0.3	-	-6.2	4.4	-1.7
1870	66.4	80.8	0.4	-0.7	-14.8	4.9	-9.9
1871	72.4	99.9	1.3	-0.4	-26.6	4.7	-21.9
1872	81.2	115.6	1.9	-0.8	-33.4	4.8	-28.6
1873	85.6	123.2	1.5	-	-36.1	7.6	-28.5
1874	80.8	121.1	2.0	-0.5	-38.8	5.6	-33.3
1875	76.7	104.6	2.7	-0.4	-25.5	5.8	-19.7
1876	76.1	93.1	2.0	-	-15.1	5.1	-10.0
1877	76.0	93.9	1.9	-	-15.9	7.1	-8.8
1878	74.0	85.5	1.5	-	-10.0	3.1	-6.9
1879	77.4	81.7	1.6	-	-2.7	7.0	4.3
1880	90.8	93.6	1.3	-0.3	-1.8	7.4	5.6
1881	98.7	109.8	1.3	-0.4	-10.2	6.9	-3.3
1882	98.7	122.8	1.2	-0.3	-23.2	7.8	-15.4
1883	92.4	120.9	1.1	-0.3	-27.6	6.6	-21.0
1884	87.2	108.5	1.1	-	-20.2	4.6	-15.6
1885	85.1	102.0	1.1	-0.1	-15.8	3.3	-12.5
1886	86.2	105.2	1.5	-0.2	-17.7	3.3	-14.5
1887	88.9	109.0	1.2	-0.1	-18.9	5.3	-13.7
1888	88.0	110.0	1.1	-0.2	-21.1	3.6	-17.5
1889	89.7	115.9	1.3	-0.1	-25.0	2.1	-22.9

Table A-3 continued

	Merchandise Trade						
	Exports (excl.Gold, etc.) (1)	Imports (excl.Gold, etc.) (2)	Net Exports of Non-Monetary Gold (3)	Net Exports of Non-Monetary Refined Silver (4)	Surplus (5)=(1)-(2) +(3)+(4)	Non-Merchandise Surplus (6)	Current Account Surplus (7)=(5)+(6)
1890	94.3	117.7	1.1	-0.1	-22.3	1.5	-20.8
1890	94.3	117.7	1.1	-0.7	-22.9	1.5	-21.4
1891	102.9	120.0	0.9	-0.4	-16.6	4.3	-12.3
1892	111.7	121.9	0.9	-0.5	-9.8	3.3	-6.5
1893	113.6	118.2	1.0	-0.4	-4.1	3.6	-0.5
1894	111.0	109.9	1.1	-0.3	1.9	1.2	3.1
1894	109.2	107.0	1.1	-0.3	3.0	1.2	4.2
1895	108.5	107.8	2.1	-0.2	2.6	1.3	3.9
1896	118.8	110.8	2.8	-0.3	10.5	2.0	12.5
1897	153.5	119.3	6.0	-0.2	40.0	2.4	42.4
1898	151.2	146.6	13.8	-0.5	17.9	1.3	19.2
1899	153.4	166.8	21.3	-0.6	7.3	7.7	15.0
1899	153.4	166.8	20.9	-0.4	7.2	7.7	14.9
1900	163.6	180.2	27.6	-0.5	10.6	8.0	18.5
1900	163.6	180.2	27.6	-0.5	10.6	12.8	23.3
1901	177.2	187.8	23.4	-0.5	12.4	9.0	21.3
1902	199.1	207.8	20.3	-0.6	11.0	12.0	22.9
1903	206.5	251.3	18.0	-0.6	-27.5	13.0	-14.4
1904	176.3	245.3	15.1	-0.5	-54.4	15.4	-39.0
1905	207.6	261.2	13.2	-0.5	-40.9	7.8	-33.2
1906	240.1	308.1	10.5	-0.9	-58.3	6.2	-52.1
1907	244.0	367.2	5.9	-1.3	-118.7	-0.8	-119.5
1908	255.5	285.7	8.4	-0.3	-22.2	-7.5	-29.7
1909	280.8	352.7	7.9	-0.5	-64.5	-2.3	-66.8

1910	287.7	434.4	7.7	-1.0	-140.1	-1.8	-141.9
1911	286.9	499.7	7.8	-0.8	-205.9	-7.7	-213.6
1912	350.6	637.8	10.3	-1.1	-278.0	-38.9	-316.9
1913	444.7	662.4	13.1	-0.8	-205.4	-49.1	-254.5

Sources and estimation methods for Table A-3

Columns (1) and (2): In principle, the Customs Department tabulated aggregate merchandise exports and imports for fiscal years. Until 1906, fiscal years ended on June 30, while from 1907 onwards they terminated on March 31. For 1868-93, only fiscal-year data are available (Hartland, 1955, ch. 1, Table II; Canada, *Report of the Department of Trade*, 1915, 6-7). From 1894 onwards, the Customs Department also published calendar-year data. However, for 1894-1904, calendar-year data are available only on aggregate merchandise exports and imports. In 1905, the Customs Department also began to disaggregate the calendar-year data (Canada, *Report of the Department of Trade*, 1903, xvii; Canada, Department of Customs, *Trade and Navigation*, various December issues). If available, calendar-year data are employed for calculating merchandise exports and imports. Otherwise, fiscal-year data are converted to a calendar year basis on the assumption of equal monthly distribution of the annual totals. Viner (1924, 32) and Hartland (1955, ch. 1) also relied on this conversion method. The break in adjusted exports and imports in 1894 is attributable to the switch from converted fiscal-year to calendar-year data.

Merchandise exports equal aggregate exports, excluding exports of coin and bullion (see sources quoted above), unrefined gold [Tables A-4 and A-5, column (1)], as well as settlers' effects (Hartland, 1955, ch. 1, Table II, and Viner, 1924, 32-33). Prior to 1901, the Customs Department underreported merchandise exports and, therefore, adjusted the data appropriately. This adjustment was recorded under the heading "Estimated short reported" (Canada, *Report of the Department of Trade*, 1915, 11). "Estimated short reported" is added to the calendar-year export data for 1894-1900, which the Customs Department did not adjust for underreporting.

Merchandise imports equal imports for home consumption and re-export, excluding imports of coin and bullion and settlers' effects (see exports for the sources). The import data are adjusted for imports of British ships, which do not figure in the Customs Department statistics. Data on imports of British ships are available for 1899-1913 (Hartland, 1955, ch. 1, Table II; Viner, 1914, 32-33). Data on imports for re-export exist for fiscal years only.

Column (3): Tables A-4 and A-5, column (3), plus Table A-7, column (11). The break in 1899 is due to the fact that data on net exports of non-monetary refined gold are unavailable for 1898 and earlier years. A slight break in 1908 is disregarded.

Column (4): Tables A-4 and A-5, columns (4) minus (5). Data for 1890-98 include net exports of gold bullion. No data exist on net bullion exports, either in the form of gold or silver, for 1889 and earlier years. For these reasons, breaks occur in 1890 and 1899. Note that the data in this column and the preceding one do not cover such items as unrefined silver exports, imports of gold and silver leaf, electro-plated ware, knives, and sterling silver ware, as well as trade in gold and silver jewellery. These items are included in columns (1) and (2).

surplus, as shown in column (6), only covers freight, non-commercial remittances, tourism and insurance. The Hartland estimates of interest and dividend flows between Canada and abroad are disregarded because they are based on an indirect estimation procedure that is liable to involve a high margin of error.[13] However, it should be noted that net interest and dividend payments to foreigners were a sizeable item in the Canadian balance of payments.[14]

Despite the omission of interest and dividend flows, the estimates in Table A-3, column (7), appear to be a reliable indicator of cyclical movements in the current-account surplus. A large part of Canada's foreign debt consisted of bonds. Since interest payments on fixed-income securities, in all probability, did not vary much over the business cycle, the cyclical attributes of the current-account surplus are unlikely to be altered very much by the exclusion of interest and dividend flows.[15]

A.4. NET EXPORTS OF NON-MONETARY GOLD

Section A.4 offers new estimates of trade in non-monetary gold, embracing exports and imports of unrefined gold, refined bullion and coin for non-monetary purposes.

A.4.1. Exports of Unrefined Gold

During the period under study, Canada was an important producer of gold. The gold discoveries in the Cariboo district of British Columbia (late 1850s), in the Yukon (late 1890s), and northern Ontario (around 1910) provided a great impetus to the Canadian mining industry. In 1900 — at the peak of the Yukon gold rush — Canada accounted for as much as 11 percent of world gold production (calculated from Robinson, 1935, Table III, and U.S. Commission, 1982, Table SC-2). Until the middle of the 1890s, Canadian production consisted mostly of placer gold.[16] Thereafter, attention increasingly shifted to lode deposits, i.e., gold embedded in solid rock.

Only a small portion of the gold mined in Canada was refined domestically. It is difficult to unearth useful information on the early history of the Canadian gold refining industry.[17] The most informative sources are reports by the Canada Department of Mines and the Ottawa Mint. They show that the first refining facility came into operation in 1904, when the Consolidated Mining and Smelting Company of Canada in Trail, British Columbia, began to refine small quantities of gold from nearby lode mines.[18] A second refining facility was added when the Ottawa Mint was opened in 1908.

Since a large share of Canadian gold output was exported in unrefined form, I would expect that exports of unrefined gold, as reported by the Customs Department, closely matched domestic production of the precious metal. In Tables A-4 and A-5, the Customs Department data on exports of unrefined gold [column (1)] are compared with the available estimates of Canadian gold production [column (2)]. Assuming that domestic inventories of unrefined gold were small, one should find that domestic gold production, net of the share refined in Trail and Ottawa, equalled reported exports of unrefined gold. Data on gold refined domestically are shown in Table A-6, columns (1) and (6). As is clearly indicated by Tables A-4 and A-5, column (3), unrefined gold exports, as estimated from production data, do not match the corresponding values reported by the Customs Department. Except in 1904, estimated exports of unrefined gold consistently exceeded their reported values. Note that the discrepancies between the two sets of data were particularly large during the Yukon gold rush (1897-1900).

The differences between the estimated and reported values imply that (a) the production statistics overstate Canadian gold output, (b) the Customs Department underreported exports of unrefined gold, and/or (c) there were large changes in domestic inventories of unrefined gold. In my opinion, possibility (c) is unlikely to account for the gaps between the estimated and reported values since the statisticians relied heavily on export data in order to estimate Canadian gold production. From 1896 to 1906, for example, gold production

TABLE A-4

EXPORTS AND IMPORTS OF UNREFINED GOLD AND NON-MONETARY REFINED SILVER, 1868-89
(Thousands of Dollars)

	Exports of Unrefined Gold (Customs Department) (1)	Gold Production = Estimated Exports of Unrefined Gold (2) = (3)	Imports of Canadian Silver Coin (Estimated) (5)
1868	95	400	-
1869	153	348	-
1870	147	387	750
1871	699	1,275	360
1872	1,135	1,866	800
1873	1,055	1,537	-
1874	1,340	2,023	500
1875	1,539	2,694	400
1876	1,331	2,020	40
1877	1,111	1,949	-
1878	988	1,538	-
1879	1,016	1,582	-
1880	927	1,305	336
1881	849	1,313	395
1882	921	1,246	286
1883	932	1,113	252
1884	976	1,058	42
1885	1,105	1,149	97
1886	1,114	1,463	220
1887	914	1,188	70
1888	717	1,099	189
1889	640	1,295	84

Sources: See Table A-5

TABLE A-5
EXPORTS AND IMPORTS OF UNREFINED GOLD AND NON-MONETARY REFINED SILVER, 1890-1913
(Thousands of Dollars)

	Exports of Unrefined Gold (Customs Dept.)	Gold Production	Estimated Exports of Unrefined Gold	Net Exports of Silver Bullion (Customs Dept.)	Imports of Canadian Silver Coin (Estimated)
	(1)	(2)	(3)	(4)	(5)
1890	606	1,150	1,150	-586[a)]	102
1891	435	931	931	-244[a)]	133
1892	282	908	908	-306[a)]	192
1893	283	977	977	-286[a)]	112
1894	466	1,129	1,129	-203[a)]	96
1895	856	2,084	2,084	-195[a)]	7
1896	1,952	2,755	2,755	-193[a)]	99
1897	3,197	6,027	6,027	-232[a)]	9
1898	3,431	13,775	13,775	-326[a)]	135
1899	8,711	21,262	21,262	-365[a)]	241
1899	8,711	21,262	21,262	-110	241
1900	19,297	27,908	27,908	-177	294
1901	22,057	24,129	24,129	-238	217
1902	18,053	21,337	21,337	-254	378
1903	17,577	18,844	18,844	-280	317
1904	18,901	16,463	16,373	-327	176
1905	13,708	14,159	13,981	-298	221
1906	11,224	11,502	11,295	-552	398
1907	8,030	8,383	8,168	-759	576
1908	7,740	9,842	9,523	-334	-
1909	5,630	9,382	8,918	-468	-
1910	5,555	10,206	8,875	-975	-
1911	7,493	9,781	8,025	-844	-
1912	10,014	12,649	10,754	-1,100	-
1913	12,771	16,599	13,048	-840	-

a) Gold and silver bullion.

Sources and estimation methods for Tables A-4 and A-5

Column (1): Canada, Department of Customs, *Tables of the Trade and Navigation*, 1868-1905; *Trade and Navigation*, 1905-13. In these sources, the series is headed "Exports of gold bearing quartz, dust, nuggets, etc." Fiscal-year data are converted to a calendar-year format along the lines suggested in the legend to Table A-3.

Column (2): Robinson, 1935, Table III. The Customs Department merchandise trade statistics do not cover Manitoba prior to April 1, 1871, and British Columbia prior to July 1, 1871. However, Canadian gold production, as reported by Robinson, includes the output of British Columbia for 1871 and earlier years. To make the data obtained from the two sources comparable, I exclude from aggregate gold production for 1868-70 the share of British Columbia. For 1871, one-half of British Columbia output is subtracted. In 1870 and 1871, aggregate gold production, including the British Columbia share, amounted to $1.7 and 2.2 million respectively. Manitoba did not produce any gold until 1917.

Column (3): Column (2) in Table A-5 less columns (1) and (6) in Table A-6.

Column (4): See column (1) for the sources. For the period 1899-1913, the series equals the difference between exports and imports of silver bullion. For 1898 and earlier years, it equals imports of bullion (gold and silver), as recorded by the Customs Department, with negative sign.

Column (5): For new issues of subsidiary coin, net of recoinage, see Canada, Public Accounts for 1915, xix-xx. No subsidiary coin was imported in 1908 and subsequent years. Seigniorage was reported under "Statement of Casual Revenue," Public Accounts for 1870-1908. Coinage and seigniorage were reported for calendar and fiscal years respectively. To put the two sets of data on a common basis, I compile average rates of seigniorage (i.e., cumulative seigniorage for a given subperiod divided by the change in the stock of coin during that subperiod). Net new issues of coin are in turn multiplied by one minus the average rate of seigniorage. This yields the cost to the government of importing subsidiary coin. The following average rates of seigniorage are applied: 1870-79: 0; 1880-84: 0.16; 1885-89: 0.30; 1890-99: 0.38; 1900-07: 0.53.

TABLE A-6
GOLD RECEIVED BY CANADIAN REFINERIES, 1904-13
(Thousands of Dollars)

	Gold Refined in Trail (1)	Gold Received by Ottawa Mint				
		Total (2)	Unrefined U.S. Gold (3)	Coin (4)	Scrap & Unknown (5)	Unrefined Canadian Gold (6)
1904	90					
1905	178					
1906	207					
1907	215					
1908	317	4	-	-	2	2
1909	377	95	1	-	8	87
1910	275	1,079	-	-	23	1,056
1911	316	1,478	2	12	24	1,440
1912	250	1,689	12	2	30	1,645
1913	248	3,375	3	24	45	3,303

Sources for Table A-6
Column (1): Canada, Department of Mines, 1914, 16. This source provides data on the quantity of gold refined in Trail. In order to determine the value of gold received by the Trail refinery, the quantities are multiplied by the gold price of $20.67 per ounce.
Columns (2) to (6): United Kingdom, *Annual Report of the Mint*, 1908-13. This source does not always show the value of the items received by the Ottawa Mint. If the value of a particular item is not indicated, I multiply the gross weight of that item by its assay value and by $20.67.

of the Yukon was estimated primarily on the basis of "receipts of gold at the United States mints and receiving offices credited to the Canadian Yukon." From 1907 onwards, the statistics of Yukon gold production rested on a royalty levied by the Dominion government on gold mined in that territory (Canada, Department of Mines, 1914, 27). The royalty payments became due when gold was shipped from the Yukon (Ross, 1922, vol. 2, 174). Similarly, the government of British Columbia (*Annual Report,* 1913, K10) relied on statistics gathered by the U.S. mints to determine provincial placer gold production. Since the statistics of Canadian gold production, for the most part, were export statistics in disguise, I doubt that much of the gold output absorbed into domestic inventories of unrefined gold is included in Tables A-4 and A-5, column (2).[19]

Provincial and federal government officials were well aware of the discrepancies between the production and trade statistics for unrefined gold. On the whole, they believed that the production statistics were more accurate than the export data supplied by the Customs Department. In their view, the Customs Department tended to underreport exports of unrefined gold (e.g., see Canada, Geological Survey, 1902, 197s). Two factors account for this underreporting. First, the Customs Department failed to capture fully exports of placer gold. While Customs Department officials did not attempt to adjust their data for unrecorded exports of placer gold, British Columbia officials added to recorded provincial placer gold production an estimate of unrecorded exports.[20] Second, as I show in Section A.4.2, the Customs Department erroneously subsumed a fraction of unrefined gold exports under the heading of bullion. For these reasons, the current-account estimates presented in this study incorporate unrefined gold exports, as shown in Tables A-4 and A-5, column (3), rather than the Customs Department data in column (1).[21]

A.4.2. Net Exports of Refined Gold for Non-Monetary Purposes

As indicated in Section A.1, net exports of non-monetary refined gold cannot be estimated from the merchandise trade statistics unless the data are adjusted in various ways. As regards trade in refined gold, the Customs Department did not differentiate between monetary and non-monetary flows but between flows of coin and bullion. Although gold bullion was traded mainly for non-monetary purposes, one cannot assume that net exports of non-monetary refined gold (GN) were equivalent to net exports of gold bullion (GB). Identities (A.1) and (A.2), which define GB and GN respectively, clearly show the difference between the two concepts:

$$GB = -GBN - GBH + GBO + GBT, \qquad (A.1)$$

$$GN = -GBN - GCN + GBO + GBT + GCO, \qquad (A.2)$$

where

GBN: Domestic consumption of gold bullion for industrial purposes.
GBH: Net increase in domestic monetary stock of gold bullion.
GBO: Gold bullion produced by the Ottawa Mint.
GBT: Gold bullion produced in Trail, B.C.
GCN: Domestic consumption of gold coin for industrial purposes.
GCO: Gold coin produced by the Ottawa Mint.

GB equals the difference between domestic production and domestic consumption of gold bullion. Identity (A.1) allows for the possibility that Canadian residents consumed gold bullion for both industrial and monetary purposes. In contrast to GB, GN is defined as the difference between domestic production and domestic industrial consumption of both gold bullion *and* coin. In line with my earlier assumption, identity (A.2) implies that domestic gold production absorbed by the domestic monetary sector is treated as an export of non-monetary gold. Rearranging identities (A.1) and (A.2), I derive a relationship between GN and GB:

$$GN = GB + GBH + GCO - GCN. \qquad (A.3)$$

GN equals GB only if (a) no gold bullion is absorbed into domestic monetary stocks, (b) there is no domestic production of gold coin, and (c) Canadian residents do not consume gold coin for industrial purposes. Identity (A.3) is employed for estimating net exports of non-monetary refined gold. On the following pages, I first review the available statistics for GB and then turn to the other items on the right-hand side of (A.3).

A.4.3. Net Exports of Gold Bullion

Net exports of gold bullion may be estimated either directly, or indirectly by determining the values of the variables on the right-hand side of equation (A.1). Direct estimates of exports and imports of gold bullion, as compiled by the Customs Department, are shown in Table A-7, columns (1) and (2). These estimates are available only for the latter part of the period under study, because the Customs Department, for a long time, published exclusively aggregated data on trade in coin and bullion. Table A-8 summarizes the coverage of the Customs Department statistics on exports and imports of refined gold and silver. For each constituent of exports and imports, Table A-8 indicates the fiscal years for which the Customs Department published data.

The Customs Department data displayed in Table A-7, columns (1) and (2), may be compared with indirect estimates based on identity (A.1). The information required for the indirect estimates is assembled in Table A-7, columns (4)-(7). Since data on GBN and GBH are available only for the period 1908-13, the indirect estimates of GB, as shown in column (8), do not cover 1907 and earlier years. Note that the GBH series presented in column (5) covers exclusively gold bullion in the hands of the Dominion government. There is little doubt that the chartered banks held a small share of their monetary gold in the form of bullion, but the extent of their holdings is unknown.[22]

Table A-7 reveals marked discrepancies between the indirect estimates of GB and net exports of gold bullion [difference between columns (1) and (2)], as calculated from the Customs Department export and import statistics. Both the direct and indirect estimates of GB suggest that over the period 1908-13, Canada was a net importer of gold bullion. However, net imports of bullion, as estimated from identity (A.1), were considerably larger than the Customs Department data would suggest. In view of the gaps between the direct and indirect estimates, the question arises as to which of the two data sets is closer to the truth. In my opinion, the indirect estimates are more reliable. A critical appraisal of the Customs Department's statistical efforts leads to the conclusion that its direct estimates are marred by at least two major errors.

First, according to the Customs Department, Canada was a significant exporter of refined gold bullion until 1900. In that year, gold bullion exports allegedly amounted to $830,000 (Table A-7). Although the Customs Department statistics published for fiscal 1899 and earlier years do not differentiate between exports of gold and silver bullion (Table A-8), they imply that gold bullion exports were substantial in the 1890s too. It is reasonable to conjecture that gold accounted for the lion's share of the bullion exports reported up to 1899, since exports of silver bullion — when shown separately — were minuscule. In view of the fact that domestic refining facilities did not exist prior to 1904, the evidence of substantial and persistent exports of refined gold bullion in the 1890s and in 1900 seems implausible. Interestingly, bullion exports, as reported by the Customs Department, rose sharply during the Yukon gold rush. Therefore, I suspect that the Customs Department, until 1900, erroneously classified under the heading of bullion exports of unrefined gold.

TABLE A-7

NET EXPORTS OF NON-MONETARY REFINED GOLD (GN), 1899-1913
(Thousands of Dollars)

	Gold Bullion								GCN	GCO	GN
	Customs Department			Estimated Net Exports							
	Exports	Imports	Adjusted Net Exports	GBN	GBH	GBO	GBT	GB Total			
	(1)	(2)	(3)	(4)	(5)	(6)	(7)	(8)	(9)	(10)	(11)
1899	n.a.	255	-255					-376			-376
1900	830	221	-221					-326			-326
1901	3	489	-486					-717			-717
1902	2	711	-709					-1,046			-1,046
1903	-	604	-604					-891			-891
1904	-	834	-834					-1,231			-1,231
1905	2	498	-496					-732			-732
1906	-	511	-511					-754			-754
1907	2	1,565	-1,563					-2,307			-2,307
1908	4	693	-689					-1,017			-1,017
1908	4	693	-589	1,328	-	-	317	-1,011	100	3	-1,108
1909	-	510	-510	1,342	-	-6	377	-971	100	79	-992
1910	-	1,344	-1,344	1,727	223	215	275	-1,460	100	136	-1,201
1911	-	925	-925	1,876	-	118	316	-1,442	50	1,236	-256
1912	-	1,361	-1,361	2,320	-	268	250	-1,802	100	1,477	-425
1913	-	840	-840	2,125	-	196	248	-1,681	103	1,885	101

Sources and estimation methods for Table A-7

Columns (1) and (2): See legend to Table A-5, column (1).
Column (3): For 1901-13, difference between columns (1) and (2). For 1899 and 1900, values of column (2) with negative sign.
Column (4): Data on Canadian industrial consumption of gold were collected by the Ottawa Mint on behalf of the U.S. Bureau of the Mint (1909-14). This source offers a breakdown of Canadian industrial consumption of gold into (a) new bullion, (b) old plate, jewellery, etc. and (c) coin. GBN covers component (a) minus scrap processed by the Ottawa Mint [Table A-6, column (5)]. The GBN data for 1908 and 1912 are estimated since the breakdown of industrial consumption is unavailable for these two years. The estimates are based on the assumption that components (b) and (c) did not change from 1908 to 1909 and from 1912 to 1913. This assumption appears to be reasonable since (b) and (c) did not vary much from year to year. Component (b) is not included in GBN as reprocessing of industrial gold does not alter aggregate consumption.
Column (5): Change in Dominion government bullion holdings. For the source, see U.S. Bureau of the Mint (1909-14), which provides data on the composition of gold and silver holdings in Canadian public treasuries.
Column (6): United Kingdom, *Annual Report of the Mint,* 1914, 1158. Like GBN, GBO is adjusted for scrap processed by the Ottawa Mint.
Column (7): Table A-6, column (1).
Column (8): For 1908-13, columns (6) + (7) − (4) − (5). For 1899-1908, data in column (3) multiplied by 1.4759, that is, the ratio of cumulative GB [column (8)] to cumulative adjusted net exports [column (3)] for the period 1908-13.
Column (9): Assumed to equal component (c) of industrial gold consumption. Data for 1908 and 1912 are estimated [see legend to column (4)].
Column (10): See column (6). GCO is adjusted for coin reprocessed by the Ottawa Mint [Table A-6, column (4)].
Column (11): For 1908-13, columns (8) + (5) + (10) − (9). For 1899-1908, column (8).

TABLE A-8

COVERAGE OF CUSTOMS DEPARTMENT STATISTICS ON TRADE IN COIN AND BULLION (Fiscal Years)

<table>
<tr><td colspan="5">Exports of Coin and Bullion
1868-</td><td colspan="3">Imports of Coin and Bullion
1868-</td></tr>
<tr><td colspan="3">Coin
1893-</td><td colspan="2">Bullion
1893-</td><td>Coin:
Gold and silver, excl. U.S. silver coin
1890-1907</td><td colspan="2">Bullion
1890-</td></tr>
<tr><td>Gold
1900-</td><td>Silver
1900-</td><td>Copper
1900-</td><td>Gold
1900-</td><td>Silver
1900-</td><td>Gold
1908-</td><td>Gold
1899-</td><td>Silver
1899-</td></tr>
</table>

Source: Canada, Department of Customs, *Tables of the Trade and Navigation*. This source also provides some data on imports of U.S. silver coin.

Second, there is reason to believe that the Customs Department failed to record exports of gold bullion by the Trail refinery. Data collected by the U.S. Bureau of the Mint (1904-14) indicate that the U.S. mints, from 1904 onwards, regularly acquired gold bullion from an unnamed refinery in British Columbia. Since the Trail refinery was opened in 1904, it must have accounted for these imports. Interestingly, there is a remarkable agreement between the series in Table A-6, column (1), and the data collected by the U.S. Bureau of the Mint.[23] Thus, the Customs Department, in all probability, underreported gold bullion exports from 1904 onwards.[24]

Considering the shortcomings of the Customs Department statistics, I rely on the indirect estimates of GB to estimate net exports of non-monetary refined gold. As indicated earlier, this procedure is applicable only to the period 1908-13 [Table A-7, column (8)]. Since indirect estimates cannot be generated for 1907 and earlier years, the pre-1908 data on GB are derived in a different way than those for the period 1908-13. Net exports of gold bullion, as reported by the Customs Department, are fairly closely correlated with the indirect estimates ($r = 0.76$), despite the fact that — in absolute terms — the direct estimates are consistently smaller than their indirect counterparts. This piece of evidence suggests that the direct and indirect estimates differ largely by a scale factor. Thus, GB may be estimated for 1907 and earlier years by blowing up the Customs Department data on net exports of gold bullion. The pre-1908 estimates of GB are not based on net exports of gold bullion, as reported by the Customs Department, but on the adjusted series shown in Table A-7, column (3). For reasons discussed earlier, the adjusted series rests on the assumption that Canadian exports of gold bullion were zero in 1899 and 1900. The pre-1908 data on GB, thus estimated, are also presented in column (8).

A.4.4. Estimation of Net Exports of Non-Monetary Refined Gold

Given the estimates of net exports of gold bullion, net exports of non-monetary refined gold may be calculated by virtue of identity (A.3). As in the case of GBH, data on GCN are available solely for the period 1908-13. Furthermore, as indicated earlier, domestic gold coins were not minted until 1908 [Table A-7, columns (9) and (10)]. Thus, for the period 1899-1908, net exports of non-monetary refined gold, as shown in Table A-7, column (11), are set equal to GB. For 1898 and earlier years, no estimates of GN are available.

A.5. NET EXPORTS OF REFINED SILVER FOR NON-MONETARY PURPOSES

Data on net exports of non-monetary refined silver are presented in Tables A-4 and A-5, columns (4) and (5). Column (4) shows net exports of silver bullion, as reported by the Customs Department. As I pointed out in Section A.4.3, the data for the period 1890-99 also cover gold. No data on net exports of bullion are available for the pre-1890 period (Table A-8). For the period 1890-99, the series displayed in column (4) is compiled on the assumption that bullion exports were zero (see also Section A.4.3.).

Column (5), presents data on imports of Canadian subsidiary coin by the Dominion government, an item not included in the Customs Department statistics. Until the opening of the Ottawa Mint, Canadian subsidiary coins were produced exclusively by the royal mints of Birmingham and London. The data shown in column (5), which cover both silver and a small amount of bronze coin, are adjusted for seigniorage. Thus, they measure the cost to the government of acquiring subsidiary coin in the United Kingdom rather than the face value of the imported coins.[25]

Endnotes — Appendix A

1. In his ingenious study on the cost of living, Coats presented the first Canadian balance-of-payments estimates (see Canada, Board of Inquiry, 1915, 889-907). His efforts left much to be desired and were condemned to oblivion after the publication of Viner's estimates.

2. Knox (1936; 1939) applied the Viner procedure to the post-1913 period.

3. See also Section A.4, notably Table A-8.

4. As regards the composition of the Dominion government gold reserve, data exist for the period 1908-13. They suggest that the government held over 99 percent of its gold reserve in the form of coin. The remainder consisted of gold bullion. The share of American eagles in government holdings of gold coin ranged from 89 to 95 percent (see U.S. Bureau of the Mint, 1909-1914, and Table A-2). No data are available on the composition of the chartered banks' monetary gold stock.

5. This point is discussed further in Section A.4.

6. Domestically produced coin only accounted for a minor share of Canadian monetary gold. From 1908 to 1913, the Ottawa Mint issued $4.8 million worth of gold coins, net of recoinage [Table A-7, column (10)]. This figure is dwarfed by an aggregate Canadian monetary gold stock of $162.0 million recorded at the end of 1913 (Table A-2).

7. Subsidiary coin seems to have amounted to less than 10 percent of aggregate specie (see Viner, 1924, 34).

8. Hartland's aim was to estimate the current-account balance, rather than gold flows by themselves. She did not believe that the estimated surplus would be affected significantly by an attempt to correct for the errors in the Customs Department gold-flow data (Hartland, 1955, ch. 1, 25).

9. Calculated from Table A-2 and Curtis, 1931a, 36.

10. Calculated as the percentage difference between the averages of the new estimates and the Curtis (1931a, 36) data for the respective subperiods.

11. Estimates of monetary gold flows by the Dominion Bureau of Statistics (1939) for the post-World-War-I period rely on the same procedure. After World War II, the International Monetary Fund recommended that its members adopt this procedure (Hartland, 1955, ch. 1, 30-33).

12. The share of U.S. silver in aggregate subsidiary coin circulating in Canada was estimated to range from 20 to 40 percent (U.S. Bureau of the Mint, 1909, 148; Great Britain, *Annual Report of the Mint,* 1913, 176; *Monetary Times,* Jan. 14, 1904, 918). Complaints about imports of U.S. subsidiary coin were voiced throughout the period under study, with the government responding by means of elaborate "silver deportation" schemes (*Monetary Times,* editorial, Sept. 12, 1867; Aug. 14, 1896, 208-09; Canada, Public Accounts for 1915, xxii).

13. Since little direct evidence is available on interest and divided flows, Viner and Hartland employed an indirect estimation procedure. To calculate interest and dividend receipts, they first compiled — from various sources — data on Canadian bank and non-bank holdings of foreign assets. Next, they estimated the average rate of return on these assets. In order to estimate payments, they employed an analogous procedure based upon estimates of foreign holdings of Canadian assets. However, unlike Canadian holdings of foreign assets, foreign holdings of Canadian assets were estimated indirectly. Viner and Hartland assumed the latter to equal the cumulative Canadian current account deficit, including net imports of monetary gold and silver, minus Canadian holdings of foreign assets.

14. Net interest and dividend payments to foreigners, as estimated by Hartland (1955, Tables XXIX, XXXI, XXXIII), increased steadily from $3 million in 1868 to $128 million in 1913. Therefore, the "true" current-account deficit expanded from roughly $10 million to $380 million over that period, provided any confidence may be placed in the Hartland estimates. Strictly speaking, it is illegitimate to estimate the "true" current-account deficit by subtracting from the data in Table A-3, column (7), the Hartland estimates of net interest and dividend payments. As indicated in note 13, these estimates depend upon her current-account estimates. In order to calculate the "true" current-account deficit, the Hartland data on net interest and dividend payments should be adjusted to conform to the new current-account estimates presented in Table A-3.

15. Subtracting the Hartland estimates of net interest and dividend payments to foreigners from the series in Table A-3, column (7), does not alter the cyclical attributes of the current account surplus. This holds true even if net interest and dividend payments are re-estimated on the basis of the new current-account data shown in Table A-3 (see also note 14). Reliable data exist on interest paid by the Dominion government on its net foreign-currency debt (available from the author upon request). While government borrowing abroad varied substantially over the business cycle (see Chapter 7), net interest payments grew at a steady pace and were insensitive to cyclical movements in economic activity.

16. "What are known as 'placer' deposits are merely sand and gravel deposits of which native gold, in the form of scales, grains and lumps ('gold dust' and 'nuggets') is one of the constituents" (Robinson, 1935, 11).

17. For a history of Canadian mining, see the comprehensive study by Innis. His discussion of the beginnings of Canadian gold refining is very vague (1936, 312).

18. Coats (Canada, Board of Inquiry, 1915, 847) overstates the output of the Trail refinery. His series appears to cover Trail's output of unrefined as well as refined gold.

19. I do not know whether there were substantial domestic inventories of unrefined gold. Some inventories were probably held by the Bank of British North America and the Canadian Bank of Commerce, which were important dealers in unrefined gold. Such inventories were reported under "other assets" in the monthly returns (Curtis, 1931a, 9).

20. To recorded output, 1/3 was added up to 1878, 1/5 from 1879 to 1895, 1/5 from 1898 to 1909, and 1/10 in 1910 and subsequent years. British Columbia, *Annual Report,* 1913, K10.

21. Imports of unrefined gold for domestic consumption or re-export were negligible. The Customs Department statistics do not show any such imports. A tiny amount of U.S. unrefined gold, however, was imported by the Ottawa Mint (Table A-6).

22. See references to this effect in United Kingdom, *Annual Report,* 1911, 163; 1914, 150.

23. From fiscal 1904 to 1914 respectively, the U.S. mints imported the following amounts of gold bullion from British Columbia (thousands of dollars): 55, 125, 175, 112, 253, 358, 135, 125, 172, 203, 176. The U.S. fiscal year lasted from July 1 to June 30. These figures are slightly lower than those in Table A-6, column (1).

24. In practice, statisticians found it difficult to decide at which processing stage bullion was to be classified as refined. Apparently, Canadian and U.S. officials did not employ the same criteria for distinguishing between unrefined and refined gold. Note that Goodhart (1969, 169) draws similar conclusions.

25. Hartland (1955, Table IV) also takes account of imports of subsidiary coin, but does not adjust them for seigniorage.

APPENDIX B

THE FOREIGN BRANCHES OF THE CANADIAN CHARTERED BANKS: STATISTICAL PROBLEMS

B.1. DEVELOPMENT AND CHARACTERISTICS OF THE BANKS' FOREIGN BUSINESS

The remarkable growth of the Canadian banks' foreign business before World War I has received its due attention from contemporary and modern researchers (Patterson and Escher, 1914, 406-10; Shearer, 1965, 330-32; Neufeld, 1972, 123-27; Naylor, 1975, vol. 2, 218-73). While the smaller banks conducted their foreign business exclusively through correspondents, the larger institutions found it to their advantage to set up their own foreign branches (or agencies). Table B-1 traces the development and location of the banks' foreign branches for the post-Confederation period.[1] It covers all the Canadian banks, including the Bank of British North America (BNA) and the Bank of British Columbia (BBC). Although the BNA and the BBC were incorporated under British charters, they must be treated as Canadian banks since they were subject to the Canadian Bank Act and required to file monthly returns.

As indicated by Table B-1, the number of foreign branches increased rapidly from seven in 1869 to seventy-nine in 1913. At first, the banks were active almost exclusively in the United States and Great Britain. They gained a strong foothold on the U.S. West Coast (especially in San Francisco) and became firmly entrenched in such major U.S. financial centres as New York, Chicago and Boston. Towards the end of the nineteenth century, they turned their attention gradually to Newfoundland, the Caribbean and Mexico. In the Caribbean, the Bank of Nova Scotia and the Merchants Bank of Halifax/Royal

Bank of Canada were the two Canadian institutions most prominently engaged in banking business. The Royal Bank acquired many banks in Cuba and other areas to gain access to the Caribbean (Baum, 1974, 21).

Although the available evidence is fragmentary, there is little doubt that the United States and London business of the Canadian banks was highly specialized. In New York, the Canadian banks were important gold and foreign exchange dealers. Moreover, they figured prominently as lenders to the New York call-loan market.[2] Unpublished data obtained from the Bank of Montreal suggest that call loans typically accounted for over 50 percent of the assets booked at the Bank's New York branch. Much of the funds invested in the New York call-loan market was furnished directly by the Bank's head office.[3] Likewise, the London branches of the Canadian banks served mainly as instruments of secondary-reserve management, with call loans accounting for the lion's share of the assets booked in London.[4] In Chicago, the Canadian banks were heavily engaged in financing exports of grain and packing-house products via the St. Lawrence route (James, 1968, 496, 575-606). On the U.S. West Coast, they were regarded as the principal foreign exchange dealers along with other foreign banks (Cross, 1927, vol. 1, 259; vol. 3, 129; Ross, 1920, vol. 1, 290-96, 326).

In Newfoundland and the Caribbean, the Canadian banks benefited from the underdeveloped state of indigenous financial markets.[5] On the Spanish-speaking Caribbean islands, in particular, the Canadian banks faced little competition from local financial institutions and, thus, were able to extract a handsome profit from their operations, as revealed by substantial spreads between the average return on loans and deposits.[7] In contrast to their U.S. and London operations, the Newfoundland and Caribbean branches of the Canadian banks offered a wide range of financial services. In Jamaica, the Bank of Nova Scotia (1932, 73) was the first financial institution to introduce savings accounts. The Canadian banks also began to issue notes on some of these islands. In Newfoundland, Canadian-dollar notes were used widely as media of exchange,[8] while in the British West Indies the Canadian banks circulated notes denominated in local currencies.[9] No data are available on notes issued by the Canadian banks abroad since the shares circulated in Canada and foreign countries were lumped together in the monthly returns.[10]

Despite the proliferation of foreign branches, the monthly returns, for a long time, did not cover the entire gamut of foreign assets and liabilities held by the Canadian banks. As was shown in Appendix A, banks were not required to report their call loans, fixed-term loans and deposits abroad until July, 1900. Moreover, it is unclear whether monetary gold on the books of the foreign branches, as well as claims on and liabilities to foreign correspondent banks, were reported in a uniform and consistent manner. In the following two sections, an attempt is made to rectify the errors and omissions in the monthly returns.

TABLE B-1
NUMBER OF FOREIGN BRANCHES OF THE CANADIAN BANKS

End of	United States				New-found-land a)	London	Paris	Brit. West Indies	Cuba, Puerto Rico, Domin. Rep.	Mexico, Brit. Hon-duras	Total
	New York	West Coast	Other	Total							
1869	2	3	-	5	-	2	-	-	-	-	7
1879	4	4	2	10	-	3	-	-	-	-	13
1889	4	6	2	12	1	3	-	1	-	-	17
1899	5	6	5	16	4	3	-	1	1	-	25
1909	6	7	3	16	6	3	1	8	15	1	50
1913	6	6	3	15	15	6	1	13	26	3	79

a) Includes St. Pierre and Miquelon

Sources and estimation methods for Table B-1

For each bank, the location of the principal foreign branches is shown. The sources indicate when and where a branch was opened. In a number of instances, I relied on bank advertisements in the *Monetary Times* to obtain the requisite information.
Bank of Montreal: New York (opened in 1858), Chicago, Spokane, London (opened in 1870, second branch in 1913), Newfoundland, Mexico. Sources: Denison, 1967, 101-02, 180, 261-81; GML (see Section B.2.1).
Bank of British North America: New York, San Francisco, London. Temporarily in Portland, Oregon and Chicago. Sources: Denison, 1967, 102; Cross, 1927, vol. 1, 257; Gilbert, 1911, 12.
Canadian Bank of Commerce: New York, Seattle, Newfoundland, Mexico. Temporarily in Chicago, New Orleans and Skagway. Source: Ross, 1920, vol. 2, Appendix XII. See also Bank of British Columbia.
Bank of British Columbia: San Francisco, Portland, Oregon, London. Temporarily in Seattle and Tacoma. Source: Ross, 1920, vol. 1, ch. 5. Taken over by Canadian Bank of Commerce in 1901.
Merchants Bank of Canada: New York. Source: *Monetary Times,* Dec. 4, 1874, 628.
Bank of Nova Scotia: New York, Chicago, Boston, Newfoundland, Jamaica, Cuba, Puerto Rico. Temporarily in Minneapolis and Calais, Maine. Source: BNS statistics 3.
Royal Bank/Merchants Bank of Halifax: New York, London, Newfoundland, Bahamas, Barbados, Jamaica, British Honduras, Cuba, Puerto Rico, Dominican Republic. Temporarily in Bermuda, St. Pierre and Miquelon, and Republic, Washington. Sources: Ince, 1970, 9-25, 110-16; Jamieson, 1955, 32; *Monetary Times,* May 12, 1882, 1390. See also Union Bank of Halifax.
Union Bank of Halifax: Trinidad and Puerto Rico. Source: Ince 1970, 113 and 115. Taken over by Royal Bank in 1910.
Banque Nationale: Paris. Source: *Monetary Times,* Aug. 1907, 252.
Dominion Bank: London. Source: Schull, 1958, 106.

B.2. MONETARY GOLD: NEW ESTIMATES

B.2.1. Description of New Data Sources

In an effort to generate a reasonably homogeneous set of data on bank gold and secondary reserves, I searched extensively for new sources of information that might help to improve the Curtis data. The following three sources turned out to be useful supplements to the monthly bank returns.[11]

First, the Bank of Montreal archives contain a series of ledgers prepared for the Bank's general manager, offering monthly data on selected assets and liabilities booked at the various branches of the Bank. The General Manager's Ledgers (GML) cover gold, Dominion notes, call and short loans, fixed loans, investments, overdue debts, demand and notice deposits, as well as (net) claims of head office on the various branches. The data are available monthly from November 30, 1887, to December 31, 1913. An attractive feature of GML is that they use the same format as the monthly returns. Although in a number of instances the monthly returns and GML do not report the data under the same headings, a comparison of the two sources suggests that the following items are equivalent:

Monthly Returns	*GML*
1. Call and short loans elsewhere than in Canada.	1. Call and short loans at foreign branches (call and short loans are shown separately).
2. Other current loans and discounts elsewhere than in Canada.	2. Fixed loans at foreign branches.
3. Deposits elsewhere than in Canada.	3. Demand at notice deposits at foreign branches (demand and notice deposits are shown separately).
4. Government securities (Dominion, provincial, municipal and foreign), railway and other bonds, debentures and stocks.[12]	4. Investments booked at domestic and foreign branches.

Second, fragmentary data exist on the assets and liabilities booked at the various branches of the Bank of Nova Scotia (BNS). They may be obtained from two ledgers preserved at the BNS archives. The first ledger, entitled BNS Statistics 3, shows for each branch total loans and deposits, the average return on loans and deposits, as well as (net) liabilities to head office. Although the data from that ledger are available annually back to 1885, they are only of limited use for identifying gaps and inconsistencies in the Curtis data. Unlike the monthly returns, BNS Statistics 3 furnishes annual averages rather than end-of-period data. Furthermore, it neither shows monetary gold held by the various branches, nor offers a breakdown of total loans into call loans and fixed-term loans. The second ledger, entitled BNS Statistics 14, comprises data on daily cash balances and call loans booked at the Bank's principal branches. Statistics 14 is based on the same format as the monthly returns but covers only a very short time span extending from the end of 1903 to the end of 1907.

Third, a fairly homogeneous set of balance-sheet data is available for the San Francisco branches of the Canadian banks. Prior to 1914, two Canadian banks, i.e., the BNA and the Canadian Bank of Commerce, possessed branches in San Francisco. The Canadian Bank of Commerce acquired its San Francisco branch as a result of taking over the BBC in 1901. Both the BNA and the BBC opened their San Francisco branches as early as in 1864 (Cross, vol. 1, 257; Ross, vol. 1, 303). All the Californian banks, including the local branches of foreign banks, were required to file periodic returns with the State Bank Commissioners (see California, *Annual Report,* 1879-1908). The returns covered such balance-sheet items as currency and coin, various categories of loans, securities, balances due from (to) other banks, deposits, and for the branches of foreign banks (net) liabilities to head office. Until 1894, the returns were filed twice a year for June 30 and December 31, with the first set of returns showing the assets and liabilities at the end of 1878. From 1895 onwards, they only appeared sporadically.[13]

B.2.2. The Curtis Data on Bank Gold: A Critical Appraisal

A critical appraisal of the data supplied by the banks maintaining foreign branches testifies to the diversity of the procedures employed for reporting gold booked abroad. As far as the Bank of Montreal is concerned, the evidence extracted from GML suggests that actual holdings of monetary gold were much larger than might be believed on the strength of the data published in the monthly returns (Table B-2).[14] The discrepancies between the two sets of data derive from the fact that the Bank of Montreal did not subsume in the figures reported to the government monetary gold on the books of its foreign branches. For the period 1887IV-1903IV, monetary gold, as shown by the monthly returns, matches closely the share at the Bank's domestic branches, as recorded by GML. Thus, prior to 1904, the Bank of Montreal only reported to the government its domestic holdings of monetary gold. In 1904, however, it began to include a small portion of monetary gold on the books of its foreign branches.[15] Aside from a minor discrepancy of $50,000, the differences between the two sets of data vanished in July, 1913, when the banks were required for the first time to show separately gold held in Canada and abroad.

While there is reasonable certainty about the reporting procedures followed by the Bank of Montreal, it is unclear how the other banks dealt with the reporting problems posed by gold on the books of their foreign branches. Useful inferences can be drawn from abnormal changes in reported gold holdings upon the July, 1900, revision of the monthly returns. Since prior to that date the banks were not required to show the assets and liabilities at their foreign branches, they might have reported gold held abroad after, but not before, the 1900 revision of the monthly returns. Had they started to include

TABLE B-2
GOLD STOCK OF THE BANK OF MONTREAL
(Thousands of Dollars)

End of Period		Monthly Returns (1)	GML (2)
1887	IV	1,725	2,752
1888	I	1,817	3,270
	II	2,389	3,500
	III	2,626	4,790
	IV	2,709	4,000
1889	I	2,403	3,610
	II	2,790	3,900
	III	2,612	4,170 a)
	IV	1,656	2,300
1890	I	1,775	2,570
	II	1,951	3,040
	III	1,995	3,250
	IV	2,222	3,390
1891	I	2,158	3,030
	II	2,327	3,520
	III	2,127	3,420
	IV	1,695	2,780
1892	I	1,790	3,000
	II	2,277	3,540
	III	2,202	4,260
	IV	2,073	3,260
1893	I	1,549	3,370
	II	2,014	3,251
	III	2,309	3,700
	IV	2,760	4,340
1894	I	2,571	4,150
	II	2,705	4,070
	III	2,770	4,500
	IV	2,747	4,170
1895	I	2,359	3,780
	II	2,184	4,380
	III	2,064	4,010
	IV	2,527	4,597
1896	I	2,098	3,820
	II	2,136	4,420
	III	2,083	4,090
	IV	2,348	4,690

Table B-2 continued

End of Period	Monthly Returns (1)	GML (2)
1897 I	2,165	4,649
II	2,492	4,650
III	2,425	4,400
IV	2,149	5,110
1898 I	2,405	5,190
II	2,514	4,600
III	2,709	6,164
IV	2,175	5,060
1899 I	2,350	4,440
II	2,179	4,984
III	2,186	4,740
IV	2,082	4,430
1900 I	2,085	3,210
II	2,138	4,130
III	2,425	4,180
IV	2,186	3,770
1901 I	2,342	3,400
II	2,358	4,520
III	2,483	6,070
IV	2,495	4,970
1902 I	3,034	5,170
II	2,499	5,410
III	2,560	6,210
IV	2,655	5,270
1903 I	3,128	5,370
II	3,166	6,210
III	3,533	6,380
IV	3,317	6,470
1904 I	4,424	6,240
II	4,116	6,630
III	3,664	6,830
IV	3,491	6,780
1905 I	3,948	6,680
II	3,738	6,710
III	5,241	7,480
IV	4,877	8,300

Table B-2 continued

End of Period		Monthly Returns (1)	GML (2)
1906	I	5,380 b)	8,550 b)
	II	5,152	7,541
	III	5,504	8,300
	IV	6,180	7,680
1907	I	5,184	7,148
	II	6,687	8,800
	III	6,330	8,000
	IV	5,147	8,770
1908	I	5,372	7,660
	II	5,216	16,110
	III	5,205	26,800
	IV	6,110	13,179
1909	I	6,499	9,989
	II	6,214	10,477
	III	8,319	12,367
	IV	5,724	9,847
1910	I	6,133	9,446
	II	5,755	10,027
	III	8,256	14,892
	IV	7,704	12,436
1911	I	8,530	15,075
	II	8,527	14,666
	III	9,742	15,862
	IV	9,126	13,555
1912	I	8,108	12,451
	II	8,595	14,119
	III	10,081	13,733
	IV	6,968	10,550
1913	I	8,799	12,245
	II	9,357	13,923
	III	10,568 c)	10,518
	IV	10,440 c)	10,390

a) Includes $130,000 worth of gold held by the New York branch, but deposited with U.S. banks.
b) Includes $400,000 worth of gold held by the Chicago branch on account of head office.
c) Includes gold held in the central gold reserves.

Sources for Table B-2

Column (1): Monthly return of the Bank of Montreal. *Canada Gazette*.
Column (2): Bank of Montreal, General Manager's Ledgers (GML). Gold booked at domestic and foreign branches. No gold is shown on the books of the London branch.

in the July returns holdings not reported previously, that revision should have been associated with a marked jump in the stock of bank gold. In order to identify possible jumps in the data, Table B-3 shows, for all the banks which maintained foreign branches at that time (with the exception of the Bank of Montreal), the percentage changes in average gold holdings between the four months immediately following and preceding the 1900 revision of the monthly returns. The evidence indicates that the banks did not uniformly exclude gold abroad prior to July, 1900. Out of the six banks covered by Table B-3, only the BNA and the BBC reported an unusual surge in their gold holdings. There is little doubt that neither the BNA nor the BBC reported gold abroad before July, 1900, since their monthly returns contain an explicit footnote to this effect.

In contrast to the BNA and the BBC, the other four banks, in all likelihood, did not alter their reporting procedures in July, 1900. The evidence of Table B-3, of course, does not rule out the possibility that the four banks failed to report gold abroad until the 1913 revision of the monthly returns. However, I doubt that they omitted from their monthly returns gold abroad at any time during the period under study. The Canadian Bank of Commerce apparently always included gold abroad in its reported figures.[16] Furthermore, the unpublished evidence available for the period 1903-07 suggests that the BNS (Statistics 14) also reported its entire gold reserve, including the portion held at its foreign branches. In conjunction with Table B-3, this evidence implies that the BNS showed in its monthly returns gold booked domestically and abroad throughout the period under study. I am less certain about the reporting procedures of the Merchants Bank of Canada and the Royal Bank. Since these two banks did not report an unusual jump in their gold holdings

TABLE B-3

CHANGE IN GOLD HOLDINGS UPON THE 1900 REVISION OF THE MONTHLY RETURNS
(Percent)

Bank of British North America	87[a)]
Canadian Bank of Commerce	4[a)]
Merchants Bank of Canada	1[a)]
Bank of Nova Scotia	- 7[a)]
Merchants Bank of Halifax/Royal Bank	- 3[a)]
Bank of British Columbia	103[b)]

a) Average of holdings over period July 31 through October 31 as a percentage of average of holdings over period March 31 through June 30, 1900, minus 100.
b) Average of holdings over period September 30 through December 31 as a percentage of average of holdings over period May 31 through August 31, 1900, minus 100. The BBC did not adjust its reporting procedures until September, 1900.
Source: Canada Gazette.

upon the 1913 revision of the monthly returns (see *Canada Gazette*), it is probably fair to argue that they consistently reported the shares booked abroad.[17]

The foregoing analysis implies that a reasonably homogeneous series on bank gold may be constructed if the Curtis data are adjusted for underreporting of gold by the Bank of Montreal, the BNA and the BBC. For the Bank of Montreal, gold not reported to the government equals the difference between columns (2) and (1) in Table B-2. For the BNA and the BBC, the Californian bank returns yield data on currency and coin held at their San Francisco branches (Table B-4). These returns probably overstate somewhat the size of the two banks' San Francisco gold reserve because they cover subsidiary coin and notes in addition to gold. No information is available on gold booked at the other foreign branches of the BNA and the BBC. Prior to 1900, the BNA and the BBC also maintained branches in New York and Portland, Oregon, respectively. Moreover, both banks were represented in London.[18] Although the BNA and the BBC were unlikely to hold their foreign reserve of precious metal exclusively in San Francisco, I believe that Table B-4 captures the bulk of the gold not reported by the two banks before July, 1900. The records of the BBC indicate that its San Francisco operation was far more important than any of its other branches either in Canada or abroad (Ross, 1920, vol. 1, 321 and 339). In the case of the BNA, the San Francisco branch probably also accounted for a highly significant part of its foreign business. The evidence of Tables B-3 and B-4 clearly implies that the BNA and the BBC held much of their foreign gold in San Francisco since the jump in the reported gold reserve of the two banks upon the 1900 revision of the monthly returns closely matched their holdings of currency and coin at their respective San Francisco branches.[19]

B.2.3. Comparison of New Estimates with Curtis Data

In Tablc B-5, I compare my estimates of bank gold with the corresponding Curtis data for the period 1887-99. Despite sizeable discrepancies, the simple correlation between annual first differences in the two series is high (r = 0.90). Moreover, nine out of twelve pairs of annual first differences are equally signed. Similar results are obtained if the comparison is based on semi-annual data. In view of the periodicity of the Californian bank returns, it is possible to construct a semi-annual variant of the new series for the period December 31, 1887, to June 30, 1895. For semi-annual first differences, the simple correlation between the new estimates and the Curtis data amounts to 0.85, with twelve out of fifteen pairs of first differences displaying equal signs. The close correspondence between the two series suggests that the Curtis data — though imperfect — are adequate for analyzing cyclical movements in bank holdings of gold. Therefore, I employ the Curtis data on bank gold whenever the new estimates are unavailable.

TABLE B-4

CURRENCY AND COIN AT SAN FRANCISCO BRANCHES OF CANADIAN BANKS
(Thousands of Dollars)

End of Period	BNA a)	BBC b)
1878 IV	285	337
1879 II	305	303
1879 IV	269	178
1880 IV	242	423
1881 IV	211	400
1882 II	341	205
1882 IV	184	191
1883 II	221	285
1883 IV	227	293
1884 II	259	325
1884 IV	286	388
1885 II	274	452
1885 IV	225	574
1886 II	188	298
1886 IV	224	200
1887 II	322	433
1887 IV	174	262
1888 II	298	775
1888 IV	173	474
1889 II	387	760
1889 IV	284	389
1890 II	269	619
1890 IV	306	538
1891 II	245	594
1891 IV	458	552
1892 II	512	862
1892 IV	430	733
1893 II	367	815
1893 IV	471	717
1894 II	651	696
1894 IV	431	644
1895 II	640	1,008
1896 II	655	662
1899 II	410	824
1900 II	441	717

a) Bank of British North America
b) Bank of British Columbia

Source for Table B-4

California, *Annual Report,* 1879-1900. Data cover currency, coin and cash items in process of collection. After 1894IV, the returns were published only sporadically. Therefore, the data for the post-1894 period are assigned to the nearest available quarter. Returns were also published in 1905, 1906, 1907 and 1908. The gaps in the data between 1896 and 1899 are attributable to the fact that the state legislature refused to appropriate funds for the bank returns.

TABLE B-5
NEW ESTIMATES AND CURTIS DATA: A COMPARISON
(Millions of Dollars)

End of	Bank Gold		Secondary Reserves	
	Curtis (1)	New Estimates (2)	Curtis (3)	New Estimates (4)
1887	6.0	7.5	14.3	20.9
1888	7.4	9.3	21.1	29.3
1889	6.0	7.3	13.6	18.2
1890	6.7	8.7	11.7	10.6
1891	5.8	7.9	23.2	27.3
1892	6.7	9.1	18.5	25.0
1893	7.7	10.5	17.4	19.1
1894	8.0	10.5	24.7	30.8
1895	8.2	11.7	21.5	23.1
1896	8.6	12.2	23.2	23.9
1897	8.3	12.4	38.1	32.4
1898	9.0	13.1	32.6	29.3
1899	9.6	13.1	29.1	29.8

Sources for Table B-5

Column (1): Curtis (1931a, 36).
Column (2): Table A-1, column (3).
Column (3): Net claims on foreign correspondent banks, as reported by Curtis [Table B-7, column (2)].
Column (4): Table A-1, column (6).

B.3. SECONDARY RESERVES: REVISED ESTIMATES

B.3.1. Call Loans Abroad

For the period prior to July, 1900, the monthly returns do not provide data on the Canadian banks' foreign call loans. The only piece of information available for that period is a series — contained in GML — on foreign call loans extended by the Bank of Montreal. However, even this series is incomplete because GML does not cover the Bank's London operation up to August, 1900. The data available for August, 1900, and earlier months, therefore, only embrace call loans booked at the United States branches of the Bank of Montreal, that is, those in New York and Chicago.[20] Annual data on call loans granted by the two branches (LM) are displayed in Table B-6. This series may be compared with aggregate call loans abroad (LA), as tabulated by Curtis for the post-1900 period. Table B-6 suggests that LM averaged 40 percent of LA between 1900 and 1909. If LM were redefined to include call loans booked at the Bank's London branches, that average would rise to 58 percent.[21] Thus, the role played by the Bank of Montreal in foreign call-loan markets was unrivalled by any other Canadian financial institution.[22].

TABLE B-6
ESTIMATES OF CALL LOANS ABROAD, 1887-1909
(Millions of Dollars)

End of	LM[a)]	LA/LM (Estimated)	Aggregate Call Loans (LA)		
			Estimated	Hartland (Estimated)	Curtis
	(1)	(2)	(3)=(1)x(2)	(4)	(5)
1887	3.58	3.38	12.1	9.2	
1888	5.32	2.92	15.5	10.7	
1889	3.66	3.28	12.0	16.6	
1890	1.33	3.35	4.5	19.7	
1891	4.04	3.17	12.8	16.4	
1892	5.05	3.43	17.3	19.3	
1893	3.04	2.87	8.7	22.6	
1894	5.23	3.18	16.6	16.1	
1895	2.63	3.13	8.2	21.8	
1896	3.34	2.51	8.4	26.6	
1897	1.42	2.39	3.4	12.2	
1898	2.00	2.54	5.1	19.6	
1899	5.63	2.05	11.5	29.6	
1900	11.53	2.25	25.9	50.2	29.3[b)]
1901	24.15	2.18	52.6	63.3	45.9[b)]
1902	22.58	2.72	61.4	60.6	43.7
1903	10.98	3.49	38.3	75.3	35.0
1904	16.16	3.05	49.3	85.0	48.8
1905	20.73	2.54	52.7	108.1	61.0
1906	15.85	3.06	48.5	132.8	59.0
1907	14.09	2.93	41.3	133.3	43.5
1908	44.66	2.33	104.1	116.4	97.1
1909	57.12	2.40	137.1	170.8	138.5

a) Call and short loans on the books of the United States branches of the Bank of Montreal.
b) Adjusted for an error in the Curtis data.

Sources and estimation methods for Table B-6

Column (1): GML.
Column (2): Ratio, LA/LM, estimated from equation (B.1).
Column (4): Hartland [1955, Table XXVI, column (15); 1960, 731].
Column (5): Table A-2, column (4).

Considering the Bank's role in foreign call-loan markets, I construct — on the basis of the data obtained from GML — an annual series on aggregate Canadian call loans for the period 1887-99. To this end, LM is multiplied by an estimate of the inverse of the Bank's share in aggregate call loans (LA/LM). The calculations are performed in Table B-6, with the resulting estimates of aggregate call loans shown in column (3). In order to estimate LA/LM for the period 1887-99, I hypothesize that changes in that ratio were due mainly to changes in DA/DM, that is, the ratio of aggregate Canadian bank deposits to deposit liabilities of the Bank of Montreal. This hypothesis is tested by the following regression equation:

$$LA/LM = \underset{(-1.60)}{-3.22} + \underset{(2.95)}{1.02}\,(DA/DM),\quad \bar{R}^2 = 0.46,\ DW = 1.00,\quad SEE = 0.44. \qquad (B.1)$$

Equation (B.1) is fitted to end-of-year data for the period 1900-09. The various goodness-of-fit tests suggest that the performance of equation (B.1) is not outstanding. While the parameter estimate of DA/DM is almost significant at the 99 percent level, the standard error of the estimate — amounting to 16 percent of the mean value of LA/LM — is relatively high. Despite its shortcomings, equation (B.1) is used for generating estimates of LA/LM for the period 1887-99, since alternative specifications do not yield superior results.[23]

In order to appraise the quality of my estimates, I predict LA for the period 1900-09 on the strength of equation (B.1), and compare the resulting forecasts with the corresponding Curtis data. As indicated by Table B-6, columns (3) and (5), the estimation procedure forecasts correctly the trend and cyclical turning points in the Curtis data. Furthermore, the simple correlation between first differences in the estimated and actual values is very high (r = 0.93). However, the estimation procedure does not track well the year-to-year changes in LA. Notable discrepancies between the estimated and actual values of LA are observed for 1902, 1905 and 1906. Nonetheless, these estimates are adequate for analyzing cyclical movements in the Canadian balance of payments, since they trace correctly the cyclical swings in the actual values.[24]

In addition to my own estimates of pre-1900 Canadian call loans abroad, Table B-6 presents an analogous series compiled by Hartland. Her estimation procedure rests on the assumption that LA was equivalent to "the difference between 50 percent of total deposits of the chartered banks and the sum of cash, government bonds, net foreign balances, and call loans in Canada" (1960, 730). The huge discrepancies between her estimates and the Curtis data suggest that her estimation procedure is extremely unreliable.[25] For this reason, I do not use her estimates of LA.

B.3.2. Net Claims on Foreign Banks

As indicated in Appendix A, the Curtis data for claims on and liabilities to foreign correspondent banks are far from homogeneous. Curtis (1931a, 5) argued that up to the 1900 revision of the monthly returns the banks included under these headings head-office claims on and liabilities to their foreign branches. A re-examination of the evidence, however, suggests that the reporting procedures employed by the banks before July, 1900, were not as uniform as Curtis believed.

Some impressions as to the diversity of reporting procedures used may be gained from a comparison of net claims on foreign correspondent banks (CC) with head-office net claims on the foreign branches (HC) of individual banks. Had the 1900 revision of the monthly returns prompted the banks to alter their reporting procedures along the lines suggested by Curtis, I would expect that CC and HC were strongly correlated before July, 1900, but not thereafter. As far as the Bank of Montreal is concerned, the evidence partly supports the Curtis thesis. The analysis is limited to head-office claims on the Bank's U.S. branches since for the London branches the required data are unavailable.[26] If quarterly data on the Bank's CC (excluding net claims on U.K. correspondent banks) are regressed on HC, the following results are obtained:[27]

$$CC = \underset{(1.34)}{1.50} + \underset{(7.74)}{0.67}\,HC,\ \bar{R}^2 = 0.54,\ DW = 1.16, \qquad (B.2)$$

sample period: 1887IV-1900II.

$$CC = \underset{(3.65)}{3.40} + \underset{(2.15)}{0.07}\,HC,\ \bar{R}^2 = 0.06,\ DW = 1.03, \qquad (B.3)$$

sample period: 1900III-1913IV.

The regression equations indicate that prior to July, 1900, changes in HC explained over 50 percent of the observed variation in CC. After the 1900 revision of the monthly returns, HC ceased to be an important source of variation in CC. Although equation (B.3) yields a much lower coefficient of determination than (B.2), the parameter estimates of HC are statistically significant for both subperiods. However, if equations (B.2) and (B.3) are re-estimated in first differences, the parameter estimate for the second subperiod is no longer statistically significant:

$$\Delta CC = \underset{(0.41\ )}{0.001} + \underset{(5.38)}{0.76}\Delta HC,\ \bar{R}^2 = 0.36,\ DW = 2.61, \qquad (B.4)$$

sample period: 1888I-1900II.

$$\Delta CC = \underset{(0.52\ )}{0.003} + \underset{(0.27)}{0.06}\Delta HC,\ \bar{R}^2 = 0.00,\ DW = 1.72, \qquad (B.5)$$

sample period: 1900IV-1913IV.

Thus, equations (B.2) through (B.5) are consistent with the view that head-office claims on the Bank's foreign branches were part of CC until the 1900 revision of the monthly returns, but not afterwards. Since the parameter estimates of HC in equations (B.2) and (B.4) are consistently smaller than unity, however, the Bank probably did not include in CC, as reported up to June, 1900, its entire stock of HC.[28]

Little is known about the reporting procedures used by the other banks. Inasmuch as any firm conclusions can be drawn from the available rudimentary evidence, the BNS, the BNA and the BBC did not subsume HC in their reported CC either before or after the 1900 revision of the monthly returns.[29] In the case of the Canadian Bank of Commerce, the Merchants Bank of Canada and the Royal Bank, I do not know how they dealt with the statistical problems posed by head-office claims on their foreign branches. Since claims on and liabilities to foreign correspondent banks were extremely volatile, it is impossible to decide whether the changes in CC reported by the latter three banks between June and July, 1900, were due to shifts in reporting procedures or other factors.

Considering the data breaks introduced by the 1900 revision of the monthly returns, I adjust the pre-1900 Curtis series on net banking claims for head-office net claims on the foreign branches of the Bank of Montreal. According to equation (B.2), the Bank — on average — included in reported net banking claims 67 percent of its HC. Therefore, 67 percent of the Bank's HC are deducted from net claims on foreign correspondent banks as reported by Curtis. Net banking claims, thus adjusted [Table B-7, column (3)], are added to call loans abroad, as shown in Table B-6, column (3), in order to derive the new estimates of secondary reserves presented in Tables A-1 and B-5.

B.3.3. Comparison of New Estimates with Curtis Data

In Table B-5, I compare my estimates of secondary reserves with the Curtis data for net claims on foreign correspondent banks, the only published piece of information on pre-1900 secondary reserves. Although the new estimates — on average — exceed slightly the Curtis data, the cyclical patterns of the two series are very similar. The simple correlation between first differences in the new estimates and the Curtis data is high ($r=0.87$). Moreover, eleven out of twelve annual changes in the two series are equally signed. The close correspondence between the two sets of data is attributable to the fact that — as mentioned earlier — the Curtis data capture indirectly movements in foreign call loans extended by the Bank of Montreal. The evidence of Table B-5 implies that the Curtis data are adequate for analyzing cyclical movements in pre-1900 secondary reserves despite the omissions in the monthly returns. Therefore, the Curtis data on net banking claims are used as a measure of secondary reserves in the pre-1887 period, for which other sources of information are unavailable.

B.4. STRUCTURE AND SIGNIFICANCE OF THE CANADIAN BANKS' FOREIGN CALL-LOAN BUSINESS

The unpublished evidence obtained from the Bank of Montreal and the Bank of Nova Scotia also serves to rectify two popular misconceptions about the

TABLE B-7
NET CLAIMS ON FOREIGN CORRESPONDENT BANKS, 1887-99: ADJUSTMENT PROCEDURE
(Millions of Dollars)

End of Year	Head-Office Claims on Foreign Branches of Bank of Montreal	Net Claims on Foreign Correspondent Banks	
		Unadjusted	Adjusted
	(1)	(2)	(3)
1887	8.22	14.35	8.8
1888	10.89	21.10	13.8
1889	10.97	13.56	6.2
1890	8.40	11.69	6.1
1891	12.98	23.17	14.5
1892	16.11	18.48	7.7
1893	10.56	17.45	10.4
1894	15.62	24.70	14.2
1895	9.95	21.53	14.9
1896	11.43	23.15	15.5
1897	13.56	38.07	29.0
1898	12.53	32.60	24.2
1899	16.14	29.10	18.3

Sources and estimation methods for Table B-7
Column (1): GML. Data do not include claims on London branch.
Column (2): Curtis (1931a, 30, 31, 44, 45).
Column (3): Difference between data in columns (2) and (3) equals 67 percent of data in column (1).

foreign call-loan business of the Canadian banks. These misconceptions concern the geographical distribution of call loans abroad and the role played by the Canadian banks in the New York call-loan market.

B.4.1. Geographical Distribution of Call Loans Abroad

Most students of the pre-1914 Canadian financial system explicitly or implicitly argue that the Canadian banks placed their foreign call loans largely in New York (e.g., Viner, 1924, 177; Beckhart, 1929, 416-17; Curtis, 1931a, 12; Goodhart, 1969, 151-56; Naylor, 1975, vol. 2, 243). Although New York call loans no doubt were important, their share in the total was smaller than has commonly been believed. As far as the geographical distribution of foreign call loans extended by the Bank of Montreal and the BNS is concerned, the unpublished evidence suggests that over the period 1904-07 the share placed in the New York market typically did not exceed 50 percent, while the London market absorbed from 28 to 44 percent of the total (Table B-8). Thus, as a recipient of Canadian call loans, the London money market was almost as important as its New York equivalent.[30] Since between 1904 and 1907 the Bank of Montreal and the BNS accounted for 50-60 percent of aggregate Canadian call loans abroad,[31] the percentage shares of Table B-8 are likely to be representative for the Canadian banking system as a whole.

B.4.2. Role of the Canadian Banks in the New York Call-Loan Market

In his narrative history of pre-1914 Canadian business, Naylor (1975, vol. 2, 219) claims that the Canadian banks dominated the New York call-loan market. Considering the unpublished evidence, I would regard Naylor's assertion as a gross exaggeration. In order to test empirically Naylor's claim, the Canadian banks' share in the New York call-loan market is estimated for April 28, 1909, for which a rough guess of the size of that market exists. On that day, total call loans granted by New York City banks amounted to $742 million. This figure probably understates substantially the size of the New York market since it excludes loans placed in New York by banks in Canada and the interior of the United States (Goodhart, 1969, 19-20). By comparison, aggregate Canadian call loans abroad stood at $114 million at the end of April, 1909 (Curtis, 1931a, 52). Considering placements by the Bank of Montreal in cities other than New York, I conclude that Canadian call loans to the New York market did not exceed $81 million.[32] Thus, at the end of April, 1909, the Canadian banks accounted for at most 11 percent of total call loans outstanding in New York. A market share of that order of magnitude hardly implies that "[w]ithout the Canadian funds, Wall Street would have had difficulty conducting its operations" (Naylor, 1975, vol. 2, 219).

TABLE B-8
GEOGRAPHICAL DISTRIBUTION OF CALL LOANS ABROAD
(Percent)

Call loans placed in	1904	1905	1906	1907
London	44	35	35	28
New York	42	52	51	55
Chicago	12	11	11	13
Other Cities	2	2	3	4[a)]

a) Mainly Boston.

Sources for Table B-8
Data cover Bank of Montreal (GML) and BNS (Statistics 14). The percentages are calculated from annual averages of end-of-quarter data.

Endnotes — Appendix B

1. See Neufeld (1972, 126) for a similar tabulation covering the post-1913 period.

2. The Canadian banks also solicited deposits in New York even though New York state law did not permit foreign banks to accept deposits. See Morgan and Parker (1920, 141) for the regulations governing foreign banks in New York. Both the Bank of Montreal and the Bank of Nova Scotia showed deposits on the books of their New York branches. The data sources underlying notes 2, 3, 4 and 7 are discussed in Section B.2.1.

3. Over 70 percent of the branch's assets were normally financed by funds from head office.

4. Data are available on the assets and liabilities of the London branch of the Bank of Montreal. The assets of that branch consisted mostly of call loans and a small amount of securities, while fixed-term loans were minuscule.

5. The Canadian banks entered Newfoundland late in 1894 and in the early part of 1895 in the wake of a total collapse of the island's banking system (Denison, 1967, 261-63; Jamieson, 1955, 31-32).

6. In Jamaica, the Canadian banks competed vigorously with the British-controlled Colonial Bank and local institutions (Callender, 1965, 53-61). U.S. banks were not active in the Caribbean since national banks were prevented from opening foreign branches until 1914 (Phelps, 1927, 3).

7. Over the period 1911-13, the Bank of Nova Scotia was able to maintain the following spreads (percent) between the average returns on loans and deposits: Branches in Canada: 3.5; Newfoundland: 3.7; Jamaica: 3.3; Cuba: 6.3; and Puerto Rico: 6.2.

8. In Newfoundland — which was on a dollar standard — Canadian coins and notes were traded at par (Harvey, 1902, 159). As a result of the influx of Canadian banks, Newfoundland's monetary system was gradually integrated into that of Canada (United Kingdom, Newfoundland Royal Commission, 29; MacKay and Saunders, 1946, 117-18).

9. Prior to 1899, Canadian banks were not empowered to issue notes denominated in currencies other than Canadian (or American) dollars. In 1899, the Bank Act was amended to enable the Bank of Nova Scotia to issue sterling notes in Jamaica (Canada, *Statutes*, 62-63 Vic. Cap. 14). A further amendment in 1904 allowed the Union Bank of Halifax to circulate notes denominated in Trinidad dollars. In principle, any bank maintaining branches in a British colony or possession could henceforth issue sterling or dollar notes redeemable in that colony (Canada, *Statutes*, 4 Edw. VII, Cap. 3; United Kingdom, Royal Commission on Trade Relations between Canada and the West Indies, 54).

10. Statement by Finance Minister Fielding (Canada, *Debates*, 1904, 7787). The Bank Act stipulated precisely how the Canadian-dollar value of foreign-currency notes was to be determined for reporting purposes. Since notes issued abroad were part of the aggregate circulation, they were subject to the statutory ceiling of the Bank Act (See Chapter 1).

11. Data extracted from these sources that are not presented in Tables B-2, B-4, B-6, B-7, B-8 and 5-1 are available from the author upon request.

12. For the period up to June, 1900, the two sources differ considerably as to the Bank's holdings of securities. Prior to the 1900 revision of the monthly returns, the banks were only required to report their holdings of government and railway securities, while GML shows the aggregate stock.

13. The states of Oregon and Washington (*Annual Report*, 1907) also required the Canadian banks to file returns, but the data were not collected prior to 1907.

14. Although GML yields monthly data, I only compiled a quarterly series on the Bank's monetary gold stock.

15. The Bank of Montreal has preserved a set of ledgers summarizing the statistical information supplied to the government. For the period 1906IV-1907IV, these ledgers specifically indicate that the monthly returns only comprise part of the gold held outside Canada.

16. Information obtained from Mr. Radford, Corporate Secretary, Canadian Imperial Bank of Commerce.

17. The Banque Nationale and the Dominion Bank opened their first foreign branches in 1907 and 1911 respectively. According to their 1913 returns, their gold holdings abroad were minuscule.

18. They temporarily operated branches in other cities. See legend to Table B-1.

19. At the end of June, 1900, the gold holdings of the BNA and the BBC, as reported in their monthly returns, amounted to $503,000 and $603,000 respectively. If these holdings are multiplied by the respective percentages in Table B-3, gold not reported at that time can be estimated. The unreported stocks, thus estimated, amount to $438,000 for the BNA and to $621,000 for the BBC. Interestingly, they are of the same order of magnitude as the respective banks' San Francisco holdings of currency and coin at the end of 1900II (Table B-4).

20. Recall that call loans, as defined in this study, include fixed-term loans maturing in 30 days or less. As far as the Bank of Montreal is concerned, fixed-term loans only accounted for a small share of the total. From February, 1897, to the end of 1913, the loans made by the Bank under this heading consisted entirely of call loans. Prior to February, 1897, the share booked at the Chicago branch consisted largely of 30-day loans, while New York loans were on call.

21. Call loans on the books of the Bank's other foreign branches were negligible.

22. During the period under study, the Bank of Montreal maintained higher cash and secondary reserve ratios than any other Canadian financial institution. The Bank's relatively high reserve ratios reflected its unique role in the Canadian financial system.

23. DA and DM exclude provincial and Dominion government deposits, as well as interbank deposits. For the sources, see Curtis (1931a, 24) and *Canada Gazette* respectively. If DA and DM are redefined to include bank notes and provincial government deposits, the coefficient of determination and the standard error of estimate remain virtually the same as in equation (B.1). Moreover, a logarithmic specification of equation (B.1) lowers slightly $\bar{R}^2$ and SEE.

24. If the estimation procedure is extended to the period 1910-13, the forecast errors rise significantly since the Bank of Montreal, around 1910, began to lose its dominant position in the Canadian call-loan business.

25. Hartland reaches a favourable verdict on the quality of her estimates. However, she does not compare her estimates with the actual values of LA, as shown in Table B-6, column (5), but with the actual values of the sum of call loans and other current loans abroad (1960, 731). She fails to explain this curious comparison.

26. Data and head-office claims on the London branches are available only for 1910IV onwards.

27. CC: Difference between balances due to and balances due from banks and banking correspondents elsewhere than in Canada and the United Kingdom *(Canada Gazette)*. HC: Net capital used by the foreign branches, other than the London branches (GML). The data are expressed in millions of dollars.

28. The hypothesis that the parameter estimate of HC equals unity is rejected at the 95 percent level of significance for equation (B.2), but not for equation (B.4).

29. As in the case of the Bank of Montreal, CC stands for the respective bank's net claims on foreign correspondent banks, other than on banks in the United Kingdom. HC is measured as follows:

BNA and BBC: Head-office net claims on the respective San Francisco branch, as reported on June 30 and December 31 (California, *Annual Report*).

BNS: Aggregate head-office net claims on the foreign branches, as shown in Statistics 3. Since that source offers annual averages of HC, the correlation analysis is based on annual averages of end-of-quarter data for CC. Recall that the BNS did not operate a branch in the United Kingdom prior to 1914.

Since CC and HC were subject to strong time trends, the correlation coefficients are compiled from first differences rather than levels. They assume the following values (sample period indicated in parentheses). BNA: 0.27 (first half of 1982 to second half of 1894); BBC: 0.20 (second half of 1886 to second half of 1894); BNS: 0.10 (1885/86-98/99) and 0.47 (1901/02-12/13). None of the correlation coefficients is statistically significant at the 95 percent level.

30. For the Bank of Montreal, complete data on the geographical distribution of call loans abroad are available for the period 1900IV-1913IV. Over this period, the share of London loans ranged from 17 to 68 percent of the Bank's total, with the average amounting to 39 percent.

31. Call loans abroad of the Bank of Montreal and the BNS, as shown in GML and Statistics 14 respectively, are expressed as a percentage of aggregate Canadian call loans, as reported in Table A-2. Statistics 14 only provides data on call loans booked at the foreign branches of the BNS. In the case of the BNS, a large portion of call loans abroad was placed directly by head office. For this reason, the monthly returns of the BNS show a much larger volume of call loans than Statistics 14.

32. I assume that call loans placed by the Bank of Montreal in foreign cities other than New York were the same on April 28 as on March 31, 1909. At the end of 1909I, they stood at $33 million (see GML). The estimate of $81 million is likely to overstate call loans placed by the Canadian banks in the New York market. I suspect that — like the Bank of Montreal — other Canadian financial institutions did not channel their call loans exclusively to New York.

APPENDIX C

DIVISION OF REFERENCE CYCLE INTO STAGES

In this study I employ a simplified variant of a technique developed by the National Bureau of Economic Research (Burns and Mitchell, 1946, ch. 5) for assigning the observations of a time series to various reference-cycle stages. In principle, I distinguish among four cycle stages. First, the reference cycle is split up into an expansion and a contraction stage, extending from trough to peak and peak to trough respectively. Second, both the expansion and contraction stages are divided up further into two substages of equal length. These substages are termed expansions I and II, as well as contractions I and II. The terminal date of expansion I (contraction I) is called the midpoint of a reference-cycle expansion (contraction).[1]

Except in a few instances, the four reference-cycle substages are not considered separately. For the most part, it suffices to distinguish among expansions and contractions, on the one hand, and booms and depressions on the other. The boom stage is assumed to cover expansion II and contraction I, that is, periods of above-average levels of economic activity. The depression stage, by contrast, embraces contraction II and expansion I.

The choice of a procedure for assigning the observations of a time series to the various cycle stages hinges on such characteristics as the periodicity and stock/flow nature of the data. Moreover, the assignment problem differs as to whether a time series is assigned to the Canadian or U.S. reference-cycle stages. The procedures most frequently used in this study are described below.

Procedure 1

This procedure is used for assigning to the Canadian reference-cycle stages quarterly first differences or rates of change in end-of-period stocks (such as assets) and in ratios (such as reserve ratios and interest rates). The quarterly observations are assigned as follows (see Tables 3-2, 3-6 and 5-2):

Expansion I: 79II-80IV, 85I-86I, 88I-89II, 91I-92I, 94I-94IV, 96III-98II, 01I-02I, 04II-05III, 08III-09II, 11III-12I.

Expansion II: 72III-73IV, 80IV-82III, 86I-87I, 89II-90III, 92I-93I, 94IV-95III, 98II-00II, 02I-02IV, 05III-06IV, 09II-10I, 12I-12IV.

Contraction I: 73IV-76III, 82III-83IV, 87I-87III, 90III-90IV, 93I-93III, 95III-96I, 00II-00III, 02IV-03III, 06IV-07III, 10I-10IV, 12IV-13IV.

Contraction II: 76III-79II, 83IV-85I, 87III-88I, 90IV-91I, 93III-94I, 96I-96III, 00III-01I, 03III-04II, 07III-08III, 10IV-11III.

Note that the observations for quarters containing a reference-cycle turning point or midpoint are assigned to each of the two adjacent cycle stages. However, if expansion II and contraction I are joined in a boom stage (just to mention one possible combination of substages), the observation for the terminal quarter of expansion II is only counted once.

Procedure 2

This procedure is analogous to 1, except that the observations are assigned to the U.S. reference-cycle stages (see Table 5-2):

Expansion stage: 79I-82I, 85II-87I, 88II-90III, 91II-93I, 94II-95IV, 97II-99II, 00IV-02III, 04III-07II, 08II-10I, 12I-13I.

Contraction stage: remaining observations and observations for the initial and terminal quarters of the respective expansion stages.

Boom stage: 80III-83III, 86I-87III, 89II-90IV, 92I-93III, 95I-96III, 98II-00I, 01IV-03III, 05IV-07IV, 09I-11I, 12III-13IV.

Depression stage: remaining observations and observations for the initial and terminal quarters of the respective boom stages.

Procedure 3

This procedure is employed for assigning to the Canadian reference-cycle stages annual flows (such as the level of real exports) and annual first differences in end-of-period stocks (such as assets). Annual observations on the level of Canadian wholesale prices — though not flows — are also assigned by this procedure, because they constitute averages of monthly data (see Tables 3-3 and 4-1). The observations of such time series are assumed to be centred on July 1 of the respective year. An observation with its central point falling into, say, an expansion stage is in turn assigned to that stage:

Expansion stage: 72-73, 79-82, 85-86, 88-92, 94-95, 97-99, 01-02, 04-06, 09, 12.

Contraction stage: remaining observations.

Boom stage: 72-76, 81-83, 86-87, 89-90, 92-93, 95, 98-00, 02-03, 06-07, 09-10, 12-13.

Depression stage: remaining observations.

The reference-cycle contraction of 1890-91 is disregarded because of its short duration.

Procedure 4

This procedure is analogous to 3, except that it is used for assigning to the Canadian reference-cycle stages such fiscal-year flow data as unit values of Canadian exports and imports (see Table 4-1). For fiscal years up to 1906, the observations of such time series are assumed to be centred on January 1 of the corresponding calendar year. The observations for fiscal 1907 — which lasted only from July 1, 1906, to March 31, 1907 — are centred on November 15, 1906, while those for fiscal 1908-14 are centred on October 1 of the corresponding calendar year minus one:

Expansion stage: 73, 80-82, 86-87, 89-90, 92-93, 95, 97-00, 02, 05-07, 09-10, 12-13.

Contraction stage: remaining observations.

Boom stage: 73-76, 81-83, 87, 90, 93, 95-96, 99-00, 03, 06-07, 10-11, 13-14.

Depression stage: remaining observations.

Procedure 5

This procedure is employed for assigning to the Canadian reference-cycle stages annual first differences or rates of change in calendar-year flow data (GNP, average return on loans) or in calendar-year averages of quarterly or monthly stock data (Tables 5-3 and 5-7). The observations on the level of such series are assumed to be centred on July 1 of the respective years. Analogously, the difference or rate of change between the levels for, say, 1907 and 1906 (denoted by 06/07), is assumed to be centred on January 1, 1907:

Expansion stage: 70/71-72/73, 79/80-81/82, 85/86-86/87, 88/89-89/90, 91/92-92/93, 94/95, 96/97-99/00, 01/02, 04/05-05/06, 08/09-09/10, 11/12.

Contraction stage: remaining observations.

Boom stage: 70/71-75/76, 80/81-82/83, 86/87, 89/90, 92/93, 94/95-95/96, 98/99-99/00, 02/03, 05/06-06/07, 09/10, 12/13.

Depression stage: remaining observations.

Procedure 6

This procedure is analogous to 5, except that it is used for assigning the observations to the U.S. reference-cycle stages:

Expansion stage: 70/71-72/73, 79/80-81/82, 85/86-86/87, 88/89-89/90, 91/92-92/93, 94/95, 97/98-98/99, 00/01-01/02, 04/05-06/07, 08/09-09/10, 12/13.

Contraction stage: remaining observations.

Booms: 70/71-75/76, 80/81-82/83, 86/87, 89/90, 92/93, 95/96, 98/99-99/00, 01/02-02/03, 05/06-06/07, 09/10-10/11, 12/13.

Depression stage: remaining observations.

Endnote — Appendix C

1. The midpoints of Canadian expansions (E) and contractions (C) are dated as follows: C 8/76, E 12/80, C 11/83, E 2/86, C 8/87, E 4/89, C 11/90, E 2/92, C 8/93, E 11/94, C 2/96, E 6/98, C 9/00, E 1/02, C 9/03, E 9/05, C 9/07, E 5/09, C 11/10, E 3/12, C 12/13. The U.S. midpoints are timed analogously. See Table 2-1 for the dates of Canadian and U.S. reference-cycle turning points.

APPENDIX D

SOLUTION OF THE DYNAMIC MODEL OF CHAPTER 4

D.1. STEADY-STATE EFFECTS OF AN EXTERNAL CYCLICAL FORCE ($v = \sin t$)

In Chapter 4, it was assumed that foreign-induced changes in the current-account surplus (v) are described by a sine wave [equation (4.32)]. Substituting equation (4.32) into (4.28) and disregarding foreign-induced changes in the Canadian non-monetary debt (w), I obtain the following non-homogeneous first-order differential equation in the Canadian cumulative current-account surplus (N):

$$k_4 N + k_2 \dot{N} = k_3 \sin t, \qquad \text{(D.1)}$$

where $k_3 < 0$ and

$$k_4 = \beta_1(\gamma_1 + \gamma_2) > 0. \qquad \text{(D.2)}$$

The general solution to (D.1) is given by $N = N_c + N_p$, with N_c and N_p denoting the complementary function and the particular solution respectively. The complementary function — which represents the general solution to the homogeneous variant of (D.1) — may be written as:

$$N_c = qe^{-(k4/k2)t} \qquad \text{(D.3)}$$

with q standing for an arbitrary constant.

The particular solution reads:

$$N_p = -k_3 \lambda_1 \cos(t + \eta_1), \qquad \text{(D.4)}$$

where

$$\lambda_1^2 = 1/(k_2^2+k_4^2), \quad \text{(D.5)}$$
$$\sin \eta_1 = k_4\lambda_1, \quad \text{(D.6)}$$
$$\cos \eta_1 = k_2\lambda_1. \quad \text{(D.7)}$$

Note that equations (D.6) and (D.7) imply (D.5) because $\sin^2\eta_1 + \cos^2\eta_1 = 1$. See Courant (1937, 509-12) for the particular solution of such a differential equation as (D.1).

As I showed in Chapter 4, a stable solution to (D.1) exists if $k_2>0$. According to equations (D.3) and (D.4), a positive value of k_2 implies that the oscillations in N approach a steady state as $t \rightarrow \infty$. In the steady state, $N_c=0$ and $N=N_p$.

In the following, I assume the Canadian economy to have attained a steady state. Therefore, only the particular solution (D.4) is considered. Setting $N=N_p$ and differentiating (D.4) with respect to time, I derive a solution for the current-account surplus:

$$c = \dot{N} = k_3\lambda_1\sin(t+\eta_1). \quad \text{(D.8)}$$

Since $\sin(t+\eta_1) = \sin t \cos \eta_1 + \cos t \sin \eta_1$,
(D.8) may also be written as:

$$c = k_3\lambda_1^2(k_2\sin t + k_4\cos t) \quad \text{(D.8a)}$$

if equations (D.5) through (D.7) are taken into account.

According to equation (D.8), the oscillations in c — as those in v — are described by a sine wave. However, the cyclical turning points in c and v do not coincide; since η_1 is a positive number, the current-account surplus leads v. This lead may also be gleaned from equation (D.8a). Provided $k_3<0$, the current account surplus reaches a trough during the second half of the expansion phase in the v-cycle (as shown in Chart 4-6). If k_2 were large (small) relative to k_4, troughs in c would occur near peaks (near inflection points preceding peaks) in v.

In Chapter 5, I concluded that real aggregate demand, in all likelihood, was unresponsive to changes in domestic interest rates, that is, $\beta_1 = k_4 = 0$ and $\lambda_1 = 1/k_2$. In this case, cyclical troughs in c should have coincided perfectly with peaks in v, as indicated by equation (D.8b):

$$c = [(1-\beta_2)/k_1]\sin t, \quad \text{(D.8b)}$$

which is derived by taking account of (4.29) and (4.30). Equation (D.8b) is identical to (5.20) with $v=\sin t$.

A solution for the price of the home good and domestic output may be obtained by rewriting (D.4) in a form analogous to (D.8a):

$$N = k_3\lambda_1^2[k_4\sin t - k_2\cos t]. \quad \text{(D.9)}$$

Substituting equation (D.9) into (4.26), setting $w=0$ and $v=\sin t$, and noting that $k_3 = k_2 - (\alpha_1+\delta_1)(\gamma_1+\gamma_2)$, I obtain:

$$P = y = \lambda_1^2 \{[(\alpha_1+\delta_1)k_2+\beta_1 k_4]\sin t - \beta_1 k_3 \cos t\}. \tag{D.10}$$

As in the case of the current-account surplus, the oscillations in P and y are described by sine waves, assuming the form of $P = y = (\lambda_1/\lambda_2)\sin(t+\eta_2)$, with $\lambda_2^2 = 1/[(\alpha_1+\delta_1)^2+\beta_1^2]$, $\sin \eta_2 = -\beta_1 k_3 \lambda_1 \lambda_2$, and $\cos \eta_2 = [(\alpha_1+\delta_1)k_2+\beta_1 k_4]\lambda_1\lambda_2$. Since η_2 is a positive number, P and y also lead v. According to equation (D.10), peaks in these two variables occur during the second half of the expansion phase in the v-cycle.

Provided real aggregate demand is unresponsive to the domestic bond yield ($\beta_1=k_4=0$), there is a perfect coincidence of cyclical turning points in P, y and v:

$$P = y = (1/k_1)\sin t. \tag{D.10a}$$

Equation (D.10a) matches (5.19) with $v = \sin t$.

In order to find a solution for the domestic bond yield, I substitute (D.9) into (4.27) and rearrange terms by taking account of (D.5):

$$r = (\lambda_1^2/k_2)\{[(\alpha_2+h')(k_2^2+k_4^2)-k_1k_3k_4]\sin t + k_1k_2k_3 \cos t\}. \tag{D.11}$$

From (4.23), (4.29), (4.30) and (D.2), it may be seen that $k_1k_3 = (1-\beta_2)k_2+k_4(\alpha_2+h')$. Thus, (D.11) becomes:

$$r = \lambda_1^2(k_5 \sin t + k_1k_3 \cos t), \tag{D.12}$$

where

$$k_5 = (\alpha_2+h')k_2 - (1-\beta_2)k_4. \tag{D.13}$$

As in the case of the other endogenous variables, it may easily be shown that the movements in r are described by a sine wave.

Equations (D.12) and (D.13) suggest that the domestic bond yield may be positively or negatively related to v. A necessary and sufficient condition for the correlation between r and v to be positive (negative) is that k_5 assume a positive (negative) value. Regardless of the sign of that correlation, the turning points in r do not coincide with those in v. Provided $k_3<0$, a positive (negative) value of k_5 implies that r peaks during the first (second) half of a contraction phase in the v-cycle.

If positive values of k_3 are ruled out, a necessary — but not sufficient — condition for k_5 to be positive is that the marginal propensity to absorb home and imported goods (β_2) exceed unity. If β_2 fell short of unity, the total output sensitivity of nominal base-money demand (α_2+h') would need to be negative in order to ensure $k_3<0$ [see equation (4.30)]. According to equation (D.13), $\alpha_2+h'<0$ and $\beta_2<1$ would be inconsistent with a positive value of k_5. Analogously, for k_5 to assume a negative value, a necessary — but not sufficient — condition is $\alpha_2 + h' < 0$. Furthermore, a sufficient but not necessary condition for $k_5 \gtreqless 0$ is that $\alpha_2 + h' \gtreqless 0$ and $\beta_2 \gtreqless 1$.

Consequently, in the steady state, both the signs of $\alpha_2 + h'$ and $1 - \beta_2$ bear on the cyclical pattern of r. This result stands in sharp contrast to equation (4.27), which suggests that in the short run the sign of the correlation between r and v is determined solely by the sign of $\alpha_2 + h'$. The importance of β_2 in equation (D.13) is explained by the fact that in the steady state an increase in v may influence r through three channels. First- and third-channel effects are captured by the sine term in equation (D.12), while second-channel effects are measured by the cosine term.

> *First channel:* Depending on the sign of $\alpha_2 + h'$, r rises or falls instantaneously as a result of an increase or decrease in base-money demand, induced by an expansion in domestic output (and the price of the home good).
>
> *Second channel:* Provided $k_3 < 0$, an increase in v causes the current-account surplus and the growth in base-money supply to decline. The level of base-money supply also shrinks, but with a lag amounting to one-quarter of the length of a full v-cycle. The decrease in the level of base-money supply is in turn accompanied by a rise in r. Thus, the initial increase or decrease in r is reinforced or counteracted by a subsequent rise prompted by a deterioration in the balance of payments.
>
> *Third channel:* Cyclical movements in r feed back on themselves by way of changes in domestic output, as well as demand and supply of base money. These feedback effects do not impinge on the cyclical pattern of the domestic bond yield, save for movements in the cumulative current-account surplus and the supply of base money prompted by second-channel changes in r. To the extent that a second-channel rise in the domestic bond yield feeds back on itself through a fall in domestic output, as well as an expansion in the cumulative current-account surplus and in the level of base-money supply, it triggers a further lagged response in r, with the lag to v amounting to one-half of the length of a full v-cycle. Specifically, third-channel effects cause r to decline during the contraction phase of the v-cycle.

If $\alpha_2 + h' > 0$ and $\beta_2 > 1$, the first-channel effects on r are reinforced by third-channel effects. During the contraction phase of the v-cycle, an instantaneous first-channel decline in r is amplified by third-channel effects triggered by the preceding expansion in v. The condition of $\beta_2 > 1$ is necessary to ensure that the current-account surplus is negatively correlated with v. Thus, in this case, the correlation between r and v is unambiguously positive. If $\alpha_2 + h' < 0$ and $\beta_2 < 1$, the first- and third-channel effects run in opposite directions. During the contraction phase of the v-cycle, the decrease in v is associated with a first-channel increase in r, while the third-channel effect is to lower that variable. However, as long as $\beta_2 < 1$, the model indicates that the third-channel effets will never fully offset their first-channel counterparts. Therefore, in this case, there is an unambiguous negative correlation between r and v. Second-channel effects do not impinge on the correlation between r and v, but introduce a lead or lag to the v-cycle.

If the assumptions underlying the analysis of Chapter 5 hold ($\alpha_2 + h' = \beta_1 = k_4 = 0$), only second-channel effects are operative:

$$r = [(1-\beta_2)/k_2]\cos t. \tag{D.12a}$$

In this case, the current-account surplus does not move countercyclically unless $\beta_2 > 1$. Therefore, equation (D.12a) implies that peaks in the Canadian bond yield coincide with the inflection points following peaks in the v-cycle.

D.2. LONG-RUN EFFECTS OF DOMESTIC MONETARY DISTURBANCES

As demonstrated by Swoboda (1972), in small open economies that are pure price takers on world markets for goods and financial assets, domestic monetary disturbances do not affect permanently such variables as the domestic monetary base, domestic prices, output and interest rates. To analyze the effects on the Canadian economy of a permanent change in a domestic monetary variable, consider an increase in the uncovered stock of Dominion notes (UD). In Chapter 4, it was assumed that in the long run, prices and wages are fully flexible, that is, equation (4.16b) rather than (4.16a) holds. Thus, domestic output equals its normal value ($y = y'$). Moreover, in long run stationary-state equilibrium, the current-account balance must be zero:

$$c = 0. \tag{D.13}$$

Otherwise, the model remains unchanged. It now consists of the eleven equations (4.7), (4.8), (4.9), (4.11a), (4.12), (4.13), (4.14), (4.15a), (4.16b), (4.19) and (D.13), determining the endogenous variables H, h, I, N, S, P, π, r, y, b and c.

In response to a permanent increase in the uncovered stock of Dominion notes, the economy, in the long run, reaches a new stationary state in which $\dot{N} = c = 0$. Thus, equation (4.14), in conjunction with (D.13) and (4.16b), may be solved for the long-run equilibrium value of the relative price of the imported good:

$$\pi = -z/\gamma_1 + (\gamma_2/\gamma_1)y'. \tag{D.14}$$

Substituting (D.14) into (4.15a) and taking account of (4.21), I obtain a solution for the price of the home good:

$$P = P_f + z/\gamma_1 + 1 - (\gamma_2/\gamma_1)y' = (v - \gamma_2 y')/\gamma_1. \tag{D.15}$$

The equilibrium value of the domestic bond yield is determined by equations (4.12) and (4.13), with $y = y'$ and $c = 0$:

$$r = r' = -(1-\beta_2)y'/\beta_1. \tag{D.16}$$

From (4.19) and (D.16), it follows that

$$S = \delta_1 r' - \delta_2 r_f + u'(P_f - 1). \tag{D.17}$$

Finally, substituting (4.16b) and (D.16) into (4.7), and taking account of (4.8), (4.11a) and (D.15), I derive the following solutions for the monetary base and international monetary assets:

$$h = h'. \tag{D.18}$$

$$H = h' (v - \gamma_2 y')/\gamma_1. \tag{D.19}$$

$$I = H - UD. \tag{D.20}$$

The solution for the cumulative current-account surplus (N) may be obtained from (4.9), (D.17), (D.19) and (D.20).

The results clearly indicate that an increase in the uncovered stock of Dominion notes, in the long run, does not affect any of the endogenous variables, save for international monetary assets. Monetary authorities are able to raise the monetary base only temporarily. This elicits temporary current-account deficits as a result of a temporary decline in the domestic bond yield and a corresponding increase in domestic output. The current-account deficits in turn lead to a permanent decline in international monetary assets, offsetting completely the impact of the rise in UD on the monetary base. Consequently, an increase in UD in the long run only alters the composition but not the level of the monetary base.

From equation (D.15), it may further be seen that a permanent increase in the price of the imported good (P_f), in the long run, raises the price of the home good by the same proportion. Moreover, by virtue of equations (D.19) and (4.21), the nominal monetary base increases by the same proportion as P_f.

APPENDIX E

QUARTERLY DATA ON CANADIAN BOND YIELDS

E.1. IMPLICIT YIELD ON BONDS ISSUED BY THE DOMINION, PROVINCIAL AND MUNICIPAL GOVERNMENTS

In this section, I describe the procedure used for estimating end-of-quarter yields on bonds issued by the Dominion, provincial and municipal governments. Dominion and provincial government bond yields are compiled for the period 1868I-1913IV, while the municipal-bond-yield series covers a much shorter time span of 1881I to 1904IV. Annual averages of the quarterly data estimated for the yield on Dominion government bonds are presented in Table 7-4. The corresponding annual averages for the yields on provincial and municipal bonds are shown in Table E-1.

The implicit yields are determined exclusively for bonds traded in the London market. Price quotations and information on the coupons and terms to maturity of the bonds are obtained from *The Economist*. The calculations are based on the highest closing prices reported for the week nearest to the end of the quarter. Price quotations derived from domestic bond markets are not taken into account since they are available only for the early part of the period under study.[1]

To determine the average yield on, say, Dominion government bonds, the estimation period is split up into overlapping subperiods of varying length, with the overlap amounting to one year. For each of these subperiods, I choose a portfolio of Dominion government bonds traded in the London market. The portfolios, thus selected, possess three characteristics:

(a) Each portfolio includes a fixed number of bonds.

(b) Each bond remains in the portfolio during the entire subperiod.

(c) The terms to maturity of the bonds included in the portfolios must not be less than five years.

Upon the start of a new subperiod, bonds whose terms to maturity approach the limit of five years drop out of the portfolio and are replaced by newly issued ones, provided the government sold any securities during the preceding subperiod. Next, I determine the unweighted arithmetic means of the end-of-quarter yields on the bonds covered by the various portfolios. This procedure generates a homogeneous bond-yield series for each subperiod. However, since the series compiled for the various subperiods are not based on the same portfolio, there are small breaks in the data upon the start of a new subperiod. To eliminate these breaks, the series for successive subperiods are chained together. The same method is employed for estimating the average yield on provincial and municipal bonds.

The data presented in Tables 7-4 and E-1 differ from similar series compiled by Neufeld (1972, Table 15:2). While Table 7-4 is based on a multitude of

TABLE E-1
AVERAGE YIELD ON PROVINCIAL AND MUNICIPAL GOVERNMENT BONDS
(Percent)

	Provincial	Municipal		Provincial	Municipal
1868	5.7		1890	3.8	4.3
1869	5.5		1891	4.3	4.5
			1892	4.0	4.5
1870	5.4		1893	3.9	4.2
1871	5.0		1894	3.7	4.1
1872	4.9		1895	3.7	4.0
1873	4.9		1896	3.5	4.0
1874	4.5		1897	3.4	3.9
1875	4.6		1898	3.5	3.9
1876	4.5		1899	3.5	4.0
1877	4.4				
1878	4.4		1900	3.7	4.0
1879	4.3		1901	3.7	4.0
			1902	3.6	4.1
1880	4.2		1903	3.8	4.1
1881	4.0	4.6	1904	3.9	4.1
1882	4.0	4.4	1905	3.8	
1883	3.9	4.5	1906	3.8	
1884	3.9	4.4	1907	3.9	
1885	3.9	4.5	1908	3.9	
1886	3.6	4.4	1909	3.8	
1887	3.6	4.3			
1888	3.4	4.3	1910	3.9	
1889	3.1	4.2	1911	3.9	
			1912	4.0	
			1913	4.4	

Dominion government securities traded in London, Neufeld's series is derived from the price quotations for a single bond (from 1870 to 1896: Canada 5 percent 1903 sterling bond; from 1897 to 1913, Canada 3 percent 1938 sterling bond). Moreover, Neufeld's table exhibits yield data for Quebec and Ontario bonds, covering the periods 1876-1913 and 1901-13 respectively. The Quebec bond yield is also computed from price quotations for a single security. The data on bond yields contained in Urquhart and Buckley (1965, series H 590 and H 606) only cover the post-1900 period.

E.2. IMPLICIT YIELD ON CANADIAN CORPORATE BONDS

Table E-2 presents quarterly unweighted arithmetic means of the yields on six Canadian corporate bonds traded at the Montreal Stock Exchange. Price quotations are obtained from the *Monetary Times*. The series only covers the period 1907I-1913IV, since Canadian corporate bonds were not traded much in earlier years. At the end of 1913, the terms to maturity of the six bonds amounted to at least seven years. The yield series is based on the following bonds:

Dominion Coal, 5 percent, due 1940,
Dominion Cotton, 6 percent, due 1922,
Dominion Iron and Steel, 5 percent, due 1929,
Laurentide Paper, 6 percent, due 1920,
Montreal Light, Heat and Power, 4 1/2 percent, due 1932,
Montreal Street Railway, 4 1/2 percent, due 1922.

The implicit yields are derived from ask prices quoted for the day nearest to the end of a quarter. Since some of these bonds were traded infrequently,

TABLE E-2
AVERAGE YIELD ON CANADIAN CORPORATE BONDS, 1907-13
(Percent)

End of Period	Yield	End of Period	Yield	End of Period	Yield
1907 I	5.42	1910 I	4.92	1913 I	5.12
II	5.47	II	4.97	II	5.10
III	5.67	III	4.93	III	5.10
IV	5.67	IV	4.98	IV	5.25
1908 I	5.55	1911 I	5.00		
II	5.57	II	4.98		
III	5.47	III	4.97		
IV	5.28	IV	4.97		
1909 I	5.00	1912 I	4.93		
II	5.00	II	4.90		
III	4.97	III	4.88		
IV	4.97	IV	4.95		

it is not always possible to extract suitable end-of-quarter quotations. To circumvent this problem, the following procedure is adopted:

(a) As a first step, price quotations are compiled for all the working days of the two-week period preceding and succeeding the end of a quarter.

(b) From the data, thus compiled, I select the ask price quoted for the day nearest to the end of the quarter. The implicit yield on the respective bond is in turn calculated from the ask price.

(c) If the data set does not contain any ask prices, I select the bid price nearest to the end of the quarter. The bid price is adjusted for the nearest available spread between bid and ask quotations.

(d) In a few cases, this procedure fails to generate a suitable ask or bid price. In this event, the ask price is estimated on the basis of the nearest available recorded prices.

Endnote — Appendix E

1. Government bonds were actively traded on the domestic stock exchanges until the 1880s. Thereafter, trading gradually shifted from the stock exchanges to the over-the-counter market. I am indebted to Ed Neufeld for this point. Also recall (Chapter 7) that domestic bond issues by the Dominion government were important only during the 1870s and 1880s.

APPENDIX F

FOREIGN BORROWING BY THE DOMINION GOVERNMENT: FURTHER ESTIMATION PROBLEMS

Appendix F addresses two further problems of estimating foreign borrowing by the Dominion government. The first one concerns the share of Dominion government bonds, payable in London, absorbed by the Canadian chartered banks. Second, the estimates of Dominion government bonds issued in London, as presented in this study, are compared with an analogous series compiled by Simon (1970).

F.1. BANK HOLDINGS OF DOMINION GOVERNMENT BONDS

For a variety of reasons, it is virtually impossible to adjust the London issues of Dominion government bonds for the share acquired by the domestic banks. For one, the monthly bank returns do not show separately bonds payable in London and Canada (Curtis, 1931a, 47). To make matters worse, bank holdings of bonds — whether payable in London or Canada — were reported in a thoroughly confusing manner. A summary of the instructions given to the chartered banks for reporting their portfolios of government bonds highlights the nature of these difficulties:

> July, 1867, to June, 1871: Over this subperiod, Dominion government bonds were reported together with other government liabilities to the chartered banks (Curtis, 1931a, 11). The share of bonds in the total is unknown.

July, 1871, to June, 1880: The data appear to cover both Dominion and provincial government bonds. Bank holdings of the two categories of securities were small and seldom exceeded $3 million.

July, 1880, to June, 1900: The monthly returns show separately bank holdings of Dominion government bonds. However, no data are available on the shares payable in London and Canada. A close examination of the series indicates that major increases invariably coincided with issues of Dominion government bonds in the London market. Therefore, it is reasonable to conjecture that the fluctuations in that series were attributable mainly to variations in bank holdings of bonds payable in London.

July, 1900, to March, 1914: Dominion and provincial government bonds were once again reported under a single heading. The modification of the reporting procedure caused reported stocks of government bonds to jump from $4.5 to 10.8 million between June and July, 1900. However, fiscal-year changes in combined holdings of Dominion and provincial government bonds were small (normally less than $3 million), notwithstanding a sharp transitory increase in fiscal 1910.[1] Nor did the series reveal a noticeable trend.

Considering the shortcomings of the available data, I do not attempt to adjust systematically the London issues of Dominion government bonds for the share absorbed by the chartered banks in order to estimate foreign borrowing. However, since that share may be estimated for the period 1880-1900, I deduct major fiscal-year changes in bank holdings of Dominion government bonds, as reported by Curtis, from the London issues for that period. The amounts by which the London issues are adjusted are shown in the legend to Table 7-5, column (6). Although these estimates of government borrowing abroad leave something to be desired, I doubt that they are far from the truth. After all, reported bank holdings of government bonds neither fluctuated much from year to year nor did they rise significantly over the period under study.[2]

F.2. THE SIMON ESTIMATES

Drawing on British sources, Simon (1970, Table I) estimated bonds issued in London by the Canadian private and public sectors during the period 1865-1914. Since Simon's published tables only show aggregate public-sector issues, Professor Irving Stone of the City University of New York was kind enough to provide me with a breakdown among Dominion, provincial and municipal issues. The unpublished data are available in the form of cumulative totals covering five-year subperiods.

Over the period calendar 1870-1909, cumulative issues of Dominion government bonds (net of conversions), as estimated by Simon, amounted to $218 million. That estimate is much larger than the corresponding cumulative total derived from Table 7-5. Provided the fiscal-year data of Table 7-5 are adjusted to a calendar-year format, cumulative foreign borrowing by the Dominion government, as estimated in this study, equalled $156.1 million for that period. Considering the rise in net government liabilities to foreign banks ($11.0 million), foreign borrowing in the form of bonds amounted to $145.1 million.[3] Thus, the Simon estimate exceeds my own by roughly 50 percent.

In my opinion, three factors are responsible for the difference between the two sets of data. First, my estimates of foreign borrowing are adjusted for bonds absorbed by the Canadian chartered banks and insurance companies. From the end of calendar 1869 to the end of calendar 1909, their holdings rose by $3.5 and 2.6 million respectively.[4] Second, unlike Simon, I estimate foreign borrowing net of bond purchases by the Dominion government on account of sinking funds and consolidated fund investments. The sinking funds and consolidated fund investments served as instruments for the retirement of outstanding debt and, therefore, consisted almost exclusively of the government's own bonds [see legend to Table 7-5, column (8)]. Holdings in sinking funds and consolidated fund investments increased by approximately $20 million during this period.[5] Third, it appears that Simon did not adjust his estimates fully for retirements of maturing bonds. He relied entirely on statistics of funds committed by British investors to new bond issues and took account of retirements only to the extent that a new issue was advertised as a debt conversion (1970, 240). For example, Simon's estimates indicate that over the period 1900-04, issues of Dominion government bonds, net of retirements, were zero. This finding is not surprising since the government issued no new bonds in the London market between 1900 and 1904. However, the government's abstention from the London market does not imply that the stock of outstanding bonds remained constant. On the contrary, that stock declined by almost $20 million, due to retirements of maturing bonds (Canada, Public Accounts for 1915, part I, 28 and 33). Therefore, Simon's estimates overstate the extent of Dominion government borrowing in London.

Endnotes — Appendix F

1. From January 31 to February 28, 1910, reported holdings of government bonds surged from $12.7 to 18.3 million. They stayed at roughly that level until the end of June, 1910, and fell again to $12.3 million the following month.

2. Even if the temporary increase in bank holdings of securities recorded in fiscal 1910 had reflected entirely purchases of Dominion government bonds payable in London, the cyclical pattern of foreign borrowing would not be altered much. The data in Table 7-5, column (8), would change to $23.9 and $4.6 million for fiscal 1910 and 1911 respectively.

3. In order to compile cumulative foreign borrowing for calendar 1870-1909, I add to the cumulative total for fiscal 1871-1909, 1/2 of the figure for fiscal 1870 and 3/4 of the figure for fiscal 1910 [Table 7-5, column (8)]. Net liabilities to foreign banks at the end of calendar 1869 and 1909, respectively, are estimated from the fiscal-year data for 1869-70 and 1909-10 by straight-line interpolation [Table 7-3, columns (5) and (6)].

4. See legend to Table 7-5, column (6), for cumulative purchases of London bonds by the chartered banks. The increase in insurance-company holdings is assumed to match the stock of bonds, payable in London, at the end of calendar 1909, as shown in Table 7-6.

5. Calendar-year data are estimated from fiscal-year data by straight-line interpolation (Canada, Public Accounts for 1915, part I, 30 and 46). The calendar-year estimates for December 31, 1909, may be inaccurate since both holdings in sinking funds and consolidated fund investments declined drastically during fiscal 1910.

BIBLIOGRAPHY

Books and Articles

Andrew, A.P. 1907. "The Treasury and the banks under Secretary Shaw." *Quarterly Journal of Economics* 21: 519-68.

Bank of Nova Scotia. 1932. *The Bank of Nova Scotia, 1832-1932*. Toronto: private print.

Barro, R.J. 1979. "Money and the price level under the gold standard." *Economic Journal* 89: 13-33.

Bates, S. 1939. *Financial history of Canadian governments*. A study prepared for the Royal Commission on Dominion-Provincial Relations. Ottawa.

Baum, D.J. 1974. *The Banks of Canada in the Commonwealth Caribbean*. New York, Washington and London: Praeger.

Beach, W.E. 1935. *British international gold movements and banking policy, 1881-1913*. Cambridge, Mass.: Harvard University Press.

Beckhart, B.H. 1929. *The banking system of Canada*. New York: Henry Holt and Company.

Berton, P. 1971. *The last spike*. Toronto and Montreal: McClelland and Stewart.

Beveridge, S. and Nelson, C.R. 1981. "A new approach to decomposition of economic time series into permanent and transitory components with particular attention to measurement of the business cycle." *Journal of Monetary Economics* 7: 151-74.

Bloomfield, A.I. 1959. *Monetary policy under the international gold standard: 1880-1914*. New York: Federal Reserve Bank.

Bonomo, V. and Tanner, J.E. 1972. "Canadian sensitivity to economic cycles in the United States." *Review of Economics and Statistics* 54: 1-8.

Bordo, M.D. 1981. "The classical gold standard: Some lessons for today." *Federal Reserve Bank of St. Louis Review* 63 (May): 2-18.

Bordo, M.D. and Schwartz, A.J. 1984. *A retrospective on the classical gold standard, 1821-1931*. Chicago and London: University of Chicago Press for National Bureau of Economic Research.

Borts, G.H. 1964. "A theory of long-run international capital movements." *Journal of Political Economy* 72: 341-59.

Breckenridge, R.M. 1895. *The Canadian banking system, 1817-1890*. New York: Macmillan. London: Swan Sonnenschein.

Bryce, R.B. 1939. "The effects on Canada of industrial fluctuations in the United States." *Canadian Journal of Economics and Political Science* 5: 373-86.

Burns, A.F. and Mitchell, W.C. 1946. *Measuring business cycles*. New York: National Bureau of Economic Research.

Cagan, P. 1965. *Determinants and effects of changes in the stock of money, 1875-1960*. New York and London: Columbia University Press for National Bureau of Economic Research.

Cairncross, A.K. 1968. "Investment in Canada, 1900-13." Hall, A.R., ed., *The export of capital from Britain, 1870-1914*. London: Methuen.

Callender, C.V. 1965. *The development of capital market institutions of Jamaica*. Institute of Social and Economic Research, University of the West Indies, Jamaica.

Carr, R.M. 1931. "The role of price in the international trade mechanism." *Quarterly Journal of Economics* 45: 710-19.

Chambers, E.J. 1958. "Canadian business cycles since 1919: A progress report." *Canadian Journal of Economics and Political Science* 24: 166-89.

———. 1964. "Late nineteenth century business cycles in Canada." *Canadian Journal of Economics and Political Science* 30: 391-412.

Clark, C. and Bond, D.E. 1972. "The behaviour of the aggregate reserve ratio of Canadian chartered banks revisited." *Canadian Journal of Economics* 3: 435-42.

Conant, C.A. 1927. *A history of modern banks of issue*. 6th ed. New York and London: G.P. Putnam's Sons.

Courant, R. 1937. *Differential and integral calculus*. Vol. 1. 2nd ed. London and Glasgow: Blackie and Son.

Cross, I.B. 1927. *Financing and empire; History of banking in California*. 3 vols. Chicago and San Francisco: S.J. Clarke.

Culbertson, J.M. 1960. "Friedman on the lag in effect of monetary policy." *Journal of Political Economy* 68: 617-21.

Curtis, C.A. 1931a. "Banking statistics in Canada." *Statistical contributions to Canadian economic history*. Vol. 1. Toronto: Macmillan.

———. 1931b. "Canada and the gold standard." *Queen's Quarterly* 38: 104-20.

Denison, M. 1967. *Canada's first bank. A history of the Bank of Montreal*. Vol. 2. Toronto and Montreal: McClelland and Stewart.

Dick, T.J.O. and Floyd, J.E. 1987a. "Canada and the gold standard, 1871-1913." Unpublished manuscript, University of Lethbridge and University of Toronto.

———. 1987b. "Balance of payments adjustment under the international gold standard. Canada 1871-1913." Unpublished manuscript, University of Lethbridge and University of Toronto.

Dutton, J. 1984. "The Bank of England and the rules of the game under the international gold standard: New evidence." Bordo, M.D. and Schwartz, A.J. (1984, ch. 3).

Easterbrook, W.T. and Aitken, H.G.J. 1956. *Canadian economic history*. Toronto: Macmillan.

Ford, A.G. 1962. *The gold standard, 1880-1914: Britain and Argentina*. Oxford: Clarendon Press.

Friedman, M. 1960. *A program for monetary stability*. New York: Fordham University Press.

Friedman, M. and Schwartz, A.J. 1963a. "Money and business cycles." *Review of Economics and Statistics* 45 (supplement): 32-64.

——. 1963b. *A monetary history of the United States, 1867-1960*. Princeton: University Press for National Bureau of Economic Research.

——. 1970. *Monetary statistics of the United States*. New York and London: Columbia University Press for National Bureau of Economic Research.

——. 1982. *Monetary trends in the United States and the United Kingdom*. Chicago and London: The University of Chicago Press for National Bureau of Economic Research.

Gilbert, J.H. 1911. "The development of banking in Oregon." *University of Oregon Bulletin* 9: Sept.

Goodhart, C.A.E. 1965. "Profits on national bank notes, 1900-1913." *Journal of Political Economy* 73: 516-22.

——. 1969. *The New York money market and the finance of trade*. Harvard Economic Studies. Vol. 132. Cambridge, Mass.: Harvard University Press.

——. 1972. *The business of banking, 1891-1914*. London: Weidenfeld and Nicolson.

——. 1984. "Comment." Bordo, M.D. and Schwartz, A.J. (1984: 222-27).

Gray, J.A. 1978. "On indexation and contract length." *Journal of Political Economy* 86: 1-18.

Hartland, P., (alias Thunberg). 1955. The Canadian balance of payments since 1868. Unpublished manuscript. New York: National Bureau of Economic Research.

——. 1960. "Canadian balance of payments since 1868." *Trends in the American economy in the nineteenth century*. Studies in income and wealth. Vol. 24. Princeton: University Press for National Bureau of Economic Research.

Harvey, M. 1902. *Newfoundland at the beginning of the 20th century*. New York: The South Publishing Company.

Hawtrey, R.G. 1928. *Trade and credit*. London, New York, Toronto: Longmans, Green and Company.

——. 1947. *The gold standard in theory and practice*. 5th ed. London, New York, Toronto: Longmans, Green and Company.

Hay, K.A.J. 1966. "Early twentieth century business cycles in Canada." *Canadian Journal of Economics and Political Science* 32: 354-64.

——. 1967. "Money and cycles in post-confederation Canada." *Journal of Political Economy* 75: 263-73.

——. 1968. "Determinants of the Canadian money supply, 1875-1958." Carleton Economic Paper 68-02. Ottawa: Carleton University.

Hayek, F.A. 1978. *Denationalization of money*. 2nd ed. London: Institute of Economic Affairs.

Homer, S. 1963. *A history of interest rates*. New Brunswick, N.J.: Rutgers University Press.

Ince, C.H. 1970. *The Royal Bank of Canada. A chronology: 1864-1969*. Private print.

Ingram, J.C. 1957. "Growth in capacity and Canada's balance of payments." *American Economic Review* 47: 93-104.

Innis, H.A. 1923. *A history of the Canadian Pacific Railway*. London: P.S. King and Son, Toronto: McClelland and Stewart.

——. 1936. "Settlement and the mining frontier." Mackintosh, W.A. and Joerg, W.L.G., eds., *Canadian frontiers of settlement*. Vol. 9. Toronto: Macmillan.

James, F.C. 1968 [1938]. *The growth of Chicago banks*. New York: Harper and Row.

Jamieson, A.B. 1955. *Chartered banking in Canada*. Toronto: Ryerson.

Johnson, H.G. 1972. *Further Essays in Monetary Economics*. London: George Allan and Unwin.

——. 1973. "The monetary approach to balance-of-payments theory." Connolly, M.B. and Swoboda, A.K., eds., *International trade and money*. London: George Allen and Unwin.

Johnson, J.F. 1910. *The Canadian banking system*. National Monetary Commission. Senate, 61st Congress, 2nd Session. Washington, D.C.: Government Printing Office.

Kessel, R.A. 1965. *The cyclical behavior of the term structure of interest rates*. Occasional Paper 91. New York: National Bureau of Economic Research.

Keynes, J.M. 1936. *The general theory of employment, interest and money*. London: Macmillan.

Knox, F.A. 1936. "Excursus." Marshall, H., Southard, F.A. and Taylor, K.W. *Canadian American industry*. Toronto: Ryerson Press; New Haven: Yale University Press for the Carnegie Endowment for International Peace.

——. 1939. *Dominion monetary policy: 1929-1934*. A study prepared for the Royal Commission on Dominion-Provincial Relations. Ottawa.

Laursen, S. and Metzler, L.A. 1950. "Flexible exchange rates and the theory of employment." *Review of Economics and Statistics* 32: 281-99.

Lindert, P.H. 1967. "Key currencies and the gold exchange standard." Unpublished Ph.D. dissertation. Ithaca: Cornell University.

——. 1969. *Key currencies and gold: 1900-1913*. Princeton Studies in International Finance No. 24. Princeton: International Finance Section.

McCallum, B.T. 1986. "On 'real' an 'sticky-price' theories of the business cycle." *Journal of Money, Credit, and Banking* 18: 397-414.

McCloskey, D.N. and Zecher, J.R. 1976. "How the gold standard worked, 1880-1913." Frenkel, J.A. and Johnson, H.G. eds., *The monetary approach to the balance of payments*. London: George Allen and Unwin.

——. 1984. "The success of purchasing-power parity: Historical evidence and its implications for macroeconomics." Bordo, M.D. and Schwartz, A.J. (1984, ch. 2).

McDougall. J.L. 1968. *Canadian Pacific. A brief history*. Montreal: McGill University Press.

McGouldrick, P. 1984. "Operations of the German central bank and the rules of the game." Bordo, M.D. and Schwartz, A.J. (1984, ch. 7).

Macaulay, F.R. 1938. *Some theoretical problems suggested by the movements of interest rates, bond yields and stock prices in the United States since 1856*. New York: National Bureau of Economic Research.

Macesich, G. 1970. "Supply and demand for money in Canada." Meiselman, D., ed., *Varieties of monetary experience*. Chicago and London: University of Chicago Press.

Macesich, G. and Haulman, C.A. 1971. "Determinants of the Canadian money stock, 1875-1964." *Rivista Internazionale di Science Economiche e Commerciali* 18: 249-57.

MacKay, R.A. and Saunders S.A. 1946. "The economy of Newfoundland." MacKay, R.A., ed., *Newfoundland. Economic, diplomatic, and strategic studies*. Toronto: Oxford University Press.

Meier, G.M. 1953. "Economic development and the transfer mechanism: Canada, 1895-1913." *Canadian Journal of Economics and Political Science* 19: 1-19.

Meiselman, D. 1962. *The term structure of interest rates*. Englewood Cliffs, N.J.: Prentice Hall.

Michell, H. 1931. "Statistics of prices." *Statistical contributions to Canadian economic history*. Vol. 2. Toronto: Macmillan.

Mills, T.C. and Wood, G.E. 1978. "Money-income relationships and the exchange rate regime." *Federal Reserve Bank of St. Louis Review* 60 (Aug.): 22-27.

Mintz, I. 1959. *Trade balances during business cycles: U.S. and Britain since 1880*. Occasional Paper 67. New York: National Bureau of Economic Research.

——. 1969. *Dating postwar business cycles*. New York: National Bureau of Economic Research.

Morgan, G.W. and Parker, A.J. 1920. eds., *Banking law of New York*. 5th ed. New York: The Banks Law Publishing Company.

Morgenstern, O. 1955. *The validity of international gold movement statistics*. Special Papers in International Finance, No. 2. Princeton: International Finance Section.

——. 1959. *International financial transactions and business cycles*. Princeton: University Press for National Bureau of Economic Research.

Morrison, G.R. 1966. *Liquidity preference of commercial banks*. Chicago: University Press.

Mundell, R.A. 1963. "Capital mobility and stabilization policy under fixed and flexible exchange rates." *Canadian Journal of Economics and Political Science* 29: 475-85.

Naylor, T. 1975. *The history of Canadian business, 1867-1914*. 2 vols. Toronto: James Lorimer.

Nelson, C.R. and Plosser, C.I. 1982. "Trends and random walks in macroeconomic time series: Some evidence and implications." *Journal of Monetary Economics* 10: 139-62.

Neuberger, H.M. and Stokes, H.H. 1979. "The Relationship between interest rates and gold flows under the gold standard: A new empirical approach." *Economica* 46: 261-79.

Neufeld, E.P. 1964., ed., *Money and banking in Canada*. The Carleton Library No. 17. Toronto: McClelland and Stewart.

——. 1972. *The financial system of Canada*. Toronto: Macmillan.

Niehans, J. 1978. *The theory of money*. Baltimore: The Johns Hopkins University Press.

Officer, L.H. 1986. "The Efficiency of the Dollar-Sterling Gold Standard." *Journal of Political Economy* 94: 1038-73.

Patterson, E.L.S. and Escher, F. 1914. *Banking practice and foreign exchange*. Modern Business. Canadian Edition. Vol. 8. New York: Alexander Hamilton Institute.

Peake, E.G. 1926. *An academic study of some money market and other statistics*. 2nd ed. London: P.S. King and Son.

Perry, J.H. 1955. *Taxes, tariffs and subsidies*. A history of Canadian fiscal development. Vol. 1. Toronto: University Press.

Phelps, C.W. 1927. *The foreign expansion of American banks*. New York: The Ronald Press Company.

Rich, G. 1976. Canadian monetary policy, 1866-1913: The failure of discretion. Carleton Economic Paper 76-06. Ottawa: Carleton University.

——. 1977. "The gold-reserve requirements under the Dominion notes act of 1870: How to deceive parliament." *Canadian Journal of Economics* 10: 447-53.

——. 1984. "Canada without a central bank: Operation of the price-specie-flow mechanism, 1872-1913." Bordo, M.D. and Schwartz, A.J. (1984, ch. 12).

Robinson, A.H.A. 1935. *Gold in Canada, 1935*. Ottawa: Canada Department of Mines, Mines Branch.

Rosenbluth, G. 1957. "Changes in the Canadian sensitivity to United States business fluctuations." *Canadian Journal of Economics and Political Science* 23: 480-503.

——. 1958. "Changing structural factors in Canada's cyclical sensitivity, 1903-1953." *Canadian Journal of Economics and Political Science* 24: 21-43.

Ross, V. 1920-34. *The history of the Canadian Bank of Commerce*. 3 vols. Toronto: Oxford University Press.

Seeger, M. 1968. *Die Politik der Reichsbank von 1876-1914 im Lichte der Spielregeln der Goldwährung*. Berlin: Duncker and Humblot.

Shearer, R.A. 1965. "The foreign currency business of Canadian-chartered banks." *Canadian Journal of Economics and Political Science* 31: 328-57.

Shearer, R.A. and Clark, C. 1984. "Canada and the interwar gold standard, 1920-1935: Monetary policy without a central bank." Bordo, M.D. and Schwartz, A.J. (1984, ch. 6).

Shortt, A. 1904a. "The history of Canadian currency, banking and exchange: Government versus bank circulation." *Journal of the Canadian Bankers' Association* 12: 14-35.

——. 1904b. "The history of Canadian currency, banking and exchange: The first general bank act for the Dominion." *Journal of the Canadian Bankers' Association* 12: 265-82.

——. 1906. "The history of Canadian currency, banking and exchange: The revision of 1880." *Journal of the Canadian Bankers' Association* 14: 7-27.

——. 1922. "The legislative development of the Canadian banking system." Chapter 7 in Ross (1922, Vol. 2).

Simon, M. 1970. "New British investments in Canada, 1865-1914." *Canadian Journal of Economics* 3: 238-54.

Smiley, G. 1975. "Interest rate movement in the United States, 1888-1913." *Journal of Economic History* 35: 591-620.

Stovel, J.A. 1959. *Canada in the world economy*. Cambridge, Mass.: Harvard University Press.

Swoboda, A.K. 1972. "Equilibrium, quasi-equilibrium and macro-economic policy under fixed exchange rates." *Quarterly Journal of Economics* 86: 162-71.

Taussig, F.W. 1927. *International trade*. New York: Macmillan.

Taylor, K.W. 1931. "Statistics of foreign trade." *Statistical contributions to Canadian economic history*. Vol. 2. Toronto: Macmillan.

Tilly, R.H. 1973. "Zeitreihen zum Geldumlauf in Deutschland, 1870-1913." *Jahrbücher für Nationalökonomie und Statistik* 187: 330-63.

Triffin, R. 1964. *The evolution of the international monetary system: Historical reappraisal and future perspectives*. Princeton Studies in International Finance No. 12. Princeton: International Finance Section.

Urquhart, M.C. and Buckley, K.A.H. 1965. *Historical statistics of Canada*. Cambridge, England: University Press; Toronto: Macmillan.

Urquhart, M.C. 1987. "New estimates of gross national product, 1870-1926: Some implications for Canadian development." S.L. Engerman and R.E. Gallman, eds., *Long-term factors in American Economic Growth*. NBER Studies in Income and Wealth, vol. 51. Chicago: University of Chicago Press (forthcoming).

Viner, J. 1924. *Canada's balance of international indebtedness, 1900-1913*. Cambridge, Mass.: Harvard University Press.

——. 1960 [1937]. *Studies in the theory of international trade*. London: George Allen and Unwin.

White, H.D. 1933. *The French international accounts, 1880-1913*. Cambridge, Mass.: Harvard University Press.

White, L.H. 1984. *Free banking in Britain*. Cambridge: Cambridge University Press.

Williamson, J.G. 1964. *American growth and the balance of payments 1820-1913*. Chapel Hill: The University of North Carolina Press.

Yamane, T. 1973. *Statistics. An introductory analysis*. 3rd ed. New York: Harper and Row.

Government Publications

(1) Canada

British Columbia. *Annual report of the Minister of Mines,* 1913.

Canada. *Annual report of the Superintendent of Insurance,* 1875-1913.

——. Board of Inquiry into Cost of Living in Canada. *Report of the Board*. Vol. 2. Ottawa, 1915.

——. *Canada Gazette*. 1867-1913.

——. *Debates of the House of Commons*.

——. Department of Customs. *Tables of the trade and navigation of the Dominion of Canada,* fiscal years 1868-1905.

——. Department of Customs. *Trade and navigation. Unrevised monthly statements of imports entered for consumption and export of the Dominion of Canada,* 1905-1913.

———. Department of Mines, Mines Branch. *The production of copper, gold, lead, nickel, silver, zinc, and other metals in Canada during the calendar year 1913*. Ottawa, 1914.

———. Dominion Bureau of Statistics. *Prices and price indexes, 1949-52*. Ottawa, 1954.

———. Geological Survey, Section Mines. *Annual report for 1902*.

———. *Monthly reports of the Department of Trade and Commerce,* various issues.

———. *Parliamentary Debates*.

———. *Public accounts for the fiscal year,* 1868-1915.

———. *Report of the Department of Trade and Commerce for the fiscal year,* 1903, 1915.

———. Royal Commission on Dominion Provincial Relations. *Report*. Book I. Ottawa 1940.

———. *Statutes of Canada*.

———. *Statutes of the Province of Canada*.

(2) Germany

Germany. Bundesbank. *Deutsches Geld- and Bankwesen in Zahlen 1876-1975*. Frankfurt a/M: Knapp, 1976.

(3) Great Britain

Great Britain. *Annual report of the Deputy Master and Comptroller of the Mint*. London: HMSO, 1908-1914.

———. Newfoundland Royal Commission 1933. *Report*. Cmd. 4480. London: HMSO, 1933.

———. Royal Commission on Trade Relations between Canada and the West Indies. *Minutes of evidence taken in Canada*. London: HMSO, 1910.

(4) United States

California. *Annual report of the Board of Bank Commissioners of the State of California*. San Francisco, 1879-1908.

Oregon. *Annual report of the State Banking Department of the State of Oregon,* 1907.

U.S. Bureau of the Mint. *Annual report of the Director of the Mint*. Washington, D.C., 1900-14.

U.S. Commission on the Role of Gold in the Domestic and International Monetary System. *Report to the Congress*. Vol. 1. Washington, D.C., March 1982.

U.S. Congress. Joint Economic Committee. *Hearings. Employment, growth and price level*. Part 4. 86th Congress, 1st Session. Washington, D.C., 1959.

Washington (state). *Annual report of the State Examiner of the State of Washington Banking Department,* 1907.

(5) International

International Monetary Fund, *International Financial Statistics*

Newspapers

The Economist, London, England.

The Monetary Times, Toronto.

Unpublished Documents

Bank of Montreal, General manager's ledgers, 1887-1913.

Bank of Nova Scotia, BNS statistics 3 and 14.

Public Archives of Canada, Finance Department records, RG 19.